HR Personnel Planning and Development Using SAP

 PRESS

SAP PRESS and SAP Technical Support Guides are issued by
Bernhard Hochlehnert, SAP AG

SAP PRESS is a joint initiative of SAP and Galileo Press. The know-how offered by SAP specialists combined with the expertise of the publishing house
Galileo Press offers the reader expert books in the field. SAP PRESS features
first-hand information and expert advice, and provides useful skills for professional decision-making.

SAP PRESS offers a variety of books on technical and business related topics
for the SAP user. For further information, please visit our website:
www.sap-press.com.

Liane Will
SAP APO System Administration
Principles for effective APO System Management
2003, 240 pp., ISBN 1-59229-012-4

A. Rickayzen, J. Dart, C. Brennecke, M. Schneider
Practical Workflow for SAP
2002, 504 pp., ISBN 1-59229-006-X

Frédéric Heinemann, Christian Rau
Web Programming with the SAP Web Application Server
The complete guide for ABAP and web developers
2003, 528 pp., ISBN 1-59229-013-2

Horst Keller, Joachim Jacobitz
ABAP Objects. The Official Reference
2003, 1094 pp., 2 Volumes and CD Set
ISBN 1-59229-011-6

Helmut Stefani
Archiving Your SAP Data
A comprehensive guide to plan and execute archiving projects
2003, 360 pp., ISBN 1-59229-008-6

Christian Krämer, Christian Lübke, Sven Ringling

HR Personnel Planning and Development Using SAP

How to get the most from your
SAP HR systems

SAP PRESS

Translation Lemoine International, Inc.,
Salt Lake City, UT
Copy Editor Nancy Etscovitz, UCG, Inc.,
Boston, MA
Cover Design department, Cologne, Germany
Printed in Germany

ISBN 1-59229-024-8
1st edition, 1st reprint

Contents

3 The Role Concept in mySAP HR — 109

4 Portals in mySAP HR — 137

8   Skill Management   201

9   Development Planning   243

10   Appraisals and Setting Objectives   287

11   Training and Event Management   315

15 Compensation Management 417

16 Personnel Cost Planning 443

17 E-Learning and Learning Management Systems — 487

18 The SAP Business Information Warehouse — 515

19 SAP Strategic Enterprise Management — 519

Goal and Organization of the Book

The Goal

In this book, we introduce employees in personnel and IT departments as well as other interested parties to the strategy, conception, and implementation of the processes of personnel planning and development in mySAP HR. Beginning with the requirements and problems that we encounter repeatedly in our projects, we will provide solutions that can also appear somewhat unconventional or innovative.

Although we have chosen to highlight the apparent weaknesses of the SAP system, its quality should not be called into question. For the reader, it is important above all else to be familiar with the weaknesses and possible ways in which to find solutions.

Again and again, you will find examples in this book where the possibilities of the system are used to support processes in ways other than originally thought. Personnel planning and development in mySAP HR offer so many options for using these processes that one book alone could never describe them exhaustively. In reflecting on the structures and functionalities of the system, you will also discover ways in which you can fulfill your requirements beyond the standard scenarios. *We invite you to innovate!*

The Target Groups

The following target groups will find valuable information in this book:

▶ Decision-makers in personnel, IT, and organizational departments will receive a critical overview of the process support of mySAP HR. They will also cultivate a sense for basic strengths and weaknesses as well as develop an appreciation for those integral to driving the projects. For them—as for some other target groups—the detailed description of customizing and the application may not be all that important. The way in which the book is organized allows for important concepts to be distinguished or separated from the details.

▶ Project managers will find the integration aspects and critical success factors for implementation to be especially important.

▶ Team members for implementation projects, consultants, and those responsible for customizing will find many hints for each process. Basic functionalities will be explained a bit more precisely, so that employees who are just assuming these roles will receive appropriate guidelines for getting started. For advanced users, there are many recommendations that are presented without all respective details. Of greater importance is understanding the basic direction of each process or project. Within the existing functionality, various suggestions are provided for its deployment.

▶ Interested users who would like to see beyond the borders of their specific activities and key users who are also responsible for the continued development of the system will get a good overview of how the activities are connected and develop a better understanding of the system's mode of operation.

▶ Students or other interested parties who are just learning about personnel development and personnel planning will develop true insight into the practice of Human Resources (HR) and its IT implementation with mySAP HR. The book's topics represent important functions of a personnel department and indicate where problems can occur. The representation of business backgrounds is particularly relevant for this target group.

▶ Programmers will learn about the professional and application-oriented background for their work. The connections between the customizing and application data are particularly helpful for the programming of reports, user exits, and extensions.

Organization and Content Delimitation

The organization of the book reflects the structure depicted in Figure 1:

▶ The general overview of mySAP HR and its integration into the total solution is kept as brief as possible to help readers understand the remainder of the book, without dwelling on the topic of integration and thus slowing down those users who are primarily interested in the HR core.

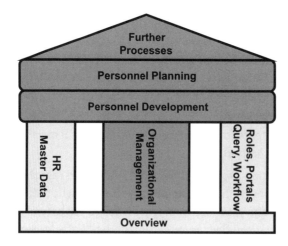

Figure 1 Organization of the Book: Overview

- Before beginning with the actual core processes, "pillars" are constructed that are relevant as a basis:

  - The personnel master data (integrated into Chapter 1, *Overview of mySAP HR*), which naturally also plays a role in the HR development. The explanations are limited to that which is required for work in personnel development.

  - The technical concepts *role*, *query*, and *workflow*, which influence work with the core processes significantly.

  - As the most important "pillar," organization management does not only provide the basis for the entire personnel planning and development; it explains the structure of these processes in mySAP HR and it is, itself, also a significant application.

- Personnel development is the largest part of this book. The organization here reflects the important processes, not the technical structure of the system. The processes of development planning as well as the organization and execution of further training are examined. The aspects of HR risk management also play an important role in this part of the book.

- In personnel planning, the primary concern is medium-term capacity planning (requirements planning) and the planning of costs and compensation. Shift planning and order-related capacity planning are excluded because they can sooner be assigned to the supported core processes (e.g., production, maintenance, sales, service). For these processes, see the chapter *Workforce Management with mySAP CRM* in the SAP PRESS book *mySAP CRM*.[1] In personnel planning, aspects of risk management are also considered.

- The last part of the book describes some continuing processes that are significant in the course of personnel planning and development. The focus of this part of the book is e-learning with the SAP Learning Solution. Finally, overviews of the Business Information Warehouse (BW) and Strategic Enterprise Management (SEM) are presented.

Working with This Book

You can read the individual chapters of this book in any sequence. For readers who are less familiar with mySAP HR, however, we recommend that you read Chapter 2, *Organizational Management*, before proceeding to Sections 2 and 3 of the book.

---

1 Rüdiger Buck-Emden, *mySAP CRM: Solution for Success*, SAP PRESS 2002.

In addition, over time, you should also get an overview of all processes — not simply the process or processes for which you are responsible or in which you work. In order to work in highly integrated processes, a basic understanding of the additional connections is absolutely essential.

Consideration of R/3 Enterprise and Release 4.6

This book is designed for users of R/3 Release 4.6 as well as 4.7 (also known as R/3 Enterprise). The main chapters show the functionality of 4.6C with the few changes in 4.7 mentioned where appropriate. The important innovations of Release 4.7, delivered via extension sets, are described in chapters or paragraphs of their own and are marked for the reader. In addition, some mySAP HR components outside of R/3 are described as well.

Process Examples

The process examples are based largely on the requirements of various companies' practices; however, in this book, they were simplified and the details were omitted. Some modeling conventions also had to be sacrificed to fit the book format. Connoisseurs of the ARIS® method must therefore excuse the impure modeling in some places. Our primary goal was to transport the relevant content in as little space as possible.

Part 1
The Basics

1 Overview of mySAP HR

mySAP HR is an extensive, powerful package for supporting the processes of personnel management. The integrated incorporation into the processes of logistics and accounting—as well as into portals in the framework of the total solution mySAP Business Suite—is among its strengths.

1.1 Incorporation of the HR Module into the R/3 System

The term *R/3 System* stands for *Realtime System 3* and is founded in the development history of this software. In addition to a multitude of industry-specific processes, R/3 is organized into the following main areas:

▶ Accounting

▶ Logistics

▶ Personnel management

▶ Basic system (Web Application Server)

You cannot view the processes of personnel management in isolation because they are inherently integrated with the other R/3 processes. The important process-specific integration aspects are:

▶ Posting of payroll results and travel cost accounting in financial accounting (FI) and cost accounting (CO)

▶ Transfer of results of personnel cost planning into the CO

▶ Assignment of cost centers and other cost units from CO into the personnel master data

▶ Incorporation of the organizational structure of the organizational management into the structures of the accounting

▶ Accounting for services (CO), cost distribution (CO) or accounting for foreign services (MM) from time management

▶ Order-related personnel deployment planning (capacity planning) for orders in production planning (PP), plant maintenance (PM), or service management (SM)

▶ Calculation of activity-based costs (CO)

▶ Invoicing of event fees (SD)

▶ Procurement of materials for the execution of events (MM)

- Validation of various fields (e.g., company car or loan) against a facility number (FI-AM)
- Generation of time tickets for incentive wages from logistics (PP, PM)
- Cross-application time sheet (CATS): Connection of many processes in which employees' time is kept, evaluated, and calculated

Just as important are the system-wide cross-sectional functionalities into which HR is incorporated. They include:

- SAP Business Workflow
- Role concept
- Development environment
- SAP Office
- Archiving
- Executive Information System (EIS)

1.2 mySAP HR in the Total Solution of the mySAP Business Suite

Within the total solution of the mySAP Business Suite, the incorporation of HR processes is even more firmly integrated. The mySAP Business Suite includes the following components (among others):

- SAP R/3 or SAP R/3 Enterprise as core of the solution
- SAP APO (Advanced Planner & Optimizer)
- SAP BW (Business Information Warehouse)
- mySAP CRM (Customer Relationship Management)
- SAP KW (Knowledge Warehouse)
- SAP SEM (Strategic Enterprise Management)
- SAP EP (Enterprise Portal)
- SAP EH&S (Environment Health & Safety)

The solution mySAP HR is therefore formed from the components R/3, BW, KW, SEM, and EP (or parts of these). The SAP Learning Solution is a component of the mySAP e-business platform; however, it can also be operated in standalone mode independently of mySAP HR. The same applies for the new solution for e-recruiting. The Workforce Management with the order-related personnel deployment planning as its core is contained in the component mySAP CRM. It is integrated with HR in many ways.

For the portal solution (Enterprise Portal 6.0), content is delivered (content packages) that makes a significant contribution to personnel management processes. These packets include:

▶ Employee Self Service (ESS)

▶ Manager Self Service (MSS)

▶ Analysis tools for HR processes

▶ mySAP HR Connectivity (for accessing HR system data from the portal)

▶ HR Queries (for executing HR queries of the BW from the portal)

▶ Additional packets that primarily serve data access by specialists, the connection of third-party products (e.g., Yahoo) or web-based communication (e.g., E-rooms, see Figure 1.1.)

All eRoom Events					
Time Period This Month ▾					
24-28/38					
	Event Name	Starting Time	Duration	Room	Calendar
↻	Mberrebi birthday	17-Dec-2001 2:00:00 PM	60 min.	Amith	Birthdays
↻	new event	18-Dec-2001	All Day Event	demo	QA
↻	test requ	20-Dec-2001	All Day Event	Lisi	QA
↻	Weekly Status Meeting	24-Dec-2001 3:00:00 PM	60 min.	Daniel	Calendar
↻	Monthly Status Meeting	12/28/01 3:00:00 PM	60 min.	Daniel	Prototype Production

Figure 1.1 Use of E-Rooms from the Enterprise Portal

1.3 Components in mySAP HR

This section will clarify the differences between R/3 up to Release 4.6C and R/3 Enterprise. In addition, the incorporation of both releases into mySAP HR should become clear. Therefore, we will first build on the "old" release status.

1.3.1 Components in R/3 Release 4.6C

The important processes of personnel work are supported. The following components form the basis for this release:

▶ **Personnel administration**
Complete personnel master data maintenance and administration

▶ **Organizational management**
Flexible mapping of the organizational structure of the company and classification of employees

Additional personnel management processes in R/3 are:

▶ **Recruitment**
Management of vacancies, advertisements, applicant selection, applicant correspondence, and applicant tracking

▶ **Personnel time management**
Maintenance and evaluation of time data, interface to time clocks, shift planning, keeping of time accounts, and evaluation of time subject to surcharge

▶ **Incentive wages**
Individual and group schemes, PDC (plant data collection) connection

▶ **Payroll accounting**
Accounting of gross and net in pay, wages, and salary; payment; legal reporting; and coverage of usually country-specific special processes such as garnishment, loans, and so on

▶ **Benefits**
Mapping of various, usually country-specific models for company pensions and other social services

▶ **Travel management** (it can also be assigned to the FI module)
Planning of trips, procurement of travel needs, application procedures, acquisition, invoicing, payment, and posting of travel costs

▶ **Training and event management**
Construction of a seminar catalog, organization of activities, booking and administration of participation, correspondence, resource administration, calculation, invoicing, and cost accounting, and Internet sales

▶ **Personnel development**
Skill management, career planning, succession planning, appraisals, development plans, objectives, and potential

▶ **Compensation management**
Total compensation approach, compensation guidelines, benchmarking, monetary job evaluation, service-oriented compensation, stock programs, and budgeting

▶ **Personnel cost planning**
Planning and projection of personnel costs

▶ **Personnel shift planning**
Quantitative and qualitative planning of the personnel deployment on tactical and operative levels

All these components and their integration into other processes are essentially available in R/3 without having to install additional components. Together with other processes, HR uses the R/3 basis / Web Application Server.

1.3.2 The Architecture with R/3 Enterprise

The previous R/3 basis, which is now being replaced with the Web Application Server (Web AS), makes available the previously known basis functionalities. The integration into a Web environment is also improved significantly. In addition to the programming language ABAP/4, Java also gains significance.

The R/3 core builds on the Web AS. There, the previous functionalities of R/3 are found and expanded with various smaller functionalities. In the future, the core will be expanded only in exceptional cases. Instead, new functionalities will be delivered as *Enterprise Extensions*. These enterprise extensions must not be licensed separately; instead, they should be installed according to the client's needs. This customization increases the stability of the core system.

Although the technical architecture will change considerably with mySAP ERP, the core statements in this paragraph will still be applicable. NetWeaver will be much more powerfull than today's Web AS, so that web integration will be easier and some components, that are external today will move into NetWeaver. But the way, HR is integrated with the other processes and the concept of core and extensions will be very similar to today.

The change from Release 4.6C to R/3 Enterprise accounts for the following additional functionalities of the core system in HR:

▶ Long Term Incentive Plans (LTIP)

▶ Expansions for pension funds

▶ The Expert Finder (as a standalone Web application)

▶ Various country-specific additions

▶ Time management applications via mobile telephones

▶ Context-dependent authorization check (see Chapter 3, *The Role Concept in mySAP HR*)

Another release change to R/3 Enterprise is not planned thus far. Smaller additions and legal changes are installed with the help of support packages. Larger expansions occur via the Enterprise Extensions, which have their own release cycle.

At first, from the HR point of view, the following functionalities are available as extensions:

- ▶ Management by objectives and appraisals
- ▶ Various country-specific additions
- ▶ Graphical user interface (GUI) for the Time Manager's Workplace (TMW)
- ▶ Management of global employees (expatriates)
- ▶ Concurrent employment (for U.S., Canada)

1.3.3 Additional Components in mySAP HR

The solution mySAP HR is organized into four areas:

- ▶ Core functions—the administrative processes such as payroll, time management, and so forth
- ▶ Strategic functions—personnel development, recruitment, compensation management, personnel planning
- ▶ Analytic functions—benchmarking and integration into the Balanced Scorecard (BSC)
- ▶ The "Enablement" area—functions that enable individual employees or individual managers to fulfill their personal requirements with the help of an easy-to-use portal (the Learning Solution is also included here)

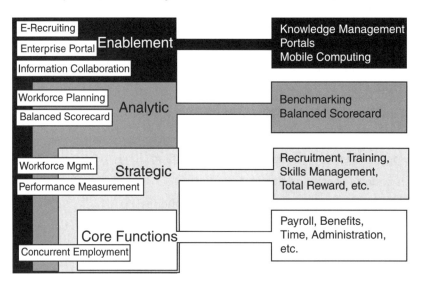

Figure 1.2 Structure of mySAP HR

Figure 1.2 shows an overview of the structure of mySAP HR. The functionalities highlighted on the left side of the figure show the focus of software development at the start of R/3 Enterprise.

This structure is based purely on content and does not indicate which functionalities are available within the core system, as an Enterprise Extension, or are available in some other way.

The mySAP application components are added to the components in the R/3 core system and the Enterprise Extensions that were named in both of the previous sections. The following components are relevant to HR:

▶ **SAP BW**
SAP BW (Business Information Warehouse) serves as an analysis and reporting tool across all processes. The special HR content is very extensive and expandable.

▶ **SAP KW**
SAP KW (Knowledge Warehouse) offers a complete knowledge management system. For the support of HR processes, however, it has little specific meaning. The primary concern for HR is the opportunity to manage HR knowledge.

▶ **SAP SEM**
In addition to the usual HR-relevant content of a BSC, the SEM (Strategic Enterprise Management) in particular allows the integration of management via objectives in the BSC and the functional chains.

▶ **SAP Enterprise Portal**
It can also serve as a single sign-on (SSO) portal for HR.

To summarize the last three sections, Figure 1.3 shows the architecture of the mySAP Business Suite.

1.4   The Personnel Master Data

The personnel master data that is kept in the personal administration component represents a significant basis for all HR processes. Therefore, we will briefly address this component, albeit it is not the initial topic of this book. Here, however, we will introduce the master data maintenance and discuss the integration aspects.

1.4.1   Basic Structure

Task of Personnel Administration

Personnel administration on the system deals primarily with the maintenance, display, and evaluation of personnel master data. Usually, these tasks occur in order to provide the required data for other processes (e.g., payroll, personnel development, and personnel planning). Therefore, the basic data of all administrative processes (time management, payroll, etc.) is kept primarily in the personnel administration. The processes of personnel planning and development use master data that is largely their own.

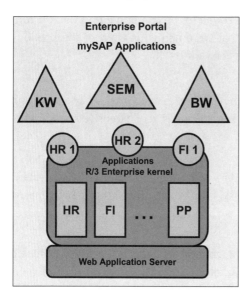

Figure 1.3 Architecture: HR in the mySAP Business Suite

The Infotype

The personnel data is stored in *infotypes*, which represent data-entry screens that summarize the content of associated data fields (e.g., address data, data about severe disability, etc.). Because the infotype concept is also used in similar fashion in organizational management, see also Chapter 2, *Organizational Management*. Figure 1.4 shows the infotype "personal data" as an example.

The Personnel Number

According to the system, the *personnel number* is the central ordering criterion for all personnel data. Each individual data record is assigned to the correct employee with the help of the personnel number. This applies to the master data organized in infotypes and also to the payroll results, time management, benefits, and travel cost accounting. There, where a link to individual employees is required in the personnel planning and development data, the personnel number is also the only link. It soon becomes apparent that it is almost impossible to change a personnel number without causing inconsistencies in the database or the loss of an employee's entire work history.

In HR, the personnel number has a maximum of eight digits and consists of numbers. With the use of "management of global employees" or of the "concurrent employment" (U.S. and Canada), an employee can have several personnel numbers (i.e., contracts) that are combined via the personal ID, which then serves as a unique identifier for that employee.

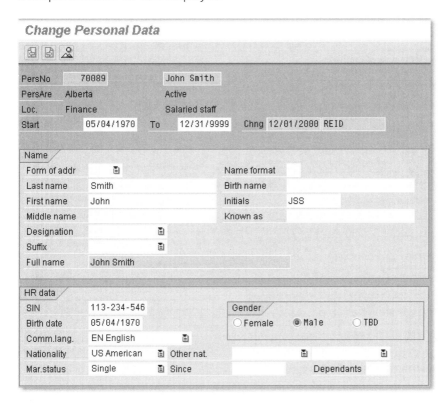

Figure 1.4 The Infotype 0002: "Personal Data"

1.4.2 Maintaining and Displaying Master Data

The maintenance of personnel data occurs almost completely via infotypes. Work with the personnel administration infotypes will be described in rough outline in this section. Hereby, we are limiting ourselves to the maintenance of individual infotypes. We will not address fast entry and the maintenance of personnel actions here.

Master Data Maintenance: Setup Screen

The maintenance of personnel master data occurs via the menu path **Personnel · Personnel management · Administration · Personnel data · Maintain**. The basic screen for master data maintenance (see Figure 1.5) is organized into the object manager (left) and the actual maintenance screen (right). The operation of the basic screen for infotype maintenance is intuitive. Essentially, you must complete the selection fields for personnel number, information type, and subtype ("STy")—as well as the time period. After that, you can select the action that you want using the menu or the button bar.

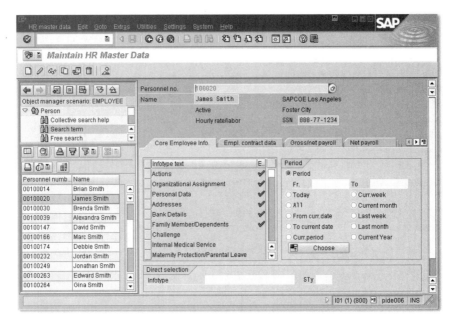

Figure 1.5 Main Data Maintenance Startup

Selection of the Infotype

To select the infotype that you want, you can choose among the following:

▶ Enter the infotype number

▶ Enter the infotype name

▶ Select the infotype field using the selection help (F4-Help)

▶ Highlight a tab

The tab selection is especially user-friendly; it can be used to construct a task-specific interface.

Selection of the Personnel Number

The selection of the personnel number is supported in many ways. This support should also be familiar to users; otherwise, a lot of time can be wasted. When calling up the selection help, several forms of search help are called up via *matchcodes* and offered via the free search (see Figure 1.6).

The search according to name is used most frequently. This can be used without F4-Help by entering "=n.lastname.firstname" or, you can enter only the initial letters of the name in the personnel number field. The search via the organizational assignment is also very helpful, especially for large organizations. You can also combine a search according to last name and personnel subarea.

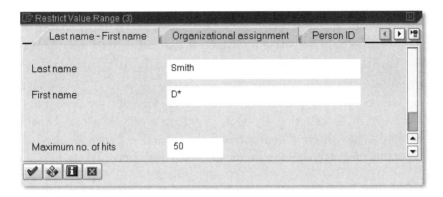

Figure 1.6 Search Help for Personnel Numbers

Basic Functions of Working with Infotypes

The actual work with infotypes occurs with the following activities:

▶ **Create**
Creation of a new record with beginning and end date. Depending on the time constraint, other records will either be deleted or delimited. Application examples: the birth of a child requires the creation of a corresponding record of the infotype 21 family. After a move, a new record is created in infotype 6 (address) as of 3/4/2002. The old address is delimited with the end date 3/3/2002.

▶ **Change**
An existing record of an infotype is changed, which means for its entire validity period. Application examples: Error corrections, for example, incorrectly spelled last name.

▶ **Copy**
Copying is comparable with the activity *Create*, with the difference that an old record is used as a template. Application example: change of last name as of 3/10/2002 due to marriage. Note: using change instead of copy often leads to errors and to the destruction of the history!

▶ **Delimit**
After entry of a limiting date, all records are offered that are valid on this date. After selection of the desired records and repeated pressing of the **Delimit** but-

ton, the end dates are set to the day before the delimiting date. Limiting is only permissible for infotypes of the time constraint 2 and 3. For infotypes of the time constraints 1 and 2, the creation or copying automatically triggers a delimitation because no parallel records are allowed. The system then makes this known with a warning message.

▶ **Display List acquisition**

The list acquisition is only permissible for particular infotypes, for which acquisition in a line is possible. These infotypes are particularly for time management.

▶ **Lock/Unlock**

On further processing, locked records of an infotype are not considered, especially in the payroll accounting. Therefore, this functionality is helpful if one is not entirely certain during data acquisition and there is still need for clarification, or if the effect of a deletion should be tested in advance.

▶ **Delete**

Infotypes of the time constraint 1 must be present throughout the timeline. Therefore, you cannot delete all data records of such an infotype. When deleting a data record for time constraint 1, the predecessor is extended by the system so that no gap occurs. This is announced by a warning message.

▶ **Overview**

Shows all entries of the infotype in the selection period as a list. From the list, some of the functions described can then be executed for individual records (see Figure 1.7).

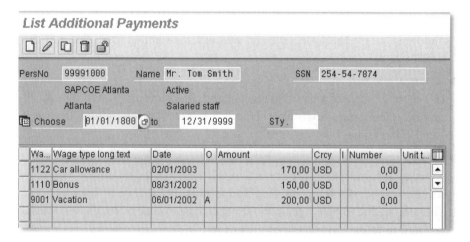

Figure 1.7 List of the Records of an Infotype

1.4.3 Integration into Personnel Planning and Development

In personnel planning and development, individual administration data is required often. For example, this data includes name, cost center, date of birth, targeted work time, and so forth. The link to an employee must be created again and again, which occurs technically via the personnel number.

The most seamless integration occurs in the organization management. Through the assignment of employees in the organizational management, their master data in infotype 0001 ("organizational assignment") also changes.

The Organizational Assignment in the Infotype 0001

Among other things, the infotype 0001 permits the assignment of employees to organizational units, positions, and jobs. This is also possible without using organizational management. The creation of the corresponding organization objects is possible via the customizing of the infotype in simple tables. Thus, however, no true structure can be created. Therefore, and due to the additional functionalities, the deployment of organizational management is absolutely recommended at the latest with a company of 1000 employees or more. Even for smaller companies, this often makes sense—one should then see that the maintenance does not become an end in itself; rather, instead, it should occur based on simpler, more pragmatic conventions.

The integration into the organizational management is activated in two steps:

1. Via the Implementation Guide (IMG) path **Personnel Management · Organizational Management · Integration · Integration for Personnel Administration · Integration with Personnel Administration**, the entry PLOGI-ORGA must be set to "x" under basic settings. In the same table, there are other additional control possibilities that are well documented.

2. If the integration is basically activated, in the second step, it must be determined which employees participate in the integration. In some companies, these are all employees; in other companies, pensioners or part-time employees are excluded. This control occurs via the feature PLOGI, which can be reached via the same IMG path.

With active integration, only the position must be maintained in infotype 0001. Job as well as organizational unit (and cost center) are derived automatically using the organizational management.

2   Organizational Management

We will describe organizational management from the point of view of personnel development. Therefore, an overview of the relevant terms and concepts will be provided.

2.1   Business Basics

In organizational theory, the inherent distinction between structure and process organization is also significant for personnel planning and development: the organization of the processes determines the need for qualifications in the employees who carry out these processes. The process organization with superior and subordinate work centers determines careers and career paths and therefore, career and succession planning. The following aspects are integral to personnel development:

▶ **Requirements profile of the work center**
  The requirements of a work center are derived from its job description. If, for example, personnel responsibility is among the requirements, then the requirements probably also include the area of *soft skills* such as leadership capability, communication capability, and so forth. The more precisely a work center is described, the more suitable are the employees who are hired for this work center.

▶ **Qualifications profiles**
  The counterpart to the requirements profile is the *qualifications profile*. It contains the required qualifications that an employee brings to the job, as well as those qualifications that this employee is lacking and needs to hone. This is where personnel development steps in, that is, when employees lack the qualifications they need to succeed in their job and therefore, need to develop additional skills. Whether via the charting of career paths or via a functioning succession planning, missing qualifications should be acquired and additional qualifications should be both maintained and encouraged.

▶ **Appraisals**
  Only via appraisal that is consistently shared and expectations that are clarified can an employee's potential and career goals be evaluated and explored.

▶ **Needs**
  The task of personnel development is to fulfill the qualitative and the quantitative needs of the company. The reorganization of the organizational structure can act as a catalyst, causing new needs to arise that must in turn be redistributed.

▶ **Careers, career paths, and succession planning** (see Chapter 9, *Development Planning*)

Careers define the development of an employee via the jobs and positions. Conversely, succession planning outlines the career path of an employee starting from the target position (i.e., the position that is now vacant) and therefore determines the optimal future staffing of this position.

2.2 The Design in mySAP HR

2.2.1 Basic Terms

To understand the concept of the mySAP HR organizational management, you must become familiar with certain basic terms. The first term we'll define is the *plan version*.

Plan Version

In personnel planning and development, a *plan version* represents a world of its own. These versions are used to test or walk through various planning scenarios. For example, an organizational structure can be reorganized into a particular plan version and its effects on the organization can be investigated. For this reorganization, the current plan version must be copied to additional versions.

The current version, also called an *integration plan version,* refers to the versions that are used productively in mySAP HR. These versions are specified once at the first implementation (usually at "01"). The integration plan version is then also the only plan version whose change has a direct influence on personnel administration if integration is active. An integration plan version specified once may never be changed again since this would cause inconsistencies to appear in the database! The plan version to be edited can be set via the menu path **Human Resources · Organizational Management · Settings · Set Plan Version.**

Infotypes

The organizational structure in mySAP HR consists of several object types. These objects, in turn, are connected with one another via different relationships. Objects are identified via a unique key that is composed of the plan version, the object type, and the object key. Example: "01 O 00000300 1" for an organizational unit (see Figure 2.1).

The data in mySAP HR organizational management is—as it exists in the personnel administration—stored in infotypes. An *infotype* is a grouping of data fields according to logical aspects. For example, in personnel administration there exist the infotypes "address" and "bank information."

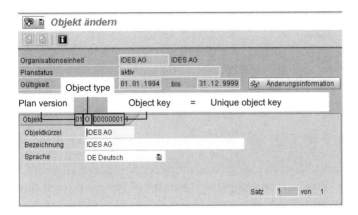

Figure 2.1 Infotype 1000, Object "Organizational Unit"

For the user, an infotype is the same as an entry mask. Within an infotype, there are plausibility checks and mandatory fields. Infotypes can also be organized into *subtypes* and they always have a validity period. Infotypes can be brought into a logical sequence, into a so-called *infogroup,* and therefore aggregated to a *personnel action*. In addition to the name, infotypes are identified with a four-digit number. The numeric range of personnel planning and development and therefore, also of organizational management lies between 1000 and 1999. Figure 2.1 shows the infotype 1000 "object as an example ."

Programmers are certainly interested in the fact that the data of the infotypes is located in tables in the database that are named after the infotype number. The infotypes of personnel administration are stored in tables with the name "PAnnnn" (nnn-infotype number), the data of the infotypes for personnel recruitment is stored in tables with the name PBnnnn, and the database tables of the personnel planning and development infotypes are called HRPnnnn. Therefore, the database table for the infotype 1000 "object" is called HRP1000.

Subtypes

Subtypes handle the subdivision of an infotype into screens for similar facts. The infotype 1001 "relationships" should serve as an example here. In organizational management, the most various relationships are between the individual objects. For each of these relationships, there is a subtype. For example, the subtype A 002 "reports to" and B 002 "is line manager for" handles the relationship of two organizational units (see also Figure 2.2).

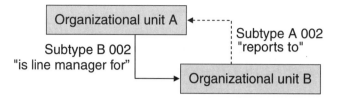

Figure 2.2 Relationships Between Organizational Units

Time Constraint

One of the most important characteristics of the infotype concept is the time constraint. Only by using the time constraint can we track the history of personnel planning and development. The time constraint specifies whether an infotype may appear several times in the system or, whether it must exist without gaps.

The following list distinguishes the various time constraint types:

▶ **Time constraint 0**
Across the entire validity period of the object, there must be precisely one record (and that is, always the same one). This time constraint is not used in personnel planning and development.

▶ **Time constraint 1**
At a given point in time, precisely one valid record must be present. Overlaps are not possible. Example: infotype 1000 "object." An object, for example, an organizational unit, is present only once with its attributes at a point in time.

▶ **Time constraint 2**
At a point in time, no more than one valid record can be present. Gaps are allowed; overlaps are not possible. Example: infotype 1007 "vacancy." At a point in time, an object can only be designated once with a vacancy. It must not be vacant across the entire time period.

▶ **Time constraint 3**
For each point in time, as many valid records as possible can be present. Example: infotype 1001 "Relationships" with particular subtypes (relation types). An organizational unit can be linked at the same point in time with several other organizational units.

The graphical depiction in Figure 2.3 further clarifies the various time constraints.

In the interface of organizational management, the infotypes rarely appear directly. The infotype 1000 "object," for example, is stored indirectly by storing an object, whether it is an organizational unit or a similar object.

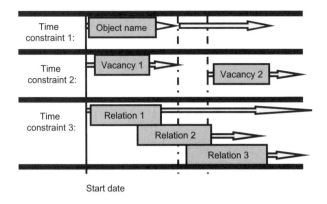

Start date

Figure 2.3 Time Constraints of Infotypes

Number Ranges

Depending on the number range that was defined, the system automatically distributes the key numbers for the objects of organizational management. Via the Implementation Guide (IMG) menu path **Personnel Management · Organizational Management · Basic Settings · Maintain Number Ranges**, you can define the number assignment. Specifically, here, is stored the number range interval for which the system assigns the object IDs in organizational management and for which manual assignment occurs. In addition, it must be distinguished whether the assignment occurs plan version-independent or, for each plan version separately. If the goal is to exchange data between various plan versions, we recommend that you define the number assignment plan version-independent; otherwise, there is the danger that objects with different meanings will be overwritten. By default, the number assignment works according to the specific version of the plan. If the object key should be distributed plan version-dependently, you must assign an individual number range for each plan version and, if necessary, for each object type. To activate the plan version-independent number assignment, you must enter an "X" in the field **Value abbr.** (see Figure 2.4). You can reach this table via the IMG menu path **Personnel Management · Organizational Management · Basic Settings · Maintain Number Ranges · Set Up Number Assignment for All Plan Versions.**

Change View "No. Assignment for All Plan Versions": Overview

Documentation

System Switch (from Table T77S0)

Group	Sem. abbr.	Value abbr.	Description
NUMRG	COMP	X	Number assignment for all plan versions

Figure 2.4 Activating the Number Assignment for All Plan Versions

To determine the type of number assignment and the number range, you must use the IMG menu path **Personnel Management · Organizational Management · Basic Settings · Maintain Number Ranges**. You have the following options:

► **Internal number assignment**
The SAP system assigns the numbers automatically. The number ranges are marked with "INT."

► **External number assignment**
The user assigns the numbers. The number ranges are marked with "EXT."

If you have decided against the plan version-independent number assignment, you must define the number range per object type and plan version. Otherwise, you can determine the number range per object type. Individual number ranges (*subgroups*) are assigned to the object types. The names of the subgroups are constructed such that the first two places determine the plan version more precisely and the last two places determine the object type (example: number assignment for plan version 10, object type S: subgroup 10S). In the definition of subgroups, *wildcards* are allowed. Thereby, the character $ stands for one place of the subgroup.

You must adhere to the following conventions:

► **Without the number assignment for all plan versions**

    ► $$$$ -   plan version and object type masked

    ► 10$$ -   plan version 10, object type masked

    ► 10S -   plan version 10, object type S

    ► $$S -   Not allowed!

► **With the plan version-independent number assignment**

    ► $$$$ -   plan version and object type masked

    ► $$S -   plan version masked, object type S

    ► 10$$ -   Not allowed!

    ► 10S -   Not allowed!

After you've acquired the relevant subgroup, you must determine whether you want an internal or external number assignment. Because the objects can also be identified using an abbreviation, it isn't necessary to give meaningful numbers. Therefore, we recommend that you use an internal number assignment. In the example in Figure 2.5, you can see how the number assignment for the plan version 10 and the subtype S is set up. The standard entry "$$$$" in the field **subgroup** stands for all number ranges that are not listed explicitly in the table. Do not delete this entry.

In typical cases, the internal number assignment should be activated. Only in exceptional cases should you use an external number assignment, for example, if there is a mixed system landscape in which the numbers are assigned by an external system and therefore no assignment should occur via the SAP system.

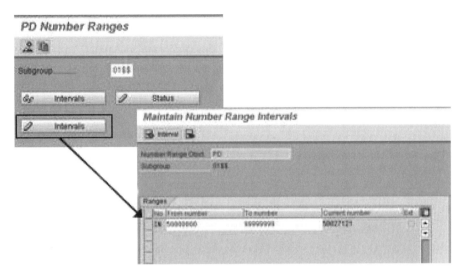

Figure 2.5 Internal Number Range Assignment

Because the number range maintenance is linked to the automatic recording for transport from a development system into a productive system, you must manually transport the changes that have been made within the number range interval. Therefore, in the start-up screen of number range interval maintenance, you should call up the corresponding function via **Interval · Transport** when you use the IMG menu path **Personnel Management · Organizational Management · Basic Settings · Maintain Number Ranges.**

In the following explanations, an *internal* and *plan version-independent* number assignment is always assumed.

2.2.2 Selecting Object Types and Relationships

While the master data of personnel administration is linked exclusively with the information object "person," there are different object types in organizational management. As a component of the unique key (see explanations of the term *infotype* in Section 2.2.1), there is an abbreviation for each type of object; for example, the organizational unit is identified with an "O," the position with an "S," and the person with a "P." Some object types are described below. Objects and relationships are stored in infotypes. An object always consists of the infotype 1000 "object" and the infotype 1001 "relationship."

Organizational Units

The basic modules of an organizational structure are the *organizational units*, which form the framework for this structure. Organizational units are objects of the organizational structure that are not particularly specified. These units can represent business areas, a team, or a factory. With this general definition, you can construct hierarchies of any depth. The hierarchy is achieved through the superior and subordinate arrangement of the organizational units, that is, the relationships "reports to" and "is line manager for" are used. For the special designation of initially neutral organizational units, the department identifier or, the identifier as staff department, can be incorporated using the infotype 1003 "department/staff" (see Figure 2.6).

Figure 2.6 Department/Staff Identifier

Positions

In order to be able to incorporate the employees into the organizational structure, there are *positions*, which represent places that are occupied by employees. Free positions that should be staffed in the future can be designated as "vacant." Therefore, they are accessible for applicant management in mySAP HR. Positions are always assigned to an organizational unit, for which the relationship "belongs to" is used. The *chief positions* that are used as chiefs of organizational units receive a special identifier. The technical identification occurs via the relationship "is managed" between the organizational unit and the position. Chief positions have a special meaning for many areas of the system; for example, in the workflow, they identify responsible supervisors within the organizational structure or, in the Manager's Desktop, they identify managers.

Jobs

Depending on how many of the following pieces of data are attached to a position, it can be worthwhile to create a type of model for the positions. In such a model, some generally valid data such as requirements and tasks could be stored.

With the concept of the *job*, SAP has created such a model. The job is therefore a template for variously characterized positions in a company. One could say that jobs are a possible grouping of positions; therefore, for example, the job "secretary" could be the model for the position "secretary Manager A." The jobs are often used for evaluation purposes, because it is easy to display, for example, how many secretaries or engineers there are in the company, regardless of their characteristics in their respective departments.

Tasks

In mySAP HR, there is a distinction between standard tasks and tasks. *Standard tasks* refer to all activities that can be carried out within the SAP Business Workflow, that is, the focus here is on the object that is linked to a method. The standard tasks are compiled into a catalog that is derived from the application component structure of the system. An example of a standard task is the execution of a profile comparison between an applicant and a position in recruitment. *Tasks*, on the other hand, describe activities that must be carried out within the organizational units.

Work Centers

Work centers are the location of where the activities or tasks are performed. In addition, you can specify information about particular basic conditions and activities in a work center. For example, via the infotype 1009 "Health Examinations," you can specify at what temporal interval the occupant of the work center should undergo a particular health check such as an eye test, precautionary examination of the lungs, and so forth. In addition, via the infotype 1010 "Authorities/Resources," you can document which resources (e.g., respiratory mask, protective goggles) must be made available for the work center or, which authorities and powers (e.g., power of attorney, power of attorney procuration, purchasing up to $50,000) are affiliated with the work center. Default values such as "Work Schedule" (infotype 1011) and "Employee group/subgroup" (infotype 1013) can be established for each particular work center.

Qualifications

Qualifications are established in organizational management or, in the personnel development component to jobs and positions. For jobs, qualifications are the default values for the positions derived from the jobs. In the positions, using qualifications, requirements profiles are created that can be used to compare the position's requirements with an applicant's or employee's qualifications. The qualifications are structured in a catalog. The qualifications catalog can be reached via the SAP menu **Human Resources · Personnel Management · Personnel Devel-**

opment · **Information System** · **Reports** · **Catalog** · **Qualifications.** Figure 2.7 shows the qualifications catalog that can be completed with self-defined qualifications. For more information about the qualifications catalog, the creation of requirements and qualifications profiles, see Chapter 8, *Skill Management*.

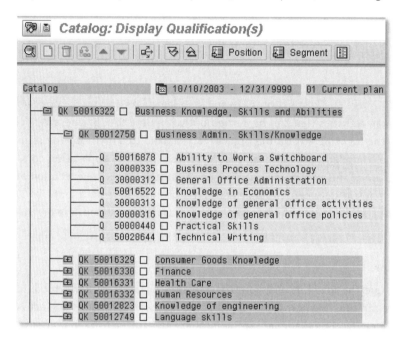

Figure 2.7 The Qualifications Catalog

2.2.3 Status Administration

Objects, relationships, and other infotypes can be stored in organizational management in a predefined status; for example, system-supported approval procedures for the setup of new objects—such as positions—can be realized (see Figure 2.8). The statuses influence the availability of objects and infotype records in the structure maintenance. There are the following statuses (each with its respective key):

▶ **1 – active**
The object or infotype record is currently usable. The processing activities for an object in the active status are unlimited. Objects or infotype records with the status "active" can be created, displayed or limited, deleted, and listed.

▶ **2 – planned**
The object or the infotype record can be suggested, but it is not active, that is, usable. Objects that have the status "planned" can be created, displayed, limited, deleted, or listed.

▶ **3 – submitted**
This is an object or an infotype record of a person or group of people for check-ing, which can be approved or declined. Objects and infotype records of the type "submitted" cannot be created or changed.

▶ **4 – approved**
This status means that a previously submitted object or submitted infotype record was accepted or approved. Processing of the data is only possible, how-ever, if the status "approved" is converted to the status "active."

▶ **5 – rejected**
If a previously submitted object or infotype record is not approved, its data can only be displayed. Processing is only possible if the object or the infotype record is converted to the status "planned."

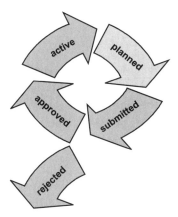

Figure 2.8 System-Supported Approval Process

Using the report RHAKTI00 or the *detail maintenance* (see explanations of the point *Entering additional data for objects* in Section 2.3.1), the status of objects can be changed after the fact. The report enables you to change many objects and infotype records at one time. Conversely, detail maintenance can only be used to change individual objects and infotype records.

2.2.4 Evaluation Paths

Evaluations of the organizational management can consider an evaluation path as selection criterion. The maintenance of the organizational structure can also be expedited on the basis of an evaluation path. For example, to be able to construct a structure from organizational units and positions, the system must be given a *start object* and a rule that describes the path that the evaluation should take from the start object and which objects should be displayed. An example is the evalu-ation path O-O-S-P (see Figure 2.9). This path lists the start object (an organizational unit) and all organizational units that lie below it hierarchically (**O-O**-S-P). In addition, all positions are displayed that are linked to the organizational units displayed (O-**O-S**-P). Finally, the structure also shows the people who occupy the positions (O-O-**S-P**).

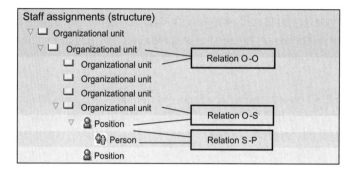

Figure 2.9 Evaluation Path O-O-S-P

In order to clarify all this once again, Figure 2.10 depicts how the system selects a particular quantity of employees that fulfill the specified selection criteria via an evaluation path. In this example, all employees in the personnel department should be selected whose position was created on the basis of the job "secretary." What results is a display of all secretaries of the personnel department.

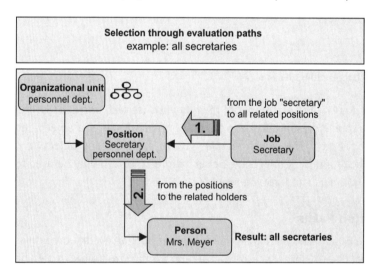

Figure 2.10 Evaluation Path "All Secretaries"

If the existing evaluation paths don't meet the demands or, individual object types and relationships were created, you can establish individual evaluation paths. For more information, see Section 2.3.5.

2.2.5 Organizational Structure

With the objects of the type "organizational unit" introduced in Section 2.2.2 and the infotype 1001 "relationships," the organizational structure of the company can be mapped. Thereby, the structure is always depicted in a tree graphic in the mySAP HR organizational management. Hierarchically subordinate organizational units are incorporated accordingly under the superior units. The user always looks across a particular start-up period at the organizational structure. Depending on whether the objects are located within or outside of the preview period, they are displayed or hidden. From here on, the beginning and ending dates of the infotype 1000 "object" and the infotype 1001 "relationship" are considered as criteria.

If there is a relationship between cost centers, on the one hand, and organizational units and positions, on the other hand, then there must be a link between the cost center structure and the organizational structure. If the information in personnel administration (i.e, the employee's master data) and the organizational management is actively integrated, the information of the cost center can be adopted from the organizational structure into the employee master data. So that particular data—such as the cost center—does not have to be maintained for each organizational unit, there is *inheritance*. The effect of inheritance is displayed when a cost center that is maintained on the uppermost organizational level is authoritative for all subordinate organizational units until a deviant cost center is maintained (see Figure 2.11).

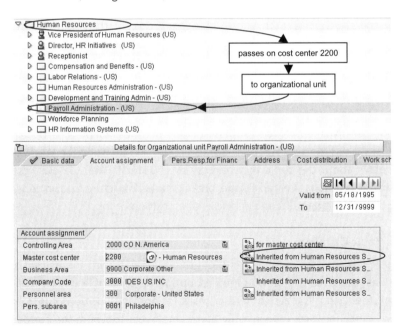

Figure 2.11 Inheritance Using the Example of Allocation

If, in addition, the account assignment features—such as controlling area, company code, and the business area of organizational units—should be handed down to subordinate positions, this must be set via the IMG path **Personnel Management · Organizational Management · Basic Settings · Activate Inheritance of Account Assignment Features.** You must enter an "X" in the field **Value/abbr.** for the group PPOM and the semantic abbreviation INHS (see Figure 2.12).

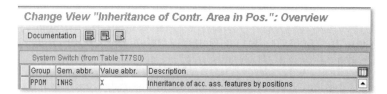

Figure 2.12 Activating Inheritance of Assignment Features for Positions

The significance of inheritance becomes apparent once again if you keep in mind that the maintenance of cost center assignment is stored completely in organizational management and in the ideal case, each cost center must only be assigned once. The maintenance effort is therefore reduced significantly and the cost centers of the employees can be acquired more easily since you can check the employee's position first and, if no cost center is maintained, you can look at those organizational units with which the position is linked.

To determine authorization administration, you should refer to the organizational structure for the *structural authorization*, which can indicate the authorization objects due to the assignment person—position—organizational unit and provide the user with, for example, the maintenance or view authorization for the corresponding organizational units. For more information on structural authorization, see Chapter 3, *The Role Concept in mySAP HR*. The organizational structure is also integral to the mySAP Workflow. For example, the workflow can be based on a chief position, identify an employee's supervisor, and therefore forward particular workflow tasks such as the approval of a vacation request to the superior. You will find more details about the topic of workflow in Chapter 5, *The SAP Business Workflow*. In the positions created in the organizational structure and in jobs, tasks can be stored that describe the activities of a position or job.

2.2.6 The Task Catalog

Tasks serve several purposes in mySAP HR. On the one hand, with the help of a task assignment to jobs or positions, a job description or job profile can be realized. On the other hand, the assignment of tasks to jobs and positions controls the workflow, which forwards tasks to only those employees to whom the performance of these tasks is assigned. Both types of tasks are located hierarchically or, grouped in the *task catalog*. In the standard version, this catalog is already filled with some tasks, but it can and should be customized to meet each customer's needs.

Within the mySAP HR system, tasks can be organized into various classes: professional, personal or, disciplinary or, they are assigned to no class. In order to ease the maintenance of the assignment of activities that are routinely carried out together to jobs and positions, you can group tasks. You can attain the task catalog from the SAP menu via **Human Resources · Organizational Management · Expert Mode · Task Catalog** or via **Tools · Business Workflow · Organizational Plan · Expert Mode · Task Catalog.**

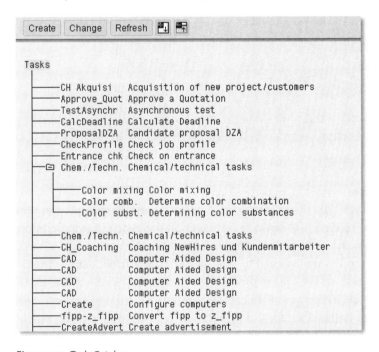

Figure 2.13 Task Catalog

In the maintenance of the task catalog, you should note that the hierarchy of the catalog arises because a new object must always be created from the object that is above it or superior to it. A completely new task on the uppermost level must therefore be created starting from the task catalog as the uppermost object. The following attributes can be assigned to the tasks in the form of infotypes:

▶ **Description**

Here, a detailed description of the task can be stored as free text. You can import already compiled texts into this infotype as long as they are in the *.txt format. This infotype has a purely informational character.

► **Character**

The assignment of tasks to particular character properties handles the categorization of tasks according to ranking, phase, and purpose. The values of the categories can be seen in Figure 2.14. These categories enable support for the salary and wage findings and deliver information, for example, about whether the tasks of a job or position contribute directly to the support of the company goals. You can evaluate the stored information using the reports RHXIAW04 "characterization of a task in an organization" and RHXIAW05 "characterization of individual tasks."

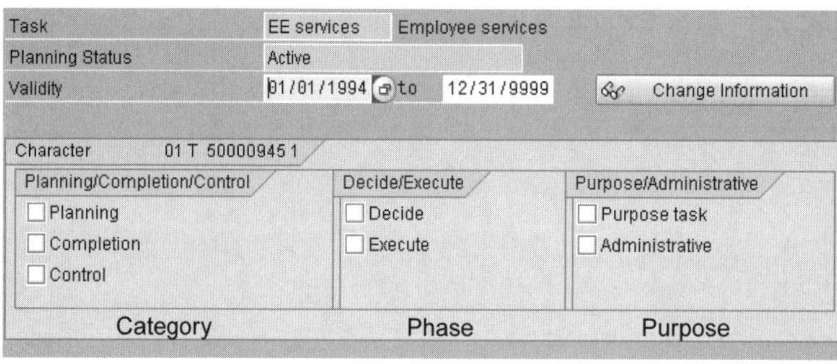

Task	EE services	Employee services	
Planning Status	Active		
Validity	01/01/1994 ⊕ to	12/31/9999	&ᵖ Change Information

Character	01 T 5000094 5 1		
Planning/Completion/Control	Decide/Execute	Purpose/Administrative	
☐ Planning	☐ Decide	☐ Purpose task	
☐ Completion	☐ Execute	☐ Administrative	
☐ Control			
Category	**Phase**	**Purpose**	

Figure 2.14 Infotype "Character"

► **Standard profiles**

Using this infotype, you assign, depending on the respective task, profiles that enable the user to carry out particular activities on the system (for more information about authorizations see Chapter 3, *The Role Concept in mySAP HR*). Authorization profiles are assigned to users of the system individually. With the infotype "Standard profile," these profiles can be assigned to an organizational unit, job, position, or task and they can be transferred to employees via inheritance. The only prerequisite for this is that the employee is linked with one of the abovementioned objects, that is, that this employee is in the corresponding position or, that the corresponding task is assigned to that employee. The assignment of the profiles specified here to the respective users is started via the report RHPROFL0. The prerequisite for a correct assignment of profile to user is the relationship between a person in the system and a user via the infotype 0105 "communication" in the personnel master data.

► **PD profiles**

As with the infotype "Standard profiles," here, also, profiles are assigned to a task. The PD profiles control the structural authorization, that is, which objects a user can display or process within the organizational structure. Via the report RHPROFL0, the infotype enables the automatic assignment of structural authorization profiles to users. Because the PD profiles only regulate access to organizational management, it is imperative that the infotype "standard profile" also be maintained.

► **Classification/lock indicator**

This infotype must be created for *workflow tasks*. The tasks can be classified according to the following criteria: "General task" means that each participant in the workflow may carry out this task. "General forwarding allowed/not allowed" expresses that the task may or may not be forwarded to users to whom this task is not assigned directly.

2.2.7   The Maintenance Interface

In Release 4.6C, the maintenance interface has changed significantly. The "old" maintenance interface from the previous release versions is still available, however, and is currently offered in expert mode or the *easy maintenance*. If you would prefer to use the old maintenance interface, you can set this as your default via **System · User Profile · Own Data** on the **Parameter tab** (see Figure 2.15)

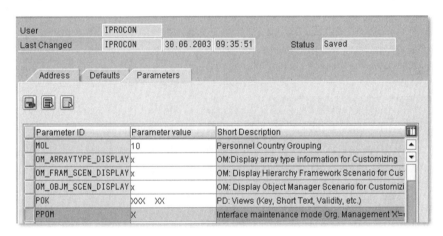

Figure 2.15 Default Setting of the Maintenance Interface

However, the new interface combines many useful functionalities on one screen. It is divided into four subareas (see Figure 2.16). Because of the *split-screen technology*, you can enlarge or shrink the individual areas of the screen with the mouse depending on in which screen area you are currently working.

Search Area

The starting basis for processing an organizational structure is the *start object*. Using the *search area*, the start object is acquired using various search tools (see Figure 2.17).

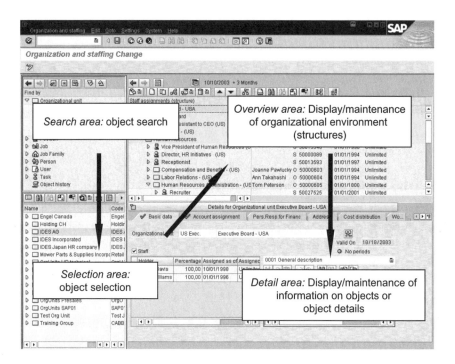

Figure 2.16 Subareas of the Maintenance Interface

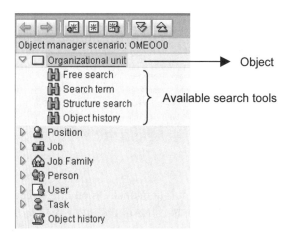

Figure 2.17 Search Area

The search enables you to conduct a search of an entire structure or object or a particular object, for example, positions. In the standard version, there are three search tools for objects:

▶ **Search term**

By entering a search term, you can search for the abbreviation and for the long name as well as for the key of an object. Another option enables you to search for objects that are assigned directly or indirectly to another object (see Figure 2.18).

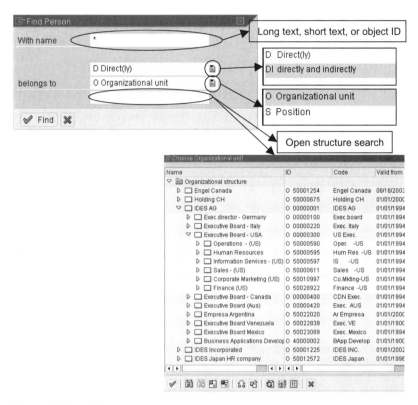

Figure 2.18 Search Term

▶ **Structure search**

The *structure search* enables you to search for the desired object using the already existing organizational structure.

▶ **Free search**

The *free search* enables you to select an object by combining a multitude of criteria (see Figure 2.19). By using the *infoset query* (see Chapter 6, *Query in mySAP HR*), you can determine which fields are used for selection and which fields are used for the task list.

You can save selections that were carried out as *search variants* (see Figure 2.20). Note that it is the selection criteria that are saved, and not the result list; that is, as soon as a stored search variant is called up, the system selects the saved criteria. You can start the search variants, which appear in the search area, by merely clicking the mouse.

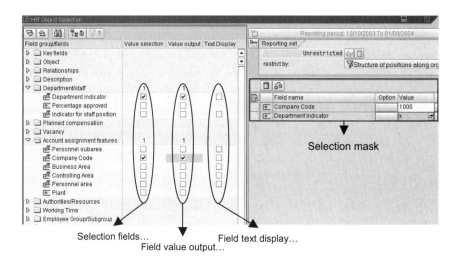

Figure 2.19 Free Search

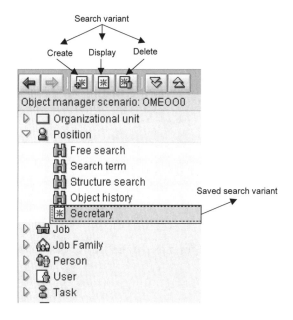

Figure 2.20 Search Variants

Selection Area

After a successful selection using the search area, the results of the selection are copied into the selection area. With the structure search, the selection area displays the entire active organizational structure. Depending on which object you are searching for, the organizational structure appears in various stages of detail.

If, for example, starting from the object "organizational unit," the structure search was called, then the structure of the organizational units is displayed in the selection area. If, conversely, the search starts from the "position" as search object, only the structure of the organizational units up to the level of the positions is visible. In contrast to the structure search, the other search tools deliver a *result list* and no structure.

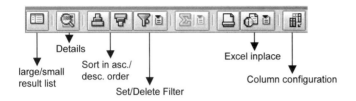

Figure 2.21 Icons of the Selection Area

Users can adjust the selection area if they want. For this customization, various functionalities are available:

▶ **Large/small result list**
The display of the list can be enlarged. The entire left area of the screen is then reserved for the list. The search area is hidden.

▶ **Details**
All available information is displayed for an entry from the result list.

▶ **Sorting (in ascending/descending order)**
The contents of the columns can be sorted in ascending and descending order.

▶ **Set/delete filter**
With the setting of filters, the result list can be limited further. Therefore, the information that is provided by the list can be used. From the column inventory, the columns are selected that should serve as filter criteria.

▶ **Excel inplace**
By default, lists are displayed in the *grid control*. This display enables, for example, the moving of columns with drag&drop. Alternatively, you can display lists in *Excel inplace*, which, if selected, transfers the list data to Excel where it is displayed. The only prerequisite is that Excel is installed on the PC in question and that a corresponding template—in this case sap_om.xls—is available.

▶ **Column configuration**
Here the user can set which information should be displayed in the columns (see Figure 2.22). The selection of information depends on which objects are currently displayed in the selection area. The column configuration exists in the selection area and also in the overview area.

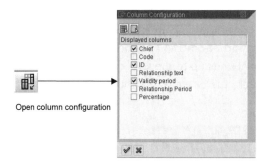

Open column configuration

Figure 2.22 Column Configuration

The search area and the selection area together produce the *object manager*. The object manager can be displayed using the menu **Settings · Hide Object Manager**.

Overview Area

By double-clicking on an entry from the selection area, that entry is copied into the overview area. From there, for example, new objects can be incorporated into the structure, and existing objects can be deleted or changed. The overview area contains various views of the selected objects (see Figure 2.23). Thus, for example, the assignment of tasks to positions or organizational units or a staffing plan can be displayed as a list or structure. The "Goto" function allows for the switching between the individual views of organizational management.

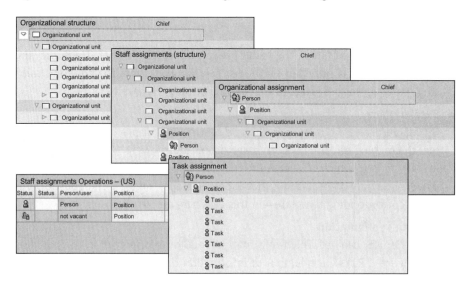

Figure 2.23 Views in the Overview Area

Detail Area

If in the overview area an object is selected with a double-click, in the detail area, individual *tab strips* appear. On the tab strips, information with content that belongs together is summarized. Data of several infotypes can appear on a tab strip. Figure 2.24 shows the tab strips from the detail area of an organizational unit.

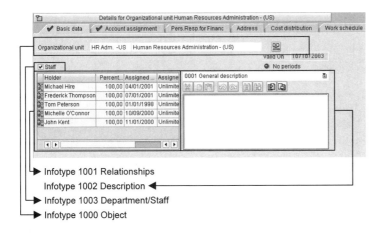

Figure 2.24 Detail Area of Tab Strip "Basic Data"

Information of the infotype 1000 "object" and of the infotype 1001 "relationships," 1003 "department/staff," and 1002 "verbal description" are displayed on this tab strip. The detail area can be adjusted. For more information, see Section 2.3.7. If information is already stored on a tab strip, it is marked with a green checkmark.

Interaction of the Areas

Objects that are selected using the search area appear in the selection area in the form of a structure or list. By selecting an object from the result list, this object is copied into the overview area. In the overview area, there are various display types via various evaluation paths. The data can be displayed as a list or as a tree structure. From the overview area, the organizational structure is maintained, that is, a new objects area can be created, and existing objects can be limited, copied, or deleted. By double-clicking on an object from the overview area, you can branch into the detail area. From there, the object properties can be maintained on the tab strips.

Using drag&drop, you can assign objects from the selection area to the overview area. For example, you can assign a person from the selection area to a position in the overview area (see Figure 2.25).

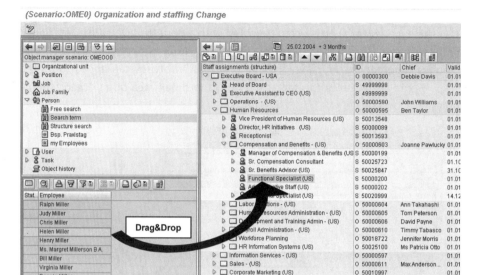

Figure 2.25 Drag&Drop Assignment

An organizational change—such as the moving of positions into another organizational unit—can be carried out using drag&drop. Because the system, by default, assumes as its beginning date for the new assignment the default date in the overview area via **Settings · Date and Forecast Period** and as its end date 12.31.9999, and it does not explicitly ask about the validity period of the new assignment, you should use caution when making any organizational change. Therefore, we recommend that you activate the time period query for organizational changes. **The query can be activated** via the path **Settings · Period Query for Organizational Changes** (see Figure 2.26).

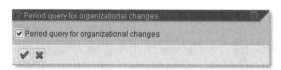

Figure 2.26 Activating Time Period Query

As soon as the time period query is activated, a transfer is only effective if the beginning date and end date are maintained explicitly (see Figure 2.27).

When it comes to maintenance and saving data, the new interface and the old interface differ greatly. In the old interface, all changes-such as the creation of an organizational unit or, the changing of the name of a position-are saved immediately after the corresponding action is carried out. In the new interface, however, all actions are carried out in memory; the data is saved immediately. Only when all previously entered information is stored using the **Save** button is the data saved in the database and therefore made available to other applications. You should make a special note of this particularly when testing the effects of changes in organizational management on other applications. Section 2.3.1 explains how you can prompt the system to remind you to save your changes at regular intervals.

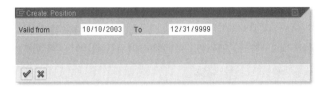

Figure 2.27 Time Period Query for Transfer

2.2.8 Organizational Management as a Basis for Planning and Development

Organizational management, with its associated object types, is vital for the processes of personnel planning and development. Figure 2.28 shows to what extent organizational management is integrated into other areas. The object types and relationships of organizational management that are integral to personnel planning and development further explain their significance to mySAP HR. Position, job, and often also the organizational unit are the basic objects that can be characterized further with respect to requirements profiles, career paths, employee goals, and so forth.

Figure 2.28 Integration Aspects of Organizational Management

Appraisals

Appraisal criteria can be acquired from positions and jobs as the basis for employee appraisal and position evaluation.

Personnel (Cost) Planning

Positions and jobs serve as input for personnel planning. For example, you can evaluate how many positions are staffed, will be vacant in the future, or even become obsolete. Furthermore, for (vacant) positions, target costs can be saved in order to be able to assign non-staffed positions a value for personnel cost planning.

Manpower Planning

Vacant, obsolete, and planned positions are the determining factors for the current number of positions and future needs.

Personnel Development

Requirements profiles that can be saved in positions determine the job descriptions and the qualifications for management in personnel development.

2.2.9 Organizational Management as a Basis for Personnel Administration

Organizational management is also well suited for structuring and evaluation in personnel administration. To list how organizational management functions as a basis for personnel administration, the pragmatic use of the following, previously explained objects will suffice:

▶ Organizational units and their incorporation into the organizational structure

▶ Positions, their incorporation into the organizational structure, and the assignment of holders

▶ Jobs as a means of describing and classifying positions

Organizational management has an additional meaning in connection with personnel administration in the authorization checking of mySAP HR. With activated structural authorization, you can assign users their authorization using their assignment in the organizational structure.

The position linked with the employee in the infotype 0001 "organizational assignment" forms the interface between personnel administration and organizational management. By assigning an employee to a position and therefore to an organizational unit, their incorporation into the organizational structure occurs.

Furthermore, in the infotype 0001, the assignment of the employee to the enterprise structure (personnel area, personnel subarea) and to the personnel structure (employee group, employee subgroup) of a company is made. With active integration, the cost center can be derived from the organizational management. It can no longer be changed in the infotype 0001.

The activation of integration into the organizational management for personnel administration occurs in two steps:

1. Via the IMG path **Personnel Management · Organizational Management · Integration · Integration with Personnel Administration** via the **Basic Settings** action, the entry PLOGI-ORGA must be set to "X" (see Figure 2.29). The table in which the integration is activated also contains other filtering possibilities and is well documented. To reach the documentation of the individual control switches, position the cursor on the entry that you want in the column **Sem. abbr.** (semantic abbreviation) and click on the **Documentation** button (see Figure 2.29). Often, the table is displayed in similar form in the customizing of personnel planning and development.

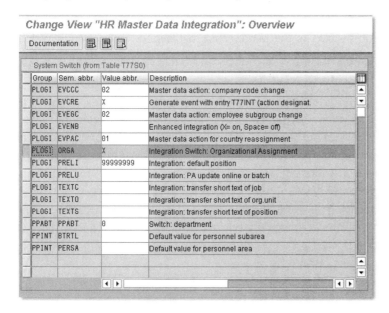

Figure 2.29 Setting Up Integration with Personnel Administration

2. If integration is activated, you must also specify which employees should participate in the integration. Some companies exclude retirees and trainees, for example. This filtering occurs via the characteristic PLOGI, which can be reached via the same IMG path. Figure 2.30 shows the integration of all employees.

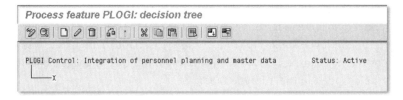

Figure 2.30 The Integration via the Characteristic PLOGI Is Generally Activated.

With active integration, only the position must be maintained in infotype 0001 "organizational assignment." The fields of the jobs as well as the organizational unit and cost center are filled automatically.

You can also manage the assignment of employees to organizational units, positions, and jobs without the use of organizational management. Instead of maintaining the corresponding organizational objects in the structure maintenance, they are maintained using customizing in simple tables. However, with an enterprise whose size is approximately 1000 employees or more, the use of organizational management is urgently recommended due to the additional functionalities.

Another integration aspect is the relationship to personnel recruitment, which accesses the data of organizational management via the vacant positions. The designation of a position as vacant is acquired in the infotype 1007 "vacancy." Therefore, it must also be noted when a position counts as vacant.

Via the IMG path **Personnel Management · Organizational Management · Infotype Settings · Activate/Deactivate "Vacancy" infotype**, the vacant position is defined using a switch. If the integration of the organizational management with personnel recruitment should be activated, the infotype "vacancy" must be activated. For this, the entry PPVAC PPVAC must be set to "1" (see Figure 2.31). If the integration with personnel recruitment is not active, the corresponding entry must be set to "0." Therefore, each unoccupied position counts as vacant.

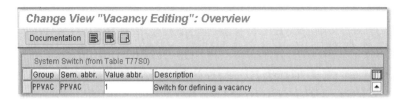

Figure 2.31 Activating Infotype Vacancy

Here are a few important notes on integration:

▶ Employees who maintain the personnel administration and organizational management in the system must be aware of the integration aspects and their effects on the work of their respective colleagues.

▶ You should note that if you conduct organizational changes to past or previous organizational management or development, these changes can trigger retroactive accounting in the payroll accounting of the affected employee; in fact, rebookings in cost accounting may go back too far in the past, assuming that through the organizational change, the employee's cost center changes.

▶ The integration into personnel recruitment and personnel manpower planning must be noted since these modules refer to the following conditions:

▷ Timely and correct maintenance of vacancies

▷ Limitation of empty positions that should definitely no longer be staffed

▷ Creation and corresponding naming of positions for new employees

2.3   Implementation in mySAP HR

2.3.1   Maintaining the Organizational Structure

You reach the maintenance interface of the organizational structure via the SAP menu path **Human Resources · Organizational Management · Organizational Plan · Organization and Staffing · Create**. You must use this path when you initially create a new structure and you want to determine the roots of the structure. Additional maintenance then occurs via the path **Human Resources · Organizational Management · Organizational Plan · Organization and Staffing · Maintain**. The maintenance interface, which is abstracted largely from the infotypes, is organized into the already familiar areas: the search area for acquisition of the desired start objects, the selection area for displaying the search results, the overview area for constructing the structure, and the detail area for displaying and maintaining information about the objects and object properties. The interaction of the individual areas of the new maintenance interface of organizational management was previously described in Section 2.2.7. The content of this section is the maintenance of the structure, the objects, and the associated object properties.

When you create the root object (see Figure 2.32) and other objects, you must ensure that you place the beginning date as far back in the past as possible. Then, all objects that should be linked with one another can be linked at the earliest as of the beginning date of the target object. If, for example, a position is valid since 1/1/2002, an employee who has worked at the company since 5/1/1998 can only be linked to this position as of 1/1/2002. The system behaves this way with all relationships that should be created in the organizational management.

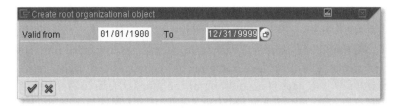

Figure 2.32 Creating a Root Object

Previous project experience has shown that some objects have been created with a beginning date that is too late. The beginning date can be changed after the fact with the help of the report RHBEGDA0. It sets the beginning date of individual or several objects (e.g., organizational units) to a new value. The report can be found in the SAP menus under **Human Resources · Organizational Management · Tools · Infotype · New Start Date.** For the selection of the relevant organizational units, the report enables you to determine the quantity of objects either explicitly by entering the object IDs or, for example, by using an evaluation path. A test function enables the viewing of the respective results without database change. The affected objects can be locked during runtime. In addition to the extension of the object validity, the relationships to the affected object are also adjusted accordingly.

After the root object has been created, one can maintain the structure from the overview area. Figure 2.33 shows the individual icons that will be referred to in the following.

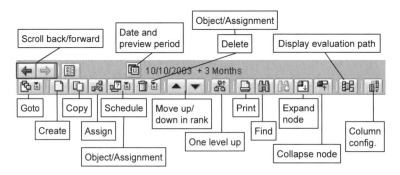

Figure 2.33 Icons of the Overview Area

The maintenance of the organizational structure always occurs using the specification of a maintenance period. When the organizational structure is called up for the first time, the current system date is suggested as a cutoff date. Via the menu path **Settings · Date and Forecast Period** or, using the corresponding button (see Figure 2.33), you can enter the beginning date and the period under consideration and an end date. This setting is valid while you are logged onto the system. When you first log on, the beginning date is reset to the system date once again.

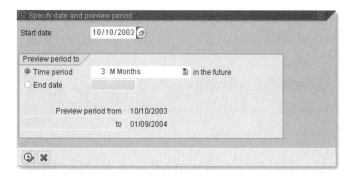

Figure 2.34 Specifying Date and Preview Period

The beginning date of the maintenance period is also a determining factor for the creation of new objects or assignments within a structure. This date is suggested automatically as the beginning date for new objects.

Before objects are created in the overview area, you should decide on a view for the structure. In the standard version, there are the following views:

▶ Task assignment

▶ Staff assignments (list)

▶ Staff assignments (structure)

▶ Managerial assignment

▶ Organizational structure

Using the Move up/down in rank button (see Figure 2.33), you can toggle from level to level.

Creating Objects

After a root organizational unit is created and you've decided on a view, another object is always created starting from an object. The system suggests the possible successor objects specified in customizing. Depending on which view you're using, for example, "organizational structure" view or "staff assignment" (structure) view, the system recommends other objects to create. Starting from an organizational unit in the view "staff assignment," the system prompts you to create an additional, subordinate organizational unit or position (see Figure 2.35).

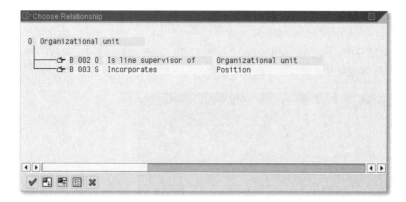

Figure 2.35 Suggestion for Creation of New Objects

From the point of view of task organization, the system suggests the creation of additional organizational units, positions, or tasks. The system takes the settings for this, depending on the view selected, from the permissible relationships of an organizational unit with other objects. The settings for this are made, for example, in the IMG path **Personnel Management · Organizational Management · Basic Settings · Data Model Enhancement · Relationship Maintenance · Maintain Relationships** and then allowed relationships. For the creation of individual object types and relationships, see Section 2.3.6.

Then, you must define the validity of the object. The system automatically suggests that you use the beginning date of the view on the organizational management as the beginning date of the object. As an end date, 12/31/9999 is recommended. However, you can also create objects—from the very beginning—that are valid for only a limited duration. Consequently, the relationship of the objects that should be assigned to the limited object created can last—at a maximum—until the end of the validity of this object. The designation as short and long text of the newly created object is acquired in the detail area on the Basic data tab strip. The key of the new object, the object ID—which, depending on the setting of the system, can be assigned automatically—as well as the validity period of the object, are not visible here at first. Using the column configuration (see Figure 2.22), you can display, among other things, the object ID and the validity period of the object and the relationships in the overview area.

When creating a new object, the associated relationships (infotype 1001) are generated automatically, therefore, A and B relationships are always generated. That is, when creating an organizational unit, a relationship B002 "is line manager of" from the starting organizational unit to the subordinate organizational unit and a relationship A002 "reports (line) to" from the subordinate organizational unit to the starting organizational unit are created.

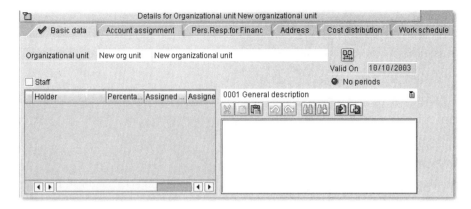

Figure 2.36 Acquisition of the Basic Data

All changes that are made to an organizational structure must be saved. Only the processing of objects makes no change to the database. Because under some circumstances, many changes are made before saving, in customizing under **Personnel Management · Organizational Management · Hierarchy Framework · Set Up Save Query**, you can define after how many actions a command can save data. An *action* refers to a user interaction that results in a change of data. To set up this command, use the IMG action and make an entry in the table for the scenario, for example, OME0 for the scenario "organization and staff" and define the number of actions (see Figure 2.37).

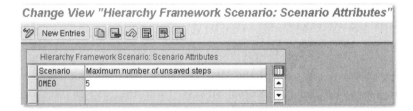

Figure 2.37 Setting Up Save Query

After the entered number of changes, you are prompted to save the data changes that you have made so far (see Figure 2.38). You also don't have to save if you don't want to. If the saving process is not executed after this command, the counter for the logging of changes begins again from the start.

Another important option when maintaining the organizational structure is the "undo" function. This function enables you to undo or restore changes made that have not yet been saved.

Figure 2.38 Safety Query on Changes

Copying Objects

Another option for creating objects is to copy existing objects. To do this, select the **copy** function starting from the object to be copied (see Figure 2.33); all data of the original object is copied and it can then be overwritten. For copying, there is a customizing setting that allows the exclusion of particular infotypes from copying an object. By default, some entries are already present in the table T77ITEX. In this way, when you copy organizational units, you can prevent linked organizational units and positions from also being inadvertently copied.

Change View "Hierarchy Framework: Copy Object: Exclude Infotypes"

New Entries

Hierarchy Framework: Copy Object: Exclude Infotypes

Scenario	Obj. type	Infoty.	Subtyp	Type of related object
	O	1001	A003	O
	O	1001	B003	O
	S	1001	A008	

Figure 2.39 Default Exclusion of Infotypes When Copying

If you would like additional exclusions, you can set this up by using the IMG path **Personnel Management · Organizational Management · Hierarchy Framework · Exclude infotypes when copying internal objects**. To do this, you can acquire entries for a particular scenario, for example, OME0 for the scenario "organization and staffing." In the **object type** column, you can select to which objects the limitation should apply. The **infotype** column must be filled with the infotype that should not be copied. Via the subtype, you can refine the selection, which is useful, for example, with infotype 1001 "relationships". The infotype 1000 "object" cannot be copied over into this table. The system ignores possible entries for this infotype.

Assigning Objects

Note that when assigning people to positions, there must be a distinction as to whether the assignment or transfer has a purely organizational cause or, whether the assignment of an employee to a new position is due to their personal performance or career. A transfer of an employee from one position to another, or a transfer of an employee into an entirely new organizational unit might be necessary from an organizational point of view. In this case, a specific procedure must be undertaken to reflect the requirements of that particular organizational department.

If this is a transfer due to an employee's personal circumstances, this transfer should be carried out via the execution of a personnel measure from the master data of personnel administration. In order to be able to trace the history of the employee in the master data without encountering problems, an action must be carried out. To adhere to this requirement, a standard workflow will do, which as a triggering event would take into account the transfer of an employee from organizational management.

The assignment from organizational management can be undertaken using drag&drop or using the **Assign** button (see Figure 2.33) of the target object. In the example depicted in Figure 2.40 and Figure 2.41, the position processor **Purchasing** and the person John Kent should be relocated from the organizational unit **Purchasing** to the organizational unit **Purchase Team A**. The teams A, B, and C have been added within the period under consideration and are therefore marked with an arrow.

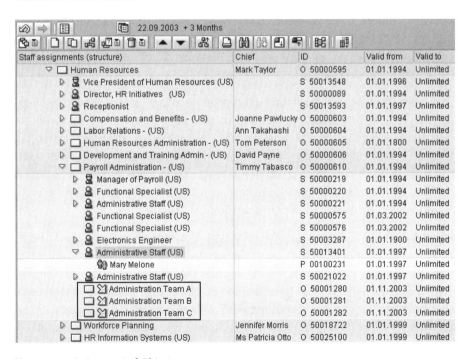

Figure 2.40 Assignment of Objects

Starting from the target organizational unit **Purchasing Team A**, via the **Assign** icons, a selection window is displayed, which offers the processor possible objects for an assignment. The selection window displayed corresponds to the one in Figure 2.35. After selecting the position as the object to be linked, the entire organizational structure is available for selection for the respective position.

Figure 2.41 Selection of the Object to Be Linked

With an activated time period query for organizational changes (recommendation from Section 2.2.7), the period for which the assignment should apply is queried (see also Figure 2.27). After the relationship period is confirmed, the transfer also becomes visible in the structure. On the now subordinate organizational unit **Purchasing**, the position is marked with an arrow. This means that the position leaves the organizational unit within the period under consideration. In addition, the position is now linked with the new organizational unit **Purchasing Team A** and there, it is marked as added with an arrow.

The transfer of people from one position to another is—as previously mentioned—only to be carried out from organizational management if the action in question is a purely organizational measure. Upon execution of such a transfer, the system asks automatically whether the action in question is a transfer or additional staffing. A transfer occurs if the relationship with the old position is replaced by the relationship with the new position. The old relationship is then to be terminated by marking the corresponding field (see Figure 2.42).

In the **Action** field, you can specify which type of personnel measure must be carried out in personnel administration. Depending on the entry, a corresponding standard workflow is started, which informs the processor of the transferred employee (entered in the master data infotype 0001 "organizational assignment") about the transfer and commands required to carry out the necessary actions. An additional staffing means that a person occupies several positions concurrently.

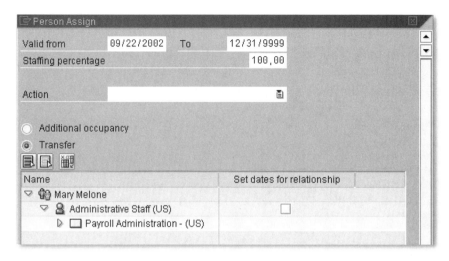

Figure 2.42 Transfer of a Person

Entering Additional Data for Objects

In the default settings, on the detail area for structural maintenance, not all info-types are accommodated on the tab strip. The maintenance of the infotype 1014 "obsolete" is, for example, not possible via the tab strips by default. Hoever, in order to maintain this infotype, you must branch—starting from the desired object—via the SAP menu **Goto · Detail Object · Enhanced Object Description in the basic transaction or detail maintenance for editing the infotype per object**. Using the SAP path **Human Resources · Organizational Management · Expert mode**, you can also reach this place without having to go through the structural maintenance. For the individual objects, there are separate transactions available:

▶ PO10 – Maintenance of organizational units

▶ PO03 – Maintenance of jobs

▶ PO13 – Maintenance of positions

▶ PO01 – Maintenance of work centers

▶ PP01 – General maintenance (from here any objects can be processed)

If, for example, the maintenance of the infotype "relationship" is not forbidden via the basic transaction (see Section 2.3.6 and from there Figure 2.64), this info-type can be created, copied, changed, or deleted here. The maintenance via the basic transaction allows the creation of infotypes in particular status, that is, info-types can be created as planned and then channeled through an approval proce-dure (see Section 2.2.3).

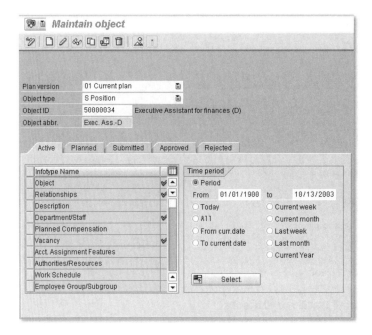

Figure 2.43 Infotype Maintenance via Basic Transaction

2.3.2 Maintaining Any Structures

In addition to the standard views of organizational management, there is the possibility of accessing any structures via the SAP menu **Human Resources · Organizational Management · Organizational Plan · General Structures** generally starting from any object (type) and by specifying a corresponding evaluation path. The list of possible evaluation paths is constructed through the specification of a start, transfer, and end object type (see Figure 2.44 and Figure 2.45). For more information on evaluation paths, see Section 2.2.4.

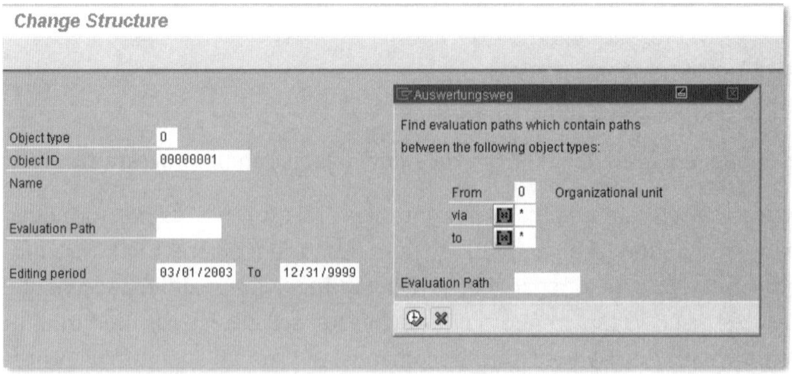

Figure 2.44 Maintaining Any Structures

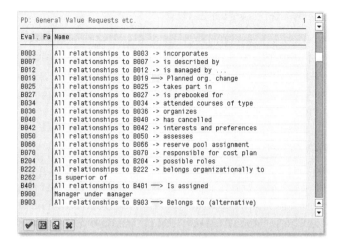

Figure 2.45 List of Evaluation Paths

After selecting the desired evaluation paths from the list, the structure is displayed according to the selection criteria (see Figure 2.46).

The maintenance of any structures enables you to use individual objects, relationships, and evaluation paths as the basis of a structural representation. The maintenance of the self-defined view of the structure also allows you to create displayed objects, as in the example of the organizational units, positions, and cost center assignments. With this type of processing, the maintenance interface is still in its old state. With the possibilities for customization of object types and relationships in the new interface, this maintenance transaction may become obsolete in the future.

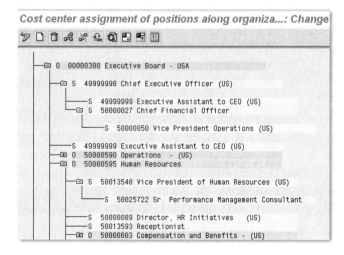

Figure 2.46 Display/Processing of Any Structure

2.3.3   Maintaining the Matrix Organization

Because the matrix organization is a very specific view of organizational management, there is a special maintenance and view transaction for this view. Matrix
organizations cannot be mapped via the standard views or via any views of the
organizational management. First, we will explain what a matrix organization is,
which customizing is assumed, and which evaluation possibilities exist.

What Is a Matrix Organization?

A *matrix organization* is an overlap of two different organizational criteria on the
same hierarchical level. Through the combination of a vertical and a horizontal
organization or dimension, intersections arise in which organizational units and
work centers (positions) can be located. An example of a matrix organization is
the *division matrix* (see Figure 2.47). In the division matrix, for example, organizational units or positions are assigned functionally/organizationally to a department (e.g., Marketing); however, they are simultaneously responsible for a particular division (e.g., Colors). Matrix organizations enable the definition of such a
dual role of employees and organizational units that exists in many companies.

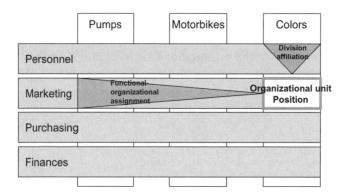

Figure 2.47 Example of a Division Matrix

Defining a Matrix Type

Before a matrix can be created, a *matrix type* must be defined. Using matrix types,
you define the object types that occur in both the dimensions and therefore the
appearance of the matrix. Using the IMG path **Personnel Management · Organizational Management · Matrix Organization · Define Matrix Types**, you reach
the corresponding customizing settings for the matrix types. First, a name is
assigned to the matrix type (key and long name). The customer namespace is
therefore defined via numbers (0-9), Y or Z as the beginning of the name. By
selecting the object types in connection with an evaluation path, you determine
the selection of object types for both dimensions (see Figure 2.48).

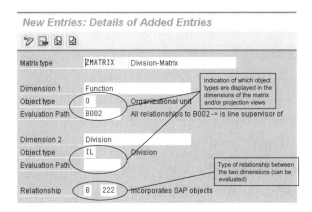

Figure 2.48 Defining Matrix Types

As soon as the matrix type is created, you can start the maintenance of the matrix. For the example of the division matrix, it is necessary that the functional-organizational dimension already be present on the system. Via the SAP path **Human Resources · Organizational Management · Organizational Plan · Matrix · Change**, you reach the matrix maintenance. First, you must select the matrix type that you want. Then, you must select the start objects for the maintenance of the matrix by specifying the corresponding object(s) for each dimension. You acquire the other system objects via the evaluation path specified in the matrix type for each dimension (see Figure 2.49).

Using the selection of the maintenance view, you specify from which dimension you want to start creating the matrix. The clear advantage of the projection to dimension 1 or 2 is the display in a tree structure from which the hierarchical organization of the individual objects arises. Unfortunately, with the matrix view, this gets lost. Figure 2.50 shows the maintenance from dimension 1 and also the maintenance from dimension 2. With dimension 1, the function stands in the foreground and the divisions are assigned accordingly. Conversely, with dimension 2, the divisions appear as uppermost objects and the functions are assigned respectively.

The third possibility for maintaining a matrix is the *matrix view*. As Figure 2.51 shows, all objects of a dimension in the matrix view are organized in *one* level, that is, the structure of the dimensions is lost for display reasons. If relationships between the dimensions are present, this is indicated with a graphic symbol. Via the menu **View · Relationship period on**, the date of the relationship can be displayed. By clicking the intersections, new relationships can be created or, existing ones can be deleted. The display of the matrix in the matrix view can be mirrored with the push of a button in order to exchange the positions of the functions with those of the divisions.

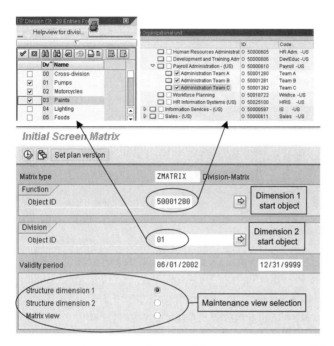

Figure 2.49 Selecting Start Objects and the Maintenance View of the Matrix

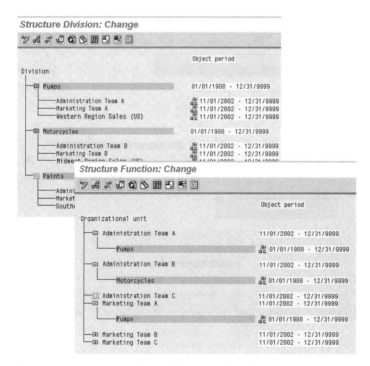

Figure 2.50 Maintenance View of Dimension 1 or Dimension 2

View: Function   and Division
Selection period: 10/14/2003 - 12/31/9999   Total number of columns: 3

	1 Pumps 01/01/1900 - 12/31/9999	2 Motorcycles 01/01/1900 - 12/31/9999	3
1 Administration Team A 11/01/2002 - 12/31/9999	■ 11/01/2002 - 12/31/9999	□	□
2 Administration Team B 11/01/2002 - 12/31/9999	□	■ 11/01/2002 - 12/31/9999	□
3 Administration Team C 11/01/2002 - 12/31/9999	□	□	■
4 Marketing Team A 11/01/2002 - 12/31/9999	■ 11/01/2002 - 12/31/9999	□	□
5 Marketing Team B 11/01/2002 - 12/31/9999	□	■ 11/01/2002 - 12/31/9999	□
6 Marketing Team C 11/01/2002 - 12/31/9999	□	□	■

Figure 2.51 Matrix Maintenance View

Evaluation Capability of the Matrix Organization

Incorporated matrix organizations can be displayed via the SAP path **Human Resources · Organizational Management · Organizational Plan · Matrix · Display.** In addition, you can use standard reports of organizational management, which enable a selection of the objects via an (individual) evaluation path, to select objects that are present within the matrix. To create individual evaluation paths, see Section 2.3.5. The evaluation of relationships between dimension 1 and dimension 2, which must be specified when the matrix type is defined, offers another possibility (see Figure 2.48). If only the display of the individual dimensions suffices, these relationships can also be evaluated via the maintenance of the "general structure" (see Section 2.3.2).

2.3.4 Selected Infotypes

All information about objects is stored in the system as infotypes, especially the object itself and its relationships. Accordingly, the infotypes "object" (1000) and "relationship" (1001) are the central personnel planning infotypes. The infotype 1000 defines the existence of an object in the system. All object types must therefore have at least the infotypes 1000 and 1001 in order to exist. Only after the infotype "object" has been created for an object can all other personnel planning infotypes be processed. Because some of the infotypes introduced here are also used in other components of personnel planning and development, we will address them again in other chapters. In the previous and following sections, some infotypes are also explained.

Planned Compensation

In the infotype for "planned compensation," information about the agreed wages of a position can be stored. This information can be referred to in personnel cost planning for the acquisition of the evaluation of a vacant position. The infotype allows for the grouping of a position in a salary or rate structure. In addition, explicit amounts can be stored as planned payments. The planned payment can be maintained for jobs as well as positions.

Vacancy

Using the infotype "vacancy," personnel recruitment receives positions that can be linked with job postings. As soon as a position in the organizational management receives the infotype "vacancy," that is, it is identified as ready for staffing, the personnel recruitment can access this position and start a personnel recruitment measure. The prerequisite for this is the active integration of organizational management in personnel administration. Vacancies are maintained exclusively for positions.

With the use of personnel cost planning, vacancies can be considered upon creation of a cost preview. Therefore, it is important that the planned compensation is maintained for a vacant position. Vacancies are also used in career and succession planning, where this information can be used to search for suitable positions for an employee. The acquisition of the infotype "vacancy" is reasonable if one of the following components is used:

- ▶ Personnel cost planning
- ▶ Career planning
- ▶ Recruiting

Account Assignment Features

Account Assignment features are defined for organizational units and positions and play a role in the assignment of cost centers to objects. Therefore, the account assignment features deliver the booking sector, the business area, the personnel area, and the personnel subarea. This data can be used for cost center finding. We recommend that you use the account assignment features in order to prevent incorrect or contradictory data entries. Through the inheritance principle, data entry is reduced because account assignment features maintained for organizational units are inherited by the subordinate organizational units. If the account assignment features should also be handed down to subordinate positions, you must set this via the IMG action **Personnel Management · Organizational Management · Basic Settings · Activate Inheritance of Account Assignment Features**. In the default settings, the inheritance of account assignment features to positions is not active. If positions are often linked directly with cost centers in a company, we recommend that you activate the inheritance principle. Otherwise, you should leave the inheritance deactivated.

In addition, the integration with personnel administration can be used more efficiently, because the account assignment features deliver default values such as personnel area and subarea for the personnel master data.

Obsolete

The infotype with positions that are required but are still occupied (for example, as a result of a reorganization) can be designated as "obsolete". Therefore, it is easy to recognize whether there is a need for action such as searching for new fields of activity for the holder of these positions.

Additional infotypes are located in the individual chapters that all build on the data of the organizational management.

2.3.5 Creating Individual Evaluation Paths

As already mentioned in the previous sections, evaluation paths help to determine the quantity of objects and relationships for an evaluation or, for the maintenance of a structure. For the objects and relationships that exist in the standard version, there are already pre-prepared evaluation paths in the system. If the existing objects and relationships are not sufficient for a company's requirements, however, and therefore new ones must be defined, the standard evaluation paths will also no longer suffice because the new objects are unknown to them.

You can attain the corresponding table for creating new evaluation paths via the IMG path **Personnel Management · Organizational Management · Basic Settings · Maintain Evaluation Paths**. You will immediately notice that each relationship by itself can display an evaluation path. The customizing table is organized in several stages that are displayed on the left side (see Figure 2.52). By selecting an entry in the table on the right side and then selecting the desired stage on the left side, you reach an additional customizing table. What is important here is that the customizing table can only be viewed for an entry. If you want to see the completely filled-out table, this occurs exclusively via the Transaction "SM31" when you specify the table name.

A new evaluation path must be named first. The reliable namespace is Y* or Z*. So that the evaluation path functions, the system must be notified as to which objects and which relationships—in which sequence—should be read out via the evaluation path. To do this, you must select an entry on the left side the action **evaluation path** (individual maintenance). The sequence in which the relationships are queried is determined by the consecutive number in the column **NR**. After that, one defines the start object in the **object type** column. If all objects should be checked for particular relationships, a "*" must be entered here. With the help of the columns **A/B** and **relationship**, you can determine which relationships should be acquired. In connection with evaluation paths, the **priority** column has a rather less important meaning. Because it is specified via priorities in which sequence objects are organized in the simple maintenance and in the structure graphic, an entry in this field makes sense if only objects are displayed as results for which a particular priority is assigned. With the entry of a "*", you can determine wheteher the objects should be organized and sorted according to their object ID. The function of the **skip** column is to consider a particular relationship in this line for the evaluation path, but not to display it. The sequence of the relationships contained in the evaluation path is what determines the output of the results.

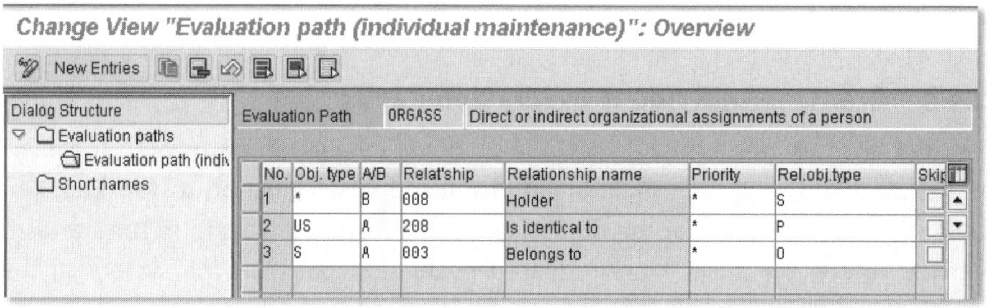

Change View "Evaluation path (individual maintenance)": Overview

New Entries

Dialog Structure	Evaluation Path	ORGASS	Direct or indirect organizational assignments of a person

No.	Obj. type	A/B	Relat'ship	Relationship name	Priority	Rel.obj.type	Skip
1	*	B	008	Holder	*	S	☐
2	US	A	208	Is identical to	*	P	☐
3	S	A	003	Belongs to	*	O	☐

Dialog Structure: Evaluation paths ▽ ☐ Evaluation paths / ☐ Evaluation path (indiv / ☐ Short names

Figure 2.52 Definition of Evaluation Path

The evaluation path depicted in Figure 2.52 acquires the holder of a position (B008 → holder of S → position), checks whether there is a system user that corresponds to the holder (US → User A208 → Is identical to P → person), and then reads the organizational unit to which the position is assigned (S → position A003 Belongs to O → organizational unit). This evaluation path serves to acquire the start object for the structural authorization.

2.3.6 Creating Object Types

In the duration of a project, it may be necessary—under certain circumstances—to expand the existing object types of organizational management to include new objects. Because organizational management is constructed like a modular construction system, with the help of which you can construct the organizational structure by selecting objects, it is relatively easy to define new objects and evaluate them. The IMG path **Personnel Management · Organizational Management · Basic Settings · Data Model Enhancement · Maintain Object Types** takes us to the table T777O (see Figure 2.53), in which all object types of the organizational management are defined. After the assignment of an object abbreviation for the object type (customer namespace 0*-9*) and a long name for the object, if it should be used with additional properties and if necessary used for the workflow, in the **OrgObj type** column, the corresponding organizational object type must be specified or previously set up. This specifies, among other things, the possible activities for an object type and events for describing state changes. As an example, here is the object type "Job family," which should be used to structure the jobs in the system.

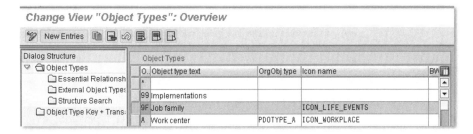

Figure 2.53 Object Type Definition

Using the **Icon name** column, you can select the display form of the object for structural maintenance that you want. Using the selection help, you can select from a multitude of object displays (see Figure 2.54).

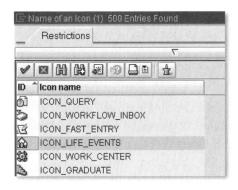

Figure 2.54 Icon Selection for Object Types

Object types that are embedded in a structure cannot be created without relationships, for example, a position can only be created in the structural maintenance if it is linked with an organizational unit. In order to ensure this requirement for individual object types, there are *mandatory relationships*. For individual object types, mandatory relationships can only be created if for the new object type the desired relationships are made accessible via the IMG path **Personnel Management · Organizational Management · Basic Settings · Data Model Enhancement · Relationship Maintenance · Maintain Relationships** (see Figure 2.55). Since the job family should be capable of grouping and jobs can be grouped under job families, it is necessary to allows relationships between job families as well as between job families and jobs.

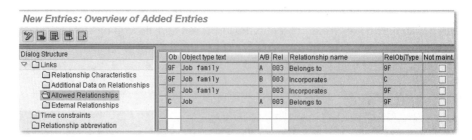

New Entries: Overview of Added Entries

Dialog Structure
- ▽ ☐ Links
  - ☐ Relationship Characteristics
  - ☐ Additional Data on Relationships
  - ☐ Allowed Relationships
  - ☐ External Relationships
- ☐ Time constraints
- ☐ Relationship abbreviation

Ob	Object type text	A/B	Rel	Relationship name	RelObjType	Not maint.
9F	Job family	A	003	Belongs to	9F	☐
9F	Job family	B	003	Incorporates	C	☐
9F	Job family	B	003	Incorporates	9F	☐
C	Job	A	003	Belongs to	9F	☐
						☐
						☐

Figure 2.55 Allowed Relationships "Job family"

The mandatory relationships are then determined in table T77SO. Figure 2.56 shows the mandatory ("Essential") relationship for the object type "Job" as an example. With this mandatory relationship, it is defined that a position must always be related with an organizational unit.

New Entries: Overview of Added Entries

Dialog Structure
- ▽ ☐ Object Types
  - ☐ Essential Relationships
  - ☐ External Object Types
  - ☐ Structure Search
  - ☐ Object Type Key + Transaction

OT	Object type text	A/B	Rel	Relationship name	Rel.obj.type	Obj.typ
9F	Job family	B	003	Incorporates	C	Job
	ⓒ					

Figure 2.56 Mandatory Relationship for Object Types

With the definition of object types, there is a distinction between internal object types whose master sets are located in database tables of personnel planning (e.g., organizational unit, position, job) and external object types whose master sets are located in database tables of other SAP applications (e.g., persons, applicants, cost centers). For external object types, in addition to table T777O, an interface program that ensures communication between the external objects and the organizational management must be specified in the table T77EO "external object types."

The structure search for object types—such as organizational units that was previously described in Section 2.2.7—is enabled through an entry in the table T77OS. The setting must be made using the action **Structure Search** (see Figure 2.57). By specifying an evaluation path and status vector (e.g., "1" for active objects), the object quantity for the structure search is determined. Activating or deactivating the **Key date** checkbox controls whether the structure search in search aids is executed on the current system date or taken into account over a period of time. If the identifier is not set, with large structures there may be very long runtimes during structure searches.

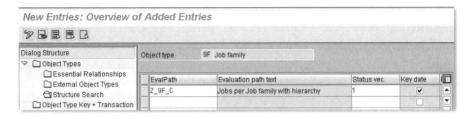

Figure 2.57 Defining a Structure Search for Object Types

The action **Object Type Key + Transactions** controls which object types are considered during evaluations and transactions. If, for example, in an evaluation, jobs are required, then the objects are considered that are assigned to the semantic abbreviation CLASS of the parameter group OTYPE; in the standard settings, the object C is considered. The behavior is the same for transactions. The Transaction PO01, for example, handles the maintenance of work centers. The semantic abbreviation PO01 of the parameter group TCODE is therefore assigned to the object type A. Previously in practice, such a step has not been necessary. If due to particular circumstances it nevertheless becomes necessary to replace the object type "job" with an individual object type, the semantic abbreviation CLASS (control of evaluations of jobs) and also PO03 (transaction for maintenance of jobs) of the object type C must be replaced with the individual object type (see Figure 2.58).

Change View "Object Type Key + Transaction": Overview

New entries   Documentation

Dialog Structure	Group	Sem. abbr	Value abbr	Text
▽ ☐ Object Types	OTYPE	APPSC	BS	Appraisal model
☐ Essential Relationships	OTYPE	BUDGT	BU	Budget
☐ External Object Types	OTYPE	CLASS	C	Job
☐ Structure Search	OTYPE	CPATH	LB	Career
⌂ Object Type Key + Transaction	TCODE	PO03	C	Maintain Job

Figure 2.58 Changing Object Type for Object Type Key and Transaction Code

The newly created object type is created in the PD master data via the infotype 1000 "object." Because all object types must have at least the infotypes 1000 *and* 1001 "relationships" in order to exist, the creation of an individual relationship type is also required for the definition of a new object.

In the following example, a relationship is created that should be used for the expansion of the structural authorization. Background: the structural authorization can give system users authorization for the organizational unit to which they are assigned and the organizational units that are, in turn, hierarchically subordinated to their organizational units. The second possibility for assignment of struc-

tural authorization is controlled by the organizational unit that somebody manages (is mapped via the chief position). Experience has shown that these options
are sometimes insufficient if, for example, somebody should process particular
organizational units in the system, although this person neither belongs to one of
these organizational units nor leads one of them. For this reason, it is necessary to
define a new relationship type, which should then be created between a position
and an organizational unit. Using the new relationship "processes in HR" and "is
processed in HR by," there is then a connection between the position of the processor in HR and the organizational unit that this person should process.

Because these are relationships to the subtypes of the infotype 1001 "relationships," it is required that you create the new relationship as subtype of the infotype 1001 via the IMG path **Personnel Management · Organizational Management · Basic Settings · Data Model Enhancement · Infotype Maintenance ·
Maintain Subtypes**.

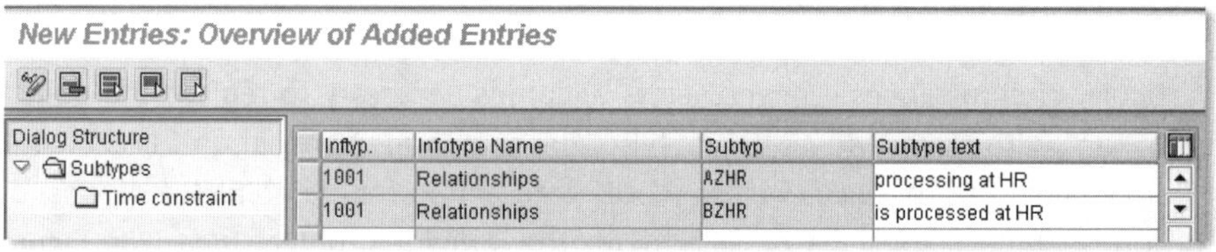

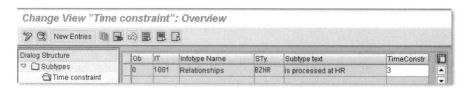

Figure 2.59 Creating Subtypes for Infotype "Relationships"

Using the time constraint that is required in a further step for the subtype definition, you can determine whether an infotype or subtype may exist multiple times
in the system or, whether it must exist without gaps (see Section 2.2.1). Because
a processor can process several organizational units simultaneously and an organizational unit can be supported by several processors simultaneously, for both
relationships, the time constraint "3" is assigned (see Figure 2.60).

Figure 2.60 Maintaining a Time Constraint for Relationships

Via the IMG path **Personnel Management · Organizational Management · Basic
Settings · Data Model Enhancement · Relationship Maintenance · Maintain
Relationships**, you reach the customizing table shown in Figure 2.61.

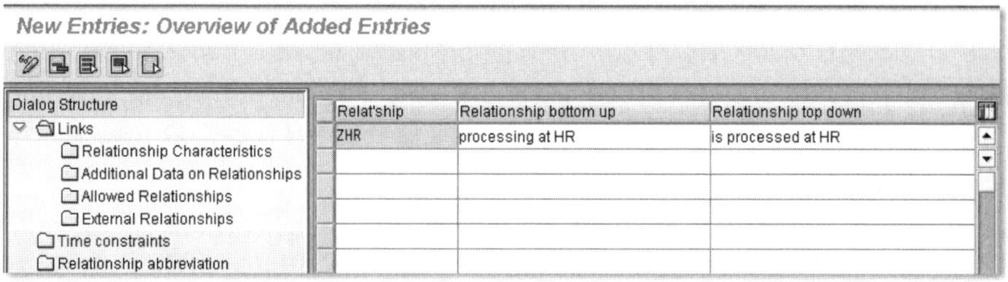

New Entries: Overview of Added Entries

Relat'ship	Relationship bottom up	Relationship top down
ZHR	processing at HR	is processed at HR

Dialog Structure
- Links
  - Relationship Characteristics
  - Additional Data on Relationships
  - Allowed Relationships
  - External Relationships
- Time constraints
- Relationship abbreviation

Figure 2.61 Maintenance of Relationships

The customer namespace for Relationships is called A** to Z** and it always has three digits. With the long name, names for the bottom-up relationship and for the top-down relationship must be specified. Using the example of the relationship 003 between positions and organizational units, this is, e.g. *bottom-up*, that is, from the position to the organizational unit the relationship "belongs to" and *top-down*, that is between the organizational unit and the position the relationship "includes" (see Section 2.2.2).

After the assignment of the bottom-up and top-down names (see Figure 2.61), using the next action, the relationship characteristics are determined on the left side of the screen. There, the A (bottom-up) and B (top-down) relationship are specified more precisely using the following fields (see Figure 2.6.2):

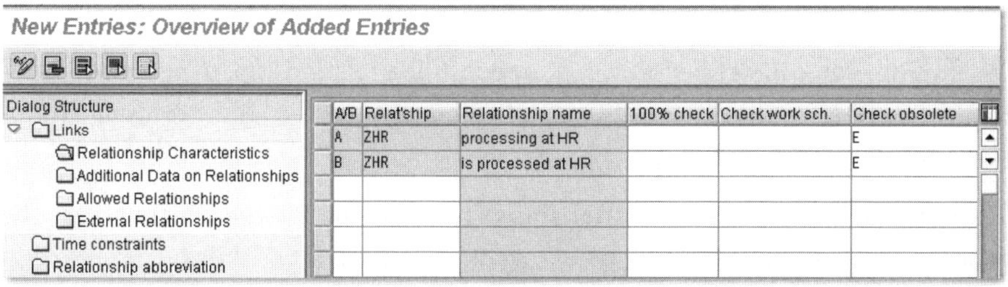

New Entries: Overview of Added Entries

A/B	Relat'ship	Relationship name	100% check	Check work sch.	Check obsolete
A	ZHR	processing at HR			E
B	ZHR	is processed at HR			E

Dialog Structure
- Links
  - Relationship Characteristics
  - Additional Data on Relationships
  - Allowed Relationships
  - External Relationships
- Time constraints
- Relationship abbreviation

Figure 2.62 Maintaining Relationship Characteristics

▶ **100% check**

It is intended for weighted relationships, where with the percent specification a check of the 100% mark should occur. This makes sense, for example, if the concern is a relationship between positions and people, since here the staffing of a position above the 100% mark is perhaps not desired and therefore, during master data maintenance, a message from the system should be displayed. This message can be specified by entering the following values: "E" = Error (saving is not possible); "I" = Information (saving is possible); "W" = Warning (saving is possible); " " = No check.

- ▶ **Working schedule check**

  If an entry is made here, with the relationship to persons in connection with the infotype 1011 "work schedule," there is a check for shortfall or exceeding. The possible values in this field are identical to those of the 100% check.

- ▶ **Obsolete check**

  Here, you can activate whether the system should check when creating this relationship if one of the objects to be linked has the infotype 1014 "obsolete." Therefore, it can be ensured that no relationship is created to an object that in the future will no longer be relevant. The possible values in this field are again identical to those of the 100% check.

In the next example, only a check for obsolete objects should occur. Via the action **Additional Data on Relationships**, additional data such as the weighting factor for a relationship can be displayed. If the weighting factor is active, then on creation of a relationship, a percentage can be specified. Now, let's look at the relationship between a person and a position (see Figure 2.63).

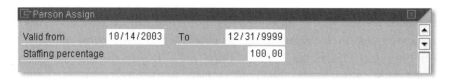

Figure 2.63 Displaying Staffing Percentage

In addition, you can define individual screens for a relationship, *dynpros* with self-programmed routines. Our relationship for the expansion of the structural authorization requires no entry here.

Using the action **Allowed Relationships**, you can specify for which object the newly created relationship will be allowed (see Figure 2.64). For our example, it is necessary that the relationship can be created for positions and also for organizational units. If one of the relationships is created, the system automatically creates the associated second relationship. The relationship B ZHR ("will be processed in HR by")—between the organizational unit O and the position S—and the relationship A ZHR ("processed in HR")—between the position S and the organizational unit O—is created. Activating or deactivating the **Not maint.** checkbox determines whether the relationship in the infotype 1001 "relationships" can be maintained via the basic transaction or, only from the structure maintenance. If the box is checked, maintenance from the basic transaction is not possible. On the topic basic transaction, see Section 2.3.1 (and once there, see Figure 2.43). For individual relationships, we recommend that you enable maintenance via the basic transaction; otherwise, the maintenance interface must be adjusted accordingly in order to enable maintenance from the structure (see Section 2.3.8).

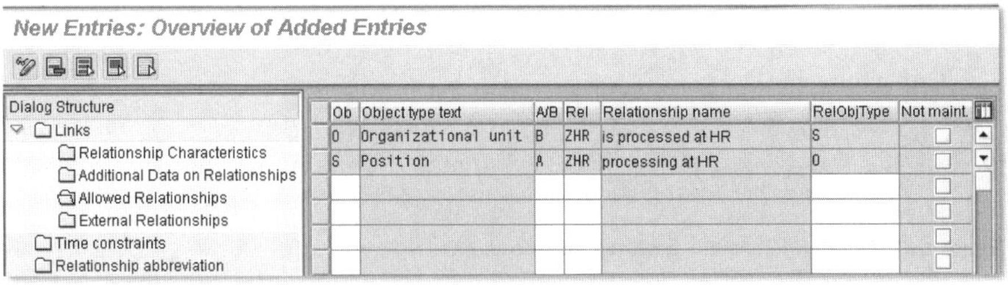

Figure 2.64 Maintenance of the Allowed Relationships

For those instances whereby relationships between two external objects should be created, in the action **External Relationships** there are additional settings required such as the specification of an interface program. The action **Time constraints** was already discussed in a previous step (see Figure 2.60). Upon conclusion of all customizing activities, the new relationship can be incorporated. The two new subtypes AZHR and BZHR are available in the infotype 1001 " relationships" via the expert mode or the detail maintenance via the basic transaction.

2.3.7 Expanding and Creating Infotypes

What in old release versions (i.e., before Version 4.0) was frowned upon and always caused problems with release changes—namely, adding individual fields to standard infotypes—is now possible, thanks to the *Customer Includes (CI)* in the database tables. Now, individual fields can be added to standard infotypes, without the danger that with a release change the additions will be overwritten by the standard entries.

Customer Includes are areas in database tables that are reserved for customer-specific fields and that are not overwritten with a release change. The database tables of the personnel planning and development infotypes always start with the designation HRPXXXX (XXXX = infotype number). Newly defined fields must then be integrated into dynpros or,+ new dynpros must be created. Because these settings require database and programming knowledge, we will not delve into them here. However, a setting that must be made—after the expansion of the database tables and the creation of new dynpros—is carried out via the IMG path **Personnel Management · Organizational Management · Basic Settings · Data Model Enhancement · Infotype Maintenance · Maintain User-Defined Settings for Infotypes**. In contrast to standard dynpros, here, the entry for the corresponding infotype can be made in order to specify which dynpro should be hidden when calling up the infotype (see Figure 2.65).

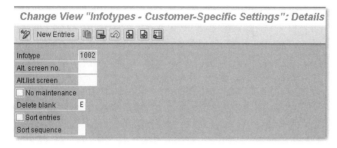

Figure 2.65 Customer-Specific Settings for Infotypes

Deviant dynpros can be specified for the individual screen and also for the list screen. The sorting of the data sets on the list screen can also be controlled via this table for each infotype.

If it is not feasible for company requirements to expand existing infotypes, individual infotypes in the customer namespace 9000-9999 can be created. A new infotype can be created with the specification of an infotype number via the Transaction PPCI (see Figure 2.66). The Transaction PPCI assumes that you have programming knowledge in ABAP/4 as well familiarity with the ABAP/4 Dictionary and the ABAP/4 Screenpainter. As a prerequisite for creating a new infotype, you must have created a data dictionary structure (DDIC) with the name convention HRIXXXX (XXXX = infotype number) in which all fields of the infotype are declared before the Transaction PPCI is executed. However, for the structure HRIXXXX, no further DDIC element can be created for this infotype. To get to the interface in which you can create structures, you must either do so via the Transaction SE11 or the SAP menu path **Tools · ABAP Workbench · Development · ABAP Dictionary**. Because structures aren't offered for selection on the screen, you must first enter the name of the structure to be created in the **Infotype Name** field and then click the **Create** button. Only then does the system prompt you for which structure you want to create. Through the selection of the object "structure," you arrive at the definition screen for structures.

Figure 2.66 Transaction PPCI

Using the **Create** button—building on the previously defined DDIC structure—all necessary module pools with the process logic, dynpros, table entries in T77XX tables, and so forth, are created. For further details, please see the documentation for the Transaction PPCI.

If the infotype is created, then in the table T777I (which can be reached via the IMG path **Personnel Management · Organizational Management · Basic Settings · Data Model Enhancement · Infotype Maintenance · Maintain infotypes**), the new infotype must still be assigned to the desired object types of the organizational management (see Figure 2.67). If the infotype is copied into the maintenance interface of the organizational management as a tab strip in the detail area, you must create the subscreen 7000 in the Transaction PPCI. Therefore, you must use the **Create** button and then choose from the menu **Infotype · Creating a Subscreen** because this screen is used for display on the tab strips. In addition, in the table T777I, you must enter "7000" in the subscreen field. The procedure for integrating new infotypes into the maintenance interface is described in more detail in Section 2.3.8.

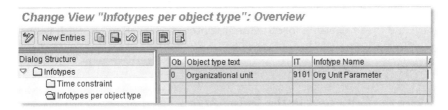

Figure 2.67 Assigning Infotypes to the Object Types

The displayed new infotype 9101 "Org Unit Parameter" arises in practice from the fact that organizational units can be specified more precisely in mySAP HR only via the department or staff identifier (infotype 1003) (see also Section 2.2.2). The requirements of personnel reporting with respect to selection possibilities and the evaluation capability of organizational units generally extend further. It is already sufficient if in a company—and this occurs relatively often—there are more than two different types of organizational units and these units are to be evaluated separately if necessary. The primary requirement that was fulfilled with the new infotype (see Figure 2.68) was that the administrative office number of the organizational unit, its functional area, and the type of organizational unit had to be capable of evaluation and available as a selection criterion for reports.

The creation of the new infotype was a natural evolution of the complex expansions for personnel reporting; only through further adjustments and programming did the kind of personnel reporting arise that would meet the business requirements of the company.

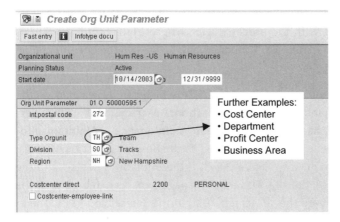

Figure 2.68 New Infotype 9101 "Org Unit Parameter"

2.3.8 Adjusting the Maintenance Interface

The maintenance interface that was explained in detail in Section 2.2.7 is very flexible with respect to customer-specific adjustments; for example, newly created object types, relationships, and infotypes can be integrated into the new interface and made available for structure maintenance. In addition, existing elements of the interface can be adjusted to meet the demands and requests of the customers.

Adjusting the Tab Pages in the Detail Area

The first adjustment possibility is the change of the tab pages in the detail area (see Figure 2.69). Via the IMG path **Personnel Management · Organizational Management · Hierarchy Framework · Adjust Tab Pages in Detail Area**, you can make the necessary settings.

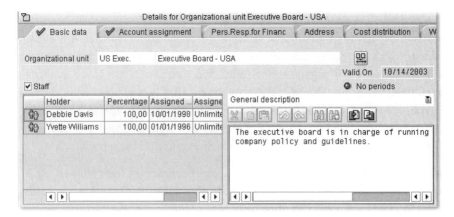

Figure 2.69 Tab Pages in the Detail Area

The adjustment of the text and icons on a tab page can be undertaken via the corresponding customizing activity. The tables to be maintained enable the overwriting of the standard entries from the tab page definition (see Figure 2.72). To identify the icons and texts, functional building blocks that are specified must meet particular requirements. So that these are adhered to, there are two model functional building blocks (CB_OM_DETAILSCREEN_ICONS for the icons; CB_OM_DETAILSCREEN_TEXT for the tab page text). The advantage of this method is that the icons and texts can be displayed dynamically. A procedure similar to the changing of texts and icons on the tab pages is also used for changing the sequence of the tab pages and for displaying and hiding standard tab pages, that is, there is a table that overwrites the entries of the tab page group definition (Figure 2.73). Figure 2.70 shows the overwriting of the sequence of the tab page BASIS_P, the basic data for the object type P. For this overwriting of the sequence of the tab page, you must enter the data of the entry in the definition of the tab page group (see Figure 2.73) in the table that can be reached via the IMG path **Personnel Management · Organizational Management · Hierarchy Framework · Adjust Pages in Detail Area · Change tab page sequence.** Only the number in the sequence field is specified as changed (see Figure 2.70).

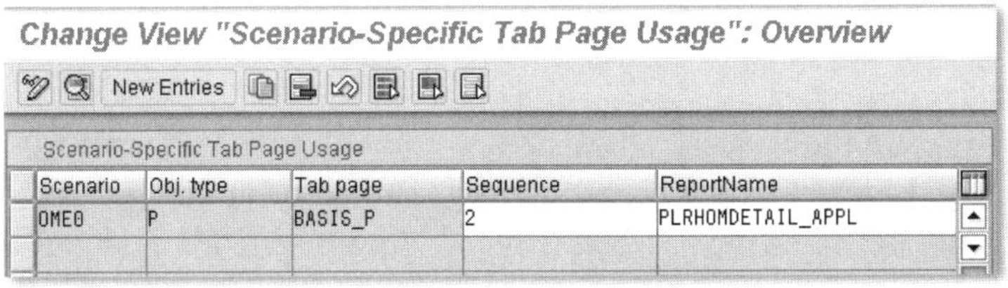

Change View "Scenario-Specific Tab Page Usage": Overview

New Entries

Scenario-Specific Tab Page Usage

Scenario	Obj. type	Tab page	Sequence	ReportName
OME0	P	BASIS_P	2	PLRHOMDETAIL_APPL

Figure 2.70 Changing the Sequence of the Tab Pages

For the tables for adjusting the tab pages in the detail area, it must be noted that here the scenario determines what adjustments are made. Which scenario is used in the structure maintenance can be displayed by setting the user parameter (SAP menu **System · User profile · Own Data Parameters tab page**) OM_FRAM_SCEN_DISPLAY = "X." If the parameter is activated, via the Transaction PPOME "change organization and staffing," you will recognize the scenario in the header of the maintenance interface (see Figure 2.71). In the default settings, this is the scenario OME0.

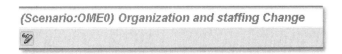

(Scenario:OME0) Organization and staffing Change

Figure 2.71 Displayed Scenario with Structure Maintenance

Expanding the Tab Pages in the Detail Area

To integrate an infotype into the detail area, you must copy the infotype into an existing tab page group via the IMG path **Personnel Management · Organizational Management · Hierarchy Framework · Integrate New Infotype · Add Infotype as Tab Page in detail area**. The definition of the tab page occurs via a customizing table, in which you can orient yourself using the existing entries and then copy a standard entry for PD infotypes (see Figure 2.72). The customer namespace begins here with Y or Z. Typically, individual infotypes appear separately and not together with other infotypes on a tab page, which is why you must activate (check) the **Infotype-specific** box. The integration of the infotype 9101 "reporting identifier," which was created in Section 2.3.7, exemplifies this situation.

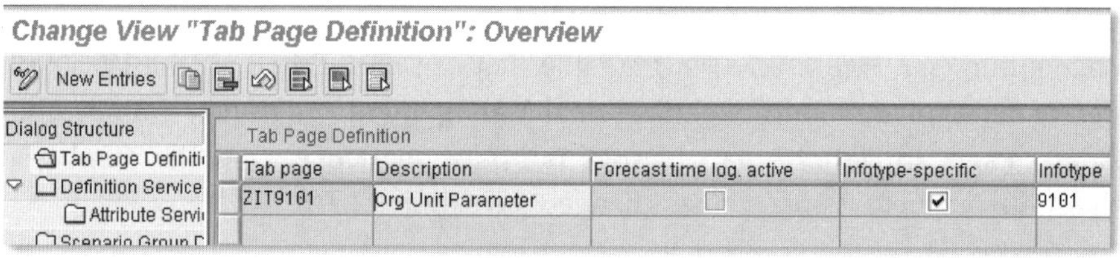

Change View "Tab Page Definition": Overview					
New Entries 📋 🗐 🖉 📑 📑 🗔					

Dialog Structure
- 🗂 Tab Page Definiti
- ▽ 🗀 Definition Service
  - 🗀 Attribute Servi
  - 🗀 Scenario Group D

Tab Page Definition

Tab page	Description	Forecast time log. active	Infotype-specific	Infotype
ZIT9101	Org Unit Parameter	☐	☑	9101

Figure 2.72 Creating Individual Tab Page

Then, you must maintain the table in Figure 2.73. In addition to the scenario, you must decide for which object type the new tab page should be available. Therefore, the placeholder "*" stands for all object types. Because the infotype 9101 "Org Unit Parameter" should be maintained exclusively for organizational units, the entry in the object type field is "O." After entering the previously defined tab page ZIT9101, you must also define the position of the tab page within the group, which is controlled by a consecutive number.

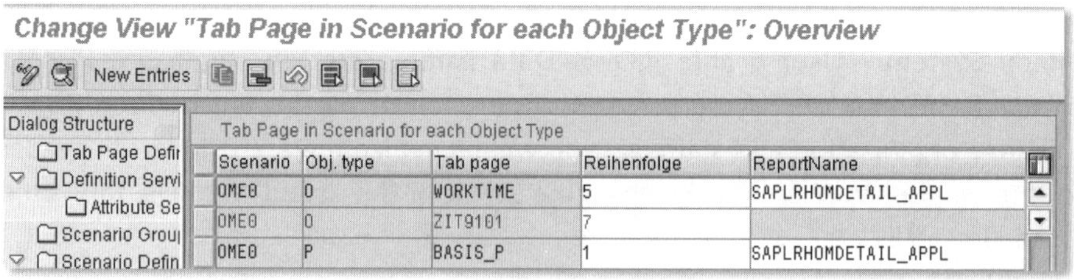

Change View "Tab Page in Scenario for each Object Type": Overview					
🖉 🔍 New Entries 📋 🗐 🖉 📑 📑 🗔					

Dialog Structure
- 🗀 Tab Page Defir
- ▽ 🗀 Definition Servi
  - 🗀 Attribute Se
  - 🗀 Scenario Grou
- ▽ 🗀 Scenario Defin

Tab Page in Scenario for each Object Type

Scenario	Obj. type	Tab page	Reihenfolge	ReportName	
OME8	O	WORKTIME	5	SAPLRHOMDETAIL_APPL	
OME8	O	ZIT9101	7		
OME8	P	BASIS_P	1	SAPLRHOMDETAIL_APPL	

Figure 2.73 Including Individual Tab Page in Tab Page Group

The entry of a report name is only required if fields of several different infotypes should be displayed on a tab page. The result of the entries is a new tab page with the fields of the new infotype (see Figure 2.74).

Figure 2.74 New Tab Page with Individual Infotype

Integration of Individual Object Types into the Maintenance Interface

The newly created object type 9F "Job Family" from Section 2.3.6 will serve as an example for the integration of a new object type into the maintenance interface. The recommended IMG path for incorporating new object types is **Personnel Management · Organizational Management · Hierarchy Framework · Object Manager** since the path provided in the standard version offers a worse and more confusing arrangement of the activities. Via the named IMG path, you arrive at the first setting that affects the search area of the object manager. The activity is called **Definition of Search Node** and is the first step toward the incorporation of the new object type into the search area. For this, the new object type is copied into the corresponding customizing table (see Figure 2.75), from which the name of the search node (customer namespace Y* or Z*), the name of the corresponding object type, and the name of the icon to be used all emerge.

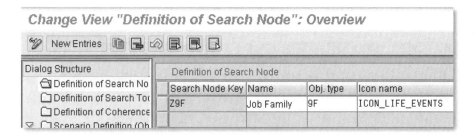

Figure 2.75 Defining Own Search Nodes

In the final action, adjust the **search area**, the scenario is once again the determining factor—this time, of the search area—to undertake the settings for the correct area. In order to see the scenario of the search area or the object manager displayed, you must once again set a user parameter: OM_OBJM_SCEN_DISPLAY (for the procedure, see the descriptions of Figure 2.71). By default, the scenario OMEOOO is used. With this information, you can undertake the corresponding settings in the table for scenario-specific definitions of the node in the search area (see Figure 2.76). Because the object manager consists of both the search area and also the result list, you can specify in this table which information of the new object should be displayed in which column of the result list.

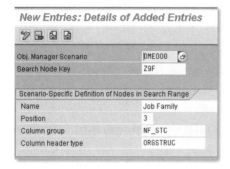

Figure 2.76 Expand Object Manager

For this, in the **Column group** field, you would enter the scenario-specific group that—depending on the object—is called and can be displayed via the set user parameter OM_ARRAYTYPE_DISPLAY. To be able to see the scenario or the column group, you must follow the path described in Figure 2.77.

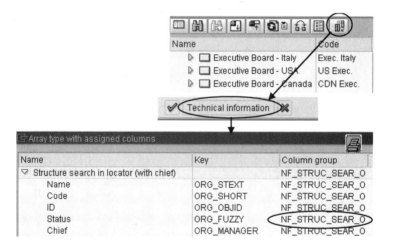

Figure 2.77 Acquiring Column Group

Enter "ORGSTRUC" as the type of the column titles. If all settings have been made, in the last step, you must assign the search tools that you want to the search node (e.g., free search, search term, or structure search) (see Figure 2.78). After you select the search tool of your choice, you can specify its position below the search node.

In addition, via the selection of the interaction tool, the actions that are possible are specified with the entries of the result list as are the results of these actions.

These actions could include drag&drop (i.e., of an entry in relationship to another entry) or, a double-click (i.e., copying the entry into the overview area). If actions that exceed the standard version are considered, programming knowledge is required because the interaction tools are implemented as an *ABAP object class*. The assignment of several search tools to one search node occurs via the acquisition of additional data sets in the corresponding customizing table. If a search tool is defined as such via the field **Search tool**, this search tool is started automatically as soon as the search node is selected. The remaining settings pertain to the display and action possibilities such as sorting or filtering, which should be available options with the result list.

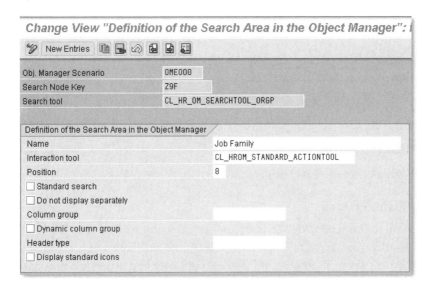

Figure 2.78 Assigning Search Tools to Search Nodes

2.3.9 Working with Different Plan Versions

As we already explained in Section 2.2.1, plan versions are simply scenarios in which organizational structures can be mapped. In the plan version designated as active, the current, valid organizational structure of a company is mapped. This is simultaneously the integration plan version that is considered if personnel administration is integrated with this scenario. Additional plan versions are used in order to map other organizational structures as planning scenarios.

Typically, a plan version contains an organizational structure, that is, only a root organizational unit. It is possible, however, to create several root organizational units and therefore, several organizational structures in a plan version. In the introduction guidelines in the Implementation Guide (IMG), the plan versions are administered under **Personnel Management · Global Settings in Personnel**

Management · Plan Version Maintenance. You cannot use or delete the plan version ".." entered in this table (see Figure 2.79) because it is used for data transport from one system into another.

The **Active** field indicates the integration plan version. Here again please note that with the active integration of the organizational management into personnel administration, you can never change the active plan version. Otherwise, inconsistencies can occur in the system! In the **Current** field, the plan version with which the system is currently working is always checked. To select the plan version to be processed within the maintenance interface of the organizational structure, use the menu path **Settings · Plan Version · Alternative or Active**.

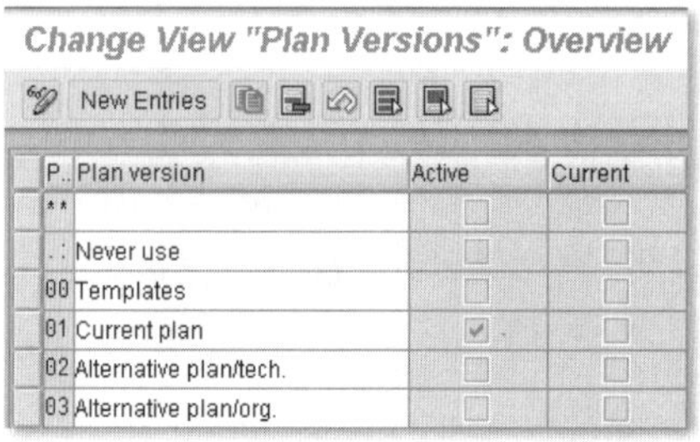

P.	Plan version	Active	Current
* *		☐	☐
. .	Never use	☐	☐
00	Templates	☐	☐
01	Current plan	☑	☐
02	Alternative plan/tech.	☐	☐
03	Alternative plan/org.	☐	☐

Figure 2.79 Maintenance of the Plan Versions

Copying Plan Versions

With the help of the report RHCOPL00, you can copy objects from one plan version into another plan version. This makes sense if the active plan version should serve as the basis for an alternative plan. You should note that the report may only be used to copy another plan version in areas that do not overlap. Therefore, the objects can either be copied into an empty plan version or, you can copy only those areas that don't overlap, which can be deleted in the target plan version if necessary. If this is not heeded, then violations of number range definitions or inconsistencies can occur in the target plan version. Problems due to overlapping number ranges can also be avoided by working with plan version-independent number ranges (see the explanations of the term "number ranges" in Section 2.2.1). Via the report parameter, you can indicate the quantity of objects and specify whether only particular substructures (evaluation paths) should be copied.

Comparing Plan Versions

The report RHCOPLPT serves to compare plan versions with one another. It works in two steps, whereby only in the second step does the actual copying occur. First, it is specified via the report parameter which objects or which substructures should be copied. Then, the selected objects and substructures are compared in the initial plan version and target plan version; the result of the comparison is output in the form of a structural evaluation on the following screen. Using traffic lights, it is indicated to what extent an object matches in the initial and target plan versions and whether it exists at all in both plan versions:

▶ **Green light**
The object exists in both plan versions and matches the selected evaluation path.

▶ **Yellow light**
The object exists in both plan versions and matches partially.

▶ **Red light**
The object only exists in the target plan version.

If you would like to compare the objects in a more detailed fashion before copying them, you can display all infotypes of the objects via the menu **Goto · Object description.** In the second step, you can select a subarea by highlighting which objects should be copied.

2.3.10 Evaluations in Organizational Management

First, you should note that with the use of organizational management, reports from other areas of the mySAP HR module receive expanded selection possibilities. Selections that were carried out previously without an organizational structure via the personnel subarea can be refined greatly with the use of organizational management. Because personnel subareas are formed differently in each company, for example, to map the individual branches of a company or the companies within a country, it is not possible via the sole criterion of the personnel area to consider an organizational unit within a branch as a selection criterion. Alternatively, via the use of organizational management, the organizational structure is available as a selection criterion. Figure 2.80 shows how—through the use of the organizational structure—a personnel administration report allows the use of individual organizational units for the selection of the employees assigned to them.

With selection via using the organizational structure, it must be noted that the selection of an organizational unit does not automatically contain the selection of the subordinate organizational units.

Only those organizational units that are explicitly checked are selected. This can be carried out automatically by using the button highlighted in the subtree in Figure 2.80 for the organizational units that lie under the highlighted organizational unit.

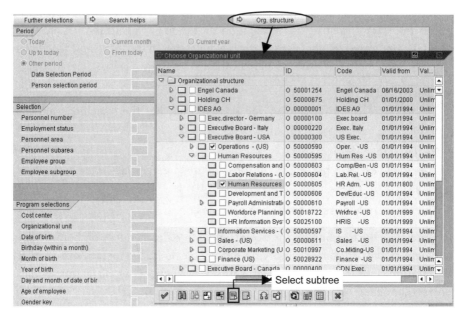

Figure 2.80 Selection via Using the Organizational Structure

In organizational management, there are reports available with which data about the elements of the organizational structure can be called up. When calling up a report, you will first see a selection screen. In addition to report-specific parameters, the following selection fields are usually available:

▶ **Object type**
Depending on the report, these are organizational units, jobs, positions, work centers, or tasks. Here it is specified with which object the report should be started. You can search for an object via the search term.

▶ **Status**
Using the status, it is determined that only objects are evaluated that have a particular status, for example, all active objects.

▶ **Evaluation period/evaluation key date**
Depending on the report, various criteria for determining a key date or an evaluation period are available.

▶ **Standard selection screen**
With many reports that are called up via the SAP menu, you can change to the standard selection screen, which makes available additional selection parameters. These parameters are, for example, the plan version, evaluation path, and the display depth, which determines up to which level of a structure a report should be executed.

In the following, some selected reports are introduced in brief, which can be called up via the SAP menu path **Human Resources · Organizational Management · Info System**. The Info System is organized in evaluations into the areas organizational unit, job, position, work center, tasks, and general.

Evaluations of the Organizational unit

The *organization plan* creates an overview of the entire structure and from this structure, it generates a structure graphic (see Figure 2.81). There are four variants of the report:

▶ Organizational structure

▶ Organizational structure with positions

▶ Organizational structure with people

▶ Organizational structure with work centers

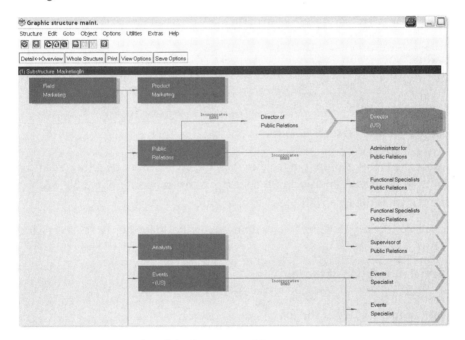

Figure 2.81 Structure Graphic of the Organizational Structure

From all evaluations, the structure can also be maintained. The generation of a structure graphic can be used conditionally to print an organizational chart of the company. However, the graphic display is not very flexible because you must use preset display methods and you cannot relocate the individual objects without additional help. Also, you cannot customize the display of the various objects such as organizational units and positions. However, there are some vendors who can enable you to use a graphic program into which you can export the organizational structure and make the necessary adjustments to meet your requirements.

Evaluations of Jobs

In Section 2.2.2, we already noted that the object type "job" can be used for evaluation purposes because, with the help of jobs, you can display how many secretaries and engineers there are in the company—regardless of their value in the respective departments. The "position" report evaluates all employees who are assigned to a job via their position and lists these respective employees.

Job index

Selection period   01/01/1900-12/31/9999

Job	Position	Holder	Staffing percentage
02 Director	02 Human Resources Director	Winnie Chung	100,00
01 Sales representative	01 Sales Representative A	Sharon Armstrong	100,00
	01 Sales Representative B	Rodney Washington	100,00
02 Administrator	02 Personnel Administrator	Iffat Patel	100,00
	02 Payroll Administrator	Sharon Whitman	100,00
00 Human Resource Manager	00 Human Resources Manager	Seamus O'Hara	100,00
02 Supervisor	02 Plant Supervisor	Jose Vega	· 100,00
Buyer JP	Buyer JP	Not occupied since: 01/01/1996	0,00
Category manager	Category manager	Not occupied since: 01/01/1997	0,00
	Category manager	Not occupied since: 01/01/1997	0,00
Construction Engineer	Motorcycle construction enginer	Position is vacant	0,00

Figure 2.82 Evaluation Position Plan

Because the report is output in *table control*, the columns can be relocated and a layout can be saved. An export of the list into a text processor or a table calculation program is possible with the click of a button.

The *job description* contains information about the following facts (see Figure 2.83):

▶ **Verbal description of the job**
The content of the infotype 1002 "Description" is output.

▶ **Tasks and activities of the job**
The tasks assigned to the job are displayed with their assigned percentages.

▶ **Requirements of the job**
The necessary qualifications from the requirements profile of the job are displayed together with the required value.

▶ **Successor/previous jobs**
From the "career and succession planning" component, the possible jobs are displayed that an employee can hold, and which jobs must be held prior to attaining the current job.

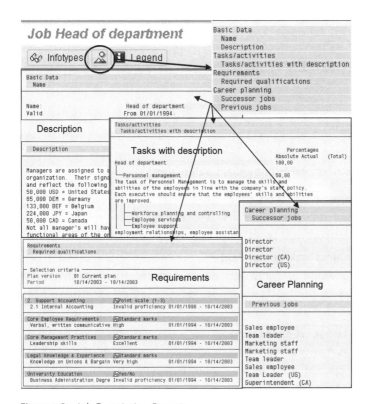

Figure 2.83 Job Description Report

For positions, there is a comparable report. In the appendix of this book, there is an overview (i.e., a brief description) of the existing reports in mySAP HR organizational management.

2.3.11 Transporting Structures

Essentially the setup of organizational management is possible in a productive system, that is, the organizational structure can be incorporated into a productive system and changed. Regarding transport, the organizational structure in a test system is set up by default such that the system always issues commands when creating, changing, or deleting objects to assign these objects to a transport order or, to create a new order.

Setting Up Transport Connection

You can change this setting via the IMG path **Personnel Management · Organizational Management · Transport · Set Up Transport Connection**. In the Table T77S0, the switch CORR in the group TRSP is responsible for the transport switch connection (see Figure 2.84).

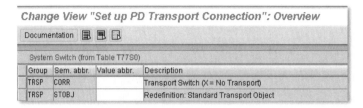

Figure 2.84 Setting Up the PD Transport Connection

The following entries are possible in the field **Value abbr.**:

▶ " " (empty) – automatic transport connection active

The system always issues a command when creating, changing, or deleting objects to assign these objects to a transport order or to create a new order.

▶ T – transport via object lock (repair flag)

With this setting, there is no query after a transport order, but via the report RHMOVE50 (transport of objects via object lock), all objects that have been changed can be selected and transported.

▶ X – no automatic transport connection

This setting ensures that with the creation, change, or deletion of objects, no query about a transport order appears. If objects should be transported, they must be transported via the report RHMOVE30 ("manual transport"). On execution of this report, it is determined manually which objects should be transported, that is, there is the danger that with extensive change, particular objects may not be transported by accident.

The semantic abbreviation ADMIN of the group TRSP, conversely, controls whether integration-relevant changes of the infotype 0001 "organizational assignment" should activate the transport connection for personnel planning objects. The field Value abbr. can assume the following values:

▶ " " (empty) – automatic transport connection active in infotype 0001

This setting assumes that the switch CORR of the group TRSP is activated, that is, it is set to ' '.

▶ X – no automatic transport connection in infotype 001

Locking Infotypes for Import

In this step, which can be reached via the IMG path **Personnel Management · Organizational Management · Transport · Lock Infotypes for Import**, infotypes can be locked against inadvertent overwriting on the importing of new data by the transport. The relevant table is delivered empty and must be filled if wanted. All infotypes to be protected must be entered in the form object type—infotype—subtype. If, for example, the infotype 1000 "object" is entered in the table, the system is informed that it imports no objects of the named object type. All object types, infotypes, and subtypes that should be protected against import must be entered explicitly since a generic entry of object types, infotypes, and subtypes is not possible.

2.4 Process Examples

2.4.1 Creation of New Positions with Application Process

The process described below shows the use of the status of objects in organizational management for mapping an approval process, beginning with the planning of positions on through to the approval or declining of the applied-for positions. Hereby, reports are presented that support the process as aids (see Figure 2.85 and Figure 2.86).

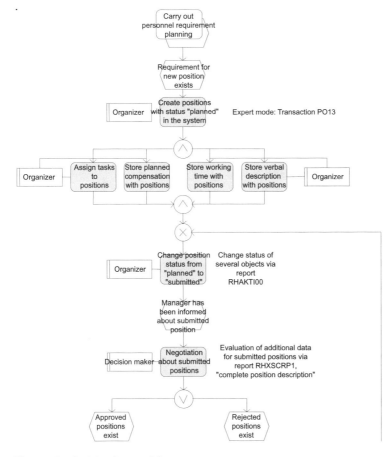

Figure 2.85 Position Approval 1

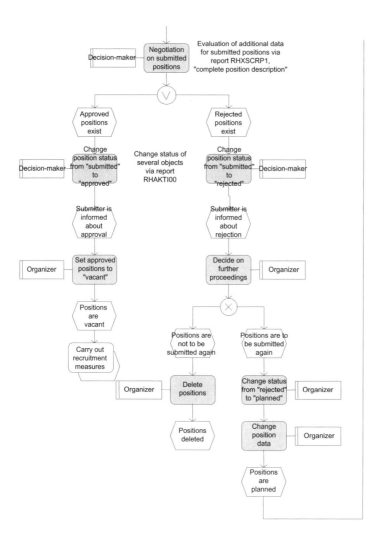

Figure 2.86 Position Approval 2

2.4.2 Scenario Planning

The process "scenario planning" shows a possible procedure for the planning of a new organizational management scenario by copying a plan version and then comparing the new with the old structure (see Figure 2.87).

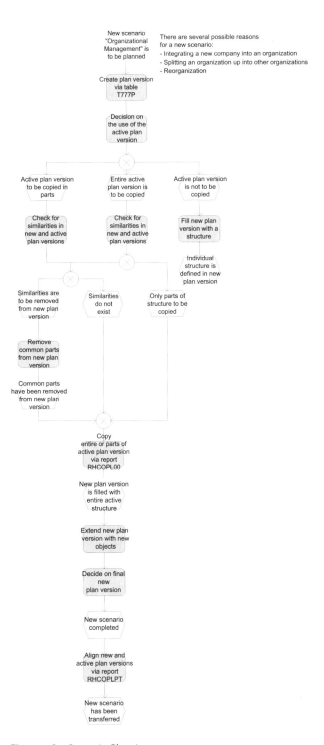

Figure 2.87 Scenario Planning

2.5 Critical Success Factors

The following critical success factors should be noted:

▶ The structures must be clarified, also with respect to the structures of other processes. It is especially important in organizational management to have the structure of the company available. This information should be available before the incorporation of the structure into the system.

▶ If the structural authorization is used, it must be checked early on whether the standard version options will suffice (see Figure 2.36) or, whether possibly new objects or relationships are necessary.

▶ The adjustment of the maintenance interface and the possibility of creating individual objects and evaluation paths allow for the optimal support of daily processes. The amount of effort that should be invested in the optimization of processes should depend on the frequency of the processes to be supported.

▶ Due to the many possibilities for storing data, for example, for positions or jobs, there is the danger of acquiring more data than is actually needed.

▶ The processes of data maintenance must be clarified early on. They must be defined in partnership with employees or consultants who have a great deal of experience in mySAP HR.

▶ The maintenance of the organizational structure is an activity that, if the organizational management is maintained directly in the productive system, requires very close examination and a documented work procedure. Knowing that via an incorrect transfer of a staffed position, the cost center assignment of an employee will change—and a retroactive calculation and correction of the bookings can result—justifies the importance of the accurate maintenance of the organizational structure.

▶ Through the strong integration of organizational management (see Figure 2.28), the maintenance of organizational management is not distributed across many areas in the company, but instead it is carried out as centrally as possible.

2.6 Innovations in R/3 Enterprise

With R/3 Enterprise, there are naturally only a few direct innovations in the area of organizational management. The following innovations affect organizational management directly:

Workforce Management – Consultant Deployment Planning

The web-based solution for the planning of consultants on projects enables the provision of a project detail plan with tasks and necessary qualifications and the linking of employees to projects via an individual staffing plan.

Management of Global Employees

From the organizational management point of view, the change of employees among various countries is especially interesting; this is well supported in R/3 Enterprise. It will no longer be necessary, as it was previously, to have an employee resign for one country and to re-employ that employee for another country. Rather, only an additional contractual relationship is created. The contractual relationships are represented by the "old" personnel numbers, which are combined via a Personnel ID.

This solution "Management of Global Employees" pertains only to foreign deployments. According to the same concept, multiple employment within a country becomes "concurrent employment mapping," which is only available in the U.S. and Canada. Both solutions are subject to release restrictions by SAP.

Context-Sensitive Authorization Check

The structural authorization check that is based primarily on the organizational management was completed with context dependency. Therefore, the mapping of a user who can carry out many activities for various groups of personnel numbers is possible, even if the limitation of personnel number access runs via the structural authorization check (see Section 3.3.4).

3 The Role Concept in mySAP HR

The ability to customize functions and interfaces to reflect the role of the user makes the role concept particularly user friendly. This concept also helps users to integrate access authorizations. Therefore, role definition is one of the most important steps in each project.

3.1 The Meaning of the Role Concept

The concept of the *Role* is a significant component of modern application software. The goal is to tailor the functionalities, menus, and interfaces provided to the user's needs. Therefore, two aspects are generally in the foreground:

▶ The requirements that users have based on the tasks (role) they must perform

▶ The requirements that users have based on personal preferences

The latter actually falls under the concept of *personalization*, which in SAP terminology is assigned to the role concept. By using the role concept in SAP environments (in older releases the term *activity group* is used instead of *role*), you can manage the following issues:

▶ The construction of the main menu (*easy access menu*)

▶ Access authorizations to data

▶ Authorization to execute particular functions

▶ Access to various systems in the mySAP environment (e.g., various R/3 systems, SAP BW, SAP SEM, etc.)

▶ Participation in workflows (see also Chapter 5, *The SAP Business Workflow*)

The broader the spectrum of available functionalities and the more users with various requirements use the system, the greater the meaning the role definition is for acceptance and security.

3.2 Implementation of the Role Concept

The emphasis of this book is not the general role and authorization administration; rather, we will focus on the special aspects of HR.[1]

3.2.1 The Definition of Roles on the System

The role definition occurs via the menu path **Tools · Administration · User Maintenance · Role Administration · Roles**.

---

1 For further information see "SAP Authorization System", SAP PRESS, 2003.

You must define two types of roles:

▶ **Single roles**

They determine the executable functions and data access immediately.

▶ **Composite roles**

They combine several single roles so that they cover the tasks of a group of users completely.

The structuring possibility that arises—thanks to this two-tiered process—should be used in every case. The reusability of the building blocks (**single** roles) improves clarity and simplifies maintenance and further development significantly. Figure 3.1 shows a section of a practical role structure.

Composite roles / Single roles	HR Analyst	HR Manager	Manager Payroll Acounting	Responsible Training Management	...
Maintenance Org. Management	⊕				
Display Org. Management	⊕	⊕	⊕	⊕	
Personnel Cost Planning (without release)	⊕				
Release Personnel Cost Planning		⊕			
HR Reports without Payroll	⊕	⊕	⊕	⊕	
All Reports for Payroll	⊕	⊕	⊕		
Everything for HR-Query	⊕				
Ad-hoc-Query only		⊕	⊕	⊕	
Maintenance Payroll Data			⊕		
Test Procedures		⊕	⊕		
Display Payroll Data	⊕	⊕	⊕		
Display Master Data, no payroll	⊕	⊕	⊕	⊕	
Day-to-day activities Training Management				⊕	
...					

Figure 3.1 Example: Role Structure—Section

In the all-encompassing view, the following points that correspond to the tabs in Figure 3.2 are maintained for a single role:

▶ A general description, which delivers the relevant information for the incorporation of the **single** role in composite roles

▶ The menu that is displayed for the user as a section of the easy access menu (if necessary, with individual transactions added)

▶ The assignment of objects of the SAP Business Workflow

▶ The authorizations as core of the role

▶ The user assignment (see also Section 3.2.2) that is generally inherited via the user assignment of composite roles

▶ The **Personalization** tab (see Figure 3.2), for which the assignment to a query user group is particularly helpful

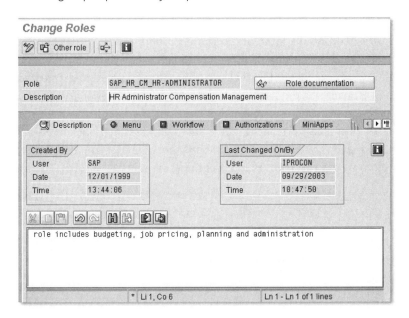

Figure 3.2 Maintenance of a Single Role

During maintenance of a composite role, it is assigned several single roles. Authorizations, personalization, and workflow properties must no longer be maintained on the composite role; instead, they are acquired dynamically from the assigned single roles. The menu of the composite role can be generated from the menus of the single role. Therefore, it may be necessary to rework the newly created composite role manually in order to avoid redundancies.

The core of role maintenance is certainly the authorizations. Therefore, the related terms should be described in brief:

▶ An *authorization object* controls access to very particular data or functions in the system, for example, to the calling of transaction codes, the editing of HR infotypes, or the editing of travel. The authorization objects are grouped according to application components for better clarity. For HR, the "Human Resources" group is available.

▶ An *authorization* is based on an authorization object and contains the permission for actual actions, for example, the call of the Transaction PA30, the maintenance of the infotypes 0001 to 0007 for all employees, or the maintenance of not-yet-approved travel.

▶ An *authorization profile* is an aggregation of any number of authorizations. It is assigned to users. This assignment can be made directly (old concept), or with the help of roles (current concept).

The creation of authorizations in an authorization profile occurs in the current concept using the **Authorizations of role maintenance** tab. Due to the menu maintained in advance, a suggestion that can then be completed and adjusted (see Figure 3.3) is made for the authorizations by the Profile Generator. Thus a profile is created automatically and assigned to the users via the role or composite role. Authorizations and also profiles can be created and assigned outside of role maintenance. In previous releases, this was the only possible procedure; however, now you should only use this method in exceptional cases.

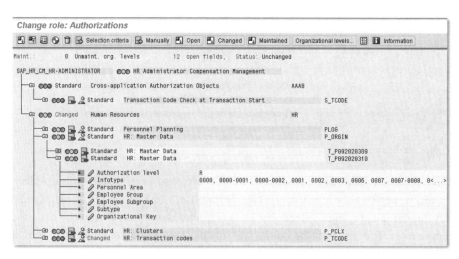

Figure 3.3 Example of an Authorization Profile

3.2.2 Assignment of Roles on the System

There are essentially two ways to assign roles to users (see Figure 3.4):

▶ Direct assignment via the **User** tab in the role maintenance or, via the user data maintenance itself

▶ Assignment via the organizational management

We want to take a closer look at the latter because it helps to clarify the meaning of the organizational management as a core function beyond HR. The basic thought behind this is that users' positions, work center, jobs, or organizational units also determine which role they occupy while working on the SAP system. This corresponds to the character of an integrated system because the same information is used in different places (organization modeling, workflow, and access rights). Indeed, this aspect must also be considered from the very beginning during the conception of the organizational management. Therefore, you must adhere to the following two aspects:

▶ Is the organizational structure—as it is required by HR—in conflict with the requirements of the role concept?

▶ Integration means that employees with maintenance authorization for the organizational management or, also only for the position assignment of an employee, can change an employee's system authorizations. Is this means justifiable to protect data?

The assignment of a role to organization objects occurs via the **User** tab of role maintenance. This button only appears if, on starting up the role maintenance, "Complete View (Organizational Management and Workflow)" has been selected. **Warning:** as of Release 4.7, select the view on the menu bar via the path **Goto Settings**. Using the **Organizational Mg...** button, the assignment of the role to organization objects is undertaken. Then, an adjustment is made, which takes over the corresponding users into the role. Therefore, for the objects "organizational unit" and "job," the directly linked positions and their holders are linked with the role. There is no link across several organizational levels.

Figure 3.4 User Assignment with Organization View

The way from the position to system user can occur in two ways:

▶ Through the direct assignment of the user (object type "US") to the position as the holder. This way should only be selected if the user is not also kept in the system as an employee, for example, for external employees.

▶ Through the assignment of an employee (personnel number) to the position (holder relationship) and via the subtype 0001 ("system user name") of the infotype 0105 ("communication") in the personnel data (see Figure 3.6). The assignment in the infotype 0105 is very important; it is not required only for the role assignment, but also for workflow, Manager's Desktop, and processor assignments. Therefore, we encourage you to handle the maintenance authorization for these subtypes carefully.

The maintenance of the assignment is depicted in Figure 3.5.

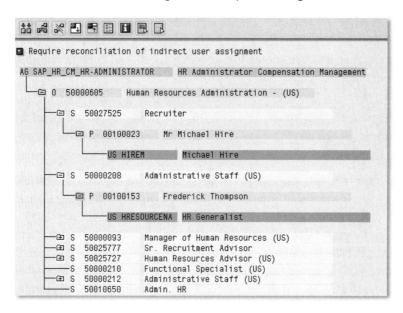

Figure 3.5 Role Assignment via Organizational Management

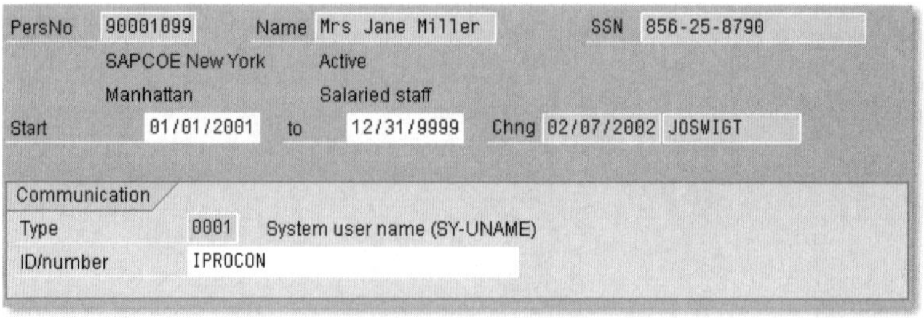

Figure 3.6 System User Name in the Infotype 0001

3.2.3 Summary

Because it would be easy to fill an entire book by describing the role concept in SAP, we chose to describe it succinctly here as the basis for the HR specifics in the sections that follow. For a better understanding of the concept, we will present the core once again using Figure 3.7. In this summary, we'll focus completely on pure authorization distribution and ignore the smaller amenities that the role concept also offers—such as personalization and menu.

In the role maintenance or user maintenance, the user is assigned composite roles. The composition of the composite roles (from several roles) is defined in the role maintenance. In the role maintenance, you select (on the **Authorizations** submenu) the authorization objects that are relevant for the role (insofar as possible, according to the Profile Generator's suggestions). For each object, one or several authorizations within the role are defined by maintaining the individual fields. The authorizations are those that ensure that the user "is permitted to do" something.

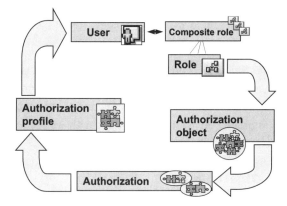

Figure 3.7 Connection Role—Authorization—Profile—User

The generation of authorizations (by simple selection of the corresponding menu option or of the button) creates an authorization profile automatically from authorizations that have been maintained. The assignment of the profile to the user also occurs automatically via the user adjustment in the role maintenance.

If one compares this process with previous releases, only the roles and composite roles have been added. These additional roles offer a comfortable opportunity to simplify and structure the maintenance of authorizations and profiles. When viewed from a technical perspective, one could certainly make do without roles and composite roles and create the decisive objects (authorizations and profiles) manually; however, then, not only would the role-dependent menus be missing, but maintaining the authorizations would be made that much more difficult.

3.3 Authorizations in HR

The authorization concept plays a pivotal role in the processes of personnel planning and development, in which many users—even those outside the personnel department—participate in various roles. The central authorization objects in HR regulate either access to employee data (that is, infotypes), or to other objects such as organizational units, jobs, activity types, qualifications, and so forth. In this context, the following four questions are particularly relevant:

1. Which person or persons (or other objects) does the user have access to?
2. Which data (i.e., data belonging to a person or persons) does the user have access to?
3. What can the user do with this data?
4. When can the user access this data?

The question that still is in the forefront is: Which system functions (e.g., "maintain personnel master data," "profile comparison," or "change creditors") can be executed? This question must be clarified via the term *transaction* and is relevant not only in HR, but across all processes. Only if certain system functions are allowed is the data that is necessary to perform these functions relevant.

In the following, first the essential authorization objects are depicted, which are also relevant in personnel planning and development. Then, the completion with the structural authorization check is described and finally, some special concepts in the HR authorization check are depicted. The chapter concludes with Appendix D, which also describes critical customizing for authorizations.

3.3.1 Central Authorization Objects in HR

Transaction Authorization

As in all other processes, HR checks the authorization of the object S_TCODE for each transaction to be called up. Many sensitive HR transactions also check the authorization of the object P_TCODE. This redundant check offers additional security in the event of a too easily accessible authorization distribution in the cross-application object S_TCODE. The Profile Generator's recommendations for the transaction check often correspond precisely to the requirement, whereby it sometimes "forgets" the object P_TCODE.

Authorization for PD Objects

The object PLOG is responsible for access to all objects of the PD. It can be controlled per object type and regulates which infotypes and subtypes may be accessed in which way (maintenance, display, approval, etc.). Due to the multitude of object types, the conception can become quite complex here. In addition, for this authorization object, many individual authorizations per role are then required. The Profile Generator's recommendations generally require extensive reworking, whereby a profound knowledge of the PD structures is essential.

It is often necessary to regulate access to particular relationships (see Chapter 1, *Overview of mySAP HR*). This occurs via the subtypes of the infotype 1001, which correspond to various relationship types. For example, a user may link an organizational unit with a position as "incorporates," but not as "manages." Generally, for medium differentiated role concepts of planning and development, control via relationship types cannot be avoided. One should begin with this part of the concept early on and factor in time for an especially high test effort.

With access to PD objects, the structural authorization is also always checked (see Section 3.3.2). The check cannot be stopped here—as shown in Figure 3.8 for access to personnel master data.

Authorizations for Personnel Master Data

Access to personnel master data can be controlled via several authorization objects. Which of these objects is active for this check is determined via the system control table T77S0 (IMG path: **Personnel Management · Personnel Administration · Tools · Authorization Management · Maintain Authorization Main Switches**). Customizing these authorization objects is conceivably easy (see Figure 3.8). However, the consistency of these authorization main switches and the maintenance of the roles must be ensured. A system check does not occur here. The authorization main switch of the view T77S0 replaces the switches in the program MPPAUTSW of earlier releases.

Change View "HR: Authorization main switch": Overview

Documentation

System Switch (from Table T77S0)

Group	Sem. abbr.	Value abbr.	Description
AUTSW	ADAYS	15	HR: tolerance time for authorization check
AUTSW	APPRO	0	HR: Test procedures
AUTSW	DFCON	1	HR: Default Position (Context)
AUTSW	INCON	0	HR: Master Data (Context)
AUTSW	NNCON	0	HR:Customer-Specific Authorization Check (Context)
AUTSW	NNNNN	0	HR: Customer-specific authorization check
AUTSW	ORGIN	1	HR: Master data
AUTSW	ORGPD	1	HR: Structural authorization check
AUTSW	ORGXX	0	HR: Master data - Extended check
AUTSW	PERNR	1	HR: Master data - Personnel number check
AUTSW	XXCON	0	HR: Master Data - Enhanced Check (Context)

Figure 3.8 Maintenance of the Authorization Main Switches

Control via Organizational Assignment

The current HR authorization check that one cannot generally escape occurs via the authorization object P_ORGIN. It allows access control via the following elements:

▶ Authorization level ("type of access")

▶ Personnel area

▶ Employee group

▶ Employee subgroup

▶ Organizational key

▶ Infotype

▶ Subtype

The authorization level can take on the value "S" in addition to "Display," "Display with entry helps," "Write," "Write locked," and "Unlock": "Unlock if the last person to change the record is not the current user." This characteristic supports a true double verification principle completely.

With the possibilities for organizational limitation (via fields of the infotype 0001), it is apparent that neither personnel subarea nor cost center are available for selection. This or other checks can, if necessary, be realized via the use of the dynamically configurable organizational key. It should be guaranteed via the customizing that the organizational key is not freely maintainable.

To limit the data, the infotype and subtype levels are available. However, no limitation on the field level is possible.

In the course of personnel planning and development, generally at least a display authorization for the infotype 0000 ("actions"), 0001 ("organizational assignment"), and 0002 ("personal data") is required—even if a display of infotypes is not directly required.

Control via the Individual Personnel Number

Because it determines the authorizations for the individual data, the authorization object P_PERNR is also significant, especially regarding decentralized scenarios. The connection between personnel number and user is created again via the subtype 0001 of the infotype 0105 ("communication").

In this scenario, there are two ways to ensure authorization control via the individual personnel number:

1. For the individual personnel number, additional rights are distributed. This variant is especially relevant in the course of an ESS application if the employee

can, for example, display his or her own salary data or change his or her own address data. In this case, the field interpretation of an assigned personnel number must be filled with "I". In the example in Figure 3.9, the user has read access to all personal master data and can also maintain his or her address data.

2. Particular rights are excepted for one's own personnel number. This affects central users such as controllers who may essentially maintain data that pertains to salary, except their own. The field interpretation of an assigned personnel number must then be filled with "E."

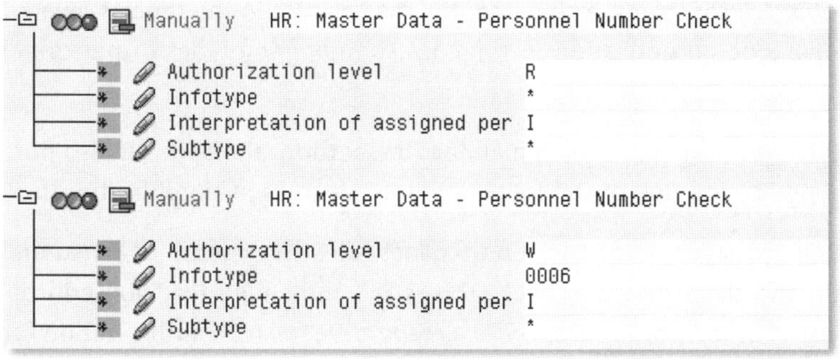

```
─🗀 ⬤⬤⬤ 🔳 Manually   HR: Master Data - Personnel Number Check
        ┌────⊞ 🖉 Authorization level       R
        ├────⊞ 🖉 Infotype                  *
        ├────⊞ 🖉 Interpretation of assigned per I
        └────⊞ 🖉 Subtype                   *
─🗀 ⬤⬤⬤ 🔳 Manually   HR: Master Data - Personnel Number Check
        ┌────⊞ 🖉 Authorization level       W
        ├────⊞ 🖉 Infotype                  0006
        ├────⊞ 🖉 Interpretation of assigned per I
        └────⊞ 🖉 Subtype                   *
```

Figure 3.9 Additional Rights for One's Own Data

The use of the authorization object P_PERNR is often misunderstood. One must also be clear that the object serves only to expand or limit authorizations for one's own personnel number. It is used *only* if the data in question belongs to the personnel number of the user who is currently logged on. Then, the object has priority over the check of the other authorization objects. It is not possible to control authorizations to personnel master data exclusively via this object—with the exception of one's own data. Typically, the object is combined with the objects P_ORGIN or P_ORGXX.

For the field interpretation of an assigned personnel number of the authorization object P_PERNR, the characteristics <Space>, "E, I", and "*" make no sense and cause undefined behavior in the authorization check.

Control via Administrator

In the infotype 0001, each employee can be assigned one administrator apiece for "time," "payroll," and "personnel." In the processes of personnel planning and development, the "personnel administrator" (custodian) is the most relevant, if necessary in compensation management, the payroll administrator is also critical. The authorization object P_ORGXX permits the access check, which is analogous to P_ORIGIN, via these three administrators of an administrator group.

Authorization in HR Reporting

Because the read authorization check for master data consumes a lot of computing time especially during the execution of reports, you can limit or turn off the check for particular reports via using the authorization object P_ABAP.

This object is also often misunderstood and also, all too frequently recommended by the Profile Generator. Note that this object does not replace the essential authorization for starting a particular report; instead, it only simplifies (and accelerates) the check of the data evaluated in the report. If one grants full authorization for this object, users can see all personnel master data in the reports, even if they actually have no authorization to the corresponding infotypes or personnel numbers.

By entering the report name, you can maintain the authorization. This is also possible by entering "*" and one of the following two "degrees of simplification":

1. The unchecked execution of the report deactivates the checks of personnel master data and the structural check. This is recommended for "non-critical" lists (e.g., list of offices) or for users who already have full read authorization for personnel master data.

2. The checks for infotypes and organizational assignment occur independently of one another, that is, if users have access to all infotypes, they have the same number of personnel numbers as they do infotypes. This accelerates the authorization check.

The authorization object P_ABAP is pertains only to reports of the logical database PNP.

3.3.2 The Structural Authorization Check

The *structural authorization check* permits control of access to any structures of personnel planning and development. If the authorization main switch AUTSW-ORGPD is active (see Figure 3.8), this check also includes personnel numbers. Because planning and development require manageable concepts for decentralized access (for example, by managers), the structural authorization check is particularly critical in this context.

Please note that no additional rights can be granted by the structural check; instead, this check can only further restrict the rights that already exist for personnel data and PD objects due to the authorization objects that were previously described.

The data to which users have access represents a section of a structure (e.g., organizational structure). This is determined by the following factors:

► The "root organizational object," the partial structure for which users should be authorized (e.g., the organizational unit "U.S. Board of Directors ")

► The evaluation path (see Chapter 2, *Organizational Management*) via which the objects can be reached (e.g., the standard path ORGCHART, which contains, beginning from an organizational unit, all subordinate organizational units, all leadership positions, their holders, and associated jobs).

In the example on the evaluation path ORGCHART, a structural authorization would be established that is suitable for an employee responsible for support of the board of directors in the U.S.

The structural authorization profile is defined in the view T77PR (IMG path: **Personnel Management · Organizational Management · Basic Settings · Authorization Management · Structural Authorization · Maintain Structural Profiles**). Here, the root object and the evaluation path are stored (see line 1 in Figure 3.10). If necessary, several lines of this type may be required if different root objects or various evaluation paths are required. In addition, object types to which users should have access independent of a structure are assigned without evaluation path (in the lines numbered 10 to 30 in Figure 3.10, these are "qualifications," "business events," "business event types," and "business event groups").

Auth.profile	No.	Plan vers.	Obj. type	Object I	Maint.	Eval.path	Status vec	De
CHICAGO	10	01	O	100	✔	ORGCHART	1	
CHICAGO	30	01	Q		✔			
CHICAGO	40	01	E		✔			
CHICAGO	50	01	D		☐			
CHICAGO	60	01	L		☐			

Figure 3.10 Authorization Profile in View T77PR

In addition, the profile maintenance of the view T77PR determines the following decisions:

► To which plan version does the access refer (for most users, this will only be the "active" plan version)?

► Can the respective objects be maintained?

► For which status is access permitted (e.g., only "planned" objects)?

► How far (across how many levels) will an evaluation path be followed if necessary (e.g., if only your own organizational unit and the directly subordinate organizational units should be maintained)?

If the profile is now defined, it must still be assigned to a user. This occurs in the view T77UA (IMG path: **Personnel Management · Organizational Management · Authorization Management · Structural Authorization · Assign Structural Authorization**) and it can be controlled by time limits (see Figure 3.11).

Figure 3.11 Assignment of a User Profile in View T77UA

The structural check is not practical when used via the "classic" organizational structure. Some application examples follow in which other structures are used:

▶ In training and event management, various personnel in charge of processing employee data are responsible for particular activity groups (see Section 11.1.1). Then, an evaluation path can lead from the start group to the group hierarchy to activity types, activities, and participation.

▶ The responsibility for particular partial budgets is mapped by an evaluation path via the budget structure (see Chapter 15, *Compensation Management*).

▶ In personnel development, various employees are responsible for the definition of various areas of the skill catalog, which maps an evaluation path via qualification groups and qualifications.

The RHAUTH00 report enables you to check which objects a user or a specific structure profile has access to. You can call up the report via the path **Human Resources · Organizational Management · Tools · Struct. Authorization · per user/profile**.

Dynamic Start Object

If you want to grant managers authorization access to the employees who are subordinate to them, you must define an individual profile for each manager because the start object differs in each case. To avoid having to define a profile for each manager, you can determine the start object dynamically. The view T77PR makes it possible to leave the field ObjectID open and instead to store a function module that finds the start object. In the standard version, two function modules are delivered for this:

▶ RH_GET_ORG_ASSIGNMENT finds as a start object the organizational unit to which the user's personnel number is assigned.

▶ RH_GET_MANAGER_ASSIGNMENT directs a user and finds as a start object the organizational unit to which the user's personnel number is assigned.

Often, these two building blocks are insufficient, for example, such is the case if the responsible personnel in charge of processing employee data (e.g., offices) is not assigned organizationally directly to the organizational unit for which they are responsible (instead, e.g., one level lower). In this example, we recommend that you do the following:

1. Create a customer-specific relationship (e.g., "is office for").

2. Define an evaluation path that considers this relationship.

3. Link the office position or the office organizational unit with the correct start organizational unit.

4. Copy one of the two standard function building blocks into the customer namespace.

5. Consider the new evaluation path in the copied functional building block (see Figure 3.12).

6. Enter the new function building block in the view T77PR.

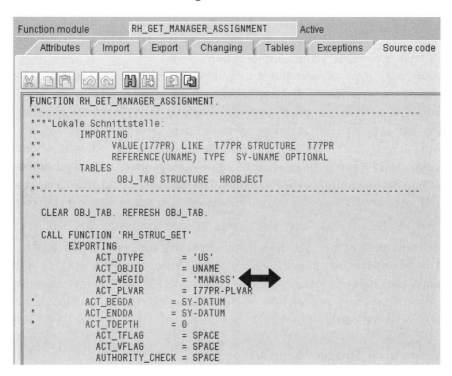

Figure 3.12 Consideration of an Individual Evaluation Path: Exchange at the Highlighted Place in the Function Building Block

As you can see, making this adjustment is easy. There are also more complicated logical possibilities for which the respective start object is found.

Default Profile

The following regulation applies: if no profile is assigned to a user in the view T77UA, the same profile is assigned to this user that the User SAP* is assigned. In the standard version, this is the profile ALL, which means "no limitation." Often, however, to ensure data protection, there is a requirement that a missing assignment must cause either an incomplete authorization or no authorization at all. In this case, a correspondingly empty profile should be assigned to the User SAP*.

More interesting still is the following case: the majority of all users should have a particular structural profile that should simultaneously serve as the default profile. Generally, there is a profile that comes into question for which the start object must be found dynamically. This profile can also be assigned to the User SAP*. However, the behavior of the two standard function building blocks is not satisfactory in this case (Release 4.6C, HR support package 49). Namely, they acquire the start object not using the identifier of the user who is logged on, but with the user name "SAP*"; however, you can prevent this problem by making a copy of the standard building block and implementing a corresponding adjustment.

Performance of the Structural Authorization Check

Because the paths stored in the structural profiles can be quite complex, the structural check can have a significant effect on performance. Because the system can store objects allowed for a user in SAP memory, this compromise in performance can be reduced. This can be controlled per user. The associated maintenance occurs via the IMG path **Personnel Management · Organizational Management · Basic Settings · Authorization Management · Structural Authorization · Save User Data in SAP Memory.** Typically, you should activate storage in SAP memory for users for whom the structural check must find more than 1000 objects.

The disadvantage of this solution is that changes that have been made since the last update of the SAP memory are not considered during the check. The SAP memory can only be updated manually—via the report RHBAUS00—for extensive or important changes that can have an immediate effect. This manual update can also be done for individual users.

Problems of the Structural Authorization Check

In addition to a degradation of performance, you should also note the following issues that can occur when using the structural authorization check:

▶ The structural check occurs in addition to the checks for personnel master data. If a user has several structural profiles, no connection between the structural profiles and particular master data authorizations is possible. Therefore, with several structural profiles per user, undesired "crossovers" may occur. Assuming a user plays two roles in the system: in that person's role as manager, the user has access to all data of the subordinate employees; as the person responsible for personnel development, that user should access particular data for all employees at a specific location. If you want to map the employees' limitation in both cases via a structural profile, you cannot avoid the fact that users can also see the same data for all users of the named location as they can for subordinate employees—that is, all of it. The only way to avoid this problem is by having employees work with two different user identifications depending on their role. R/3 Enterprise solves this problem via the context-sensitive authorization (see Section 3.3.4).

▶ If not all personnel numbers are integrated into the organization management (as a rule employees and pensioners who have left the company), the check is difficult. In the standard release, the check is against the organizational unit stored in infotype 0001. If the field is empty, access is denied. With the OSS Note 339367, a solution was provided for this problem. In the view T77S0 for the authorization main switch AUTSW – ORGPD, four different possibilities are available for the active structural check for non-integrated persons:

  ▶ *Switch setting 1:* if an organizational unit is assigned in infotype 0001, the check is against this organizational unit. If no organizational unit is assigned, the authorization is denied.

  ▶ *Switch setting 2:* the organizational unit is not evaluated. The authorization is denied.

  ▶ *Switch setting 3:* if an organizational unit exists, the check is against this organizational unit. If no organizational unit is assigned, the authorization is granted.

  ▶ *Switch setting 4*: the organizational unit is not evaluated. The authorization is granted.

▶ In the course of the structural check, access to possibly-sensitive data depends on many factors. These factors can also often be influenced by many users. It is imperative that all essential elements that touch authorization checks can be changed by only the minimum possible number of users. The essential elements are:

  ▶ Assignment of the system user name in the infotype 0105

  ▶ Maintenance of the infotype 0001 for non-integrated personnel numbers

- Position assignment of an employee

- Organizational structure of the organizational management

- Additional structures

- Definition of the profile in the view T77PR

- Assignment of the profile in the view T77UA

▶ The view of the organizational structure generally reflects the disciplinary assignment. If necessary, in the case of the matrix organization there is a second view, which represents the division. For the distribution of access authorizations, another view that deviates from these views—at least in some cases—is often required. Most frequently, the location view emerges. It is relevant, for example, if the office of a location is responsible for booking seminars in training and event management. In this case, you would have to maintain an individual location structure or establish a location check in another way, for example, using a customer-specific authorization check (for more information, see the explanations in Section 3.3.3).

3.3.3 Special Concepts in HR Authorization

In the HR authorizations environment, there exist special concepts that adhere to very specific requirements. They include the following:

The Time Period Problem with Authorization Check

The authorization check accesses decision criteria at various points, which change in the course of time. This is especially true for the data of the infotype 0001 as well as the PD structures. For example, the HR personnel administrator in charge of processing employee data can vary for an employee if that employee relocates. With such a change, an extremely complicated ruling applies, which must ensure that this different HR administrator can handle certain tasks as needed for the respective employee; however, it should also ensure that the authorization check does not occur too broadly, and therefore prevents this HR administrator (who is new to the employee who relocated) from having complete access to the employee's personal data.

Essentially, three cases must be distinguished:

1. The HR administrator's responsibility only begins in the future. Then, administrators may only maintain data that falls completely in their realm of responsibility, that is, they can work in advance, but may not "botch the handiwork" of previously responsible colleagues. In addition, these administrators who process employee data see all data whose validity begins before they assume responsibility, but also reaches into their period of responsibility.

2. The administrator is responsible for the employee on the current calendar day. Then, according to the role of said administrator, he or she can process personal data regardless of the validity period of the data.

3. The HR administrator's responsibility ends in the past. Then, the administrators have essentially no write access, but can see the data that extends into their period of responsibility.

With responsibility there also comes a tolerance period, which must ensure that the particular work that is left over or remains to be done can still be executed by the former HR administrator. The default for this concluding work is 15 days; however, it can be changed via the authorization main switch (AUTSW – ADAYS) (see Figure 3.8).

The check of the period of responsibility occurs essentially only for infotypes for which the "identifier for access authorizations" is set in the table T582A ("infotype properties" – IMG path: **Personnel Management · Personnel Administration · Customizing Procedures · Infotypes · Infotypes**) (see Figure 3.13). Because this setting of the identifier sometimes is also lacking with sensitive data in the standard version (e.g., "on-the-job doctor service" as well as various accounting data of several country versions), it should be verified if the period-dependent check is regarded as important.

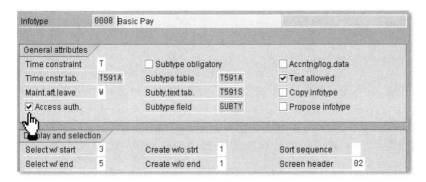

Figure 3.13 The Time-Independent Check for the Infotype 0008 Is Active.

The time-dependency of the authorization check has to do with authorizations based on the duration of the organizational assignment and not simply with who was the personnel administrator in charge of processing the employee's personal data at the point in time in question.

That is, if an employee has been assigned to the personnel area 4711 for two years, but the administrator responsible for processing the employee's personal data is only today assigned the authorization for that personnel area, that person nevertheless has access to the full two years of the employee's personal data.

Otherwise, continuity would be impossible with the succession of each new personnel administrator who is in charge of processing employees' personal data.

Test Procedures

The test procedure is a special form of a time-dependent authorization check. It assumes that particular data is checked at a particular point in time and then may no longer be changed. This test is documented in the infotype 0130 ("test procedures") (see Figure 3.14). Data that is assigned to the test procedure before the release date can no longer be changed, except the users who have maintenance authorization for the infotype 0130. They can change the data even after the release date.

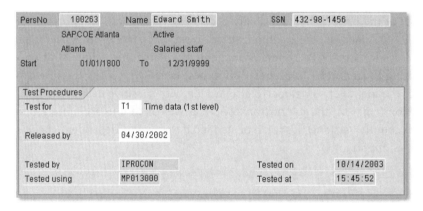

Figure 3.14 Infotype 0130: Test Procedure

The definition of test procedures occurs in customizing in the table T591A or under the IMG path **Personnel Management · Personnel Administration · Tools · Authorization Management · (4.6C: special authorization of personnel administration) · Test Procedures · Create Test Procedures**. Figure 3.15 shows the creation of new test procedures.

Subty...	Name
9PD	Personnel Development
9WS	Wage and salary data
T1	Time data (1st level)

Figure 3.15 Creation of New Test Procedures

Then the data is determined that falls under the test procedure. This occurs on the level of infotypes and subtypes. Figure 3.16 shows the assignment of two instruction types (that is, two subtypes of the infotype 0035) to the test procedure "Personnel Development."

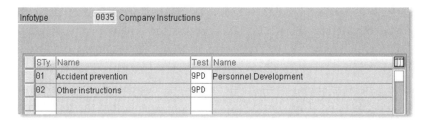

Infotype		0035	Company Instructions		

STy.	Name	Test	Name	
01	Accident prevention	9PD	Personnel Development	
02	Other instructions	9PD		

Figure 3.16 Definition of a Test Procedure

Customer-Specific Authorization Check

A customer-specific adjustment of the authorization check can be required for three reasons:

▶ The checks in the standard version do not offer enough possibilities.

▶ The standard checks, especially the structural authorization check, do not perform well enough.

▶ The required check could be mapped in the standard release, but this would be inconvenient and therefore require a great deal of high maintenance and effort.

The explanations in this section are by necessity quite technical. For readers without programming experience in the SAP environment, the procedures described here are less interesting. What is most important is the response to the question "what is possible?"

The easiest method is to create a customer-specific authorization object and integrate it into the standard test for HR master data. The fields of the infotype 0001 ("organizational assignment") are especially easy to check, as are those of the personnel subarea or the payroll area. The procedure in this case is quite easy; however, a user with a sufficient knowledge of development is required. In addition, for the generation and adjustment of the coding, an object key must be entered for the report MPPAUTZZ. However, this is a modification, which occurs at a point provided by SAP and should therefore be regarded as uncritical. We will not delve into the programming details here.

You must perform the following steps:

1. Create an authorization object in the class HR via the Transaction SU21 or the path **Tools · ABAP Workbench · Development · Other Tools · Authorization Objects · Objects**. Then, all fields of the infotype 0001—in addition to

the authorization level, infotype, and subtype fields—can be used analogously to the authorization object P_ORGIN.

2. Incorporate the new object into the authorization profiles (in general via the roles)

3. Automatically generate the program coding for the test of the new object with the help of the report RPUACG00. This creates the coding in the program MPPAUTZZ, which removes any programming work the customer would have had to do.

4. Adjust the generated coding so that other additional customer-specific requirements can be mapped. Thus you can, for example, ensure that the test of the objects should turn out positive if the first four places of the main cost center of the employee to be processed and the user who is logged on match. Four additional similar logics are conceivable.

5. Activate the customer-specific check via the authorization main switch AUTSW – NNNNN (see Figure 3.8).

Because the incorporation of the check of the customer-specific authorization object is provided from the very start in the program MPPAUTZZ, the integration into the standard application is quite easy. It would be much more difficult to incorporate an individual object that one defined "out of the blue" in the correct places. The previously generated test coding eases the procedure further.

In addition to the concept of the customer-specific object and the program MPPAUTZZ, there is also the BAdI (Business Add-In) HRPAD00AUTH_CHECK for HR authorization check in the current release. The necessary settings must be made in IMG under the path **Personnel Management · Personnel Administration · Tools · Authorization Management · BAdI: Set Up Customer-Specific Authorization Check**. The checks are realized in the methods of a class. For the implementation, knowing the classes in ABAP objects is required.

After you create an implementation of the BAdI, you can let individual checks run customer-specifically and delegate those checks that should occur by default to the corresponding standard class.

The following possible uses for customer-specific authorization checks become apparent:

▶ A user who cannot maintain his or her own data according to object P_PERNR can also not maintain any data about family members stored in infotype 0021 who are also employees of the company.

- The maintenance of the infotypes 0008, 0014, and 0015 can only occur up to a particular upper limit, which, for example, is stored in a customer-specific infotype in the user's personnel data.

- Users can only maintain particular data if they have a corresponding qualification (e.g., tax data, social insurance data, old age benefits, etc.) in their qualification profile.

There is also a BAdI for the adjustment of the structural authorization check of customer-specific concerns. It can be reached via the following IMG path: **Personnel Management · Organizational Management · Basic Settings · Authorization Management · Structural Authorization · BAdI: Structural Authorization**.

Special Authorization Questions for Evaluations

With lists and statistics, sometimes other requirements arise than with the direct display or maintenance of data.

Aggregate Data Versus Individual Data

In statistics, it is often necessary to factor the data of a particular circle of people; however, this data might not be available. Example: a personnel controller shouldn't know what the members of the board of managers earn; however, in statistics, the controller provides the payroll, which should also contain the board of directors' salaries.

Initially, accessing this data is not possible, because in order to read the board of managers' salaries a corresponding data authorization is required—if the reading occurs via an evaluation. If this evaluation is present, direct insight into the individual data is possible.

There are two workarounds for this problem:

- For the affected application, the authorization check is switched off via the authorization object P_ABAP. Then, there is the danger that the evaluation will only be executed for one person. Because the payroll corresponds to the individual salary, the "secret" data is therefore disclosed.

- For the evaluation, a customer-specific report that doesn't execute an authorization check is programmed. Using this approach, you can also exclude the targeted selection of individual persons used in the statistics compiled.

Authorization Check in Your Own Developments

Contrary to what one knows—perhaps from some other systems—the authorization distribution in R/3 occurs exclusively in the application system and not on the database level. Consequently, the access checks for particular data must be incorporated explicitly into each program.

The programs of the standard delivery generally contain sufficient test routines. The same applies for queries and also for customized developments that rely completely on the "logical databases" delivered by SAP. Any other customized development—in which a test routine was not incorporated—delivers the data to executing users without any check insofar as they have the authorization to execute the program, which means that users with authorization for ABAP programming can read out all data this way. And they can do this in all systems on which they may either create or transport programs. Hereby, access to a client suffices in order to be able to read the data of all other clients.

Behavior of Evaluations with Flawed Authorization

If users execute a list evaluation that contains data outside their authorization, then all lines are skipped that contain the "forbidden data." Example: a list should contain the names and privileges of all employees. However, for some of the selected persons, the user who is executing the list only has read access rights for the names of those users. The list then does not output the persons affected (also not the names) and displays at the end only the warning message "Personnel numbers skipped due to flawed authorization."

3.3.4 The Context-Sensitive Authorization in R/3 Enterprise

The context-sensitive authorization solves the problem described in Section 3.3.2 in the area of the personnel master data. It enables the linking of authorizations for personnel master data with structural profiles.

The Concept

As a basis for this solution, corresponding to the previously existing authorization objects, the objects P_ORGINCON and P_ORGXXCON are also delivered. Unlike P_ORGIN and P_ORGXX, the objects P_ORGINCON and P_ORGXXCON both have the additional field PROFL, in which a structural profile from the table T77PR is entered. Therefore, the distributed master data authorization is attached to the structural profile. The corresponding master data authorization applies only for those personnel numbers that are accessible via the assigned structural profile.

Figure 3.17 clarifies the concept with a simple example: users should have access to both the employees of the organizational unit O1 and to the employees of the organizational unit O2. One accomplishes this by awarding the structural profiles PROFL1 and PROFL2 via the table T77UA. However, users should not have the same authorizations for all employees. For the employees of O1, they should maintain the infotypes 0000 to 0007; for the employees of O2, however, only the infotypes 0008 and 0015 should be maintained. This is not achieved by mapping both the different authorizations via the object P_ORGIN, but instead via P_ORGINCON in connection with a reference to the structural profile PROFL1 and PROFL2. What results are two self-contained profiles that yield the total profile according to the described requirement. If, in the same example, you were to use the object P_ORGIN instead of P_ORGINCON, then users would have maintenance authorization for all employees of O1 and O2 for the infotypes 0000 to 0008 and 0015.

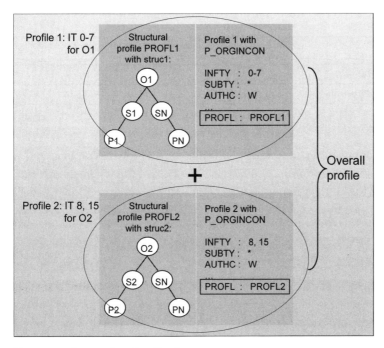

Figure 3.17 Context-Sensitive Check

The Configuration

Prerequisite for the assignment of the structural profiles to the master data authorization is the configuration of the structural profiles as described in Section 3.3.2. In particular, the assignment of the profile to the users must always occur via the table T77UA—even if this appears redundant due to the entry in the master data authorization.

In addition, you must activate the checks via the different authorization objects. To do this, there are additional authorization main switches in the table T77S0:

▶ AUTSW – INCON: activates the context-dependent check via the object P_ORGINCON

▶ AUTSW – XXCON: activates the context-dependent check via the object P_ORGXXCON

- AUTSW – NNCON: activates the context-dependent check via the customer-specific object P_NNNNNCON

- AUTSW – DFCON: controls the system behavior in the context-dependent check for persons who are not linked in the organization management, analogous to the main switches AUTSW – ORGPD for the non context-dependent check. Figure 3.18 helps you to decide on the value of this switch in dependency on the content of the field "organizational unit" in the infotype 0001.

	Evaluate organizational unit (if available)	Never evaluate organizational unit
Reject authorization by default	1	2
Grant authorization by default	3	4

Figure 3.18 Authorization Main Switch DFCON

The authorization main switches must be maintained in a logical combination. A check by the system does not occur. Especially the switches that correspond with one another for the context-dependent and non-context-dependent objects may not be active at the same time, that is, if the switch INCON is active, ORGIN must be inactive.

The Availability

The context-dependent authorization check is delivered with R/3 Enterprise as an Enterprise Extension. For Release 4.6, an advance delivery on a project basis is possible for a fee if the customer agrees on this individually with SAP.

3.4 Critical Success Factors

The authorization concept itself can be regarded as a critical success factor of each larger project with mySAP HR. Especially worthy of emphasis are the following points:

- The processes and responsibilities in the authorization concept must be clarified before detailed work begins.

- In addition to representatives of system administration and the participating departments, an employee with extensive knowledge of and project experience in the role concept of SAP should participate in the authorization concept. All participants in the conception must familiarize themselves early on with the rough structure and relevant terms of the SAP role concept.

- The authorizations that span across processes (i.e., printing, variant maintenance, SAP Office, download to MS-Office, etc.) may not be forgotten in the conception.

- A clear, modular structure with roles and composite roles and as few roles as possible can considerably reduce the maintenance effort required considerably.

- Sufficient time must be allocated for the test of the roles. In a larger project, all integration tests and trainings must be executed with the role that will also be used later in the productive environment.

- In their roles, users should have the authorization for the Transaction SU53 ("display authorization data") for which they should be trained. Then, if there are authorization problems, the cause can be located quickly.

- Most authorization concepts in HR only become complicated if the usual exceptions are considered. If this only occurs with the emergence of the first problems in productive operation, the concept quickly loses its structure and becomes unclear due to the time pressure. Conceivable exceptions such as representation rules, delegation, trainee programs, multi-activity relationships, transfer times, display rights within the personnel department, and so forth, must be considered integral to the authorization concept from the very beginning.

- With migrations from R/2 or from the earlier R/3 release versions, the concept should reflect—from the very beginning—the current solution on the system. If you reduce the conversion effort via a one-to-one conversion of the old concept, this savings will be overcompensated quickly by a later maintenance effort.

- The number of roles, composite roles, and structural profiles is responsible for a significantly increased effort during later maintenance. Concepts that help reduce this number should therefore always be used if possible. In addition to the structural authorization with dynamic start object, are the customer-specific authorization objects and the named BAdIs for customer-specific adjustment of the check.

- Customizing settings (e.g., T77S0, T582A) and application data (e.g., "Org-structure," infotype 0105) that have influence on the authorization check must be documented and tested.

4 Portals in mySAP HR

With the advent of the new mySAP Release Enterprise, came the real-ization of integrating R/3 into Internet platforms. This chapter pro-vides an overview of the conception of the SAP Enterprise Portal and the integration of Employee Self-Service (ESS) and the Manager's Desktop (MDT).

4.1 The General SAP Concept

As we discussed in Chapter 1, *Overview of mySAP HR*, with the new R/3 Release Enterprise, the previous R/3 basis is replaced with the Web Application Server (Web AS), whereby the integration of the basis into a Web environment is improved significantly. The mySAP components HR, FI, CO, and so forth are still retained in the core system, which also builds on the Web AS. In future, new functionalities will be delivered as *Extensions*.

Thus, the basis for the Enterprise Portal (EP) is laid, which allows a company to integrate information, applications, and services in a browser-based interface. For users, uniform access to various SAP systems and other providers' systems is real-ized. Therefore, the users of an EP have a web-based work environment, which is tailored to their tasks and enables them to access a heterogeneous system land-scape. The portal is based on the latest technologies such as MS.NET, JSP, J2EE, and LDAP.

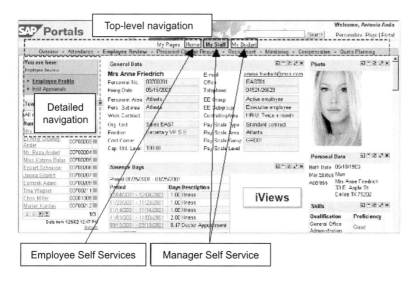

Figure 4.1 Interface SAP Enterprise Portal

With some additions, the Enterprise Portal helps to integrate services on a new technical platform that was not possible with the mySAP Workplace. To understand the Enterprise Portal, see Figure 4.1, which shows the structure of the portal from the user's point of view. You can see the integration of the self services, which we will discuss in more detail in the next section.

Previously, that is before the R/3 Enterprise Release, the self services and thus also the Workplace were operated via the *Internet Transaction Server* (ITS). This will change with R/3 Enterprise because the self services will also run via the Web AS. Nevertheless, in the following section, we have chosen to explain self-services operated on the ITS because it is currently more widely used and therefore more relevant to our discussion at this time. We will also address the future integration of the self services into the EP.

4.2 The mySAP Workplace

The *mySAP Workplace* is a central point of entry for employees from which they can access the self services as well as information from the Internet and store these as favorites. The Workplace contains an inbox that can be used for e-mails and workflow tasks. Like the Enterprise Portal, the Workplace is also intended as a way to enable access to R/3 application screens, which are transmitted in a Web-capable interface via the Web-GUI. Using *roles,* employees can execute activities in the browser that they would typically perform directly in R/3. Another goal is the incorporation of foreign systems into the mySAP Workplace.

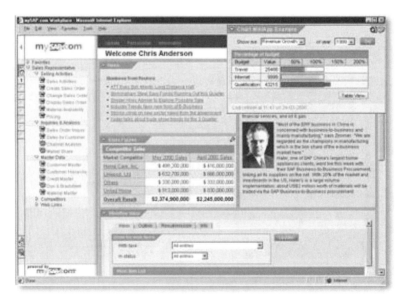

Figure 4.2 mySAP Workplace

In use, mySAP Workplace looks like Figure 4.2. On the left side, the individual roles are listed. In the present example, Employee Self Services (ESS) users "only" have the role of employees and under this, the individual *service categories* that are well suited for their role. Users can select a service from those offerings on the right side of the screen in order, for example, to apply for vacation or book a training. These services are part of the ESS.

The Workplace can now be considered obsolete. For any new implementation, the Enterprise Portal will be used instead. Nevertheless, the Workplace will have some merit in the years to come as companies that have invested in it will need time to migrate to the Enterprise Portal.

4.3 The mySAP Employee Self Services (ESS)

4.3.1 Why ESS?

The requirements demanded by companies and employees provide the best argument for using *Employee Self Services (ESS)*. Today, employees require that personnel management ensure that each employee's data is transparent, up-to-date (for example, new address, new bank information), and much more the responsibility of the respective employee. It is also understood that the personnel department will function more as a service department, and less as an overseer of each individual's data.

Companies make similar demands of modern personnel management and require more service and service-oriented work from personnel departments and that they focus on the company's strategy and its goals. Another requirement is, as in other departments, cost reduction in the execution of HR processes.

ESS enables employees to keep their own data current. The personnel department is only contacted if the employee needs to consult them about a particular issue. Thus, personnel management—unburdened by administrative activities—can now concentrate on its consulting activities and place planning processes such as personnel development more in the foreground.

In addition to fulfilling the requirements of companies and employees, the following benefits become apparent from using ESS:

▶ Increased timeliness of data

▶ No long idle periods

▶ Unburdening of the personnel department from routine administrative work

▶ More space for qualitative personnel work

▶ Saving of administrative costs

▶ Decentralization of personnel work

▶ ESS can be used "standalone" with the R/3 system or within the Enterprise Portal or Workplace. In the following examples, we show ESS only with R/3 via ITS without mySAP Enterprise Portal or mySAP Workplace.

4.3.2 The Internet Transaction Server (ITS)

In order that Employee Self Service (ESS) can be used, additional hardware is necessary, on which the software for the *Internet Transaction Server (ITS)* is installed. The ITS provides the Web interface for the self service and controls the communication with the R/3 (see Figure 4.3).

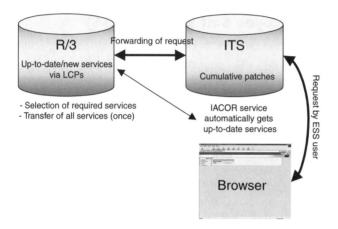

Figure 4.3 ITS Concept

Before the ITS can be operated, you should download the most up-to-date patches: */general/its/patches/46DC3/NT/I386/setupits_7.exe* from the sapserv3. With the *support packages*, SAP continuously delivers updates to the self services. Because these updates are always completely held in R/3 (this is the concept since R/3 release 4.6C), a constant exchange between R/3 and the ITS is necessary. This function is handled by a service on the ITS side (IACOR), which constantly supplies the ITS automatically with the updated services (see Figure 4.3).

If one assumes that a "normal" system structure in a company—in addition to having a productive system—contains at least a development/test system, a quality assurance (QA) system, and an additional test ITS, then, transmitting the services simultaneously on all ITS servers or instances does not make sense. Instead, the R/3 test system should be connected with the test ITS and this should be equipped with the updated and new services. Via the transport of the settings to the services from the test system into the productive R/3 system, the productive

ITS is supplied with the updated settings (automatically via the IACOR service). Therefore, it will suffice to make settings for the services on the test system and then transport these settings.

Before the first operation of the ITS, you must select the self services in R/3 and transmit them to the ITS. In order to do this, you must make the ITS known to the R/3 via the **Object Navigator (Transaction SE80)**. There, under **Utilities · Settings**, on the Internet Transaction Server tab, the server that has to be entered or "on all defined sites" must be selected (see Figure 4.4).

Figure 4.4 Connecting ITS

Since the Web interface is completely administered and maintained in R/3, the adjusted services must be transmitted once to the ITS. If the server is known to R/3, the program W3_PUBLISH_ALL_SERVICES can be started, which ensures that all services are transmitted to the ITS.

Furthermore, in R/3 via the view V_T77WWW_CDE (Transaction SM31) under PZM3, all service categories must be deactivated that aren't needed (see Figure 4.5). To deactivate those categories that are no longer needed, check the corresponding Deactivate field.

ESS menu	Text	ServCat	Text	M...	Deact
PZM3	ESS	APPR	Appraisals	20	☑
PZM3	ESS	BENE	Benefits	9	☑
PZM3	ESS	OFFI	Office	1	☐
PZM3	ESS	PAY	Payment	13	☐
PZM3	ESS	PERS	Personal Informati.	15	☑
PZM3	ESS	QUAL	Skills	19	☐
PZM3	ESS	RECM	Jobs	11	☑
PZM3	ESS	TIME	Working Time	3	☐
PZM3	ESS	TRAV	Business Trips	5	☐
PZM3	ESS	VMAN	Training	17	☐

Change View "ESS Deactivate Catalog and Change Menu Item"

Figure 4.5 Deactivating the Service Categories

Service categories refer to the groups of self services that are displayed when ESS is started. Figure 4.6 shows the startup in ESS with such selected service categories as OFFI (Office), TIME (Working Time), TRAV (Business Trips), PAY (Payment), VMAN (Training), and QUAL (Skills).

Figure 4.6 Service Categories in the ESS

In addition to the service categories, you must select services belonging to each category. This occurs via the view V_T77WWW_SDE (see Figure 4.7).

Change View "ESS Deactivate Service and Change Catalog Item"

ServCat	Text	Service	Name of service	C...	Dead
TIME	Working Time	4	Display Time Statement	70	☐
TIME	Working Time	8	Display Work Schedule	60	☐
TIME	Working Time	9	Display Leave Information	50	☐
TIME	Working Time	21	Create Leave Request	20	☐
TIME	Working Time	23	Leave of Absence Requ...	30	☐
TIME	Working Time	33	Leave Requests - Overvi...	40	☐
TIME	Working Time	40	Record Working Time	10	☐
TRAV	Business Trips	68	Travel Management	10	☐
TRAV	Business Trips	114	Travel Manager	20	☐
TRAV	Business Trips	995	Exchange Rates	12	☐
TRAV	Business Trips	996	Travel Weather	11	☐
TRAV	Business Trips	998	Route Planning	5	☐
VMAN	Training	62	Training Center	10	☐
VMAN	Training	63	My Bookings	20	☐

Figure 4.7 Deactivating the Services

Services are actions that can be carried out in ESS. These are, for example, in the service category VMAN (Training) the services 62 (Training Center) and 63 (My Bookings). Figure 4.8 shows that the services are located below the service category. On the right side, the content of the selected services can be seen.

Services that are not defined as Internet services in the object browser are interpreted by the ITS as Web-GUI-Transactions, which means the transaction is directly started on the R/3 system and translated into a Web-page by the Web GUI functionality of the ITS.

Figure 4.8 Services in ESS

4.3.3 Self Services

With the previously mentioned settings, you can use the services as they are, that is, without any adjustment. The following explanations show, however, that in practice, requirements can arise that in turn require you to customize or expand the services. Here, some self services will be introduced and then, we will provide a few examples with possible solutions.

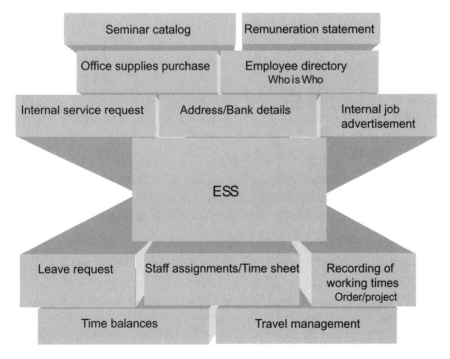

Figure 4.9 Self Services: Overview (Selection)

We will now provide you with a little information about navigation in ESS, which you will need to know more about later on in the book. Navigation between the individual ESS areas is possible via the service categories and services on the left side of the browser. In addition, above the services, there are buttons that you can use to cancel actions and return to the ESS start screen. These buttons should be used to navigate in ESS. When you use the back button, you may inadvertently lose synchronization. You can use the parameter "NoResync" to prevent this problem from occurring, unfortunately it is seldom used as it is not always readily detected that synchronization has been lost. Then, suddenly incorrect data, for example, from the last visit of the screen, will be displayed. You can resolve this problem with additional coding (JAVA script), which is transmitted when ESS is called up and which ensures that the back button is not displayed. A selection of the standard self- service offerings is shown in Figure 4.9.

Self-Service Time Worked: Error List

In time management, there are two aspects that we shall consider: the error list and the time statement. It should be noted that there are additional services for time management in the standard version. There is, for example, the possibility of acquiring a notification of absence or a vacation application (connected to a workflow for approval).

The error list shown here is no standard service; instead, it was enabled by the creation of a new service. The new service was defined in the corresponding customizing table (view T77WWW_SRV). Hence, the service number, service type "S" (ITS server), and the associated transaction must be specified. The transaction for the error list was created anew and linked with an ABAP/4 program that was especially programmed for this purpose. In addition, the Web GUI was activated for this transaction.

Another note on the Web GUI: by default for the Web GUI transactions, the field for entering transactions (OK code field) is displayed. If this is not desired, you can remove the field with the entry "~noheaderokcode 1" in the file *global.srvc* on the ITS.

Using the error list, the employee receives the messages generated in R/3 for his or her time-clock bookings if an error has occurred there. A classic example here is the missing "clock-in" or "clock-out" booking. By selecting the details of the error message, the employee receives more detailed information about the day in question. In the example in Figure 4.10, the employee was obviously at work on what was supposed to be a holiday.

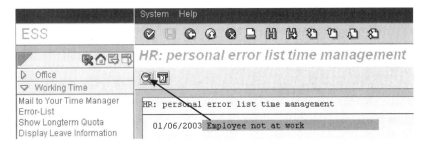

Figure 4.10 Time Management Error List

You can view this more precisely for the case in question (see Figure 4.11) via the detail view. The personal work schedule is in the upper area; this shows that the day in question is marked as "A1."

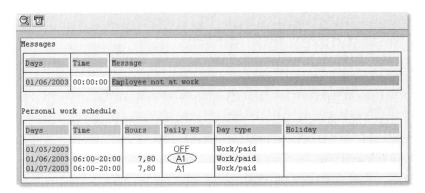

Figure 4.11 Details on Time Management Error

Now, the employee can inform the time administrator and explain the situation via an individual screen (see Figure 4.12). This screen is also not present in the standard ESS version; it was customized to meet the requirements of specific customers. For this, particular fields were read out of R/3 and made available for the screen as default values.

Figure 4.12 Notification of the Time Processor

The employee can now explain to the time administrator why he or she was present on this day. In the event that an employee forgot a booking, the employee can enter the missing time in the screen and send this information directly to the time administrator. In the time that administrators receive an executable mail in R/3, they can jump into a newly created transaction. This transaction provides the time administrators with an interface that will help them check the correction in the e-mail (jump to error list, time verification, main data). After a successful check of the facts, the administrator can execute the master data change from the e-mail with the click of a button. As soon as the error has been corrected, the error message disappears from the employee's error list.

The functionalities of the error list permit employees to see their time management errors (for example, forgotten bookings, missing notification of absence) directly on the system and to send the correction notification directly to the personnel department using an easy procedure. Because this process is standardized, the processing is accelerated.

Self-Service Time Worked: Time Statement

The second aspect of time management, time statement, is a standard service that was adjusted in some places. To display the time statement correctly, there must be no more errors in the error list for the period to be evaluated.

In typical cases, the time evaluation that creates the time statement is started at regular intervals in R/3. It is only after the time evaluation that events that have been added subsequently (such as absences, clock-in/clock-out,...) be seen on the time statement. The standard service for time statement reads the results of the last time statement created and passes them along to the ITS, regardless of whether changes have been made in the system since the last accounting period.

In order for employees to see the most current time data displayed when they start time statement from the ESS, you must make a small adjustment in the program SAPMESSREP. The adjustment has the following effect: when calling up the time statement from the ESS, there is a check of whether relevant changes in the system have been made for the time evaluation. If the relevant changes have been made, a new time evaluation will be started before the output of the time statement.

When calling up the time statement, initially, there is a query for the chosen accounting period (see Figure 4.13). After selecting the time period, the time statement is displayed in the browser and it can be printed out if desired. If the time data is flawed, the time statement is only displayed up to the day on which the error prevented further evaluation.

Time Statement

Report options

Display time statement form for

○ Current month
○ Current and last month
⦿ Period from   01/09/2003
   to   09/09/2003

Display report

Figure 4.13 Time Period Selection Time Statement

Self-Service Payment: Remuneration Statement

To display the remuneration statement, there is a standard service that enables the offering in the ESS of the previous accounting results for an employee for selection. The employee therefore can select the desired accounting results from the list and see the remuneration statement (see Figure 4.14).

Quit   Help

Remuneration Statement

Payroll results

Period	Payment...	Payroll type	Payroll reason
01/09/2003-30/09/2003	11/09/2003	Regular payroll run	
01/08/2003-11/08/2003	11/08/2003	Regular payroll run	
01/07/2003-11/07/2003	11/07/2003	Regular payroll run	

1 / 3

Display remuneration statement   New selection

Figure 4.14 Calling Up the Accounting Results

For companies in which not all employees have access to the ESS and therefore not everyone can print out their remuneration statement themselves, it will continue to be necessary to print out these statements and send or distribute them. In order not to generate and send a printed version of their remuneration statement for the employees who have access via the ESS, there is a new infotype in the personnel master data. In the infotype 0655 "ESS Settings Remuneration Statement," you can store a value that indicates that an employee uses the ESS and therefore no printout of the remuneration statement is necessary (see Figure 4.15).

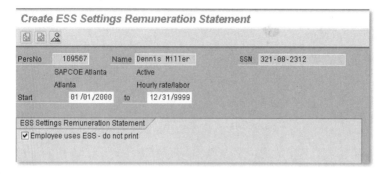

Figure 4.15 Infotype 0655 "ESS Settings Remuneration Statement"

Self-Service Training: Training Offerings

The standard self-service training offerings enable employees to select a training from the R/3 training catalogue according to the criteria *topic*, *event time*, *event location*, and *language*.

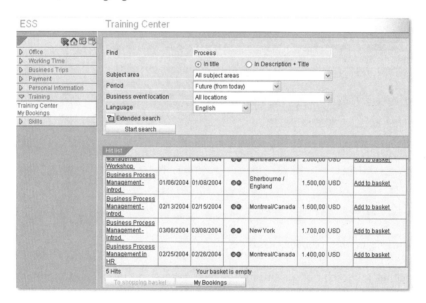

Figure 4.16 Display Training Offerings

The events found are displayed in the Hit list. By selecting the event name, additional information that is stored in the R/3 training and event management in the event type can be displayed (see Chapter 11, *Training and Event Management*). The desired event can be placed in the shopping basket and then additional events can be selected.

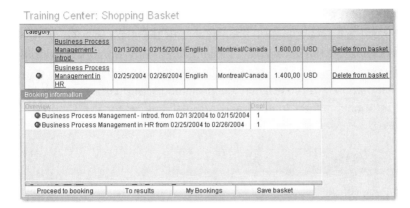

Training Center: Shopping Basket

category								
⊙	Business Process Management - introd.	02/13/2004	02/15/2004	English	Montreal/Canada	1.600,00	USD	Delete from basket
⊙	Business Process Management in HR	02/25/2004	02/26/2004	English	Montreal/Canada	1.400,00	USD	Delete from basket

Booking information

Overview | Displ.
⊙ Business Process Management - introd. from 02/13/2004 to 02/15/2004 | 1
⊙ Business Process Management in HR from 02/25/2004 to 02/26/2004 | 1

| Proceed to booking | To results | My Bookings | Save basket |

Figure 4.17 Display of the Shopping Basket

From the shopping basket, more detailed information about the events can be displayed and the booking can be executed (see Figures 4.17 and 4.18). After a successful booking, the booking overview "my bookings" appears together with a success notification.

Training Center: Book Business Event

When you choose "Book Business Event", the following business events will be booked:

Name	Start date	End date	Language	Location	±Price	Curre ^
Business Process Management - introd.	02/13/2004	02/15/2004	English	Montreal/Canada	1.600,00	USD
Business Process Management in HR	02/25/2004	02/26/2004	English	Montreal/Canada	1.400,00	USD

| Book business event | To basket | To search results | My Bookings |

Figure 4.18 Executing a Booking

As should be evident from the foregoing explanations, the ESS is a good opportunity to decentralize administrative work and also provide employees with more individual responsibility.

For managers of a company, who naturally also utilize self services, there is another user interface that delivers data that managers require in order to carry out their daily work, employee management, supervision of budgets, decision making: the Manager's Desktop (MDT).

4.3.4 Integration of Self Services into the Enterprise Portal

These self services can be integrated completely into the Enterprise Portal (see Figure 4.19). In addition, the self services are completed with additional functions that support employees in carrying out their tasks in the company, such as cross-company collaboration with colleagues, team members, and customers, or the provision of information from internal and external sources for the support of decision-making.

Figure 4.19 Employee Self Service in the Enterprise Portal

4.4   The mySAP Manager's Desktop

The *Manager's Desktop (MDT)* developed from the managers' need for an easy-to-use tool that supports them in their daily administrative, organizational, and strategic tasks. Here we focus on the MDT and not on the *Manager's Self Service (MSS)* within the Enterprise Portal (see 4.4.3), because the MDT is available for far lower costs and thus is a reasonable solution for nearly every company that wants to manage the (technical *and* cultural) change—from paper-reporting to decentralized online-reporting.

4.4.1   The User Interface

The MDT is organized into two main areas: on the left side are the functions or topic categories that the manager can execute; on the right side are the "objects" with which the functions can be executed. Thus, for example, on the left side in the area of personnel development, you can call up the training history. The call is done with the selection of an object, for example, an organizational unit or a person and the assignment to the desired function via drag&drop (see Figure 4.20).

The main points displayed on the startup screen and also in the MDT such as *Personal Data*, *Organization*, *Requisition* are called *topic categories*. These topic categories in turn are divided into individual subcategories such as Reports, Education and training, Employee appraisals, and Personnel development for the topic category Personal Data (see Figure 4.21).

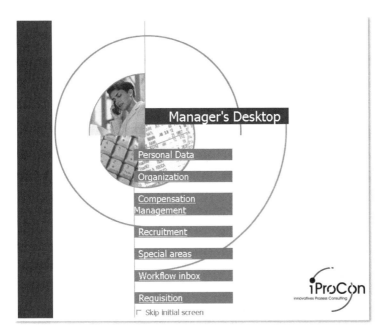

Figure 4.20 MDT Startup Screen

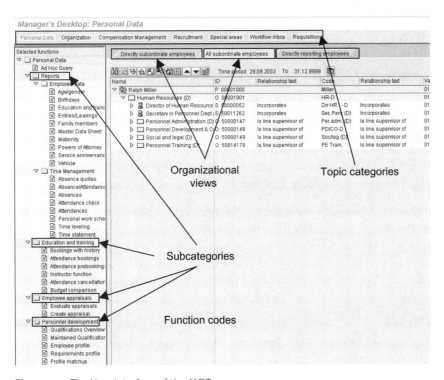

Figure 4.21 The User Interface of the MDT

4.4.2 Configuration

In addition to adjusting the design by selecting an individual background image for MDT startup, additional adjustments can be undertaken via the IMG: **Personnel Management Customizing Settings · Managers Desktop · Customer Adjustments · Define Scenario-Specific Settings**.

Scenarios, Topic Categories, Subcategories

Modifications to standard scenarios should be added via the step "Define Standard Scenarios" because other modifications will be deleted when the system is updated. However, it is recommended that you copy a standard scenario via the step "Define Application Scenario" and therefore define all settings for an individual scenario (see Figure 4.22).

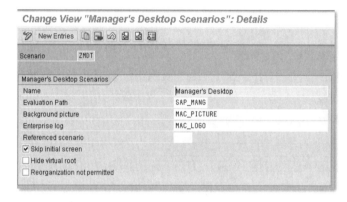

Figure 4.22 Defining Manager's Desktop Scenarios

The MDT startup screen offers an overview of all available topic categories. By checking the box **Skip initial screen**, the startup screen (see Figure 4.20) is no longer displayed when MDT is started; instead, the program branches directly from the first topic category in customizing to the first tab specified.

If you check the box with the identifier **Reorganization not permitted**, you specify that the line manager cannot execute any organizational changes with the help of drag&drop within his or her area of responsibility on the right side of the screen. This also means that the subcategory **Reorganization** will also no longer be displayed in the function tree of the topic category **Organization**.

Views

In Customizing, via the activity **Personnel Management · Manager's Desktop · Customer Adjustments · Define Views of Organizational Structure**, you can define which evaluation paths can be used to determine the employee structure displayed in the MDT. Therefore, the possible views (displayed in tab rows) in the MDT are defined. Figure 4.21 shows, for example, that you can display the following views in the MDT: **Directly subordinate employees**, **All subordinate employees**, and **Directly reporting employees**. Another view used by many companies is **Project assignments**—if the project organization is maintained in the organizational management, too.

Function Codes

Another possibility is the enhancement of the function codes. Therefore, it is possible, for example, to integrate individual reports in the MDT. You can expand the hierarchy of topic categories via **Customizing Personnel Management · Managers Desktop · Enhancement of Function Codes · Define Function Codes/Define Structure of Function Codes** (see Figure 4.23). For example, as shown in the following figure, if you want to customize a specific MDT scenario, you can supply the structure of the topic category "employees" with its own hierarchy of function codes. The comparison of the settings with their effects makes clear again the functioning of the hierarchy of the function codes.

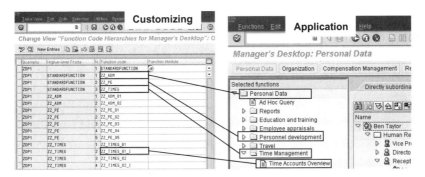

Figure 4.23 The Relationship Between Customizing and the MDT Interface

4.4.3 Integration of the Manager Self Services into the Enterprise Portal

The Manager's Desktop is easy to configure within the R/3 system. Another way to access management functions within HR is via the Manager's Self Service (MSS). MSS is a web-based solution that is similar to the ESS; however, it can only be used within the Enterprise Portal in the areas My Staff and My Budget (see Figure 4.24), where the budget area in particular will be enriched with new extensions and reports from the SAP Business Information Warehouse (BW).

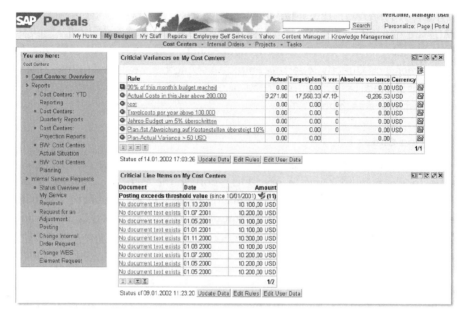

Figure 4.24 Manager's Self Service in the Enterprise Portal

This chapter alone could fill an entire book; unfortunately, due to the number of other interesting topics that need to be addressed, we must end our discussion of portals and self services here. These topics will certainly play a large role in the future and we are anxious to see where the development will lead. Please note that the decision to implement the Enterprise Portal will generally not be driven by HR alone; rather, it is a part of the companies IT strategy. ESS and MDT, however, are tools that don't affect the company-wide IT-architecture, and therefore can be determined in HR.

5 The SAP Business Workflow

The necessity of optimizing processes and making them more transparent with respect to quality and stability, when coupled with the requirement of shortening wait, idle, and processing times means that the use of workflow systems is becoming more important all the time.

5.1 Spectrum of Services and Connections

SAP Business Workflows include the following aspects of a process:

▶ The process flow itself (that is, the business activity)

▶ The participating people within the organizational structure

▶ The effects of the process (e.g., change of particular data in the system)

▶ Therefore, they ease the electronic processing of structured processes that include a series of activities. These processes occur in similar or identical form; they relate to several people or departments; and they require a high degree of coordination.

The business workflows control processes according to a predefined model and are especially suited for structured organizations. In mySAP HR, workflows are organized into three groups:

▶ **Workflows for controlling information flows**

   ▶ Change and status notifications

   ▶ Early archiving

   ▶ Form-based processes, mapping of circulation slips

   ▶ Help in error situations and during customizing

▶ **Workflows for controlling individual processes**

   ▶ Next process upon reaching particular limit values
    (e.g., maximum number of participants reached)

   ▶ Support in master data maintenance

   ▶ Printing and sending reports

   ▶ Automatic booking

   ▶ Automatic archiving

▶ **Workflows for controlling complex processes**

   ▶ Approval process during booking and cancellation of events

   ▶ Issuing of invoices

- ► Escalation procedure

- ► Applicant management

The approval and information workflows in training and event management are good examples of how workflows can efficiently reduce manual effort. These workflows can automatically ensure that supervisors are informed of their employees' bookings and cancellations and that they receive this information for approval without having to write an individual e-mail or, lose time by transporting forms via inter-company mail.

Simple, clearly defined subprocesses such as those already mentioned can be implemented easily with workflow; and, if needed, they can be adjusted quickly. Because of the improved efficiency, they generally amortize themselves quickly.

5.2 Integration of Workflow into mySAP HR

The SAP Business Workflow is integrated across different applications into the Web Application Server (Web AS) and can therefore support the business functions optimally.

Its central building blocks are:

- ▶ The Workflow Builder—a graphical definition environment for workflows (see Figure 5.1)

- ▶ The runtime system that monitors and controls the workflows

- ▶ Finished workflow models that are delivered with the system and can be reused
  For the completed workflow model, it will suffice to assign possible processors and to activate the event linkage to start the workflow.

The component *Organizational Management* (OM) of mySAP HR is accorded a special role. It delivers the entire information for the structural organization of the company and its staffing with employees for SAP Business Workflow. With a cleverly chosen, person-independent assignment of workflow steps to objects from OM (e.g., organization unit, position, job, etc.), changes to the structural organization can even occur without having to change the workflow definitions. Finally, the *Business Object Repository (BOR)* must be mentioned, in which objects (the central components of a workflow) can be defined and implemented.

The main purpose of the SAP Business Workflow is to direct the correct task at the correct time to the correct processor (organization unit, position, job, or user). This helps to expedite business processes. The OM component delivers the framework for a routing structure that the SAP Business Workflow uses for task assignment at runtime. In order to reduce the number of processors found to the actual processors, you can also use role resolution.

There are two possible ways to use OM in connection with workflow:

▶ The company uses OM for personnel management purposes. If the integration between OM and Workflow is set up, one cannot only assign users, but also employees' tasks (via the infotype 0105 "communication" = users).

▶ The company does not use organizational management within its personnel management processes. In this case, respective small parts of the organizational structure are created in order to make the workflows executable. Because no persons can be kept as HR objects in the organizational structure, tasks or organizational units can be assigned to the users directly.

5.3   The Workflow Builder

The *Workflow Builder* is the central tool of the SAP Business Workflow (see Figure 5.1). Its graphical interface enables, among other things, the creation, changing, testing, and displaying of a workflow definition.

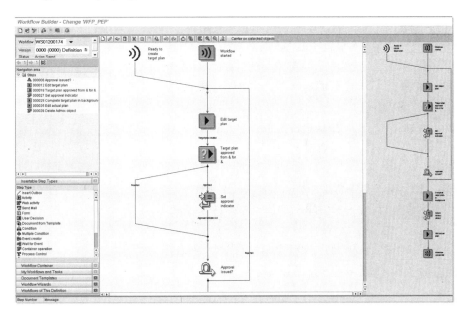

Figure 5.1 Setting Up the Workflow Builder

The *Workflow Definition (WF definition)* controls the business process (e.g., the approval of a training course). A WF definition consists of the following steps that build on one another, each describing precisely one action in the process, for example:

- ▶ Making a request
- ▶ Checking a request
- ▶ Running through a resubmission loop
- ▶ Waiting for the result of another process

Workflows are generally triggered by events, which are independent of the workflow. They are generated by the system when a company reaches certain business goals. They must be actively linked with the workflow. Actions in the workflow can be control steps. They can refer to actual tasks that are carried out by selected HR administrators who process personal data for employees. For example, the supervisor generally approves a training action.

Figure 5.2 Overview of the Individual Step Types

Each step type has its own icon in the workflow in order to make the definition legible immediately (see Figure 5.2). A detailed list of these icons and their meaning would exceed the limits of this chapter; however, you can locate such a list in the workflow portion of the SAP documentation. The data is forwarded automatically from workflow step to workflow step. The workflow container is the interface for these steps.

5.4 Standard Elements in Personnel Planning and Development

The following workflow models for personnel planning and development are available in the standard version:

▶ Qualification monitoring (workflow model Expired Qualification, abbreviation PDExpiredQua, ID 1000089): monitoring of the process of qualifications with limited validity period

▶ Approval and post-processing of appraisals (Appraisal, PcvAppraisal 1000105): approval or declining of a completed appraisal through by the appraised and automatic activation of post-processing activities

▶ Inform holder about changed subprofile (HR development subprofile changed, PCVChanProfi, 1200124)

▶ Automatic profile comparison with requirements profile of the new position for position change (Transfer, PdvTransfer, 1200145)

▶ Approval and activation of compensation adjustments (Approval process compensation adjustment, CMPApprProc, WS100083)

▶ Notification of personnel processor about the exercise of an employee participation via ESS (Follow-up action after award exercised, CMPExerc, 1200169)

▶ Automatic notification of the employee in timely fashion before the expiration of an employee participation (award Expiration, CMPExpire, 1200178)

▶ Notification of the processor of flawed correspondence in training and event management (correspondence Error handling, ERROR PD-SCM)

▶ Approval of the participation of an employee in ESS booking (Approve employee's attendance booking, PE_APPROVE01)

▶ Approval of a participation cancellation via an ESS employee (attendance cancellation, PE_APPROVE02)

▶ Approval of a rebooking via ESS (employee's rebooking, PE_APPROVE03)

5.5 Critical Success Factors

The following critical success factors should be noted:

▶ The business processes to be supported with workflow must be defined clearly in the flow.

▶ The processor responsibilities must be clearly regulated and the necessary competencies must be distributed.

▶ The higher the frequency of a process flow, the higher the benefit from the realization of a workflow.

- Wherever possible, you should work with standard workflows or copies of the standard workflow that are easy to customize. The effort required to develop completely new workflows is generally much higher than it is to adjust standard templates.

- The Works Council must be convinced of the advantages. (For example: Warning! Workflow can enable performance monitoring of individual employees)

5.6 Innovations in Enterprise

A special emphasis in the new SAP Web AS (R/3 Enterprise) are innovations in the workflow area. Because processes that are carried out across different systems are supported via the Internet, the term *WebFlowEngine* has come into being. A terminological separation between the R/3-internal workflow and workflows (WebFlows) that also include the Internet does not exist officially. The book *Workflow-Management with SAP* delivers a detailed description of the WebFlowEngine.

The most important innovations and changes are:

- The WF-XML standard is completely supported in Version 1.0. You can now start workflows on other systems and respond immediately to the answers and messages.

- The Workflow Builder will, in future, support the import and export of workflow definitions in the XML format. To make this component be able to run, the imported activities must, however, be linked to corresponding tasks in the respective SAP system.

- The identification will, in future, occur asynchronously, which means that there can be a work item without a corresponding recipient. This is generally acquired by a rule that is integrated into the work item.

- WEB services that can be called directly via the intranet can be called directly from a workflow.

- In the workflow definition, properties can be defined for all work items. The values that are assigned to these properties can be read out via programmer exits and reused.

- For selected step types, a condition can be stored in the step definition, which is checked if the work item ends without errors or an ending event arrives. If this condition is met, the work item is reused; otherwise, the recipients will be identified again and the item is re-sent for processing.

- For many types of work items, programmer exits are available, in which reactions to particular states can be implemented.

6   Query in mySAP HR

In mySAP HR, as in most applications, an evaluation tool is required to define reports easily and rapidly. SAP Query is such a tool; it offers the user a broad range of options to define and create different types of reports and lists.

6.1   The Design in mySAP HR

6.1.1   Connections and Terms

To simplify things, we'll define queries as self-definable queries of data sets (defined by infosets), whereby both the query's selection parameters and also the fields that display in the output—within the bounds of the underlying data set—can be freely selected.

The first and central building block of the definition of SAP Query or ad-hoc/infoset query are *infosets*. They form the data basis for queries. In the infosets, data is combined according to professional aspects in field groups (e.g., address data, organizational association, taxation data), which is intended to help the user find what he or she is looking for more easily. Therefore, the structure of the infoset corresponds to the infotype structure of HR, as you can see in Figure 6.6.

The technical (data-delivering) foundation of infosets is generally a logical database or parts of a database (for example, the PNP or PNPCE in personnel administration, or the PCH in personnel planning and development). For the purpose of simplification, think of logical databases as programs that access the data of a particular application (e.g., PNP for personnel administration), which also have an individual selection screen and make the data they acquire available to superior reports and also to queries. Therefore, there is a great advantage to using logical databases because all queries and reports that are based on them automatically work with the same data-retrieval mechanisms. Another advantage to using logical databases is that all necessary authorization checks have already been performed.

The second important building block of the definition of SAP Query or ad-hoc/infoset query are *user groups*. In a user group, users (SAP users) are grouped professionally (e.g., the employees of personnel development). The user group is then assigned to one or several infosets (see Figure 6.1). This means that the employees of the user group can see and use all queries that use the assigned infoset (or the assigned infosets) as their data basis.

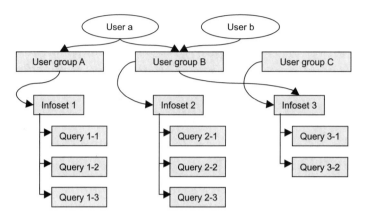

Figure 6.1 Users, User Groups, Infosets, and Queries in Context

The basic check for the authorization concept is not affected by this assignment. This check regulates whether or not a user has access to particular data. SAP Query does not enable you to access data that you do not have the proper authorization to access.

The ad-hoc query allows easy, one-step lists, for example, on the basis of the logical databases PNP and PCH. Therefore, the following data is available:

▶ All infotypes of personnel administration

▶ Results and infotypes of time management

▶ Long texts for most relevant keys that are used in the infotypes

▶ All infotypes of personnel planning and development of the logical database PCH (infotypes 1000 to 1999 as well as customer-specific infotypes)

The use of the ad-hoc query by a broader group of users depends on a clear definition that is based on specific requirements of the infosets and user groups. Even if the application appears easy to use at-first-glance, training or at least good, company-specific documentation should not be omitted. Otherwise, as past experience has shown, frequent confusion will arise, along with conflicting lists due to errors in the selection of data and the interpretation of the results.

6.1.2   Integration into mySAP HR

As we already stated in the previous section, infosets in mySAP HR are defined on the basis of the logical databases. Therefore, the advantage that the queries inherit—in the completed selection screen of the logical database—contains the extensive and convenient selection possibilities regarding the time range and those parts of the organizational structure selected for evaluation. With the use of the logical database PCH, the selection screen includes an editor for the definition of structural conditions (see Figure 6.2).

Figure 6.2 Selection Screen of a Query on the Basis of the Logical Database PCH

6.2 Implementation in mySAP HR

6.2.1 Use and Deployment Areas of Query in Personnel Planning and Development

The *ad-hoc query* with its relatively simple user interface is well-suited for ad-hoc reporting. Within a few minutes, existing queries can be adjusted to reflect changed or expanded questions. This ability for easy customization affects both the selection possibilities and also the displayed fields in the output.

The *SAP Query* is better suited for reports that must be standardized for a larger number of users. Conditioned by its extensive definition possibilities and a correspondingly sophisticated definition tool, SAP Query requires more maintenance; however, it does offer a myriad of possibilities and the appearance of a standard report. Furthermore, once the SAP Query is defined and generated, the actual application of it requires no other familiarization on the part of the user. In addition, some questions can be answered that the infoset query does not cover. In comparison to self-developed reports, this query is more cost-effective in development and maintenance.

Another advantage of SAP Query is that it enables the user group to determine—via the authorization concept—which queries of an infoset are assigned to which specific users.

In summary, SAP queries and ad-hoc queries are suitable tools for constructing self-defined standard reports in personnel planning and development.

6.2.2 Working with SAP Query

SAP Query can be found via the menu path **Tools · ABAP Workbench · Utilities · SAP Query** (see Figure 6.3).

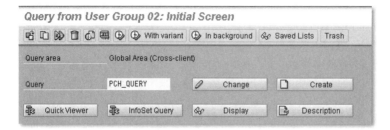

Figure 6.3 Starting Up SAP Query Processing

After starting the definition environment, you must first decide which infoset that you want to use as a data basis (see Figure 6.4).

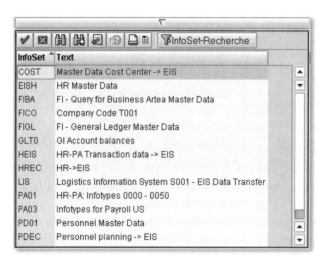

Figure 6.4 Selection of the InfoSet When Creating an SAP Query

In the next step, you create the general parameters of the query such as title, list format, table format, and general output format (see Figure 6.5). Then, you select the field groups that you want to use in the query. *Field groups* are partial quantities of an infoset and generally group the fields of an infoset professionally (similar to infotypes that group data in personnel administration).

After this selection, you select the individual fields as well as specify the parameters and which selection should appear in the output. Then, you define the output lists (see Figure 6.6). Here, you can also check and adjust the naming of the individual output fields if necessary.

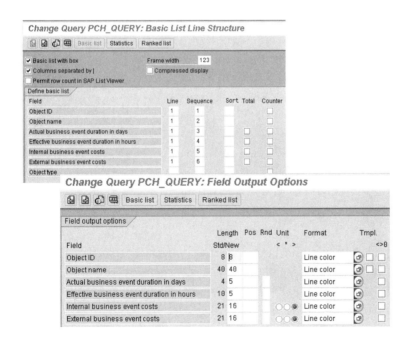

Create Query PCH_QUERY: Title, Format

Basic list | Statistics | Ranked list | Output sequence

| Title | SAP Query Personnel Development |
| Notes | |

List format

| Lines | |
| Columns | 83 |

Special attributes

| Standard variant | |
| ☐ Execute only with variant |
| ☐ Change lock |

Table format

| Columns | 200 |

Print list

| ☑ With standard title |
| No. of characters left margin | |

Output format

- ◉ SAP List Viewer
- ○ ABAP List
- ○ Graphic
- ○ ABC analysis
- ○ Executive Information System EIS
- ○ File store

- ○ Display as table
- ○ Word processing
- ○ Spreadsheet
- ○ Private file

Figure 6.5 Creating the Properties of a New Query

Change Query PCH_QUERY: Basic List Line Structure

Basic list | Statistics | Ranked list

☑ Basic list with box   Frame width 123
☑ Columns separated by | ☐ Compressed display
☐ Permit row count in SAP List Viewer

Define basic list

Field	Line	Sequence	Sort	Total	Counter
Object ID	1	1			☐
Object name	1	2			☐
Actual business event duration in days	1	3		☐	☐
Effective business event duration in hours	1	4		☐	☐
Internal business event costs	1	5		☐	☐
External business event costs	1	6		☐	☐
Object type					☐

Change Query PCH_QUERY: Field Output Options

Basic list | Statistics | Ranked list

Field output options

Field	Length Std/New	Pos < • >	Rnd	Unit	Format	Tmpl. <>θ
Object ID	8 8				Line color	☐ ☐
Object name	40 40				Line color	☐ ☐
Actual business event duration in days	4 5				Line color	☐
Effective business event duration in hours	10 5				Line color	☐
Internal business event costs	21 16			○○◉	Line color	☐
External business event costs	21 16			○○◉	Line color	☐

Figure 6.6 Definition of a Basic List in SAP Query

Depending on the selection of the output format, for example, list viewer, when the queries are later used individually, the user can adjust the layout (sequence, display and hide fields) and the formatting (filter, subtotals, aggregation levels) to meet the requirements of the people to whom it is addressed.

6.2.3   The Ad-Hoc Query

You can reach the ad-hoc query via the menu path **Personnel · Personnel Management · Administration · Infosystem · Ad-Hoc Query**. The term *infoset query* in HR is used interchangeably with *ad-hoc query*.

As in SAP Query, you first select the infoset. As you can see in Figure 6.7, the screen is divided into three parts: the field selection from the infoset structure on the top left, the selection criteria on the top right, and on the lower area of the screen, a preview of the output.

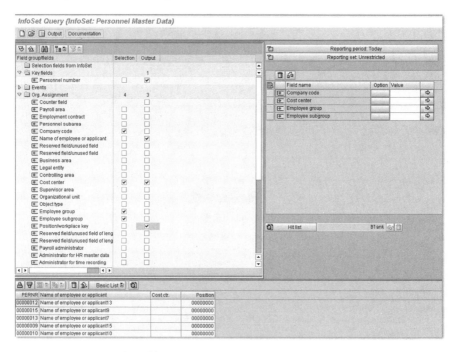

Figure 6.7 Starting Up the Ad-hoc Query

If you click on the **Reporting set** button, another convenient selection option is displayed via the tree structure of organizational management (only with "object selection" switched on via the menu"). To select the time period for the validity of the selected data, you must go to the next higher level where the selection of the reporting period is available. The selection criteria that you have chosen will appear to the right, in the middle of the tree structure.

The output using list viewer can be adjusted individually to meet specific requirements and offers the following possibilities:

▶ Sort, display, and hide columns

▶ Output of keys and/or long text

▶ Aggregation according to freely selectable columns in the output list with details that can be hidden

▶ ABC analyses and graphical display (diagrams, pies, etc.)

▶ Save self-developed layouts

▶ Transfer the output list in prepared form to Excel and MS Word

▶ Send the lists via SAP mail, with the mail connector activated also to external mail addresses

Pers.no.	Title, first name and surname	Postal code	City	Company name	P.subarea text
00010154	Trevor McDonald	19111	Philadelphia	IDES US INC	Chicago
00010155	Paul Ashe	60609	Chicago	IDES US INC	Chicago
00010270	Henry Miller	19111	Burlington	IDES US INC	Philadelphia
00010271	Karen Holzblatt	19111	Burlington	IDES US INC	Philadelphia
00010451	Lou Windham	30123	Atlanta	IDES US INC	Atlanta
00010452	Glenn Baxter	30112	Atlanta	IDES US INC	Atlanta
00010453	George Adams	30123	Atlanta	IDES US INC	Atlanta
00010454	Jo Sallis	30112	Atlanta	IDES US INC	Atlanta

Figure 6.8 List Viewer Output of an Ad hoc Query

6.2.4 Ad-Hoc Query Versus SAP Query

SAP Query is a complex tool that enables you to formulate complex queries. You can also extract several kinds of lists from the query result. One distinguishes between basic and ranking lists and statistics. From its appearance, the SAP Query appears to be identical to standard reports. With the aid of SAP Query, employees without programming knowledge can develop complex queries. In this way, expensive individual programming can often be eliminated.

The effort required to define a complete SAP Query, however, is often too great for the clarification of simple ad-hoc requests. The ad-hoc query does this (outside HR it is called the *infoset query*). The ad-hoc query is based on SAP Query; however, it is much simpler to operate and therefore much easier to learn and use in the departments. Because you can also save the selection criteria, there are no variants with the ad-hoc query as there are with standard reports or SAP queries. Different *variants* must be saved as different ad-hoc queries. Statistics and ranking list are also included with R/3 Release 4.6C or higher.

Both the ad-hoc query and the SAP Query reach their capacity if the task at hand is to report on interdisciplinary questions or, to enable branching options for other applications and detail information about objects (drilldown). In this case, programming is necessary or SAP Business Information Warehouse (SAP BW) must be used.

6.3 Critical Success Factors

Individual queries based on delivered infosets or self-created infosets can be created without devoting a lot of time to the conception. However, if the instrument of the query should be made available to a broad group of users, you should consider the following points:

▶ In naming the fields in output lists, great attention must be paid to clarity. First, the naming of the field appears from the Data Dictionary and this name can say nothing: for example, the title "Name" appears first over columns with long texts about cost center, organization unit, position, and many others. Here, definitions must be added to the list subsequently.

▶ Due to the requirements of the various user groups, before the creation of individual infosets and queries, a clear structure of the query user groups and the associated infosets is absolutely necessary. Therefore, not just the content but also the complexity of the infoset must be tailored to the individual user.

▶ The development of SAP queries already requires a significant training effort on the part of each user.

▶ The authorization concept must be checked carefully after clarification of the data-protection background; under certain circumstances, it must be developed further.

6.4   HR Query in R/3 Enterprise

In R/3 Enterprise, there are some innovations that make the use of SAP Query and especially of the ad-hoc query in HR still more interesting. Because SAP Query is not the focus of this book, we simply want to list the individual innovations briefly:

▶ The behavior of SAP Query can be controlled via various switches that either act generally or specific to infotype.[1] These switches are built into the infoset with a simple, fixed syntax and then act, for example, so that:

  ▶ locked infotype sets are also displayed

  ▶ only the last data set for a key is displayed

  ▶ without the proper authorization for a particular subtype, the other subtypes are nevertheless displayed

  ▶ The documentation about the switches listed can be found in the Implementation Guide (IMG) via the menu path **Personnel Management · Human Resources Information System · HR Settings for SAP Query · Create Infosets for HR Infosystem**.

▶ Documentation can be compiled for each query, which eases using completed queries considerably for most users.

▶ The logical database PNP will be replaced by the PNPCE. The PNP will continue to function; however, the PNPCE should be used for new infosets. This is indispensable for the use of the "Concurrent employment" and "Management of global employees" solutions (see Section 1.4.1).

---

1 Via HR support packages, these switches were also delivered for additional release versions. The following notes are required:
Release 4.5B: Note No. 152684
Release 4.5B: Note No. 187767
Release 4.5B: Note No. 305118

Part 2
Personnel Development

7 The Process of Personnel Development

The significance of personnel development as an inevitable component of continuous processes of change is increasing constantly. In addition, employees' capabilities and motivation are some of the most important "Intangible Assets" and as such are recognized as making a significant contribution to the value of a company. Systematic, IT-supported personnel development is therefore becoming known to an ever growing circle of people far beyond the realm of personnel departments.

7.1 This Chapter's Goal

With the introduction of the personnel development components of mySAP HR, many companies are facing extensive support of personnel development processes with an EDP system for the first time. Often, isolated systems for seminar organization and individual screens for training data have, thus far, formed the only IT support in this area. Therefore, in this chapter, the process of IT-supported personnel development (called *PD* in the following) is built from the ground up.

In Figure 7.2, an integral approach is established and described. Figure 7.3 then develops a procedure for constructing a skill management with the help of an integrated information system. This skill management forms the basis for the entire personnel development and must consider the constantly changing business processes and environmental conditions.

The complete PD process is then described in Figure 7.4. This purpose of this chapter is to represent a professional conceptual basis for the functionalities, strengths, and weaknesses of mySAP HR, which are described below. The initially SAP-independent view makes it easier to evaluate the possibilities of the system without being influenced by SAP. The representation in this part of the book thus corresponds to the procedure in a project in which the professional requirements are first defined without being system-specific.

Section 7.5 summarizes the important requirements of IT support in personnel development and compares these requirements with the options of mySAP HR.

7.2 The Integral Approach to Personnel Development

7.2.1 Central and Decentral Elements of Personnel Development

The terms *personnel development* and *organizational development* are becoming ever fuzzier. What is needed here is an integral approach that focuses on the goals of the company and also values the employees as individuals. The speed with which environmental conditions and business processes change also requires personnel development to be an integral component of business process management.

The quick response to requirements of operative business processes demands the appraisal of individual employees and a decentralized approach: the relationship between employees and their managers or mentors is the central and pivotal point.

Simultaneously, a central personnel development team is required in order to ensure adherence to the company goals and the proactive consideration of strategy changes as necessary. In addition, expertise, methods, and tools for optimal performance of their tasks are made available to those who participate in the decentralized process.

The significant influencing factors on personnel development are transported, on the one hand, via the company strategy (centrally), and on the other hand, via the staff dialogue (decentrally) (see Figure 7.1). Both approaches must be considered to define goals and design processes. Otherwise, either the reference to the company goals is lost (personnel development becomes an end in itself) or, the transporting of the strived for improvements fails in the real work situation.

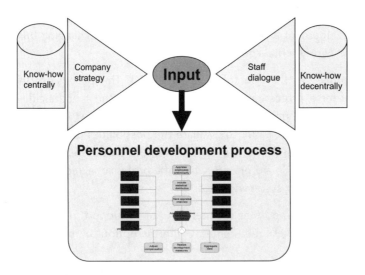

Figure 7.1 Company Strategy and Staff Dialogue as Input

It is a core task of the central personnel development instance to integrate both these aspects. If this occurs, then one can speak of an integral approach that fulfills the following requirements:

▶ It is relevant for the actual work situation.

▶ It enables the ongoing or project-related change of the business processes.

▶ It makes a significant contribution to the entire organization by helping it reach its goal.

7.2.2 Integration of Central and Decentral Elements

In the following, the term *central process participants* refers to personnel development as a department or competence center. These participants need not necessarily be located geographically in a central place; however, in a company group or in an international company, it will always be necessary to distribute personnel development teams geographically. Conversely, *decentral process participants* are employees outside the PD department, particularly each individual employee with his or her manager or mentor.

In addition, locations—such as department or branch offices (for organizational support)—and trainers participate (in the implementation). Because these first and foremost serve as support, they are generally not assigned to the *central personnel development instance*.

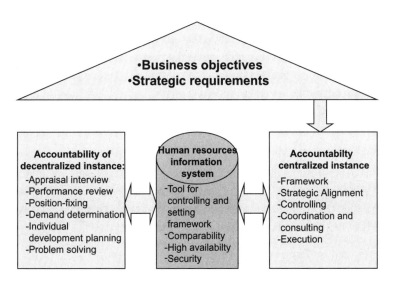

Figure 7.2 Integration of Central and Decentral Processes via a Personnel Information System

Figure 7.2 depicts the interplay between central and decentral processes or process steps in a first approach. The central personnel development instance (in the following "central PD") lets the company strategy flow into its planning and it uses the personnel information system to set the framework for decentral processes (e.g., by storing a skill catalog). The decentral responsible persons, that is first and foremost the managers, carry out their tasks independently in this framework and, if necessary, exercise their own initiative. Insofar as necessary, they are supported in their efforts by the central PD. The results of decentral dialogue flow constantly into the personnel information system, which then delivers to the central PD instance the basis for the planning and execution of courses and other PD activities, in addition to the basis for controlling.

Here, it is not important that the process be defined in detail; instead, what matters is a rough depiction of the integration framework:

▶ Strategy flows in via the central PD.

▶ The employees' goals flow in via the staff dialogue.

▶ The integration occurs with the help of a decentrally available personnel information system. It is apparent that a strongly decentralized process would not be possible without such a system to ensure quality and strategic direction by the central PD.

It is worth noting, however, that with this approach, the company strategy arrives at the decentral participants filtered via the central PD. This is certainly not sufficient due to one-sidedness and will in general not be the case. The company goals will be communicated at least as target values "from the top downwards." With the approach of the *Balanced Scorecard* (BSC), see Chapter 19, *SAP Strategic Enterprise Management*, all participants are incorporated into the target definition after an extensive communication process and a reorientation of the company's goals is achieved. In this desirable scenario, the role of the central PD regarding the company goals is limited to the development and communication of an appropriate personnel development strategy.

Furthermore, it is worth noting that the central PD is privy only to the desires and opinions of employees who have been filtered by the managers (aside from individual cases in which the employee seeks direct contact with the PD). This information can also bias the PD, and in the network of meetings, this data may not always be timely, which presents yet another problem.

These weaknesses can be removed via the following two measures:

▶ Implement periodic or event-related employee surveys

▶ Enforce the direct maintenance of the information system by the employee (e.g., new development goals or newly acquired skills) via an employee portal (ESS)

Figure 7.3 shows the improved communication of company goals and employee goals. In the following sections, the decentral and central tasks are described in the overview of each section.

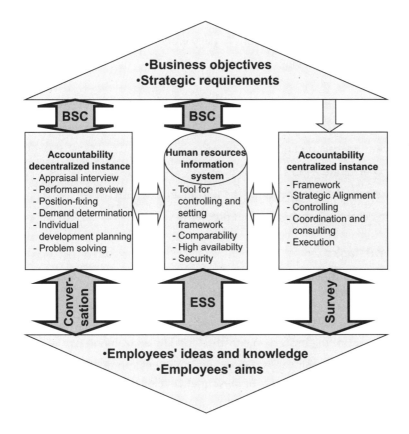

Figure 7.3 Rounding-Off of the Integral Approach Through Improved Communication

7.2.3 Decentral Tasks

This section focuses on managers and mentors, but also individual employees, as participants in the personnel development process. They must carry out the following tasks that they—if necessary–can execute without requiring any activation by the central PD and which can occur outside of the usual time period:

▶ Incorporate on-the-job training

▶ Execute staff dialogue on various occasions

▶ Create an employee appraisal

▶ Create development plans

▶ Select individual training actions

▶ Coach

▶ Determine the actual state of employee qualifications (periodically with the managers and constantly via the employees themselves)

- ▶ Provide immediate feedback on training actions
- ▶ Check effectiveness of training actions in daily work
- ▶ Determine and discuss changes in job requirements (e.g., due to changed business processes)
- ▶ Communicate and discuss goals on the company and department level
- ▶ Agree on goals on an individual level
- ▶ Determine employees' potential and desires
- ▶ Propose or precipitate a job change
- ▶ Maintain the relevant information in the information system
- ▶ Activate the central PD in the event of problems

7.2.4 Central Tasks

The following tasks are performed by the central PD, sometimes in cooperation with other departments or external providers:

- ▶ Derive a personnel development strategy
- ▶ Activate and control the process to construct a skill management
- ▶ Consider trends in the company strategy and in the environment that have an effect on the strategy and process of personnel development
- ▶ Define the organizational and content framework of the decentral PD process
- ▶ Provide a suitable information system with access for the decentral process participants
- ▶ Provide methods for the decentral process participants
- ▶ Train/coach the decentral process participants
- ▶ Perform quality assurance of the process; ensure the comparability of results
- ▶ Execute training activities
- ▶ Execute employee surveys
- ▶ Control personnel development

7.3 Construction of a Skill Management as a Basis of the Personnel Development

7.3.1 The Questions in Skill Management

The goal of personnel development is to ensure that individual employees, teams, and the entire organization are all able to carry out the business processes that you are in charge of optimally and to integrate these business processes into the overall processes of the entire organization. Additionally, all employees should be able to change business processes, when needed, to reflect the company goals, and if necessary, question their purpose, omit them, or replace them with completely different processes. All personnel should also be able to acclimate readily to changed or new processes.

Generally, the first point—the optimal expediting of the current processes—is overemphasized. Regarding the integration of personnel development, organizational development, and business process change, the other points listed have become more significant and will continue to grow increasingly more important. In all cases mentioned, however, this means that the employees must arrange the necessary "skills" (in the broadest sense) in order to manage these tasks.

For personnel development, the first thing to do is to define this task more precisely, which assumes that the following four questions can be answered:

▶ Which tasks must be accomplished now and in the future?

▶ Which skills are required for the accomplishment of the known tasks ?

▶ Which skills do our employees possess?

▶ What potential for not-yet-existing skills do our employees presently have?

Answering these basic questions is not akin to solving an academic riddle; instead, it is the indispensable requirement for qualified work in personnel development. Freely translated, these questions are:

▶ Where do we want to go?

▶ From where are we beginning?

Any development work without answers to these questions is equivalent to playing soccer without a goalie. On closer inspection, one deduces that these questions were answered with at least a general strategy in mind, despite the lack of a systematic and deliberate approach and the absence of a connection between the strategic and operative levels. Now, we will show you a systematic procedure to construct a skill management, which the personnel development can perform in the way it is required.

7.3.2 The Approach of Integral Skill Management

The input for the skill management and therefore for the PD strategy as a whole is derived from two sources (see Figure 7.4):

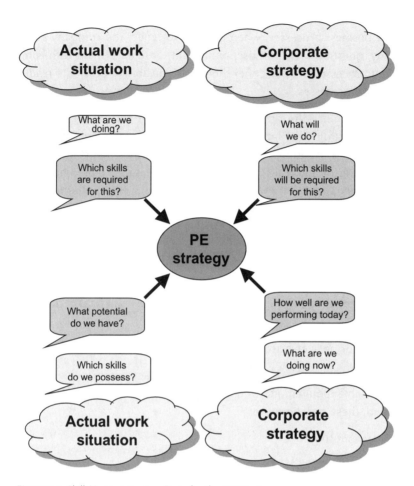

Figure 7.4 Skill Management as Basis for the PD Strategy

▶ **The actual work situation (decentral)**
   It delivers to the decentral participants detailed knowledge about the tasks to
   be performed and the knowledge and skills necessary to perform these tasks.
   This knowledge must be used for skill management because no central instance
   has better information that accurately reflects the individual workplaces. In
   addition, the individual employees and managers can best assess the existing
   skills and their room for growth, even if the consulting services and support
   that provides the framework of the central PD are required.

▶ **The company strategy**
   Changed goals and development trends lead to new tasks that must be accomplished by the organization and its employees. Here it must be assessed on the
   strategic level which skills are required for the future task structure and the

changed business processes. Because there is no corresponding experience on the operative level for the future situation, this can only be done by the central PD. Also, for the actual state, the quality of the company-wide task fulfillment should be checked on the strategic level. Unsatisfactory quality can point to a gap in the personnel development that is not recognized due to incorrect assessments on the operative level.

The approach developed in Section 7.3.2 combines a bottom-up strategy with a top-down strategy. Using two simple examples, we will show you again why combining these two methods is necessary:

► **Bottom-up**
In a particular company, no Spanish courses have been offered as yet. Therefore, the central PD assumes that only a few employees have Spanish skills worth mentioning. Before the company expands into the Mexican market, therefore, "Beginner Spanish" courses are factored into the training course planning. In reality, however, many employees already have advanced skills (e.g., because there are many Mexican guest workers). Therefore, the PD planning misses the mark completely because personnel didn't know the state of the company's existing skills. Furthermore, in most cases, the central PD's lack of knowledge about the skills that are actually required in the workplace is surprisingly greater than would be expected.

► **Top-down**
In a company that is about to expand into the Japanese market, many employees are booking Japanese language courses. Additional training planning reflects this operative need and therefore, the number of Japanese language courses is expanded to reflect the number of preregistrations for this demand. However, what is not considered is that the medium-term company strategy requires targeting the Japanese market via the takeover of a regional competitor in order to keep the company's own resources free for expansion into the Canadian market. In this case also, the additional training offerings—although they reflect employee demands—circumvent the actual need. What is particularly critical in this example is that the error in judgment may only be detected after many work hours have already been invested in these courses.

In both of the aforementioned examples, flawed information and miscommunication lead to a PD strategy that does not accurately reflect each of the company's actual needs and ultimately, does not contribute to the overall goals of each enterprise. The following section shows you how the required information basis can be established.

7.3.3   Skill Management Procedure Model

Basic Steps

Essentially, a systematic skill management must expedite the following steps:

1. Determine the current existing skills and potential via decentral inquiry.
2. Determine the current required skills via decentral inquiry.
3. Verify the statement made regarding the coverage of requirements using the actual goal achievement on the company level.
4. Determine the forecasted skills required on the strategic level.

Therefore, the description of the skills required for a particular job usually appears on the corresponding requirement profiles, which helps an individual employee or applicant determine, via a profile match, how well suited her or she is for a particular job. The more dynamically the business processes change, the sooner one should free oneself from static requirements profiles and examine the need for particular qualifications independently of actual jobs. This changes nothing in the basic construction of the skill management, so that both views are regarded as exchangeable in the following.

The Importance of the Personnel Information System

A constant update is required with the first-time construction. On the one hand, this occurs periodically (e.g., in the staff dialogue and in the PD strategy planning), and on the other hand, it is ongoing (e.g., with strategy changes or the acquisition of qualifications that a new employee brings to the job).

After more careful consideration of the processes of updating and controlling, it becomes apparent that support from an integrated, decentrally-available information system is indispensable. The argument that an EDP system is too inflexible and too much in need of maintenance is really incomprehensible. If you decide that what is needed is an integral and systematic approach in personnel development, you will require a sufficient information basis. The consistent pursuit of this approach is only possible with integrated personnel information systems with correspondingly-extensive functionality. Of particular importance is the decentral availability via portals (Manager Self Service, Employee Self Service), which brings the administrative effort—assuming there are efficient processes in place—into a dimension that is manageable.

Procedure Model

The procedure model shown in Figure 7.5 is organized into four main phases. There are certainly other ways to organize the phases or deviate from the procedure model shown here. At the core, however, the steps and especially the results for optimal IT support are always very similar. The main phases of the procedure model are described in detail in the following.

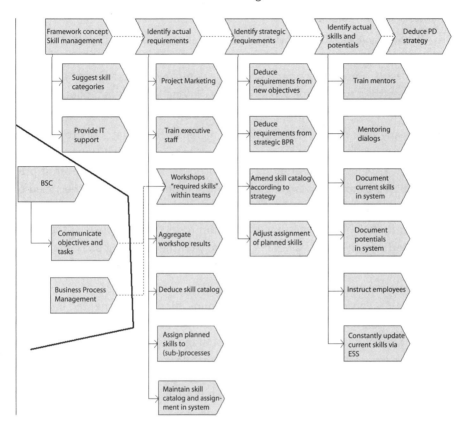

Figure 7.5 Construction of a Skill Management: Procedure Model

1. **Framework concept**

   In addition to project planning based on the procedure model, the framework concept delivers the following two results:

   ▶ The skills demanded in the company are divided roughly into categories, which ease the structuring—especially in the decentral workshops—and simplify the later aggregation of the workshop results.

   ▶ The skill management process receives its organizational framework via the design of the IT support.

2. **Current requirements**

   In this phase, the primary concern is to ensure that the information received regarding the skills needed accurately reflects the current requirements of the real work situation, and also reflects in what context these skills are used by the current business processes. Here, the focus is on the following core issues:

- ▶ Moderated workshops within the individual teams or departments deliver the skills demanded.

- ▶ The aggregation of the workshop results delivers a skill catalog with uniform terminology and the skills required that meets the demands of the business processes. Depending on the size of the company, a first aggregation should occur after a part of one workshop (e.g., in one location as a pilot) in order to provide a framework for the following events.

- ▶ In many companies, instead of the assignment of target skills to business processes or process steps, the assignment to "workplaces," "jobs," or "positions" is widespread. Adopting this procedure is possible; however, it presupposes a more rigid organization, which cannot truly reflect the speed of change or the employee as an individual.

- ▶ The results (and, if necessary, the interim results) are mapped in the information system and are available uniformly for the following phases and continuous change company-wide.

3. **Strategic requirements**

Even if a BSC process with excellent communication is implemented in a company: the goals that have been broken down (=detailed) to the lowest level often lag behind the company's overall strategic vision. Therefore, the central PD must ensure that the target skills and therefore, the goals of the personnel and organizational development, also consider the most up-to-date strategic goals and ensure that they are realized. This third phase completes the previous results "only" by adding the strategic component.

4. **Current skills**

Only after the desired state of the company-wide qualifications is known does the fourth phase deliver the corresponding actual state:

- ▶ Based on the existing skill catalog, the status of each employee is determined individually via discussions; for example, the regular annual staff dialogue can be used as a determining factor. Because the focus of these annual discussions is typically about such job aspects as salary, advancement, or even disposition at the company, however, we see a conflict of goals here. A way to resolve this conflict exists via implementing another annual development review at another time, which is not carried out by the manager, but instead by a mentor.

- ▶ The agreement about skills and potentials is stored in the system by the mentors.

▶ From this point on, all employees document changes to their actual qualification in the system independently via an easy-to-operate portal (ESS). With a well explained system and due to the annual alignment in mentoring dialogues, the quality of the self-assessment is usually much higher than generally expected.

In addition to the main phases, Figure 7.5 also reveals the dependency on the target structure (develops and communicates, e.g., via a BSC) and on the business process management.

After the four phases described, the target skills and existing skills are known and therefore a PD strategy and detailed PD planning can be created. The big advantage of a skill management constructed therefore lies especially in the broad availability of information that is continuously updated. Therefore, strategy changes can be planned just as professionally as restructurings on the lowest level. The following PD components, among other things, then build on the system-supported skill management:

▶ Risk management (e.g., "Is significant expertise only present in a particular age group?")

▶ Assurance of succession and representation of professionals and managers

▶ Employee perspective of the BSC and an agreement of objectives

▶ Advancement of employee satisfaction

▶ Individual development planning

▶ Planning, execution, and controlling of seminar offerings

▶ Identification of broadly needed seminars, for which e-learning is especially well-suited

▶ Planning, execution, and controlling of additional PD measures

The total process, which contains these components in particular, will be constructed in the following section.

7.4 The Personnel Development Process: Overview

Figure 7.6 provides an overview of the personnel development process with its relationships. This depiction regards the individual level and assumes a complete skill management. The skill management and also the BSC are influenced after the first construction by changes on the strategic level. In the process shown here, the influences of the operative level are considered. In the following sections, individual process steps will be explained in detail.

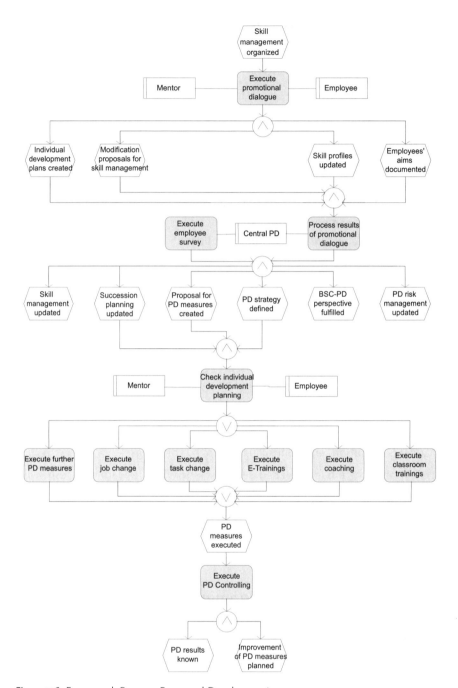

Figure 7.6 Framework Process: Personnel Development

7.4.1 The Promotional Development Dialogue

As the process shows, the dialogue is the central element. It delivers the significant input and must therefore meet the requirements shown in Figure 7.7.

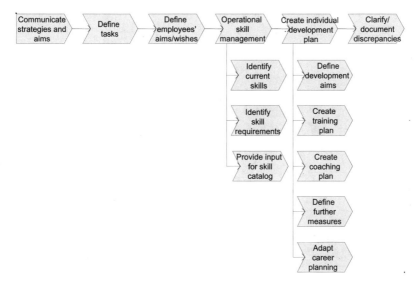

Figure 7.7 Content of the Promotion Discussion

The results of all promotional dialogue—if necessary, completed with employee surveys—serve the central personnel development for the construction of its planning in the context of the strategic requirements. In particular, the following aspects can cause a need for adjustment in the individual development planning in the dialogue between employee and mentor:

▶ Succession planning

▶ Offering of personnel development actions

▶ Personnel development strategy

7.4.2 Risk Management

We should emphasize the importance of *risk management*, which is often neglected when the subject is personnel development. Only succession planning, which makes risks recognizable on the individual level, is carried out systematically in some companies. In the future, this will certainly change. The risks that threaten a company from the "HR" factor are also increasingly being perceived by analysts and investors and thus have a direct effect on the shareholder value. Rating agencies are also increasingly considering these aspects. Figure 7.8 shows the most important questions of risk management in personnel development.

Figure 7.8 Components of Risk Management in Personnel Development

7.4.3 Personnel Development Actions

After the individual development plan has been reworked according to the development-action offerings and the PD strategy, the largest task block is the actual execution. The awareness that the action execution requires the most effort by far (see also Chapter 11, *Training and Event Management*) is very important here. It justifies the effort required for systematic planning in the previously discussed process steps, which enables the greatest possible efficiency of the actual actions.

Personnel development actions can include the following:

▶ In-class trainings

▶ Workshops

▶ Individual promotional development dialogue

▶ Moderated group discussions

▶ Conferences

▶ Online workshops

▶ Trainings on the Internet/intranet (WBT)

▶ Trainings via CD-ROM (CBT)

- ▶ Online discussions
- ▶ Planning games, role-playing games
- ▶ Learning groups
- ▶ Team-formation actions
- ▶ Self-discovery actions
- ▶ Language trips
- ▶ Coaching
- ▶ Management on probation
- ▶ Job rotation (getting to know various processes)
- ▶ Job enlargement (expansion of the task area to include similar processes)
- ▶ Job enrichment (deepening of the task area along the previously processed process)
- ▶ Relocation
- ▶ Foreign assignment
- ▶ Trainee programs that consist of many individual actions

Three groups are integral to the processes to be implemented here:

- ▶ **Employees**
  They participate in an action in coordination with mentors or managers.
- ▶ **Central personnel development**
  It organizes the actions and expedites or delegates them to third parties.
- ▶ **Managers or mentors**
  They approve and are in charge of seeing that the actions are carried out.

Depending on the kind of action, the processes distinguish themselves. First, the process for in-class training (whereby "training" should also include workshops, moderated discussions, etc.) will be described because this is currently used most frequently in companies and can therefore serve well as a basis for the other process variants. The depiction of the process in Figure 7.9, Figure 7.10, and Figure 7.11 occurs in simplified form because numerous possibilities (cancellation, rebooking, switching of appointments, consulting, resource problems, alternative sequence of the individual steps, etc.) would consume a lot of space. Note that the reading of the process may appear difficult because several levels are depicted as being grouped with one another: the individual case level of the employee who attends a training, as well as the superior level of the central PD, which carries out an action for several employees. This integrated view is necessary, however, in order to recognize the dependencies clearly.

Even this rough process already shows how many different functions—and particularly dependencies—can occur. These functions are essentially administrative activities that can be simplified significantly with an EDP system. The logical or appropriate degree of EDP support depends first and foremost on how often processes are used or implemented and the degree of standardization.

Figure 7.9 illustrates the first section of the process, in which the offering is created and the need is defined. Figure 7.10 depicts the second section of the process, in which the actual notifications from the participants occur and the extent of the planning is orchestrated or implemented by the central PD.

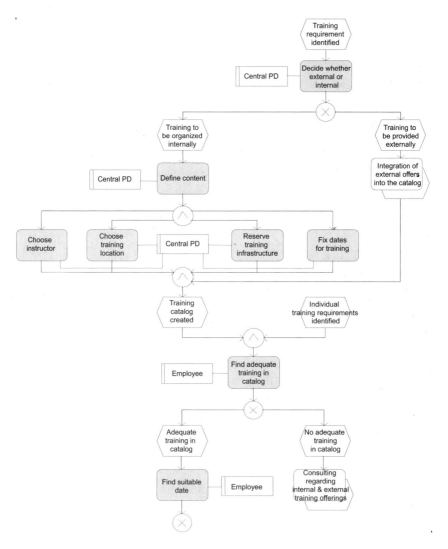

Figure 7.9 Presence Training Part 1: Training Offerings

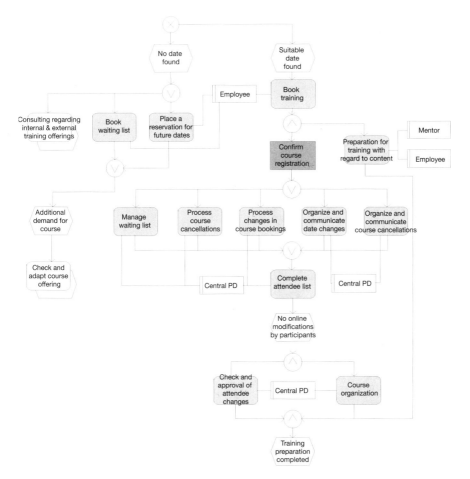

Figure 7.10 Presence Training Part 2: Booking and Preparation

The last and most important section (from the IT's point of view) is the wrap-up described in Figure 7.11. Here, the data that is necessary for planning and quality assurance is acquired and evaluated. This depiction simplifies the temporal sequence of the activities because of its flexibility and its lack of importance here.

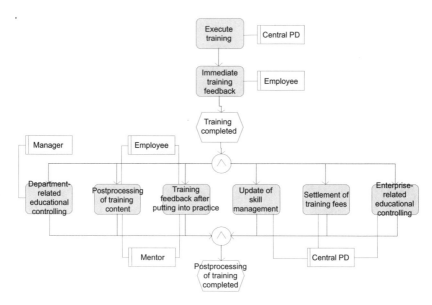

Figure 7.11 Presence Training Part 3: Wrap-Up

7.5 Conclusion of the Implementation in an Information System

The requirements of IT support can be organized in essentially two areas: the content requirements describe which functions the system must provide and therefore also which data must be saved. The requirements regarding role-specific access describe how the various groups of users actually use the system. There are also additional requirements—such as security and performance capability—that are not specific to personnel development.

The points described in the following section lead us then immediately to the functionalities in mySAP HR and allow us to reveal the strengths and weaknesses of the system. We will briefly summarize our evaluation here in advance.

7.5.1 Role-Specific Access

Essentially, you must distinguish the following three groups of users:

▶ The individual employees who want to access their own data

▶ The managers and mentors who want to access the employees in their area of responsibility

▶ The employees of central personnel development

Access, especially for the first two groups, must be simple and specifically designed because the work with the personnel development system does not count as one of their main tasks. Therefore, what would be most desirable is access via a Web portal. SAP fulfills these requirements essentially with its role concept and the portals Employee Self Service (ESS) and Manager Self Service (MSS). Without the use of the Enterprise Portals 5.0 or higher, the MSS is not yet available as a Web portal. However, managers can access the relevant data pretty comfortably via SAP GUI in the form of the Manager's Desktop (MDT). Role-specific and also individualized access is also especially well developed in the SAP Learning Solution (see Chapter 17, *E-Learning and Learning Management Systems*).

7.5.2 Content Requirements

In general, an EDP system must support the following task blocks:

▶ Integration into strategic company planning

▶ Skill management

▶ Planning and controlling of personnel development

▶ Organization and execution of PD actions

The detailed representation occurs here once again separated according to the important user groups.

Employee Self Service (ESS)

In particular, employees require the following possibilities:

▶ Maintenance of their own profiles

▶ Selection and booking of PD measures

▶ Evaluation of PD measures

▶ Search for suitable contact people

▶ Selection, booking, and execution of online trainings

▶ Overview of planned and ongoing events and events attended

▶ Recommendation of trainings

With the exception of evaluation, mySAP HR makes these functions available in the standard edition together with the expansions *Learning Solution* and *Expert Finder*. The lack of event evaluation in the SAP ESS indeed is a significant weakness in the mapping of processes and can only be bridged with an individual programming effort. Outside of the employee portal ESS, the compilation of an evaluation is absolutely possible; however, direct system access without ESS may soon be the exception.

Manager Self Service (MSS)

Within a manager portal, various roles for managers and mentors should be available. Therefore, it is highly conceivable that the same person can fulfill both roles for different employee groups. Specifically, the following functionalities are required:

▶ Overview of the development history of individual employees

▶ Succession planning and career planning

▶ Administration and control of training budgets

▶ Overview of booked PD actions

▶ Documentation of the success of actions

▶ Overview of the success of actions

▶ Overview of cancellation behavior

▶ Maintenance of employee profiles and desires

▶ Availability of and need for particular skills

▶ Further training statistics

These functions are mapped in mySAP HR and can be provided in the MDT. The representation is not always as intuitive as one might want. The required evaluations must then be incorporated into the MDT in suitable form. Moreover, generally, some evaluations with company-specific design and content are required. Therefore, you will note that the construction of the PD view in the MDT requires some conceptual and technical effort which, with the consistent use of standard reports, can be kept low. These actions and behaviors are also applicable to the MSS in the mySAP Enterprise Portal.

Functions of the Central Personnel Development

In the central personnel development, there is generally the greatest variety of roles. Roles are conceivable for the following groups of people; typically, however, individual employees occupy several of these roles:

▶ Strategic PD planner

▶ Training program planner

▶ Consultant/Counselor of employees and managers

▶ Organizer of actions

▶ Trainer

▶ Authors of online trainings

▶ Personnel officer

While most of these employees execute the lion's share of their work on the HR system, others will use it only seldom or in limited ways (e.g., as trainers) and therefore require very simple access to the functions required. The smaller the company in question, the more the roles named above will meld together. In the central location, the same functionalities are required that have already been described in ESS and MSS—only without the limitation to individual employees or departments. In addition, the following requirements are added:

▶ Support of strategic PD planning with incorporation into the BSC
▶ Creation of a skill catalog, which must contain the following points:
  ▶ Hierarchical structure of skill categories (e.g., language abilities, knowledge of own products, etc.)
  ▶ Various scales for the proficiencies (depending on categories or individual skills)
  ▶ Explanations that enable a uniform understanding of the skills and their proficiencies and therefore ensure comparability
  ▶ Connection of skills with positions (jobs, workplaces), tasks/processes, and PD measures
  ▶ Additional information per skill (for example: "version" for software or products, "expiration duration")
▶ Support of employee surveys, especially with the option to remain anonymous
▶ Creation of a catalog of PD measures that must contain the following points:
  ▶ Hierarchical structure of categories/areas (e.g., language courses, courses on own products, etc.)
  ▶ Description of content, target group, etc.
  ▶ Integration into skill management
  ▶ Integration of actions that represent no classic in-class training
  ▶ Requirements that the respective actions make of the organization (required infrastructure, possible trainers, etc.)
  ▶ Price and cost information
  ▶ Support for planning and date finding requirements
  ▶ Combination of actions into packets
  ▶ Mapping of more complex organizational forms such as series of dates with imprecise rhythm, parallel seminar elements, etc.
▶ Organization and execution of PD actions
  ▶ Resource planning for rooms, technology, etc.
  ▶ Material planning and procurement

- ▷ Special problem of rooms that can be divided into separate rooms
- ▷ Participant management, especially:
  - – Efficient compilation of participation even with mass registration
  - – Processing of cancellations, participant changes, nn. bookings, date change
  - – Participation in partial events
  - – Wait lists, lists of desires/reservation lists
  - – Management of external participants
  - – Simple procedure for controlling and if necessary approving bookings via ESS
- ▷ Integration into a knowledge management system so that access to associated media is possible immediately from the processing of measures
- ▷ Documentation and organization of participants in external actions
- ▶ Automation of the required correspondence, if possible in electronic form
- ▶ Reworking of PD actions
  - ▷ Appraisal of evaluations
  - ▷ Creation of certificates
  - ▷ Evaluation of action types, action groups, participant groups, department, presenters, trainers, etc.
  - ▷ Assignment of newly acquired skills
  - ▷ Internal accounting for services or invoicing to the outside
- ▶ Compilation and evaluation of
  - ▷ Potential
  - ▷ Tendencies
  - ▷ Positions wanted, activities, and locations
  - ▷ Potential successors and representatives
  - ▷ Education and earlier jobs
- ▶ Evaluation of
  - ▷ Overtime hours, time accounts
  - ▷ Absences
  - ▷ Salary histories
  - ▷ Position histories
- ▶ Maintenance and simulation of succession plans/career plans

▶ Special requirements for the creation, planning, and maintenance of e-learning activities (detailed description in Chapter 17, *E-Learning and Learning Management Systems*)

These requirements are also essentially well met by the solution in mySAP HR. In addition to R/3 Release Version 4.6C or Enterprise, for some points the SAP Learning Solution, the SAP Knowledge Warehouse (KW), and the SAP Strategic Enterprise Management (SEM) (see Chapter 19, *SAP Strategic Enterprise Management*) are required. The area of evaluations can be supported by the SAP Business Information Warehouse (BW) (see Chapter 18, *The SAP Business Information Warehouse*).

Minor limitations must be made for the following points:

▶ The support in the planning and organization of actions has its strength in the mass processing of frequently repeated events where people have to be physically present. With the Learning Solution, e-trainings can then be mapped well. Essentially, the operation for lower frequency (e.g., the participation of individual participants in special events by the most various external training providers) is often somewhat inconvenient. In Chapter 11, *Training and Event Management*, it will be revealed how one can work around these limitations pretty well.

▶ The following points are not optimally resolved in the organization of actions, but they can be mapped:

  ▶ Participation in particular event portions

  ▶ Very long-running events with low intensity (e.g., language course once a week over the course of a year with flexible dates)

  ▶ Divisible training rooms

▶ Training cost controlling also demonstrates some weaknesses. Therefore, travel times and travel costs cannot be assigned to training participation without a second thought. This applies also for additional costs or preparation times that arise in the course of participation in a PD action. Evaluations of training costs are very simple and are limited to the direct costs that arise due to the need for resources for a training. The work time of the participants, for example, is not integrated. Here, one must make individual programming or seek solutions outside of R/3 (e.g., compilation of various evaluations in Office products).

▶ An integration of skill management into the Balanced Scorecard (BSC) of the Strategic Enterprise Management (SEM) is not possible. The SEM in its standard delivery will only be integrated with the components of the management by objectives. But with some customizing or programming, it should not be too difficult to get key figures from skill management as well as event management into the SEM via the BW.

▶ The greatest weakness lies in the lack of a process view. Therefore, we will address this aspect in more detail in the following section and introduce a possible solution.

Overall, one can call the support of the PD process good—especially, if one compares mySAP HR with competing ERP products.

7.5.3 Integration into the Business Processes

Neither the skill management nor the knowledge management have a clear reference to the company processes in the mySAP HR solution. In the skill management, this can be achieved in limited fashion via the object "task." However, the incorporation of the tasks into the business processes is lacking.

An incorporation of the aspects *skill management*, *process management*, and *knowledge management* is hardly offered in the required form by other HR information systems. A possible approach here is the use of a third-party product such as "DHC Vision" by *DHC GmbH* (see Figure 7.12), which integrates the three aspects into a modern tool. Knowledge in the form of the most various files is available along the documented business processes or via direct access. The "division of labor" of such a tool with mySAP HR must be defined via the tasks, which are contained in SAP and also documented in the form of "functions" in the business processes.

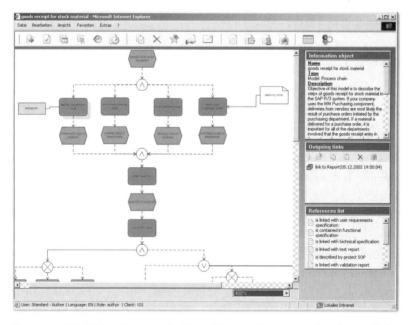

Figure 7.12 DHC Vision Connects the Views "Process Management" and "Knowledge Management"

In most cases, it will suffice to use DHC Vision technically independently of mySAP HR for integrated knowledge management and process management. The cooperation with the skill management executed in SAP can then be ensured organizationally. Due to the openness for interfaces to other systems, a coupling of DHC Vision with mySAP HR is certainly conceivable: A mirroring of the tasks between both systems then allows, among other things (not without significant technical effort):

▶ The evaluation of required skills in a process

▶ Recognition of need for change in the skill management and thus in the strategic PD planning for business process changes

▶ The evaluation of "knowledge documents," which are required for the fulfillment of a task

Figure 7.13 shows an example of the possible teaming of both products. Certainly other concepts and the use of other tools are conceivable, insofar as these can map process-oriented knowledge management. With such a scenario, you can achieve a situation where knowledge management and PD strategy reflect the business processes and therefore support the company goals optimally. Therefore, whether you establish a technical integration between both products becomes secondary.

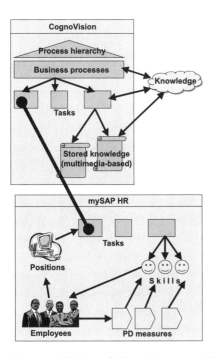

Figure 7.13 Division of Labor Between mySAP HR and DHC Vision

7.5.4 Summary

An integrated personnel development process can be mapped well with mySAP HR, especially when using the new products of the mySAP product family. The weaknesses mentioned may be compensated for with reasonable technical or organizational effort. For smaller companies, the complete mapping of the processes described would not enter into question anyway. For them, the most important success factor is the recognition of the areas and functionalities for which IT support is truly worthwhile.

8   Skill Management

In the previous chapter, skill management emerged as the basis for personnel development. In this chapter, you will learn that mySAP provides a very good basis for the IT support of skill management.

8.1   The Design in mySAP HR

The basis for skill management is the qualifications catalog of the HR component *Personnel Development*. It houses the entire pool of qualifications that then forms the various profiles. The profiles, in turn, are linked with the individual employees, the elements of the structural organization or—with limitations—also with process organization. Figure 8.1 shows the relationship between the qualifications catalog and the profiles as well as their relationship to the important information objects in the overview.

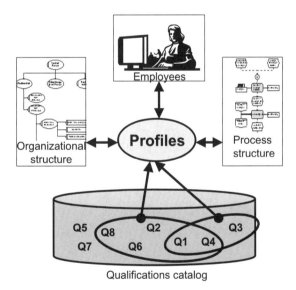

Figure 8.1 Connections of the Skill Management in the Overview

8.1.1   The Qualifications Catalog

Basic Structure of the Qualifications Catalog

The qualifications catalog is not simply a listing of all relevant skills in the company. Because of the object type of the *qualification group*, the qualifications (or skill) catalog can be structured by subject. With the help of qualification groups, you can build a hierarchical structure of any depth (see Figure 8.2). The construction of this basic structure is an important step at the beginning of building a qualifications catalog and often, it can be corrected only with great effort afterwards.

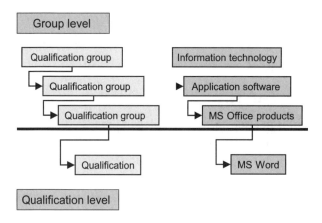

Figure 8.2 Structure of the Qualifications Catalog

The qualifications themselves can be formed into additional hierarchies. Therefore, you can assign an employee both the general qualification "Microsoft Office" and also the specific qualifications "Microsoft Excel," "Microsoft Word," and so forth. Figure 8.3 shows a corresponding alternative structure. In contrast to the catalog depicted in Figure 8.2, in this example, the qualification "MS Office" can be assigned to an employee directly. In this case, however, the interpretation must be unambiguous: does an employee with this qualification have basic knowledge of all MS Office products or, is this person familiar with only one of the products? The entire organization must adhere to this convention. For appraisals and employee-qualification matches, the formation of hierarchies based on levels of qualification can prove to be very awkward.

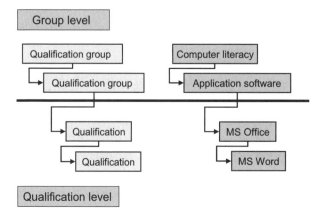

Figure 8.3 Alternative Structure with Formation of Hierarchies on the Level of Qualifications

Use the following guidelines when building the skill catalog (some of these guidelines are alternatives to each other):

▶ Focus on the process architecture of the company (in general, several additional groups with general qualifications—such as key qualifications or language skills—are required)

▶ Focus on the organizational structure of the company

▶ Use the training catalog as a basis for the skill catalog (see Section 11.1.1)

▶ To determine how qualification groups and qualifications should be defined, examine whether a direct assignment to an employee makes sense, as well as whether an appraisal scale should be used (see the following section)

▶ Combine the qualifications that are appraised with the same scale for the same group

▶ Focus on the availability in the Employee Self-Service (ESS) (see Section 8.3.1)

Scales

The penultimate guideline, in particular, is significant in the configuration of HR. The qualification group is linked directly with an appraisal scale (called a *value scale* or simply a *scale*). All qualifications of a group are then appraised according to this scale when they are assigned, for example, to an employee. Two such examples are:

1. The qualification group "driver's license" contains as qualifications all relevant driver's license classes. As values for these qualifications, the values "yes," "no," and "currently confiscated" make sense.

2. For the qualification group "languages," other values make sense, for example, from "not present" to "basic knowledge" to "native language."

In neither of the aforementioned two examples would the classic school-grade scale be the optimal choice. The scales are handed down from the qualification group to the qualification, which is the most important system-conditioned restriction for the construction of the qualifications catalog.

Free Texts

In addition to a description with scales, qualification groups and qualifications are also described with free texts. For groups, these free texts serve first and foremost the purpose of orientation during the incorporation of new qualifications or, during a search within the skill catalog. With the qualifications themselves, a detailed description in the form of a free text is indispensable if several persons should appraise the value of qualifications independently of one another. As described in the previous example, it is unclear as to whether the qualification "MS Office" should only be given if all products are known or, whether knowledge of one product will suffice. Also, in other cases—above all with so-called *Soft Skills*—a clear description is essential. Only then can a uniform appraisal and interpretation of the appraisals be achieved (this is seen most clearly in the self-assessment done by each employee).

Structure of Scales

There are two basic types of scales in personnel development in HR:

▶ **Quality scales**
These scales consist of well-defined values such as "very good," "good," "bad," and "very bad." Each value corresponds to a numeric ranking, which is required in order to calculate average values or suitability percentages.

▶ **Quantity scales**
These scales consist of an interval in which any value can be assumed (only limited by a step size to be determined). The individual values must not be defined explicitly. Therefore, a quantity scale must be numeric.

In the qualifications catalog, only quality scales can be used. Quantity scales are only permitted in appraisals (see Chapter 10, *Appraisals and Setting Objectives*). Like the qualification groups and the qualifications, the individual values of quality scales can also be described by a free-form text. Here also, the use of this possibility is highly recommended. If you use the decentralized approach, developed in Chapter 7, *The Process of Personnel Development*, then both managers and individual employees must be in a position to interpret the values according to a company-wide standard. If, for example, the qualification "project management" should be appraised, the value "good" says little and will certainly be understood in many different ways. For a common understanding, an additional description is warranted, such as: "Can develop reliable time and resource plans for projects with up to 100 participants"; "Can ensure the achievement of milestones and the optimal use of all resources"; and "Still requires support in conflict situations on the top management level and in project marketing."

The description of the values is stored in the scale definition itself. It can be overwritten on the level of the qualification groups and on the level of the qualifications and then handed on down. Therefore, a qualification always inherits the value description of the superior group—even if the direct superior object is a qualification. A group, however, inherits the description of the original scale definition directly—even if another group is superior. This somewhat unusual inheritance is evident in Figure 8.4, which describes a hierarchy with four levels (two groups and two qualifications). In this figure, you can also see precisely which inherited values can be overwritten (except for the scale itself; on the level of the qualifications, everything can be overwritten).

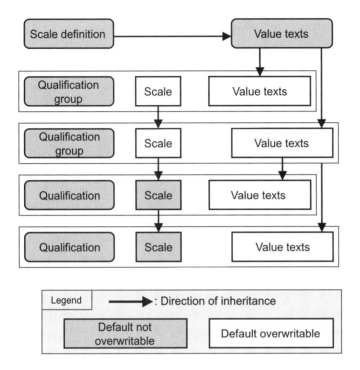

Figure 8.4 Inheritance Logic for Scales and Value Description

Alternative Qualifications

For the execution of a profile matchup or during the search for a suitable employee for a particular task, the search for precisely defined qualifications is often insufficient. Generally, employees are considered who possess qualifications similar to those sought. Thus, for example, knowledge of business English could substitute for knowledge of technical English, at least in part. With the concept of alternative qualification, HR takes this factor into account. For each qualification, other qualifications can be stored that can be used as alternatives up to a certain degree.

Validity and Depreciation

Typically, one loses knowledge and capabilities once acquired if they are not refreshed regularly. This can be mapped with the concept of the depreciation. Each qualification can be stored for a duration, after which the value of the qualification should be reduced by half the value. However, this depreciation occurs only for employees who don't need this qualification to meet the requirements of their position. In contrast to the depreciation time, the validity of a qualification specifies the period after which the qualification expires definitively. The validity must be used if a qualification has to be refreshed periodically due to a regulation or law (for example, a test for the transport of hazardous materials).

8.1.2 Profiles

Profiles are created via the assignment of qualifications of the qualifications catalog to other objects. Therefore, requirements profiles, in particular, which are assigned to organizational objects, are distinguished from other profiles that are assigned to people (in the broadest sense—not in the sense of the object type "person"). Requirements profiles are created via the assignment of qualifications to the following objects:

▶ Jobs
▶ Positions
▶ Work center
▶ Tasks
▶ Capacities
▶ Requirements profiles

The last object must seem a bit strange; however, here, you must distinguish between the object type "requirements profile" and the requirements profile as a business term. With the help of the object type, you can maintain requirements profiles independently of actual organizational objects. Therefore, it is possible to search freely according to particular, repeating criteria combinations. The profiles of persons consist of the following subprofiles:

▶ Qualifications
▶ Potential
▶ Preferences
▶ Dislikes
▶ Additional profiles that will be described later in this book

Even if the actual qualifications profile is integral to the framework of the skill management, the other three profiles are also equally important. The potential makes a statement about which nonexistent qualifications a person can acquire in a particular time period. It is also important to know which qualifications an employee is striving for or, which qualifications that employee does not want to acquire.

In addition to qualifications, other objects are provided for these profiles (e.g., jobs or positions). Via the customizing of the relationships (see Chapter 2, *Organizational Management*), you can make additional objects available for the profiles (e.g., the location in order to document geographic preferences). The named profiles can be formed for the following objects:

▶ Persons (employees who are kept in the personnel master data)

▶ Applicants

▶ Companies

▶ External persons

▶ Contact persons

▶ System users

In the following, we will primarily describe how these processes can be applied to persons—the processes are similar to the connection with other object types. The interaction between the qualifications profile and the requirements profile opens up the possibilities for a profile matchup, which highlights gaps and those persons or applicants who are overqualified. This profile matchup can be executed visibly (e.g., for an employee with a job that person is striving for); however, most often, it is transparent as it occurs during the search for employees who meet particular requirements.

Regarding the requirements, an inheritance logic is active, which is depicted in Figure 8.5. Therefore, the assignment of requirements, particularly to positions, must not be maintained redundantly. The assignment to jobs is sufficient, so that all requirements that are generally valid for this job are inherited by the positions connected with this job. Special requirements of an individual position can also be added. In addition to the three-stage inheritance logic depicted graphically here, there is also a two-stage chain: requirements are also inherited from tasks in work centers, which occurs primarily during shift planning and workforce management.

On the one hand, the incorporation of tasks permits a modularly-divided assignment of requirements and therefore requires less maintenance effort. On the other hand, a connection to the process organization or the business processes is possible if the tasks are reflected in the business process documentation (typically outside of R/3, see Section 7.5.3).

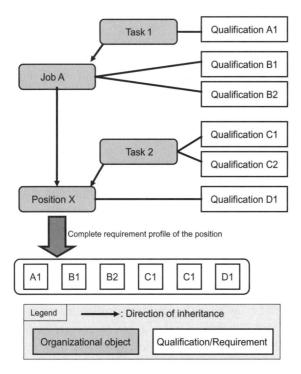

Figure 8.5 Inheritance of Requirements

8.1.3 Reporting

The reporting possibilities on the basis of the qualifications catalog and the profiles are the primary immediate objective of skill management. The selection of reporting possibilities is ideal and provides responses to questions that may arise regarding the stored skills and requirements. These questions can be divided into three categories by subject:

▶ Biased considerations, for example: "Which skills does Mrs. Miller have?" or "Which requirements does the position of Personnel Director have?"

▶ Matchups that constantly require two-sided consideration, for example: "Which employees correspond to an actual profile?" or "How well would Mrs. Miller fit in the Personnel Director position?" (classic profile matchup)

▶ Administrative reports, for example, a list of all alternative qualifications stored in the system

The application of the essential reports will be discussed in detail in the following sections.

8.1.4 Integration

Organizational Management

We already described the integration of the skill management into the organizational management in the previous sections. The entire area of requirements depends on the relevant organizational objects. In addition, essential elements of the selection in reporting are based on organizational management. If, however, the concern is purely the documentation and evaluation of the as-is qualifications and employees' potential, then using the skill management without the organizational management is absolutely conceivable. In most cases, however, the advantages of integration win out.

Personnel Administration

The integration of the skill management into the personnel administration is also fundamental. There the important "objects" of personnel development are kept with their master data: the employees. From the processing or display of the personnel master data, you can therefore branch immediately into an employee's profile.

If you limit yourself to rudimentary master data, you can use the skill management without the administration. Then, the employees can be maintained as objects of the object type H ("external person"). This object type is also available in the components organizational management and training and event management. Typically, however, the use of personnel administration may be the best solution. If the processes of payroll, time management, and administration of personnel master data are run in another system, a very simple version of personnel administration will suffice.

Numerous personnel administration infotypes (e.g., address, disability, etc.) are also relevant for personnel development. The following infotypes contain special data for education or training:

▶ "Education" (0022)
▶ "Other/Previous Employers" (0023)
▶ "Corporate Function" (0034)
▶ "Company Instructions" (0035)

With active integration, the infotype "qualifications" (0024) leads to the profiles of personnel development (also to the appraisal). With inactive integration, this infotype enables you to maintain qualifications from an unorganized list with poor reporting possibilities. The infotype "education" is represented using the example of school attendance in Figure 8.6. It is the only named infotype for which the customizing can prove to be a bit more complicated. In addition to school attendance, especially professional training, university education, and course participation can be documented there.

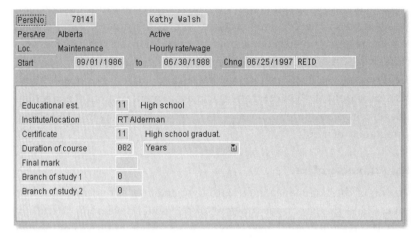

Figure 8.6 Infotype 0022 "Education"

Training and Event Management

With training and event management, there are the following points of contact:

▶ Particular qualifications can be defined as a prerequisite for participation in an event.

▶ For each event, it can be specified which qualifications it imparts.

▶ After participation in an event, these imparted qualifications can be transferred to the participant by the system automatically.

▶ Within a profile matchup that reveals gaps of an employee, the system can generate suggestions for training events automatically. This also occurs on the basis of the qualifications to be imparted as they are stored in the training and event management.

The use of these aspects is described in more detail in Chapter 11, *Training and Event Management*.

Shift Planning

In shift planning, employees are planned into particular workplaces for particular times. Therefore, you can limit yourself to the classification of employees via the job plan or to a profile matchup of suitable employees. To do this kind of planning, requirements profiles must be maintained for the work centers and qualifications profiles for the employees.

Logistics: Capacity Planning

In the logistics component of R/3 (e.g., production planning or plant mainte-nance), workplaces are described technically. They can also be linked with the HR object "work center." Therefore, profiles and qualifications can also be used for the planning of employee capacities in logistics.

8.2 Implementation in mySAP HR

8.2.1 Basic System Settings

Before we can turn to the skills and profiles, some basic settings must be noted. First and foremost, these skills and profiles are to be made via customizing and these settings control the interfaces during work in the skill management.

Integration

The integration aspects were described in detail in the previous section. To acti-vate the integration for personnel administration and recruitment, it is necessary only to set a customizing switch that is located under the IMG path **Personnel Management · Personnel Development · Integration · Set Up Integration with Personnel Admin. and Recruitment**. In addition, there are also some tools there for the conversion of master data that was acquired before the activation of inte-gration.

General Control Parameters

The following settings must be made via the IMG path **Personnel Management · Personnel Development · Functions · Set Up Control Parameters** :

▶ Number of entries in hit lists as a result of a search for employees suitable for particular requirements

▶ Valuation of overqualification (in the calculation of suitability, overqualifica-tions can flow in positively, negatively, or neutrally)

▶ Default value for the percentage at which the maintenance of alternative qualifications (see Figure 8.13) is suggested

▶ Decision whether the abbreviations should be displayed in the qualifications catalog

Selection of the Subprofile s

The profile view of an employee generally contains several profiles, each of which is displayed or maintained on a separate tab strip. You can get to the profile view used in personnel development from many different screens. One possible way is to call the infotype 0024 ("qualifications") in personnel administration. Figure 8.7 shows the *personnel development* profile view for an employee and the maximum information that is provided in that view. It contains qualifications, potentials, preferences, dislikes, received and created appraisals, the individual development, and the development plan history.

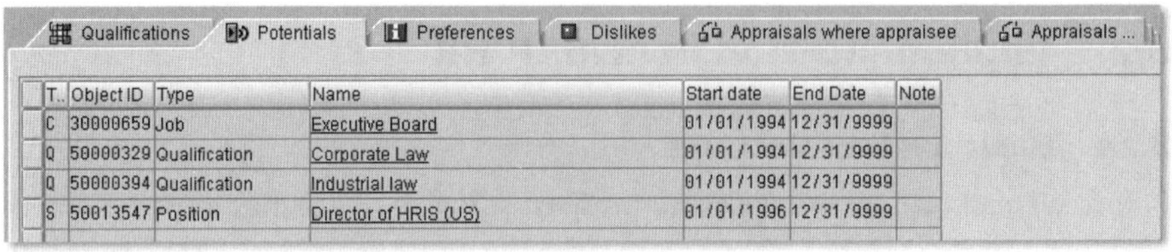

			Qualifications	Potentials	Preferences	Dislikes	Appraisals where appraisee	Appraisals ...

T..	Object ID	Type	Name	Start date	End Date	Note
C	30000659	Job	Executive Board	01/01/1994	12/31/9999	
Q	50000329	Qualification	Corporate Law	01/01/1994	12/31/9999	
Q	50000394	Qualification	Industrial law	01/01/1994	12/31/9999	
S	50013547	Position	Director of HRIS (US)	01/01/1996	12/31/9999	

Figure 8.7 "Personnel Development" Profile View for an Employee

The structure of the profile view can also be adjusted via the IMG path **Personnel Management · Personnel Development · Functions · Define Profile View**. There, first the header information is defined for each object type and the possible subprofiles. Do not adjust these definitions initially because fixed program coding is stored there. Typically, intervention is only warranted here if the functionality of the user interface is ostensibly altered. Then, instead of the standard interface, individual developments can be stored.

What you must adjust in most cases, however, is the selection of the relevant subprofiles. In order, for example, to construct the *personnel development* view for employees, you must first select the PD view ("personnel development") in the dialog structure on the views level. On the header assignment level, you then highlight the object type P ("person") and open the screen depicted in Figure 8.8 via the subprofile assignment level. There, you can deactivate the unnecessary subprofiles or add other subprofiles (e.g., the display of salary data through the subprofile No. 21). If, for example, you do not maintain dislikes, you should deactivate the corresponding subprofile in order to avoid confusion in the user interface.

In this chapter, we are limiting ourselves to the *qualifications profile*. The other subprofiles can also contain qualifications (e.g., an employee has the potential to become an ABAP objects expert), however, we will only address this topic in the next chapter.

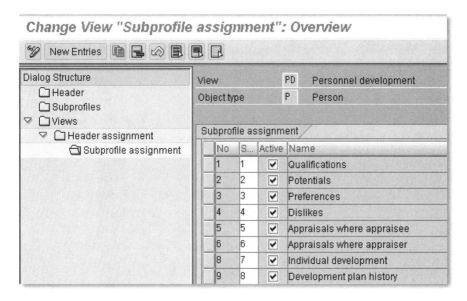

Figure 8.8 Assignment of the Relevant Subprofiles

Selection Possibilities

For the selection of persons, SAP delivers—similar to object manager for personnel administration—a group of selection criteria. If these criteria don't meet the requirements, you can create an infoset with the necessary selection criteria. You must store this criteria via the IMG path **Personnel Management · Personnel Development · Functions · Define Criteria for Detail Selection**.

Personal Settings

In order for the results in reports and matchups to reflect your or a user's expectations, all users must maintain their personal settings for personnel development (menu path: **Personnel · Personnel Management · Personnel Development · Settings · User-specific**). In PD, the following settings are determined (see Figure 8.9):

▶ Default period for reports

▶ Consideration of alternative qualifications

▶ Consideration of essential requirements

▶ Consideration of depreciation in reporting

In addition to the fixed adjustment of these parameters, a temporary change for a special request is possible, which can then be reset once more.

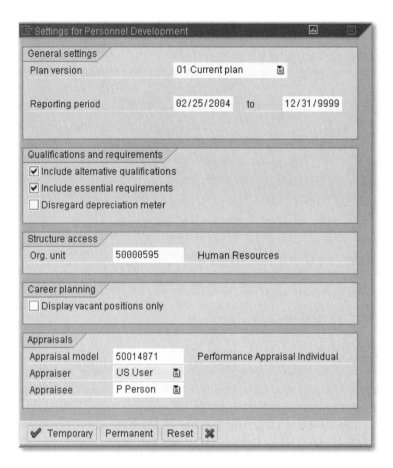

Figure 8.9 Maintenance of Personal Settings

8.2.2 Maintenance of the Qualifications Catalog

The qualifications catalog is the basis of the skill management and is also important for additional processes. Therefore, its maintenance and especially its conception must be given special attention. Figure 8.10 shows an overview of the process.

First, the structure of the qualification groups must be defined. The question of which appraisal scales must be used within the groups is a technical criterion for the organization of the catalog (see Section 8.1.1). In the course of this structure definition, therefore, the scales themselves must be defined. Only after the determination of the scales to be used and the rough structure of the catalog should you begin with maintenance on the system. Therefore, it must also be noted that qualifications, after they have already been used once in profiles, can no longer be moved into a group with another scale assignment.

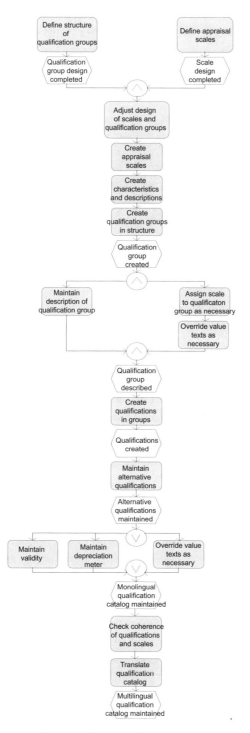

Figure 8.10 Process: Structure of the Qualifications Catalog

The first step in the system is the maintenance of the scales (IMG path: **Personnel Management · Personnel Development · Master Data · Edit Scales**). To create a scale, three actions are required:

▶ First, create a scale with a numeric abbreviation and a name. With the corresponding system request, select a quality scale since quantity scales cannot be used in the skill management.

▶ Then, on the level "Characteristic Values," maintain the proficiencies with value and short text (see Figure 8.11).

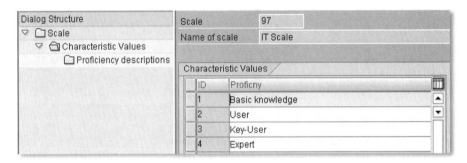

Figure 8.11 Maintaining Values of a Quality Scale

▶ Next, on the proficiency description stage, define each individual value completely. These descriptions, when paired with the texts, produce the overwritable default values for the scale of a qualification group.

Scales should always be constructed such that the lower capabilities correspond to the smaller numbers. Because a nonexistent qualification is appraised with "0," no sensible calculation of differences and average values is possible.

The construction of the catalog itself also occurs in the customizing (IMG path: **Personnel Management · Personnel Development · Master Data · Edit Qualifications Catalog**). Therefore, this will seldom correspond precisely to the ideal typical process, which is displayed in Figure 8.10, because the total catalog is not created at one time. Nevertheless, you should adhere to the basic procedure and sequence.

When creating a qualification group (see Figure 8.12), explanations can be maintained immediately. Groups on the uppermost level must be assigned to a scale; for groups starting on the second level, the inherited scale can be taken over. Regarding the use of deviant scale texts, the inheritance logic from Figure 8.4 should be considered.

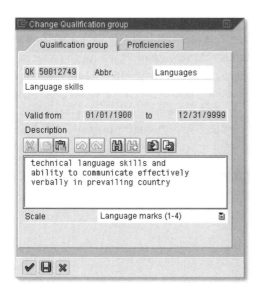

Figure 8.12 Maintenance of a Qualification Group

If the group structure or the currently relevant portion of the structure is maintained, then the individual qualifications must be integrated. These qualifications are created immediately in the structure, so that no subsequent assignment to a group is required. If the concept of alternative qualifications is used extensively, the sequence depicted in the process model is highly recommended. If the qualifications—at least of one main group—are all created, next is the assignment to alternative qualifications, which is maintained. Note that the relationship between two qualifications as possible alternatives is always interpreted as bidirectional, even if technically only a one-way relationship is stored. This technical peculiarity must be considered during the programming of individual reports and also during the creation of appraisal paths in customizing.

The texts for qualifications and qualification groups should be selected so that the essential content is expressed within the first 15 characters. If possible, you should limit yourself to 15 characters. There are many more characters available; however, they aren't displayed on all screens. If, for example, all language skills begin with "Language skills in…", in the profile matchup, only the words "language skills" will be displayed. The essential part is truncated. If this is only detected after the complete maintenance of the catalog, a painful reworking is required.

The additional properties of the individual qualifications should only be maintained subsequently. Therefore, it is guaranteed that the attributes of two reciprocally-substituting qualifications do not contradict each other. You should especially design the scales and descriptions homogenously here because only the numeric value is considered as an alternative qualification. If, for example, for the qualification "MS Word" the value 4 stands for "very good," then for the alternative qualification "text processing," the 4 may not stand for "good end-user knowledge." The same thing applies for validity and depreciation time, for which maintenance is relatively easy (see Figure 8.13). The importance of clear names and explanations for the scale values—particularly with decentral use—is referred to expressly yet again here.

Figure 8.13 Maintenance of a Qualification

If the qualification is completely maintained, then, when you click on the **Overview** button, a small "list of characteristics" with all their relevant properties is displayed. Before this last step, check the entire catalog again. The scales, their values, and the explanations must reflect the respective qualifications. For this accurate correspondence, we recommend that you employ new users who have not previously participated in the maintenance of the catalog. Figure 8.14 shows an example of the complete catalog.

Only if this quality test was successful do we arrive at the topic of "translation." If we arrive at the translation topic prematurely, we must make all the corrections in all the languages presented. The translation works similarly here as it does in many other areas of HR (see Figure 8.15). Its quality, however, is nowhere as critical as it is here—in the qualifications catalog. It is the determining factor for the comparability of profiles, which were created in various languages.

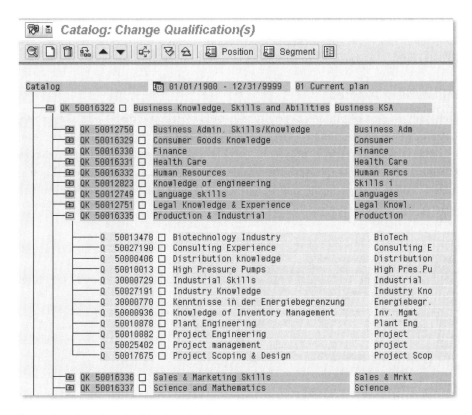

Figure 8.14 Complete Qualifications Catalog

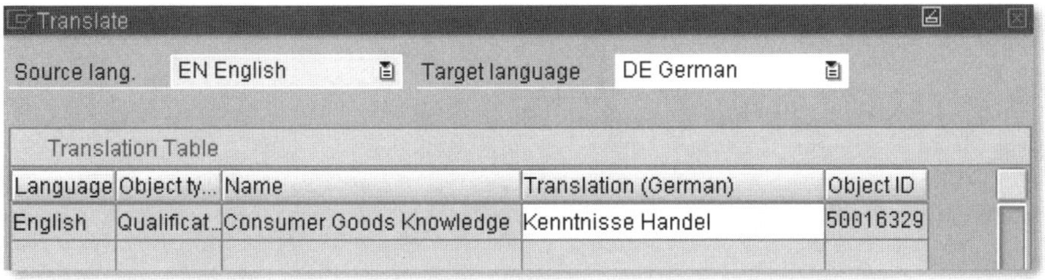

Figure 8.15 Translation in the Qualifications Catalog

In addition to the previously described core functions, the maintenance screen of the qualifications catalog offers additional tools like those that are familiar with similar maintenance interfaces. Because the application of these tools is via a menu path or a right mouse button click (context menu) and therefore intuitive, we will not describe them in detail here.

8.2.3   Working with Profiles

When working with qualifications and requirements profiles, the primary concerns are the maintenance of profiles and various evaluations.

Maintaining Profiles

The maintenance of profiles of any type is possible via the menu path **Personnel · Personnel Management · Personnel Development · Profile · Change**. Here, you must select the object for which a profile should be maintained. If, as shown in Figure 8.16, a job is selected, the profile maintained is automatically a requirements profile. In the profile maintenance, all relevant skills are selected on the basis of the catalog (see Figure 8.17).

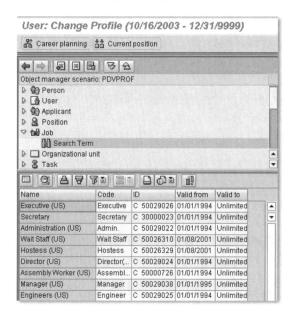

Figure 8.16 Profile Maintenance: Select Object (here: Job)

Then comes the appraisal and the marking of mandatory qualifications (see Figure 8.18). Since the requirements are maintained as time-dependent, the changes of need over the course of time can be mapped very well. A **Note** field also allows for the compilation of free texts, for example, to explain the assigned requirements.

The maintenance of actual profiles from the same interface is also possible. For internal people, the complete profile offerings are displayed as described in Section 8.1.2. In addition, the process example in Section 8.3.1 provides insight into the maintenance of actual profiles.

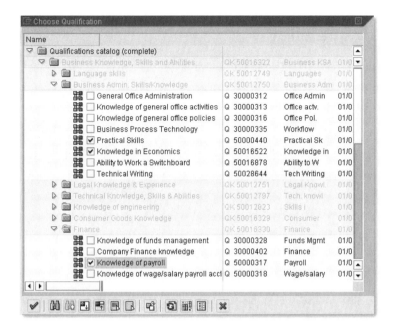

Figure 8.17 Selecting Qualifications from the Catalog

Qualification Group	T..	ObjectID	Name	St..	ID	Proficny	E..	Start date	End Date	Not
Core Employee Requirements	Q	30000444	Verbal, written communicative skills		7	High	☐	01/01/1994	12/31/9999	
Core Management Practices	Q	30000453	Leadership skills		9	Excellent	☐	01/01/1994	12/31/9999	
Legal Knowledge & Experience	Q	30000761	Knowledge on Unions & Bargaining Uni..		8	Very high	☐	01/01/1994	12/31/9999	
Physical Abilities	Q	30000450	Endurance and stamina		8	Very high	☐	01/01/1994	12/31/9999	
University Education	Q	30000679	Business Administration Degree		8			01/01/1994	12/31/9999	

Figure 8.18 Target Profile: Appraising Skill Need

Displaying Profiles

The display of profiles occurs in the same way as does the maintenance, that is, via the menu path **Personnel · Personnel Management · Personnel Development · Profile · Display**.

Executing Profile Matchup

If qualifications profiles and requirements profiles are maintained, profile matchups can be executed in various ways. The general menu path for this is: **Personnel · Personnel Management · Personnel Development · Information System · Reports · Profile Matchup**. Here, several people can be compared with one requirements profile or vice versa (see Figure 8.19). The actual profile matchup contains the following information:

▶ Degree of fulfillment of the individual requirements

▶ Essential requirements

▶ Additional, not required qualifications

▶ Training recommendations (if this option was activated for the matchup) via which one can immediately book a training course for the identified deficits

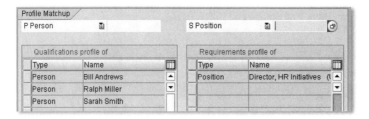

Figure 8.19 Selecting Several Persons for Profile Matchup

For a better overview, you can also display the matchup graphically (see Figure 8.20).

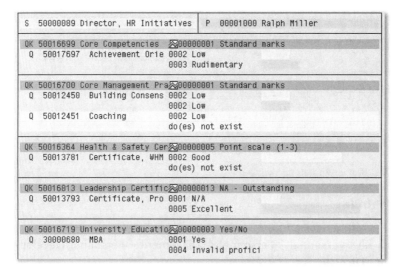

Figure 8.20 Profile Matchup with Additional Training Recommendations

Searching for Employees According to Profile or Individual Qualifications

Searching for a suitable employee for a particular position is a requirement that is made often. Therefore, this functionality is integrated into various interfaces of personnel development. The general menu path is: **Personnel · Personnel Management · Personnel Development · Information System · Reports · Search · For Qualifications**. In this interface, one can search for employees via individual qualifications as well as via requirements profiles. In addition, a combination of these search criteria is possible, in that one searches for an employee according to the requirements profile of the position "Personnel Director," but who also has a sound understanding of MS Excel. In the example in Figure 8.21, the qualifications didn't have to be entered individually into the search boxes. Selection occurred via the requirements profile of the position "Personnel Director." Only the qualification "Knowledge of Excel" was added manually.

	Object ID	Name	E...	O...	Proficny	Maximum ...	
	30000400	Marketing Skills	☐	▣	Average		
	30000401	HR Management skills	☐	▣	Very high		
	30000444	Verbal, written communicative skills	☐	▣	Average		
	30000449	Independence and initiative	☐	▣	Excellent		
	30000453	Leadership skills	☐	▣	Excellent		
	50000317	Knowledge of payroll	☐	▣	High		
	50000452	Sociability	☐	▣	High		
	50000551	Knowledge of Excel	☐	▣	Average		

Figure 8.21 Search According to Qualifications

Additional limitations that can be maintained via the additional tabs on the screen are, for example:

▶ "Only internal employees" or "Only applicants"

▶ From a particular organizational unit

▶ Without absence in a particular period

Consequently, the search then delivers a list of people who partially or completely meet the requirements—sorted according to the number of requirements fulfilled. People who don't meet an essential requirement are not displayed.

Skill Management for a Department

Essential functionalities that managers in the area of skill management require are provided in the Manager's Desktop (MDT). They are described in the process example in Section 8.3.1. However, tools for department-related skill management are offered outside of the MDT. These tools aren't only used by managers, but by personnel developers or HR support people especially, those individuals who advise a particular department.

The essential activities are bundled via the menu path **Personnel · Personnel management · Personnel development · Planning for organizational unit**. The entry-point into the organizational structure used here is defined in the user-specific settings (see Figure 8.9). The screen (see Figure 8.22) offers the following functionalities:

▶ Profile matchups for employees, positions, and jobs of the organizational unit (with corresponding authorization, you can also use the **Comparison** button to compare with positions and jobs in other organizational units)

▶ Display of all or selected profile types for all or selected employees or positions of the organizational unit in a list (**Appraisal** button)

▶ Display and maintenance of any profiles for individual employees or positions of the organizational unit (that is, requirements profiles, qualifications profiles, potentials, dislikes, preferences, appraisals, development plan) via the **Change profile** or **Display profile** button

▶ Career planning (see Chapter 9, *Development Planning*)

▶ Succession planning (see Chapter 9, *Development Planning*)

▶ Search for employees according to particular qualifications

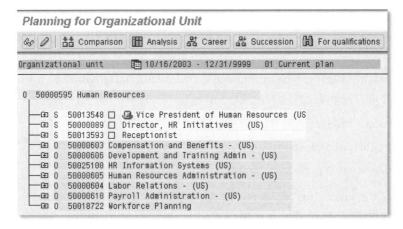

Figure 8.22 Personnel Development for a Department

Additional evaluations of particular organizational units are available via the menu path **Personnel Management · Personnel Development · Information System · Reports · Organizational Unit**. Here, the following aspects are important:

▶ The qualification overview delivers a list of all qualifications present in the department with their holders. The layout suggested by default is very unclear; however, it can be changed easily by any user via the normal layout design. Figure 8.23 shows the overview sorted according to qualification groups.

▶ The report of expired qualifications displays which qualifications will become invalid in a particular period of time. In addition, further training suggestions to refresh one's skills can be displayed and booked.

Qualifications Overview

Organizational unit O 50000595 Human Resources
Key date 10/16/2003

Qualification Group	Qualification	Average prof...	Name	Average	Proficiency text
Language skills	English language skills	Fluent	Jennifer Esposito	3,000	Fluent
			Lisa Felix	3,000	Fluent
	Technical Spanish Language Skills	Mediocre	Mr. Matthew Black	2,000	Mediocre
Leadership Certification	Certificate, BEI Selection Interviewing	N/A	Michelle O'Connor	1,000	N/A
	Certificate, Prob Slvng & Decision Mking		Michelle O'Connor	1,000	N/A
Legal Knowledge & Experience	Regulatory Knowledge	Very high	Tom Peterson	8,000	High
			Ann Takahashi	8,000	High
			Timmy Tabasco	8,000	Excellent
			Jerry Wagner	8,000	High

Figure 8.23 Qualifications Overview for a Department

8.2.4 Central Control

For central personnel development, some tools and reports are also offered that are helpful for the performance of control tasks:

▶ To check the completeness of data maintenance, two reports are available under the menu path **Personnel Management · Personnel Development · Infosystem · Reports · Profile**. Both reports are very well-suited for monitoring process quality within a decentralized environment.

   ▷ The "Objects without qualifications or requirements" list delivers people without qualifications profile or positions without requirements profiles and allows for an immediate branching into the profile maintenance.

   ▷ The "Objects with unevaluated qualifications or requirements" list also delivers all qualifications for a selected object type for which the value must be maintained.

▶ A list of all alternative qualifications can be called up via the menu path **Reports · Others**. Therefore, this part of the qualifications catalog can be checked in an overview.

▶ The previously described report of expired qualifications (see Section 8.2.3) is of use for the monitoring by the central PD.

▶ Similarly, the qualification overview is essential for central control. Instead of the layout depicted above, for the consideration of larger areas, a layout should be selected that contains the field "Qualification fulfilled." This is always set to "1" and can therefore be used ideally to incorporate interim totals per qualification into the layout. Thus you have an overview for an area of any size of how many employees have a particular qualification and what the average value is.

▶ You can assign individual or several qualifications to a quantity of employees via the menu path **Personnel Management · Personnel Development · Settings · Current Settings · Qualifications Profile: Mass Data Maintenance**. Figure 8.24 shows an example in which four employees who all worked together on the same project are assigned the qualification "ABAP/4."

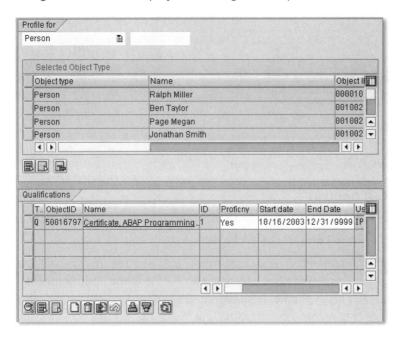

Figure 8.24 Mass Data Maintenance for Qualifications

▶ Another interesting function can only be reached via the customizing using the IMG path **Personnel Management · Personnel Development · Tools · Copy Requirements Profile to Position Holder(s)**. Typically, it isn't feasible to maintain qualifications and requirements identically. This tool is very helpful, however, if you're just beginning with the maintenance of skill management and would like to use both qualifications profiles and requirements profiles. To minimize the maintenance effort, therefore, the following procedure is advisable:

▷ Maintain the requirements profiles for the jobs

▷ Complete the requirements to the position holder as qualifications with the named tool

▷ Adjust the automatically-maintained qualifications profiles to reality, for example, by the employees themselves via the ESS

8.3   Process Example

8.3.1   Decentral Skill Maintenance

As described in the previous chapter, a broad skill management is only possible with decentrally organized processes. In mySAP HR, this is supported with various services of the *Employee Self-Service* (ESS) and the *Manager's Desktop* (MDT). This process will be described in great detail here with the help of figures. Therefore, readers should get a good impression of the support afforded by this important and specifically decentral process. Figure 8.25 shows an overview of the process.

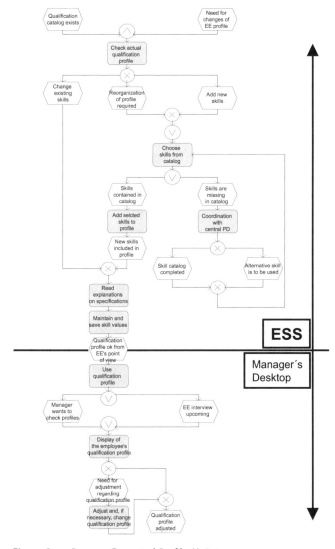

Figure 8.25 Process: Decentral Profile Maintenance

First, employees can check their qualifications profile that is stored in the system. In addition to the simple display, matchup against the requirements profile of their own position is possible, that is, they can find a requirements profile for their job and determine if their qualifications profile matches this requirements profile. Figure 8.26 shows this in an example in which the employee is completely lacking three qualifications. In addition, overqualifications (difference positive) and underqualifications (difference negative) occur.

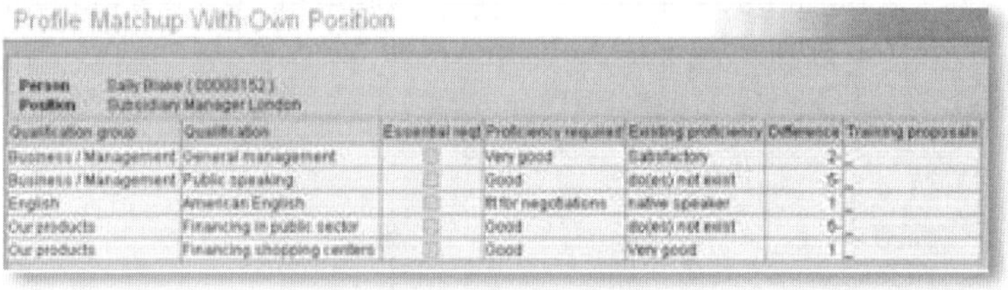

Figure 8.26 ESS: Profile Matchup Against Requirements of One's Own Position

Figure 8.27 ESS: Selection of Qualifications

If the qualifications profile is to be maintained completely anew or, if individual skills are to be added, the employee can select the qualifications from the qualifications catalog (see Figure 8.27). Then, there is an appraisal of the selected qualifications or, a new appraisal of the skills already contained in the profile (see Figure 8.28).

During the appraisal, the necessary detailed information pertaining to the qualifications is available to the employee. This information includes all the descriptions of the proficiencies of the appraisal scales as shown in the following example (see Figure 8.29).

Figure 8.28 ESS: Appraisal of Qualifications in the Profile

Qualification	**Swedish conversation** (Qualification group: Swedish)
Area of validity	01.01.1900 - 31.12.9999
<Blank proficiency>	
basic skills	Sufficient for survival with additional use of gestures
some dialogue possible	Simple dialogue possible
adequate for small talk	Can make himself understood in most situations. Adequate for polite conversation with many mistakes in vocabulary and structure and that do interfere with

Figure 8.29 ESS: Detail Information About a Qualification

In the course of this appraisal of the qualifications, an employee may want to enter a skill into his or her profile that is not listed in the qualifications catalog. In this case, the employee must contact the personnel development (e.g., via SAP mail directly from the ESS). To resolve this problem, note the following possibilities:

▶ The central personnel development must make an addition to the qualifications catalog.

▶ The outcome of the conversation is that an already existing qualification should be used, which the employee did not find. In this case, it may be necessary to adjust the structure of the catalog or the explanations.

▶ The skill in question is not relevant to the company and is therefore not compiled.

▶ If only a part of the skill catalog is released for the ESS: the skill in question may not be maintained via the ESS and, if necessary, is compiled directly by the personnel development.

If, per the employee, his or her qualifications profile is maintained correctly, it is immediately available in the system for a search and evaluation. However, a simple sharing procedure is not supported here. For one thing, this process is dependent on the timeliness of the data. If every change had to be released immediately by the manager, the timely availability of the new data would no longer be possible, provided the manager uses a practical time management system.

The second part of the process affects the manager first and foremost. In the MDT, the managers can, for example, check the profiles of the employees assigned to them and, if necessary, change the profiles. Depending on the definition of the process, the central personnel development might then function as the "broker" if the manager needs advice. Figure 8.30 shows the entire default menu for skill management in the MDT.

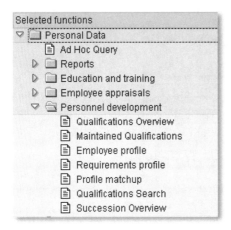

Figure 8.30 Default Menu of the MDT for Skill Management

Here, the qualifications overview is very helpful. The manager receives an overview of how widespread the various qualifications are in his or her department as well as an appraisal of the qualifications overview (see Figure 8.31).

Qualifications Overview

Organizational unit O 50000595 Human Resources
O 50000603 Compensation and Benefits - (US)
Key date 02/25/2004

Organizational unit	Qualification Group	Qualification	Average	Average proficiency	Name	Proficny	Proficiency text
Compensation and Benefits - (US)	Human Resources	Knowledge of Compensation & Benefits	9.000	Excellent	Joanne Pawlucky	9	Excellent
	Language skills	English language skills	3.000	Fluent	Joanne Pawlucky	3	Fluent
	Professional Certifications	Certified Human Resources Professional	1.000	Yes	Joanne Pawlucky	1	Yes
			1.000		John Parker	1	Yes
	University Education	B.Ed.	1.000		John Parker	1	Yes
		Business Administration Degree	1.000		Joanne Pawlucky	1	Yes
		Master's Degree	1.000		Liam Morton	1	Yes
		MBA	1.000		John Parker	1	Yes
Human Resources	1. Support Secretary	1.1 MS Office	8.000	Very high	Tom Peterson	8	Very high
			8.000		Ben Taylor	8	Very high
		1.2 Event Organization	7.000	High	Ben Taylor	7	High
	2. Support Accounting	2.1 Internal Accounting	3.000	Very good	Tom Peterson	6	Invalid proficiency
			3.000		Joanne Pawlucky	6	Invalid proficiency
			3.000		Ann Takahashi	6	Invalid proficiency
			3.000		Timmy Tabasco	6	Invalid proficiency
			3.000		Ben Taylor	1	Average
		2.3 Knowledge Taxes	3.000		Tom Peterson	7	Invalid proficiency
			3.000		Joanne Pawlucky	2	Good
			3.000		Ann Takahashi	3	Very good
			3.000		Timmy Tabasco	7	Invalid proficiency
			3.000		Ben Taylor	1	Average
	3. Translation	3.2 Spanish written	3.000		James Maritz	7	Invalid proficiency
			3.000		Michelle Firenze	7	Invalid proficiency
			3.000		Daniela Wilson	7	Invalid proficiency

Figure 8.31 Qualifications Overview in the MDT

Customizing

For the ESS, in the view V_T77WWW_CDE, the service category QUAL must be activated in the relevant menu (Default in R/3 4.6C: Menu PZM3). Then, in the view V_T77WWW_SDE, the following services of this category must be released (for the process described here, the first two services will suffice):

▶ For matchup with one's own position: Service 66

▶ For matchup with one's own qualifications profile: Service 35

▶ For display of one's own qualifications profile: Service 64

▶ For the display of the requirements profile of one's own position: Service 65

If the entire qualifications catalog is not usable for the ESS, the root node of the section available in the ESS should be defined (IMG path: **Personnel Management · Personnel Development · ESS · Define Root Qualification Group**). This requirement must be addressed during the conception of the qualifications catalog because there must be a distinction between the ESS catalog and the Non-ESS catalog.

Warning! When maintaining the root node, the behavior of the user interface can be unpredictable. This "bad behavior" causes unrecognizable empty spaces in the field, because no qualifications catalog is displayed in the ESS. If this problem occurs, one should empty the field by placing an exclamation point ("!" this is an abbreviation for "empty a field" in the entire system) in the first position and pressing the **Enter** key. Then, one can ensure that the field is truly empty and -- if desired -- enter a new root node.

In the MDT, one can incorporate different function codes from the area of skill management. In order to integrate the menu in Figure 8.30 into the customer-specific MDT scenario, you must copy the following function codes from the default scenario in Customizing (IMG path: **Personnel Management · Manager's Desktop · Enhancement of Function Codes · Define Structure of Function Codes**):

▶ PA_PD_QR (as superior node)

▶ ORG_QUALI_OVERVIEW (qualifications overview)

▶ ORG_QUALI_MAINTAINED (maintained qualifications)

▶ PERS_PROFILE (maintain qualifications profile)

▶ POS_PROFILE (maintain requirements profile)

▶ PERS_PROFILE_MATCHUP (profile matchup)

In addition, the incorporation of more reports can make sense, for example, the list of expired qualifications (see Section 8.2.3). According to Figure 8.32, a new function code must be created for this (IMG path: **Personnel Management · Manager's Desktop · Enhancement of Function Codes · Define Function Codes**) and then organized in the customer-specific scenario under the node PA_PD_QR.

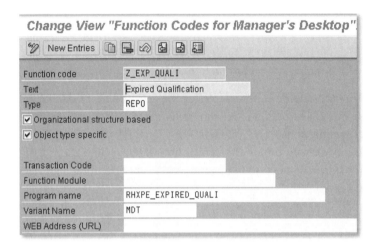

Figure 8.32 New Function Code for Expired Qualifications

8.3.2 Project Occupation with Internal and External Employees

An important use of skill management is the search for employees for actual tasks, such as filling the skill requirements for a project. To pair employees with needed tasks, maintaining the employees' qualifications profiles on the basis of the qualifications catalog makes a lot of sense. The definition of requirements profiles for jobs and positions is not necessary for this kind of application (and also for the following process example in Section 8.3.3).

In order to consider not just a company's own employees but also external employees, the qualifications for the relevant external employees must also be maintained. Therefore, typically, only the specific skills are maintained for which you would engage the external employees. If you primarily work with particular partners (e.g., consulting companies), it may also be advisable to store not only the qualifications for the individual external employees, but also a profile for the company as a whole. If needed, it is then the responsibility of the company in question to introduce a suitable employee. Figure 8.33 shows the profile of a company, whereby the qualifications considered are limited to the area that is necessary for national and international HR projects. Other skills that exist in the company are not relevant and therefore, are not compiled. For both external persons and companies, the profile maintenance occurs via the menu path **Personnel Management · Personnel Development · Profile · Change**. The creation of companies and external persons is possible via the menu path **Training and Event Management · Settings · Current Settings · Attendee · Create**.

Company	McBer & Associates				U	50013664		
Start	10/03/1997	-	12/31/9999					

🏢 Qualifications

Qualification Group	T..	ObjectID	Name	ID	Proficny	Start date	End Date
Application software skills	Q	30000364	Knowledge of ABAP/IV	9	Excellent	09/29/2003	12/31/9999
Enterprise software	Q	50013007	Overall Knowledge of SAP HR _	8	Very high	09/29/2003	12/31/9999
Human Resources	Q	30000401	HR Management skills	4	Adequate	09/29/2003	12/31/9999
Human Resources	Q	50025414	HR: knowledge personnel dev_	7	High	09/29/2003	09/28/2004
Human Resources	Q	50025413	HR: knowledge recruitment	8	Very high	09/29/2003	09/28/2004
Language skills	Q	50025463	Basic Italien	1	Basic knowledge	09/29/2003	12/31/9999
Language skills	Q	30000430	Business French language skil_	3	Fluent	09/29/2003	12/31/9999
Language skills	Q	50025448	Business German language s_	3	Fluent	09/29/2003	12/31/9999
SAP Payroll	Q	50016777	Certificate, U.S. Payroll	1	Yes	09/29/2003	12/31/9999
SAP Planning & Administration	Q	50016756	Certificate, Config of Master Da_	1	Yes	09/29/2003	12/31/9999
SAP Planning & Administration	Q	50016769	Certificate, Programming in SA_	1	Yes	09/29/2003	12/31/9999
SAP Planning & Administration	Q	50016770	Certificate, Recruitment	1	Yes	09/29/2003	12/31/9999
SAP Planning & Administration	Q	50016763	Certificate, SAP Human Resou_	1	Yes	09/29/2003	12/31/9999

Figure 8.33 Profile of a Company

Figure 8.34 shows the process of creating an overview of a project occupation. To simplify this depiction, we avoided including the object type "company" in the process model. However, the basic procedure remains the same.

After the profiles are maintained as a prerequisite and the requirements of the project are known, one can begin the search via the menu path **Personnel Management · Personnel Development · Information System · Reports · Search · For Qualifications**.

In this search, the required qualifications are first selected and appraised; then, some of the qualifications are designated as essential (analogous to Figure 8.21). Next, the limitation to the object type P occurs, since at first only internal employees should be considered. Then, the capacity need in the project period is specified (see Figure 8.35). Therefore, absences such as vacation or illness are considered for internal employees.

If no suitable staff is found in this selection, you can make the selection less restrictive, for example, by omitting essential qualifications or considering external persons or companies (see Figure 8.36).

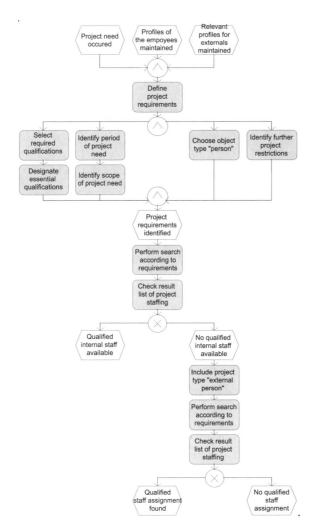

Figure 8.34 Process: Project Occupation

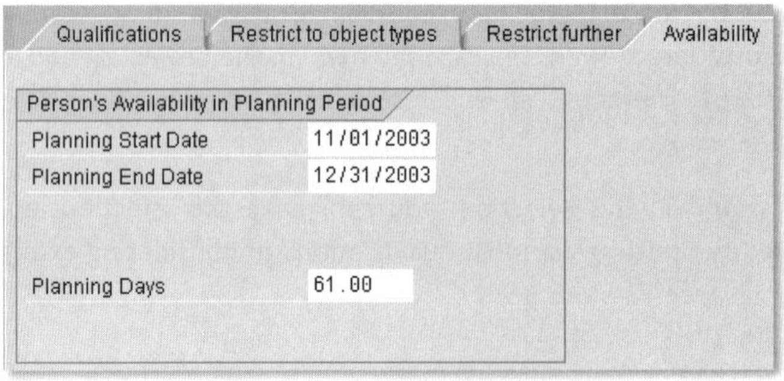

| Qualifications | Restrict to object types | Restrict further | Availability |

Person's Availability in Planning Period

| Planning Start Date | 11/01/2003 |
| Planning End Date | 12/31/2003 |

| Planning Days | 61.00 |

Figure 8.35 Checking Availability According to Capacity Need

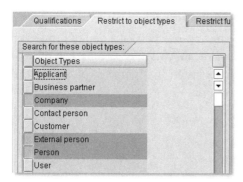

Figure 8.36 Search for Various Object Types

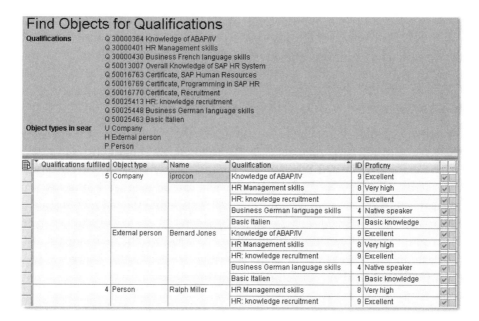

Figure 8.37 Result List with External Person and Company

Consequently, you now receive a list like the one shown in Figure 8.37. Because the external person fulfills the requirements, you must ask this person first as you are familiar with their personnel qualifications. The qualifications that are assigned to the company, however, may not occur in this combination in an individual employee. Because the system cannot check the availability of external persons or companies, this must occur independently of the system before one can be certain of the project staffing. Overall, the system support is a big help. As with external partners, the appraisal of the qualifications should adhere to the same standard as used for internal employees. It therefore makes sense to appraise skills only if they can be validated by one's own experience.

8.3.3 Risk Management and Strategy Change

To monitor risks in the skill area, using the person-related evaluation of profiles or the usual profile matchup will not suffice. Instead, you must compare, independent of the following factors, the overall quality of the human capital with the essential and critical requirements of the future:

▶ Individual persons

▶ Individual jobs and positions

▶ Project requirements

▶ Present-day situation in the area of qualifications as well as in the area of requirements

To make this comparison, you can create strategically-important areas or "qualification bundles," which don't describe any special positions or projects. For a plant construction company, these two qualification bundles could be:

▶ Key qualifications in the area of product development

▶ Strategically-important knowledge of the company's most important markets

A similar procedure is required if a strategy change is planned. If a company changes its IT strategy completely to MS Office products, it must also clarify how much expertise in this area already exists. For this comparison also, you can create a *qualification bundle*. This qualification bundle can be mapped in the form of requirements profiles in the system. The profiles are either formed by assignment of qualifications to a *qualifications profile* (object type QP) or to a *task* (object type T). In both cases, the concern is ultimately the strategic requirements for a strategically important task. Which object type that you select for the mapping is secondary. Figure 8.38 shows the object "requirements profile."

Requirements profi... MS Office applications			QP 50010169		
Start 01/03/1996 - 12/31/9999					

Requirements

Qualification Group	T..	ObjectID	Name	St..	ID	Proficny
4. IT Development	Q	50014775	4.1 Knowledge C++		3	Very good
Application software skills	Q	30010189	Knowledge in Wordprocessing/Winword		9	Excellent
Application software skills	Q	50000551	Knowledge of Excel		9	Excellent
Application software skills	Q	50010177	Knowledge of Powerpoint		8	Very high
Knowledge of network adminis...	Q	50012100	Knowledge of PC Network Technology		9	Excellent
Knowledge of network adminis...	Q	30010019	NT Server		9	Excellent
Knowledge of operating syste...	Q	50010179	Knowledge of Windows NT		9	Excellent

Figure 8.38 Strategic Requirements Profile: Change of IT Strategy

Therefore, the first part of the process described in Figure 8.39 is already worked through: the strategic requirements are recognized and compiled in profiles on the system and documented. Then, two tasks must be performed in parallel:

▶ Through the matchup with the existing skills, the present-day situation can be appraised.

▶ Through the consideration of potentials and dislikes, the possibilities for future development can be estimated.

We will discuss working with potentials and dislikes in more detail in the next chapter. Here, the check of the present-day state as an example will suffice.

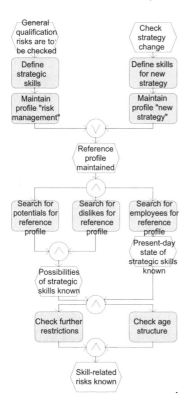

Figure 8.39 Process: Recognizing Risks in the Qualifications Area

The familiar search for persons using their qualifications is best suited for the matchup. Thus, the strategic requirements profile, which was just compiled, is selected. The result—after adjusting the layout on the output screen—is a list like the one shown in Figure 8.40. It's easy to see how many employees cover each of the strategic requirements. You will note that the requirements in the area of development (Visual Basic and .NET) are not covered. On the same screen, you could quickly determine—by considering the object type AP ("applicant") in the selection—whether to close the gap discovered with applicants from the current pool.

Find Objects for Qualifications

Key date	02/25/2004
Qualifications	Q 30010019 NT Server
	Q 30010189 Knowledge in Wordprocessing/Winword
	Q 50000551 Knowledge of Excel
	Q 50010177 Knowledge of Powerpoint
	Q 50010179 Knowledge of Windows NT
	Q 50012100 Knowledge of PC Network Technology
	Q 50014775 4.1 Knowledge C++
Object types in sear	P Person

Σ Qualification fulfilled	ID rel.obj	Object type	Name	Qualification	Qu...
1	00100239	Person	Ben Taylor	Knowledge of Windows NT	2
1	00070147	Person	Bill Andrews		1
▪ 2				Knowledge of Windows NT	
1	00010451	Person	Lou Windham	Knowledge of PC Network Technology	1
1	00085006	Person	Tom Little		1
▪ 2				Knowledge of PC Network Technology	
1	00100239	Person	Ben Taylor	Knowledge in Wordprocessing/Winword	2
1	00070146	Person	Sarah Smith		1
1	00100002	Person	Dave Demmerle		1
1	00109803	Person	Steve Waters		1
▪ 4				Knowledge in Wordprocessing/Winword	
1	00109358	Person	Oliver Wendell Douglas	4.1 Knowledge C++	1
▪ 1				4.1 Knowledge C++	
9					

Figure 8.40 Result: Search for Strategic Requirements Profile

This is the core of risk monitoring. Nevertheless, additional restrictions would then have to be checked, such as the geographic distribution. The most important point here is the age structure of the sufficiently qualified employees. If the emphasis is on employees who are nearing retirement, a distribution of the knowledge to the lower end of the age structure is very important. If one omits high-gloss representations and graphics, risk management in the area of skills can be performed very well in dialog with the system. With relatively little effort, you have at your disposal an early-warning system and can take countermeasures in a timely fashion or adjust the strategy to meet the possibilities of the human capital.

8.3.4 "Small Solution" for Environmental Audit

As in the two previous process examples, here, the solution should not be one that entails the entire effort needed for the maintenance of all requirements and qualifications profiles. Instead, it should only reflect those specific requirements and qualifications needed for that particular solution. The goal here is to describe a particular section of the skill management in the HR system Frequent examples for such requirements are *certification s* and *audits*. With an environmental audit, for example, only those workplaces—for which adherence to environmental regulations is relevant—are checked. In addition, the full spectrum of qualifications is also not required. Rather, you can limit yourself to only those requirements that are relevant to the demands of environmental protection.

These requirements are often specified precisely in certification regulations. The documentation of these requirements in the system should produce the following proof for the certifier:

▶ The relevant workplaces are identified and documented.

▶ The requirements of the employees are documented.

▶ The fulfillment of these requirements is constantly monitored.

▶ Qualifications that require regular updating are also monitored correspondingly and the employees are retrained in a timely fashion.

The following can be mapped without a problem with the familiar functionalities of mySAP HR:

▶ The relevant qualifications are stored in the qualifications catalog—preferably in an individual qualification group.

▶ For qualifications for which regular retrainings are required, the validity duration is maintained.

▶ If training and event management is in use, the possible refresher courses are stored there and linked with the qualifications they represent.

▶ Requirements are assigned to the relevant positions.

▶ The employees' qualifications are maintained.

▶ The qualifications are compared regularly with the requirements (profile matchup of SAP personnel development), especially before each new occupation of a relevant position.

▶ The expiration of qualifications is monitored proactively (see Section 8.2.3).

Figure 8.41 shows a procedure model that summarizes the skill management for special audits.

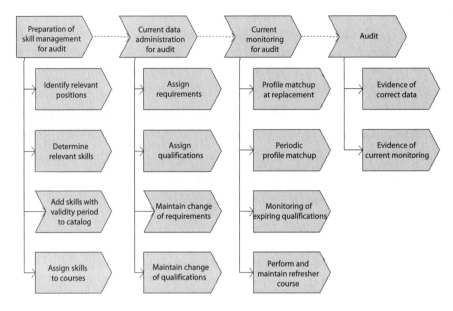

Figure 8.41 Skill Management for a Special Audit

The automatic execution of a profile matchup on a position change is also supported by the SAP Business Workflow. The workflow model "position change" (1200145, PdvTransfer) shows the result of the matchup of the affected employee. We recommend that you make a copy of this workflow model that also forwards the result to the responsible manager or to personnel development. In addition, the workflow supports the monitoring of expired qualifications in the standard edition. In this case, the workflow model *expired qualification* (1000089, PDExpiredQua) informs the responsible personnel officer.

8.4   Critical Success Factors

Project success in skill management depends first and foremost on process design, and less on the technical aspects. The critical success factors are as follows:

▶ The goals of skill management must be clarified at the beginning.

▶ You can determine the area to be considered from the goals. If, for example, the concern is only the development of managers, you don't need to build an all-inclusive skill catalog; only a segment of the employees and positions need to be considered. Miscalculating this point may be the main cause for project plans exceeding time and budget as well as for the failure of projects in skill management. Therefore, a realistic limitation of the area under consideration is recommended in the first step.

- For the tracing of the goals of skill management, sufficient capacities for maintenance and advising must be provided. These capacities can often be compensated for because uncoordinated activities are replaced in this environment by the integrated solution. For this to occur, however, two prerequisites must be fulfilled:

  - The redundant, uncoordinated activities must also be stopped. Often, line managers insist on hiding or not sharing their data. Then, the reason for keeping their data secret must be discovered. If the concern is only formalities or the hiding of authority knowledge, then help must come via the top management and the HR director. If there is actual functionality missing with the central solution, the decentral units must be more tightly incorporated in the conceptual phase of the project.

  - The capacities becoming available must be known and also booked on the "credit side" of the skill management project. This is often not the case because the capacities become available in places (e.g., department secretaries) other than where they will be needed in the future (e.g., central HR department).

- The process should, if possible, be implemented in the decentral variant (see process example in Section 8.3.1).

- In the implementation project, the definition of the qualifications catalog should be paramount. Decentral process participants must be incorporated sufficiently. The knowledge that employees and managers have regarding the requirements of daily business must be used.

- The other extreme must also be avoided: a pure focus on the present-day situation neglects strategic requirements. Since these present-day needs are a significant element of skill management, however, the central PD must incorporate these requirements.

- For the mapping of the qualifications catalog, attention to detail must be paid in the definition of the structure and the scales as well as in the naming of qualifications and groups. Otherwise, the structure and the alphabetical sorting in the appraisals can always cause problems.

- Explanations in the system and recommendations provided by the central PD must guarantee the comparability of the data maintained. Here, with systems used internationally, translation must also be heeded. Depending on how widespread a uniform company language is (e.g., English), it can prove to be feasible, in some circumstances, to maintain the catalog only in the company language. Therefore, meaning shifts in translation can be prevented.

▶ With integration into shift planning, training and event management, and recruitment, the qualifications catalog must be developed with the corresponding project teams.

▶ Employees and managers must be provided with easy-to-operate tools so that they can use and expand skill management in daily business, that is, ESS and MDT must be configured optimally. For content questions, advice from central PD must be available.

9 Development Planning

Development planning for individual employees or groups of employ-ees is supported by various mySAP HR functions.

9.1 The Design in mySAP HR

9.1.1 Elements of Development Planning

The process of development planning includes all the planning steps that define the advancement of employees with individual personnel actions or career plan-ning. First, the process is determined on an individual level; it considers individual employees or positions. However, instruments that create an overview for devel-opment planners are also required, such as an overview of specific employee groups or succession chains. In general and in its focus on critical positions, devel-opment planning is an essential element of risk management in HR and an ele-ment to be considered on the strategic level.

SAP uses the essential terms as they pertain to SAP and distinguishes between the following planning concepts:

▶ Career planning
Defines the development of an employee by positions or jobs.

▶ Succession planning
Performs a similar examination, but begins from the other side, that is, at the target position. Succession planning then searches for the optimal future staff-ing of the position, which also ultimately means that a career is planned for the selected employee.

▶ Development plans
Stipulates the individual development of an employee with training and trans-fers. Development plans can also contain sequences of positions and jobs. Individual and general plans can be created; the latter can serve as a blueprint for an individual employee or position.

To some extent, "career planning" and the "development plan" create thoroughly competing designs, because both plans can map an employee's career steps in the company. However, because each plan offers additional functions, the exist-ence of both is justified, as will become apparent later in this section.

Although the title of this chapter may contribute to the reader confusing devel-opment planning with the SAP concept of the "development plan," we want to retain this terminology. In the process-oriented view, the three SAP concepts that we just described form an overall process best defined by the term *development planning*. In SAP terminology, the term *personnel action plan* can be used interchangeably with "development plan." SAP itself creates another terminological problem: both succession planning and career planning are based on the same chains, which are called *careers*. Readers should recall that careers form the basis not only of career planning, but also of succession planning.

Overall, development planning is based on four foundations:

▶ **Skill management**
The previous chapter described skill management in detail. Of course, qualifications profiles and requirements profiles must be considered during individual development planning; the system supports this task.

▶ **Organizational management**
Includes the management of organizational units, jobs, positions, and work centers. Organizational management is required to map the steps of a career or a development plan.

▶ **Training and event management**
Delivers the training personnel actions required by an employee's development.

▶ **Preferences, potentials, and dislikes of an employee**
Planning can and should consider these elements.

Figure 9.1 summarizes these aspects. The following briefly describes the three main components of development planning. But first, we will examine the concept of an employee's individual attributes (preferences, potentials, and dislikes) and the career concept in general. The division of tasks between the three main components is addressed at the end of the conceptual section.

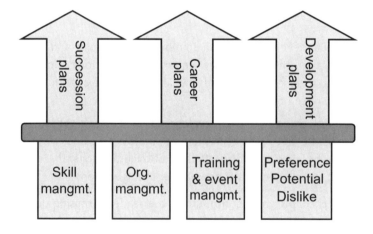

Figure 9.1 Elements of Development Planning

9.1.2 Individual Attributes

System features

Employees' essential attributes, which influence their development planning, are their preferences, potentials, and dislikes. To record the attributes, the system links the person to another object. The target object can be a position that the person wants or, a position that one doesn't want. Figure 9.2 summarizes the default options. Enhancement is another option, which includes other object types; however, we cannot assume that standard reports will factor in customer-specific relationships.

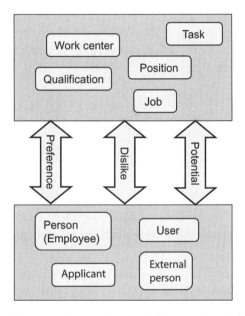

Figure 9.2 Relationships by Preferences, Potentials, and Dislikes

Designation (for example, for a position) is a fourth attribute. Typically, designation is not maintained beforehand; it is only derived from and maintained as a result of career planning.

Problems with Interpretation

To use these constructs, clear conventions are required. You first need to decide which attributes to use. Then, you can create detailed conventions that will help you to interpret the data in a meaningful way.

We recommend that you maintain the information on preferences and dislikes only sporadically, for example, when it happens to become available during a meeting with an employee. You can also limit the determination of potentials to the results of comprehensive potential analyses (in assessment centers, for example) and to exclude informal assessments of supervisors. However, these conventions must be known when evaluating the information. If preferences are maintained only sporadically, succession planning cannot be systematically built on this information. It can be considered only as helpful, additional information during a planning process that is based on other foundations (e.g., qualifications profiles). In addition, you must decide which of the options should be used (see Figure 9.2). The use of positions and work centers can create a significant workload for systematic maintenance.

Examples of Meaningful Conventions

Now, we'd like to offer as examples some meaningful conventions, which, in light of company-specific requirements, may require further examination; however, they can still serve as a foundation or starting point:

▶ All three attributes are used for internal employees.

▶ Potentials and preferences are maintained for candidates in the long-term candidate pool.

▶ Potentials are maintained systematically based on the results of staff dialogs and assessment centers. If the results come from an assessment center, store a note in the system to record their origin.

▶ Potentials are maintained for jobs. The same is done for positions from the second level of management. In addition, potentials are maintained for strategically important qualifications.

▶ Employees maintain their own preferences and dislikes and discuss them with their managers once a year. Dislikes and preferences can be jobs, positions, qualifications, and locations. (The last item requires an enhancement of standard Customizing.)

▶ To obtain a realistic image that supports planning, 5 to 10 entries per employee are needed for preferences and dislikes. A maximum of 20 entries per employee is allowed.

▶ The use of information in individual planning (particularly succession planning), skill management, and personnel risk management is based on these conventions.

9.1.3 The Career Concept

Careers are integral to career planning and succession planning; however, setting up careers is not required by both processes in mySAP HR. As the following two sections indicate, planning can occur based on the additional elements illustrated in Figure 9.1. In very flexible structures that don't allow the definition of a fixed career, this convention will be the norm.

A career is essentially built from jobs or positions. As illustrated in Figure 9.3, parallel branches can appear, but they don't have to reconnect. Each element of the career has a length, given in years, months, and days. Looking down from a career step provides the view of succession planning. In the graphic, all persons who hold inferior jobs and positions are potential successors of the person holding the highest position. Similarly, looking up indicates the career prospects of the person currently holding an inferior position: the view of SAP career planning.

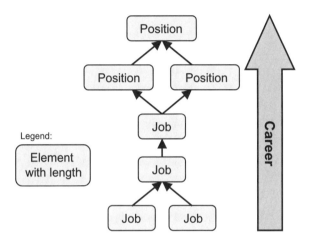

Figure 9.3 Structure of a Career

Both statements clarify the problems of this view: only a small portion of employees will follow a path all the way to the top. In succession planning, it's a fallacy to believe that all employees at the lower end of the career model are truly potential successors. Accordingly, actual succession planning must always consider other factors.

As a principle in constructing careers, you should avoid inserting positions (but only jobs) because the results are too rigid and unmanageable. However, in certain exceptional cases and at the upper levels of the hierarchy, limiting selection to special positions is recommended. For example, an IT career can consist of various IT-specific jobs (IT trainee, programmer, administrator, IT group leader, and IT department head), which ultimately lead to the one position of IT department head. The options here depend primarily on the structure of the jobs and positions.

The connection between an employee and a career consists of an employee who has a position that is directly assigned to the career or assigned to it via its position.

9.1.4 Career Planning

Career planning enables you to recognize and then display the career prospects of an employee. Based on various restrictions along a career path, it seeks to find the potential positions or jobs to be considered in the future development of the employee. Furthermore, additional steps should be checked or planned (in dialog with the system), based on the jobs and positions that have been found.

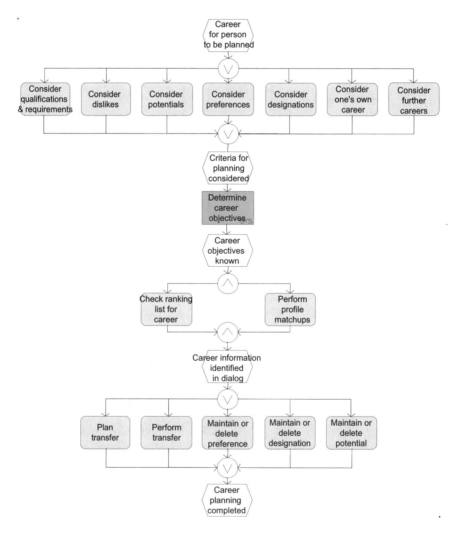

Figure 9.4 Process: Career Planning in mySAP HR

You can use the following criteria in the search for development options:

▶ Qualifications profile and requirements profile

▶ Preferences

▶ Potentials

▶ Designations

▶ Dislikes

▶ Career (the employee's current career)

▶ Any other careers

Dislikes are considered only to exclude potential results: they should only be used in connection with other criteria. Very flexible queries are certainly possible. The *career* is the least practical instrument for a flexible query: the other concepts can often replace it completely.

The result of the query is a list of potential goals as jobs or positions, which can serve as the basis for searching for concrete options. Personnel actions can be planned or carried out, and interim results can be documented. When the result of this tool is not interpreted as a definitive recommendation, but as a helpful basis for discussion, it can serve to support open dialog with employees. Figure 9.4 provides an overview of how the planning process can be performed in dialog with the system.

Career planning is available not only for employees (object type "person"), but also for other object types. For example, the use of the object type "applicant" in the case of unsolicited applications helps to find an appropriate position for the applicant. The use of careers is generally relevant only for internal employees; however, it is also helpful when you are looking for development options for external, temporary help listed in organizational management who later become employees.

9.1.5 Succession Planning

As noted, *succession planning* is the counterpart to career planning. It allows you to find suitable employees for a specific position. The mechanisms are essentially identical to those described in the previous section on career planning. Because of its strategic significance and risk management, succession planning is usually the more important view. The essential difference between the two is that succession planning enables you to filter the hit list (list of applicants) according to user-defined criteria, as long as the criteria have been maintained as master data in personnel administration. The following examples can prove helpful:

- Selection by age (This may be restricted in many countries as it is in the U.S. However, if you're looking for a successor for a specific position that will be vacant only in 8 years, you won't consider employees, who are already retired by that time. Conversely, there are jobs that require a certain minimum age by law.)

- Selection by gender (if you want to use affirmative action to find female candidates, for example)

- Selection by handicap (if you want to use affirmative action to find handicapped candidates or, when the tasks required by the position exclude specific handicaps, for example

- Selection by residence (if a position has a residency requirement)

- Selection by employment percentage (if you want to fill a half-time position)

You can perform succession planning for more than actual positions. The following additional objects are especially relevant:

- Positions
- Work centers
- Tasks

Succession planning delivers a ranking list sorted by percentage of suitability. The percentage is calculated from the comparison of profiles.

You can also perform succession planning for more than a single position. You can use a simulation to map complete *succession chains*. For example, if the system proposes a successor for a specific position, it will automatically look for a successor for the position that has just become vacant because of the proposal. Individual succession planning can occur for every position in the chain, as previously described. Figure 9.5 illustrates this nested process, the core of which ("individual" succession planning) is quite similar to career planning.

Succession simulation is certainly an interesting tool; however, because of the complexity of the relationships involved, the results are simply a nice tip on the solution to the problem—therefore, you must interpret the results with great care. Using succession simulation makes the most sense when individual succession planning has captured designations or, at least potentials, and when you limit succession simulation to these two criteria. With this approach, you would get a rather good overview of the effects of individual planning steps. If required, you can also switch between individual succession planning (with maintenance of a designation or potential) and the succession chain (simulation) to arrive at a suitable result. The strength of the system lies in its ability to dialog, because you can play with various ideas and approaches. Whether this approach is simpler than planning on paper depends partially on personal preference.

9.1.6 Development Plans

In any case, the most multifaceted instrument for individual development planning is the *development plan*. You use this instrument to plan, monitor, and document an employee's individual development. In addition to an employee's *individual development plan,* you can also use *general development plans*. The latter plans describe well established sequences of personnel actions related to development, such as those actions that follow similar lines in an orientation program for new employees or to reach a specific position. You can use them as a template for an individual development plan, which you then can modify to reflect the employee's specific needs. You can also create individual plans by combining elements from several general plans. When modifying the general plan for an individual employee, you can disregard elements if you so choose.

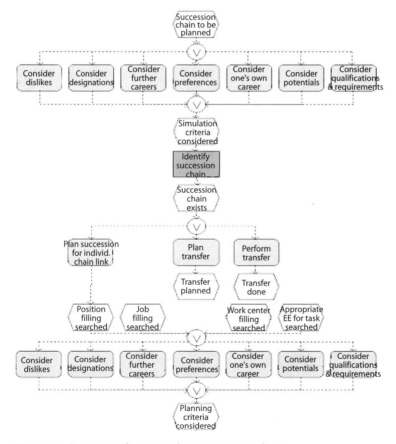

Figure 9.5 Succession Planning with Succession Simulation

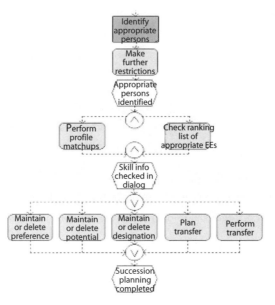

Figure 9.5 Succession Planning with Succession Simulation (cont.)

The *development plan catalog* contains general development plans. Similar to the qualifications catalog, it is structured hierarchically. Plans on similar topics are summarized in development plan groups. Figure 9.6 illustrates the relationships between development plan groups, general development plans, and an individual development plan.

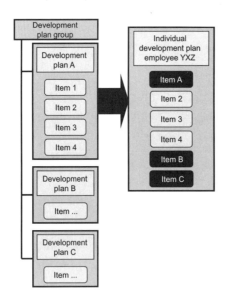

Figure 9.6 General and Individual Development Plans

The General Development Plan

A *general development plan* consists of any number of steps. Each step contains one or more development plan items, which can include the following:

▶ Event types in which the employee must participate

▶ Locations where the employee must spend a specific period of time (particularly when related to language and cultural skills)

▶ Jobs for which the employee must hold a position

▶ Work centers where the employee must work

▶ Positions that the employee must hold during the program (this item should be avoided because it's more flexible to involve jobs)

▶ Organizational units in which the employee must work for a certain time

▶ Appraisal model, which is used to evaluate the employee at specific points in the program (initial, intermediate, and final appraisal, for example)

▶ Other career development items (The standard delivery includes the development plan that one plan can be built on from several sub-plans. Depending on the Customizing settings, this point can also include other types of development items.)

Each development item is identified along with its duration and whether it is mandatory; however, you can define more than one career development item as mandatory. For example, you can easily require that an employee must go through at least two of the four career development items in a specific step. To do so, you would identify the step by the number of mandatory development items. Figure 9.7 illustrates a general development plan.

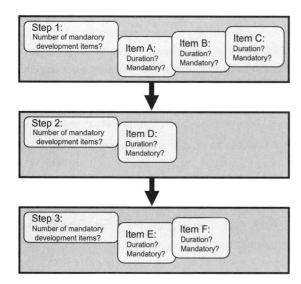

Figure 9.7 Structure of a General Development Plan

The qualifications imparted by the plan also are important attributes of the general development plan. You can insert the qualifications manually, but you can also have the system generate a proposal from the types of events and positions contained in the plan. Whether attaching the qualifications to a development plan is a good approach depends on the specific requirements. It can be helpful when selecting a plan with a very short duration. A detailed list of individual qualifications will be less useful in plans that stretch over several years.

The Individual Development Plan

The *individual development plan* is created by assigning various types of development items to an employee. In this process, every item has a defined period that the employee must spend in it. Unlike a general development plan, the individual development plan is subject to ongoing change. In long-term plans, the individual items and, in particular, their duration, will often change. You can make the changes easily when maintaining the individual development plan.

The *status* of the individual items is particularly important. The status is used to document how far the employee has already progressed in the development plan item. Moreover the status can directly trigger actions in other components. For example, if the status of an assigned position or an event is set to "current," the user can trigger an immediate transfer in Organizational Management or book a training course in Training and Event Management.

9.1.7 Collaboration Among the Three Components

The three main components of development planning don't have to relate to each other as shown in Figure 9.1. The distribution of tasks between careers and development planning can also be set up in two different ways:

▶ The development plan is used for a shorter period and describes how employees move from one development item to the next in their careers. Accordingly, the individual items are not elements of any general development plan and are listed in the individual plan only for documentation, not for planning. The career provides a rough overview of an employee's planned development.

▶ Career planning serves only as a sandbox to enable you to recognize additional development steps. The development plan is always used for actual planning.

Among the comprehensive options available, we recommend the development plan as the primary planning vehicle for the employee. You must decide in individual cases if you can define general plans that surpass the length of a trainee program. Most often, general plans tend to cover periods of several weeks to two years. Beyond this, the individual plans would then suffice, because the structures of a company generally change quickly to define a model that remains valid over several years. In this scenario, career planning actually serves only as a vehicle to generate ideas. Succession planning would then play a more active role here: it is best suited to finding appropriate employees for important positions. Because of the varied selection and filtering options offered by succession planning, it often can replace a search with requirements profiles, as described in Chapter 8, *Skill Management*.

9.2 Realization in mySAP HR

9.2.1 Basic System Settings

As is the case in skill management, development planning requires some general Customizing activities so that the interfaces and integration reflect the requirements of the company.

Profile Views

To maintain preferences, dislikes, and potentials, you must define the corresponding partial profiles as active with the IMG path **Personnel Management · Personnel Development · Functions · Define Profile View**. We already addressed this process in the previous chapter. However, if you want to maintain subprofiles that have not yet been defined in the standard settings, you must make more comprehensive adjustments. For example, it would be helpful to do so for designations that are not displayed in the standard profile views or for customer-defined facts (customer-specific relationships). To do so, you would then have to define a new tab (a new subprofile), which requires the following steps:

▶ Create a new screen in program SAPLRHPP as a copy—from screen 2200 (potentials) for example. This is a modification, but it will remain stable if you use a screen number above 9000.

▶ Change the programming of the new screen and its logic so that the desired type of relationship is displayed and maintained. This is by far the most expensive step.

▶ Enter the new subprofile with the new screen number and an appropriate icon in the IMG path given above.

▶ Assign and activate the new subprofile under the view "PD" and under the header for object type P ("person") in the PD view. Other object types might also be relevant.

Integration with Recruitment

You must activate the "vacancy" Infotype if integration with Recruitment is active. To activate this infotype, use the IMG path **Personnel Management · Personnel Development · Functions · Activate/Deactivate "Vacancy" Infotype**.

Criteria for Detail Selection

To filter the results list of succession planning by additional criteria, as described in Section 9.1.5, you must first define the criteria. First, you should verify if the criteria available by default is sufficient for your purposes. To define new criteria, you need an InfoSet (see Chapter 6, *Query in mySAP HR*) for personnel master data and one for applicant master data. You can then assign the InfoSets to the PDVFINE scenario with the IMG path **Personnel Management · Personnel Development · Functions · Define Criteria for Detail Selection** (see Figure 9.8.)

Figure 9.8 Enhancing Detail Selection for Succession Planning

Because detail selection is an essential function for succession planning, you must design this point optimally. You can also make any changes later if necessary.

9.2.2 Working with Preferences, Potentials, and Dislikes

Maintenance

You can maintain these attributes with the menu path **Personnel Management · Personnel Development · Profile · Change**. Figure 9.9 illustrates the maintenance of potentials. The interpretation of validity period is important here. When employees have the potential for a specific position today (in normal parlance), this can mean that you are confident that they will be able to fill the position in two years. It may be helpful to perform a maintenance that deviates from this parlance. If you set the starting date to begin when the employees—according to today's estimates—can actually perform the requirements of the position, you gain additional information. Then, you can (and must) also work in career planning and succession planning with the exact key dates.

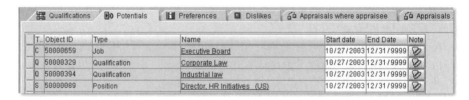

Figure 9.9 Maintenance of Potentials

The actual maintenance of preferences, potentials, and dislikes is intuitive. You use the **Note** icon to insert any text that you would like. Here, you should work with a convention that defines the cases that require a note. Generally, it's preferable to create notes sparingly. Whenever anyone creates a note, there's always a great deal of follow-up work required. Ultimately, all those who retrieve information from the screen must read the note to ensure that they're not missing something important. If you have a convention that regulates the creation of notes, everyone will know what kind of information the notes contain.

Enhancements in Customizing

The standard objects available to record preferences are often insufficient. To allow additional object types, you must know that the following relationships in the system map them:

▶ Preferences: A042/B042

▶ Potentials: A038/B038

▶ Dislikes: A043/B043

Use the IMG path **Personnel Management · Personnel Development · Basic Settings · Maintain Relationships** and from there the entry for **Allowed Relationships** to define the object types for which the relationships noted are allowed. Here, you can also enhance additional internal object types; however, be aware that both relationship directions are always required. Figure 9.10 illustrates this point with an example for preferences. Standard reports don't necessarily consider these new possibilities.

Dialog Structure		Ob	Object type text	A/B	Rel	Relationship name	RelObjType
▽ ☐ Links		D	Business event type	B	042	Interests and preferences	P
☐ Relationship Characteristics		F	Location	B	042	Interests and preferences	P
☐ Additional Data on Relationships		0	Organizational unit	B	042	Interests and preferences	P
🗐 Allowed Relationships		P	Person	A	042	Interests and preferences	D
☐ External Relationships		P	Person	A	042	Interests and preferences	F
☐ Time constraints		P	Person	A	042	Interests and preferences	0
☐ Relationship abbreviation							

Figure 9.10 Allowing Three Additional Object Types for Preferences

9.2.3 Maintenance of Careers

You can maintain careers from the following menu path: **Personnel Management · Personnel Development · Settings · Current Settings · Edit Careers**. The path leads to a directory of all careers (see Figure 9.11), which cannot be structured by groups, as is the case with the development plan catalog. If you use several career definitions, you should work with a naming convention. Using a key at the start of a name (such as "IT" for IT careers and "MA" for management careers, and so on), you get a manageable structure with the help of the alphabetical sorting.

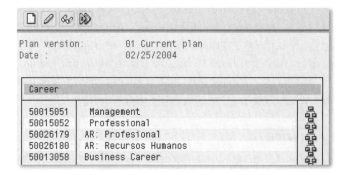

Figure 9.11 Initial Directory of Careers

Maintenance of career items then occurs in the graphical editor shown in Figure 9.12. In the standard view, the editor consists of the following elements:

▶ **Display area**

The career items are linked to the career here. In this area, you can also remove career items from the career or maintain their duration in years, months, and days. The display area also includes a legend.

▶ **Navigation area**

This area displays a smaller overview of the career and allows you to set the pane in the display area.

▶ **Node area**

You can click on the elements in the node area to select an object type that you can then place into the career. You then select an actual object in the display area after it has been placed there. Because parallel branches are possible, you can place one career item next to another.

▶ **Button Bar and Menu Bar**

As usual, the screen displays the required general and special functions of the user interface. The view menu is particularly important. Experiment a bit with the entries there to find the best view for your work. Because most users usually use a greater height than width of the display area, it's helpful to set the display as it appears in Figure 9.12, whereby the navigation area and the node area are to the right of the display area.

Overall, career maintenance is rather simple. Once you know the meaning of the three areas (Display, Navigation, and Node), the user interface can be used intuitively.

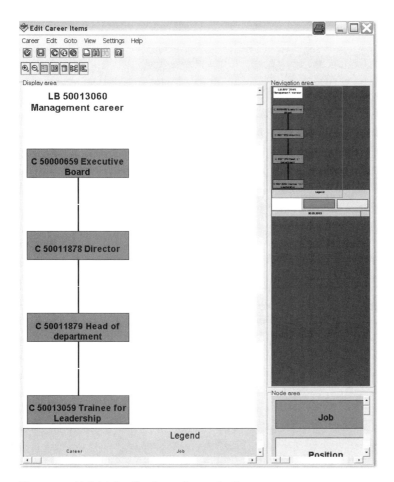

Figure 9.12 Maintaining the Career Items of a Career

9.2.4 Performing Career Planning

Executing a Planning Run

Section 9.1.4 describes the contents of the process of career planning in detail. You reach this tool via the menu path **Personnel Management · Personnel Development · Planning · Career**. In addition to selecting the object for which you are planning (that of the employee or applicant), you must also specify the planning criteria (see Figure 9.13). We recommend that you first select all the criteria to be maintained and then, if necessary, reduce the selection. If the selection is too small when you begin (selection based only on the career, for example), the viewing area constricts too much. Ultimately, the planning results should be viewed as a catalyst and springboard for additional work rather than as a recommendation that is set in stone.

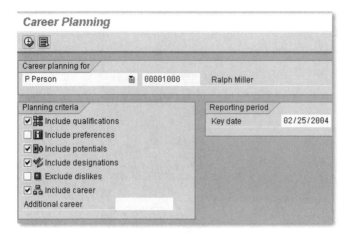

Figure 9.13 Initial Screen of Career Planning

The key date is also important, especially when potentials and the like are maintained with a future starting date. You should also note that certain positions or jobs are only created in the future. This feature is a weakness of career planning. Because career planning usually spans multiple career items, selecting only one key date cannot meet all the requirements of planning. Accordingly, you might have to work with several key dates ("Where is the employee in one, three, or five years?"):

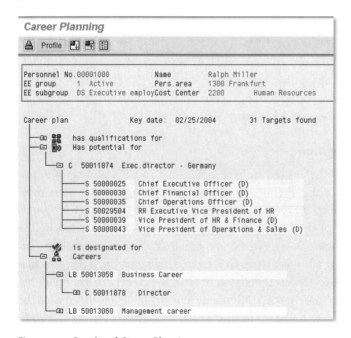

Figure 9.14 Results of Career Planning

Creating an Overview

The first result of the planning run produces the possible goals (positions and jobs, for example, arranged according to the selection criteria used to find them (see Figure 9.14). It's entirely possible for the same position to appear more than once. The selection criterion "dislikes" works as a filter. When it's active, the display does not even show the corresponding goals at first. The strength of the tool lies in your ability to work with it in dialog with the system in order to collect information and document planning results. You should take advantage of this capability and then use the following tools to create a view of the development options:

▶ Check the requirements profiles of the development goals displayed.

▶ Compare the employee profile with the selected requirements profiles (or with all profiles simultaneously).

▶ Display the related careers.

▶ Display a ranking list of all the development goals that come into consideration (see Figure 9.15). In addition to the development goals, the positions of the ranking list contain the following additional information:

  ▷ A specification of the suitability range that can be switched to the concrete suitability percentage by changing the view

  ▷ An indication of the selection criteria used to find each development goal

Documenting Results

Once you have created the required overview in this manner, you can document the results by creating or later deleting potentials, preferences, or designations. The designation (mapped with the A027/B027 relationship) is particularly well suited to documenting career and succession planning. Creation and deletion occurs within the planning results interface by placing the cursor on the desired goal and selecting the menu entries **Planning · Create · ... respectively Planning · Delete · ....** Anyone familiar with the numerous security queries and results notifications in SAP R/3 is likely to be somewhat confused at this point. Only the window illustrated in Figure 9.16, which requests the entry of the period, appears. After you enter the information and confirm it with the **Enter** key, only a short notification in the status line documents the result: "The preference has been noted," for example. Accordingly, you should ensure that you have selected the correct goal before you begin this action.

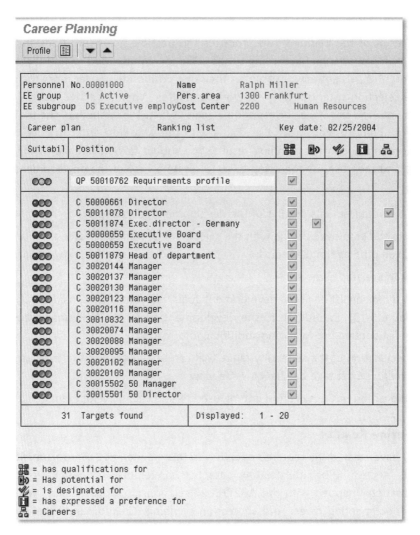

Figure 9.15 Ranking List in Career Planning

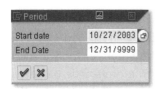

Figure 9.16 Maintaining a Preference, Designation, and Potential from Planning

An option for checking no longer exists. Once you have performed this action, you can call only the corresponding subprofile for the employee. You can do so with the **Profile** button whenever the cursor is not positioned on a target object, but only with the view of the key date used to perform planning. Designations and similar items created for the future are not visible here. New designations, potentials, and preferences appear directly in the corresponding category, as long as the category was active during selection. An additional point that often causes confusion is that the new designations also appear in the dialog if they become active only after the planning key date. Then, if you perform a new planning run, it contains only the goals that correspond to the key date selection.

Creating Personnel Actions

In addition to the (initially non-binding) maintenance of designations and so on, you can also create personnel actions directly:

▶ You can create a transfer directly or in "planned" status with the menu entry **Planning**. The dialog that appears is identical to the one used for a transfer in organizational management (see Figure 9.17).

▶ You can generate a proposal for education directly from the profile comparison and book a training course.

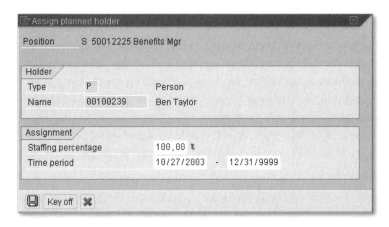

Figure 9.17 Creating a Planned Transfer from Career Planning

Customizing

To display a ranking list (also in other areas, such as succession planning), you can define *suitability ranges* for career and succession planning, which determine the icon displayed in front of each item in the ranking list. By default, a red, yellow, or green traffic light is displayed for suitability percentages up to 33%, 66%, and 100%. You can modify the setting with the IMG path **Personnel Management · Personnel Development · Functions · Define Suitability Ranges**. Figure 9.18 shows a changed configuration with four suitability areas to highlight a suitability of more than 90%.

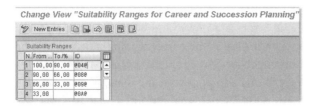

Figure 9.18 Customizing the Suitability Area

Figure 9.19 illustrates the effects of changing the configuration in the ranking list. The available icons are displayed graphically in the Customizing view (Figure 9.18) via the selection help.

Career plan	Ranking list					
Suitabil	Position	⊞	🞂	✔	ℹ	🔗
⊕	A 50001398 TS service workshop	☑				
⊙⊙⊙	QP 50010169 MS Office applications	☑				

Figure 9.19 New Ranking List Icon

9.2.5 Performing Succession Planning

Use the following menu path to perform the process described in Section 9.1.5: **Personnel Management · Personnel Development · Planning · Succession**. As long as you plan for individual objects, working with succession planning is very similar to career planning. However, when you use this helpful tool, do not interpret the term too literally. In addition to qualifications profiles, additional selection criteria are available, so that you can also use it instead of searching with profiles, as already noted. The sample process in Section 9.3.1 describes this procedure more precisely.

Generally, you perform succession planning with positions or work centers; however, planning with jobs is also an option. With this approach, you can recognize bottlenecks in the future staffing of these jobs independently of an individual case.

Planning for Individual Objects

As shown in Figure 9.20, the list of possible successor candidates usually delivers persons (employees). You can also include applicants or external employees if you plan to acquire freelance employees or consultants for full-time employment.

The options for career planning described above are also available here and should be used similarly:

▶ Create an overview in dialog with the system.

▶ Document planning results, especially with designations.

▶ Create direct personnel actions as transfers, planned transfers, or training bookings.

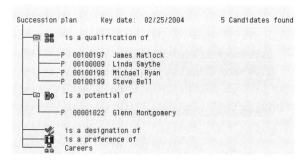

```
Succession plan      Key date:  02/25/2004      5 Candidates found

    ─⊟ ▦▦  is a qualification of

            ──P  00100197  James Matlock
            ──P  00100009  Linda Smythe
            ──P  00100198  Michael Ryan
            ──P  00100199  Steve Bell

    ─⊟ ▶▶  Is a potential of

            ──P  00001022  Glenn Montgomery

        ✔✔  is a designation of
        ▯  is a preference of
        ▣▣  Careers
```

Figure 9.20 Result: Succession Candidates

Detail selection offers another tool for a dialog search; Section 9.2.1 addresses Customizing for detail selection. You should always use detail selection to filter a small set of candidates from a larger set by various criteria. Figure 9.21 illustrates how—by clicking on the **Detail Selection** button—you can decrease a group of 20 candidates by filtering them according to a specific handicap ("Challenge group") group. Selection corresponds to enhanced object selection, such as that found in the maintenance of personnel master data or the selection screen of InfoSet Query. You can then continue to work in dialog with the reduced list of candidates that has been generated. Generally, selection criteria can be used only with specific object types (such as a person), so that the filtering does not affect other candidates.

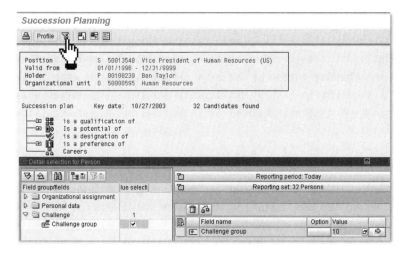

Figure 9.21 Detail Selection in Succession Planning

Succession Overview

To display succession candidates for all the positions of an organizational unit, you can use the menu path **Personnel Management · Personnel Development · Info System · Reports · Organizational Unit · Succession Overview**. The overview offers a quick way to look for any weaknesses in succession planning. This tool is also helpful to verify the results derived from a detailed planning that has been fully documented in designations. Figure 9.22 also shows how little, in general, the SAP concept of the "career" helps here. Generally, many employees occupy a position that can potentially lead to a job as a department head; however, that says nothing about their actual potential.

Succession overview

Organizational unit   O 50000595 Human Resources

Object ID	Object name	Suitable qualification	Prebookings	Careers	Number of candidates found
50000089	Director, HR Initiatives (US)	67	0	106	164
50000093	Manager of Human Resources (US)	144	0	650	427
50000199	Manager of Compensation & Benefits (US)	151	0	650	434
50000200	Functional Specialist (US)	87	0	123	197
50000202	Administrative Staff (US)	9	0	134	102
50000205	Manager of Labor Relations (US)	144	0	650	426
50000206	Functional Specialist (US)	87	0	123	197
50000208	Administrative Staff (US)	9	0	134	102
50000210	Functional Specialist (US)	87	0	123	197
50000212	Administrative Staff (US)	9	0	134	102
50000213	Manager of Development & Training (US)	144	0	650	426

Figure 9.22 Succession Overview of an Organizational Unit

Succession Simulation

If you select the **Perform Simulation** button instead of the **Perform Planning** button, a succession chain is generated, as shown in Figure 9.23. The display shows the proposed new holder of each position in the chain along with the same additional information that appears in the simple ranking list. You can select a position and then use the **Planning criteria** to perform individual succession planning for the position, as shown in Figure 9.23. This approach provides a wider selection of candidates than the succession chain itself, which specifies only one candidate for every position.

Integration into the System-Supported Processes

You can call both succession planning and career planning from various screens. The system provides excellent support for the user here—it makes the functions available in almost every context in which they are required. This approach avoids the need for complex navigation between windows. Both tools—and others for planning based upon a department—are available via the menu path **Personnel**

Management · Personnel Development · Planning for Organizational Unit. We also recommend placing these and other tools in the MDT (see Chapter 4); doing so is usually quite simple.

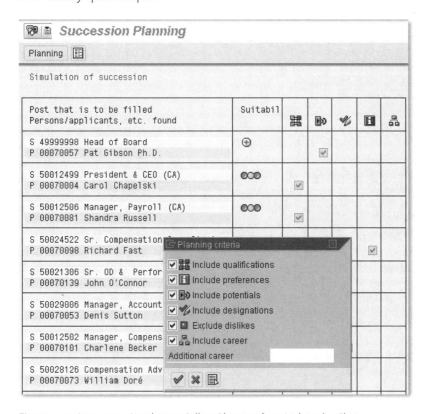

Figure 9.23 Succession Simulation: Calling Planning for a Link in the Chain

9.2.6 Development Plans

Maintaining General Development Plans

Follow the menu path **Personnel Management · Personnel Development · Settings · Current Settings · Edit Development Plan Catalogs to maintain general development plans**. To ensure a clear outline from the very beginning, you should first define development plan groups. To do so, position the cursor and click on the **Create** button. The group structure can include several levels, although this approach is usually unnecessary. A group is very easy to define and is described only by a name, a validity period, and a free text (see Figure 9.24).

Within the group structure, you can then use the same button to create individual development plans as shown in Figure 9.25. At first this is done without assigning the career items or the qualifications to be earned.

Figure 9.24 Definition of a Development Plan Group

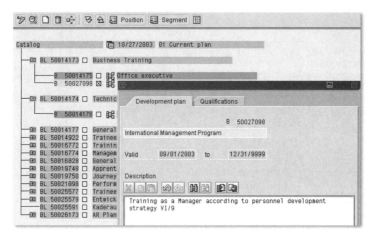

Figure 9.25 Creating a Development Plan within a Group

Only the maintenance of the individual steps and the respective items is somewhat more complicated. The graphical maintenance interface basically works much like the maintenance of careers (see Section 9.2.3). From the node area, you select the type of item that you want to create. You can find all types not listed explicitly in the Node area in the "Others" node. You then place the career items into the desired location in the display area; after this placement, you select the actual object (the position of "group leader," for example). You must also specify the duration and maintain the flag that indicates if the item is mandatory. To make a specific number of items mandatory for a step, but without specifying the career items themselves, double-click on the step number and then enter the number. The minimum or mandatory number of items is then displayed in red beneath the step number. Figure 9.26 illustrates a development plan that has been maintained completely.

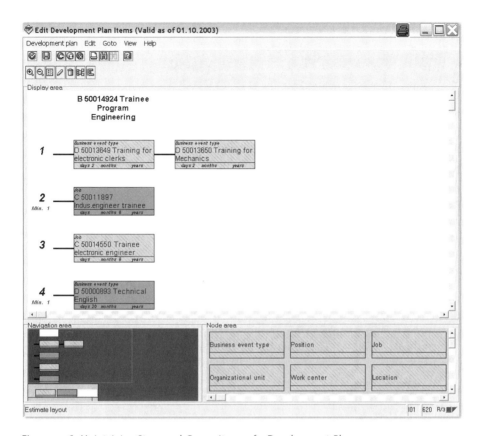

Figure 9.26 Maintaining Steps and Career Items of a Development Plan

You maintain the qualifications to be earned for the development plan only after you have maintained the items because the system can now propose values based on the related event types, jobs, and positions.

Individual Development Plans

You can call individual planning for an employee with the menu path **Personnel Management · Personnel Development · Planning · Individual Development**. This screen offers the following options:

▶ Calling an individual development plan without a template

▶ Calling an individual development plan with a general development plan as a template

▶ Displaying the completed development plans for a person
  (from the "Edit" entry in the menu)

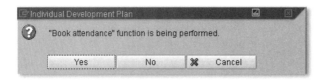

Figure 9.27 Automatic Branching to Book Attendance

You can enter the items described in Section 9.1.6 into the individual development plan. You can also expand the list of items permitted. Enter the present-day state and the planned period for each item. The state is of particular importance, because it can trigger automatic system functions. For example, if a career item with an event type is marked as "current," the system proposes that you book a training course (see Figure 9.27). You can branch to the corresponding course offering from this dialog window and perform a booking or a reservation. You can also use the Note button to create a note for each entry of the development plan.

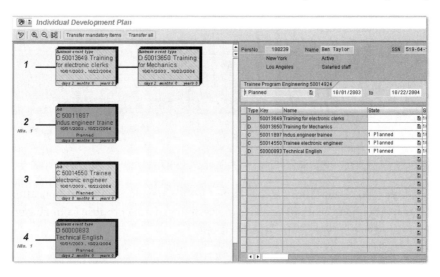

Figure 9.28 Transferring a General Development Plan

In principle, planning with a general development plan with a template does not differ from planning without a template. If you work with a template, the left half of the screen displays the general plan that you have selected so that you can double-click on items to transfer them into the individual plan (see Figure 9.28). You must also have entered a state and a period for the plan.

In addition to transferring individual items, you can also transfer all items or all mandatory items with one click. In this case, you would then have to tailor the validity periods and states in the individual plan. Note the following when transferring all mandatory items: a general development plan can include a step with three items, whereby at least one of the items must be completed. These items are not transferred; rather, you must decide which of the career items should be transferred in a dialog.

When both plans are displayed adjacently, an essential difference between them is made apparent. The individual plan does not distinguish between steps and items. The distinction is not absolutely necessary, because you can maintain a unique period for each element. Another difference is that the individual plan does not recognize any mandatory career items, but it does mark every entry with a state.

Managing States in Development Plans

By default, the following development states are available:

▶ Planned

▶ Current

▶ Completed

▶ Completed unsuccessfully

▶ Completed successfully

▶ Not carried out

You can define this list as you want with the IMG path **Personnel Management · Personnel Development · Development Plans · Define Development Plan States**. You can insert, delete, and rename states. This feature allows you to use additional states; for example, you can distinguish between mandatory and optional items of the individual plan.

In any case, for every change of the states from the SAP-standard, you must check the Customizing (described in the following) of automatic further processing and of the automatic change of state. Automatic state management creates a bottleneck because the available automation can be active only upon the basis of a starting state. If you itemize the states in too much detail, you might limit the options for automatic state changes (besides this, the list will become unmanageable, and you will need unwieldy conventions to maintain states). You can use two automatic mechanisms in the context of states: *automatic further processing* and *automatic state management*.

Automatic further processing of plan states ensures that certain configurations trigger a dynamic system action. By default, these actions include the following:

▶ Transfer of the qualifications attributed to the employee once the development plan has been completed successfully

▶ Booking a training course when a career item event type is set to the "current" state

▶ Transfer of an employee when a career item position is set to the "current" state

You can change the configuration for further processing with the IMG path **Personnel Management• Personnel Development · Development Plans · Further Processing of Plan States**. You can create a function module that controls the corresponding further processing for every combination of object type and state. For example, Figure 9.29 illustrates an additional entry that is easy to create and ensures that a personnel appraisal is called automatically when the corresponding development item is set to "current."

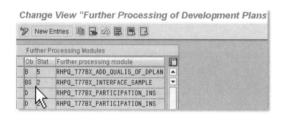

Figure 9.29 Further Processing of Development Plans: Creating a Personnel Appraisal

The situation is more complicated if you want to configure a further processing, for which SAP does not provide a standard function module. In this case, you must program a customer-specific function module, for which standard function module RHPQ_T77BX_INTERFACE_SAMPLE can serve as a template. You can store new function modules with IMG path **Personnel Management · Personnel Development · Development Plans · Define Permissible Further Processing**.

Examples for the use of customer-specific function modules include the following:

▶ Calling an appraisal after leaving a position

▶ Maintaining qualifications after the completion of specific items

▶ Sending e-mails or triggering workflows at the beginning or end of specific items

One adaptation that you can easily undertake in Customizing is the replacement of function module RHPQ_T77BX_PARTICIPATION_INS with function module RHPQ_T77BX_PART_INS_NO_DIALOG. Then, trainings will be booked in the background rather than online.

By default, a confirmation appears before every instance of automatic further processing (see Figure 9.27). You can bypass this by deactivating the corresponding parameter in IMG path **Personnel Management · Personnel Development · Development Plans · Set up Control Parameters**.

Automatic state management saves the user from maintaining sates in certain configurations. By default, the following state changes are performed automatically:

▶ An appraisal item is changed from "current" to "completed" when the appraisal is closed.

▶ An event item is changed from "current" to "completed" after the follow-up-procedure of the event.

▶ A job career item is changed from its current setting to "not carried out" when the job assignment is deleted.

▶ A job career item is changed from "planned" to "current" when the employee is assigned to the job; it is later changed to "completed" when the employee leaves the job.

These options can hardly be enhanced. If you don't want state changes to occur automatically, you can deactivate the corresponding entry in the IMG path **Personnel Management · Personnel Development · Development Plans · Automatic State Management** (see Figure 9.30).

Generally, you can work only on the basis of the existing state keys. When a corresponding event occurs ("Holder leaves position," for example), the system checks to see if the corresponding initial state (in this example 2, for "current") is present and then changes it to the target state (3, for "completed"). The initial state and target state can be changed, and must be changed, when the Customizing of the development plan states is changed. You cannot simply create new state keys without considering these consequences.

Change View "Development Plans: State Keys": Overview

New Entries

Development Plans: State Keys

State key	Actv.	A...	Zi...	Text
APPR_HISTO	✓	2	3	Create Historical Record for/Complete Appraisal
EVENT_BOOK	✓	1	2	Book Business Event Attendance
EVENT_FIN	✓	2	3	Business Event Follow-Up Processing
EVENT_STOR	✓	2	1	Cancel Business Event Attendance
S_DEL	✓		6	Staffing assignment for position was deleted
S_NEW	✓	1	2	Position is restaffed
S_OLD	✓	2	3	Holder leaves position

Figure 9.30 Automatic State Management

Each participation in an event that is entered directly in Training and Event Management results in an entry in the employee's development plan. In general, the state of the entry is set to 3, for "completed" when the event ends. You can change this setting in the IMG path **Personnel Management · Personnel Development · Development Plans · Set up Control Parameters**.

Reporting on Development Plans

The following describes the three most important reporting tools in more detail:

▶ Search "for development plan"
This report lets you determine how many employees are linked to a specific development plan and the state of their participation in the plan. You can call the report from the menu path **Personnel Management · Personnel Development · Information System · Reports · Search · For Development Plan**. Figure 9.31 shows that two employees currently participate in the plan, one is planned to participate, and one has already completed the plan successfully. If the dataset is large enough, you can also create a success key figure for a development program to see the relationship between successful and unsuccessful participation.

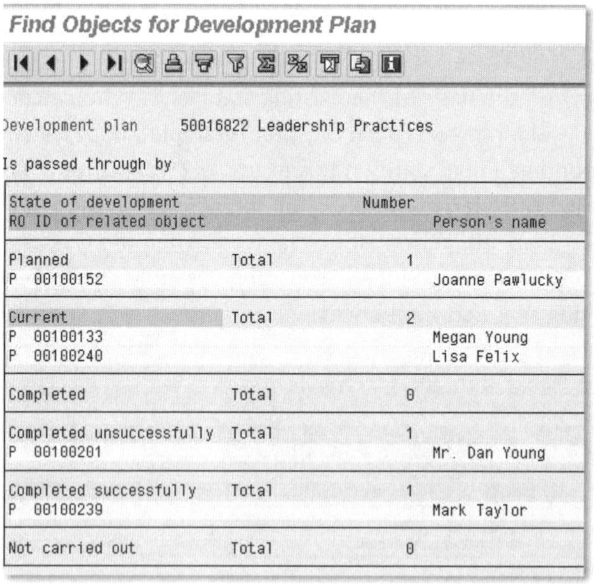

Figure 9.31 Statistics and Participant List of a Development Plan

▶ Search "for development plan item"

Similarly, you can also use menu path **Personnel Management · Personnel Development · Information System · Reports · Search · For Development Plan Item ·** to create statistics on the participants in a career item. Figure 9.32 expressly shows the selection of an organizational unit. It also shows that the report correctly considers the items added with simple Customizing. In the example, one participant has already completed the internship in the selected company successfully, one is currently doing it, and two are still waiting for this item.

▶ Development Plan History

The development plan history is a subprofile of the typical personnel development profile of every employee; you can navigate to it in various ways. If you want to report on the histories of several employees simultaneously, use the menu path **Personnel Management · Personnel Development · Information System · Reports · Profile**. As Figure 9.33 shows for an example with two employees, the development plans assigned to an employee are displayed along with their status.

This report is helpful only when the development plans are not seen as merely as a model, from which you can remove individual elements at will. Development plans must be used for the purpose indicated by their name and completed in their entirety in order to make this report informative.

Find Objects for Development Plan Item

```
Organizational unit  50000595 Management Consultants Ltd., Seattle

Is passed through by

State of development                    Number
RO ID of related object                          Person's name

Planned                     Total          2
P  00100152                                       Joanne Pawlucky
P  00100241                                       John Parker

Current                     Total          1
P  00100240                                       Lisa Felix

Completed                   Total          0

Completed unsuccessfully    Total          0

Completed successfully      Total          1
P  00100239                                       Mark Taylor

Not carried out             Total          0
```

Figure 9.32 Statistics and Participant List of a Career Item

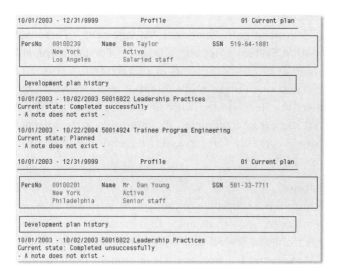

```
10/01/2003 - 12/31/9999          Profile                    01 Current plan

 PersNo   00100239     Name  Ben Taylor         SSN  519-64-1881
          New York           Active
          Los Angeles        Salaried staff

  Development plan history

 10/01/2003 - 10/02/2003 50016822 Leadership Practices
 Current state: Completed successfully
 - A note does not exist -

 10/01/2003 - 10/22/2004 50014924 Trainee Program Engineering
 Current state: Planned
 - A note does not exist -

10/01/2003 - 12/31/9999          Profile                    01 Current plan

 PersNo   00100201     Name  Mr. Dan Young      SSN  581-33-7711
          New York           Active
          Philadelphia       Senior staff

  Development plan history

 10/01/2003 - 10/02/2003 50016822 Leadership Practices
 Current state: Completed unsuccessfully
 - A note does not exist -
```

Figure 9.33 Development Plan History for Several Employees

9.3 Sample Process

9.3.1 Risk Management Based on Strategic Tasks

You can use succession planning to check the potential of the overall company or, of single departments to fulfill strategically important tasks. To do so, you must first identify the strategically decisive tasks in the company. The system provides good support for the process (see Figure 9.35) based upon that identification. You must simply stretch the term *succession planning* somewhat further than usual. As soon as the strategic tasks are known, enter them into the task catalog of Organizational Management. You should not have too many tasks; otherwise, they are not truly "strategic" and will prove to be very time—consuming when you must list them hierarchically. One branch of strategic tasks in the general task catalog will suffice. To conclude maintenance here, you must also assign requirements profiles. Figure 9.34 shows an excerpt from such a profile.

Because we're dealing with a strategic task of the company, in the next step we don't want to look for an individual employee who can perform the task. Instead, we want to find all the employees who can contribute to the fulfillment of the task. Accordingly, setting mandatory qualifications is generally not helpful because it would exclude employees who (after additional training) can make important contributions. In a few cases, however, flagging individual requirements as "essential" might prove worthwhile.

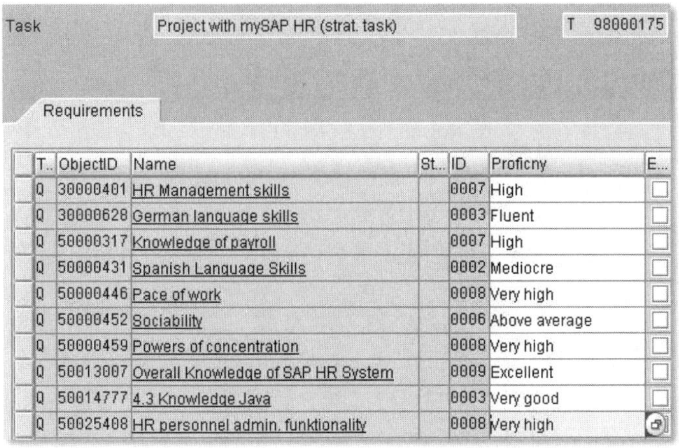

Task Project with mySAP HR (strat. task) T 98000175

Requirements

T..	ObjectID	Name	St..	ID	Proficny	E...
Q	30000401	HR Management skills		0007	High	
Q	30000628	German language skills		0003	Fluent	
Q	50000317	Knowledge of payroll		0007	High	
Q	50000431	Spanish Language Skills		0002	Mediocre	
Q	50000446	Pace of work		0008	Very high	
Q	50000452	Sociability		0006	Above average	
Q	50000459	Powers of concentration		0008	Very high	
Q	50013007	Overall Knowledge of SAP HR System		0009	Excellent	
Q	50014777	4.3 Knowledge Java		0003	Very good	
Q	50025408	HR personnel admin. funktionality		0008	Very high	

Figure 9.34 Requirements Profile of a Strategic Task

You must also communicate the tasks with their strategic significance. The process of maintaining profiles must be set up so that potentials, preferences, and dislikes can be maintained in consideration of strategic tasks (see Figure 9.35).

Based on this data, you can use succession planning to evaluate the potential of the company. To do so, start "normal" succession planning with a strategic task as the target object. If possible, you should first use all selection criteria—except for careers. The result gives you a first impression of the available potential. The selected employees are once again listed according to selection criteria. The results in Figure 9.36 show a rather large number of candidates, most of whom were found by qualifications profiles, which can occur because of an incomplete maintenance of the potentials.

You can branch to the ranking list for a better overview; however, you should display it with percentages of suitability rather than with suitability areas. Otherwise, most employees would fall in the lower area because individual employees would hardly be able to fulfill such a broad requirements profile. Figure 9.37 shows that all employees are below the 33% mark. Only teams of employees or—as shown here—external firms can cover such a wide spectrum. But that is not the goal of this "succession planning." The ranking list shows that some employees can fulfill a rather large portion of the tasks while others can make only small contributions.

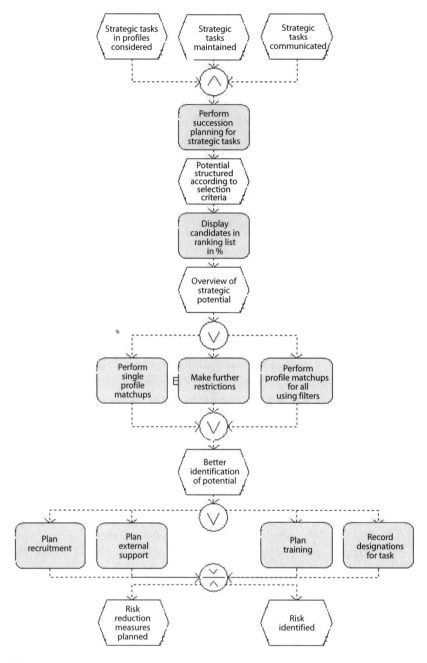

Figure 9.35 Risk Management Based Upon Strategic Tasks

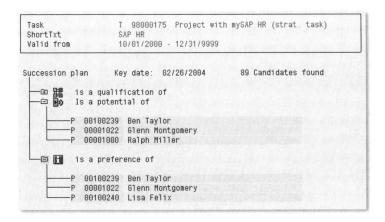

```
Task                 T  98000175  Project with mySAP HR (strat. task)
ShortTxt             SAP HR
Valid from           10/01/2000 - 12/31/9999


Succession plan       Key date:  02/26/2004         89 Candidates found

   ┌─⊞ 🎛    is a qualification of
   ├─⊟ 🔂    Is a potential of

         ┌───P  00100239  Ben Taylor
         ├───P  00001022  Glenn Montgomery
         └───P  00001000  Ralph Miller

   └─⊟ 🖥    is a preference of

         ┌───P  00100239  Ben Taylor
         ├───P  00001022  Glenn Montgomery
         └───P  00100240  Lisa Felix
```

Figure 9.36 First Impression of the Potential in a Company

Succession Planning

Profile 🏴 ▤ | ▼ ▲

```
Task                 T  98000175  Project with mySAP HR (strat. task)
Valid from           01/10/2000 - 01/12/9999

Succession plan              Ranking list        Key date: 01/10/2003
```

Suitabil	Person/applicant, etc.	🎛	🔂	🌿	🖥	🗄
0,00 %	P 00100130 John Jefferson	✓				
0,00 %	P 00100228 Karen Altobelli	✓				
0,00 %	P 00100240 Lisa Felix				✓	
0,00 %	P 00100012 Maryann Hutton	✓				
0,00 %	P 00100016 Michael Kennedy	✓				
0,00 %	P 00100015 Michelle Firenze	✓				
0,00 %	P 00100151 Richard Jones	✓				
0,00 %	P 00100209 Timmy Tabasco	✓				
0,00 %	P 00100134 Tom Peterson	✓				
0,42-%	P 00100123 HaroldXCarson	✓				
3,33-%	P 00109402 Brian Boudin	✓				
3,33-%	P 00109403 Connie Cook	✓				
3,33-%	P 00109404 Daniel Davis	✓				
3,33-%	P 00100033 Joseph Rossi	✓				
3,33-%	P 00100034 Madeline Marino	✓				
3,33-%	P 00100007 Mike Eckert	✓				
3,33-%	P 00100035 Terri Brown	✓				
6,67-%	P 00100204 Douglas Darwin	✓				
6,67-%	P 00100311 Neil Nesenblatt	✓				
10,00-%	P 00109405 Ernie Edwards	✓				

```
     88  Candidates found    Displayed:   69 - 88
```

Figure 9.37 Ranking List for Strategic Tasks

You must therefore examine the results more closely. You can use the profile comparison for all employees. The first output of this tool is quite confusing, but the button "List" provides a complete listing of all the employees under consideration with the fulfilled and non-fulfilled qualifications. Skillful sorting (according to qualification) and filtering (hiding non-fulfilled qualifications) will provide you with a list similar to the "Display Profile Matchup" shown in Figure 9.38. Here, you can quickly determine how many employees can fulfill each of the required qualifications, and which qualifications cannot be fulfilled at all. In particular, you can also easily distinguish among internal employees, external employees, and candidates.

Display profile matchup

Task	Project with mySAP HR (strat. task)
Key date	01/10/2003
More settings	Alternative qualifications were not included
	Depreciation meter was not included

	Object type text	Object name	Qualification Group	Qualification	Required	Existing Proficiency	Difference
	Person	John Benton	Enterprise software	HR personnel admin. funkt...	Very high	Very high	0
	Person	Robert Hoffman	Enterprise software	HR personnel admin. funkt...	Very high		0
	Company	McBer & Associates	Enterprise software	Overall Knowledge of SAP ...	Excellent		1-
	Person	Amy Worthington	Finance	Knowledge of payroll	High		1
	Person	Mr Steven Chambers	Finance	Knowledge of payroll	High		1
	Applicant	Garth Morris	Human Resources	HR Management skills	High		1
	Person	Ralph Miller	Human Resources	HR Management skills	High		1
	Company	iprocon	Human Resources	HR Management skills	High		1
	External person	Bernard Jones	Human Resources	HR Management skills	High		1
	Person	Frederick Thompson	4. IT Development	4.3 Knowledge Java	Very good	Very good	0
	Person	Steve Goldberg	4. IT Development	4.3 Knowledge Java	Very good		0
	Person	Jennifer Esposito	4. IT Development	4.3 Knowledge Java	Very good		0
	Person	Ann Takahashi	4. IT Development	4.3 Knowledge Java	Very good		0
	Person	Arthur Dent	4. IT Development	4.3 Knowledge Java	Very good		0
	Person	Mr Ryan Reval	4. IT Development	4.3 Knowledge Java	Very good		0

Figure 9.38 Overview List of a Profile Comparison (Filtered)

You might want to create an overview based on various filter criteria-by age or location, for example. Succession planning offers comprehensive filtering options to complete this task, as described in Section 9.2.5. In addition to looking at the overview, you should also examine individual employees more closely. A profile comparison, such as the one shown in Figure 9.39, quickly reveals the contributions that an individual employee can make.

Based on this information, you can now plan personnel actions, which include (in particular) designating the employees who have been found suitable for the strategic task. You can also customize the relationship type and designate candidates or external employees. At this early stage in the process, you can also use the proposals for training courses that the profile comparison indicates for designated employees to book or plan training.

These concluding personnel actions, however, are not the most important part of the process. It's much more important to use the option to recognize the potential, and therefore the risk, in dialog with the system and then, to derive the need for action. Actual and direct documentation of the follow-up planning of personnel action in the system is of secondary importance. Skillful definition of the strategic requirements profiles can provide important information with relatively little effort. As a precondition, however, you must work in dialog and make concessions to the layout of the printed results.

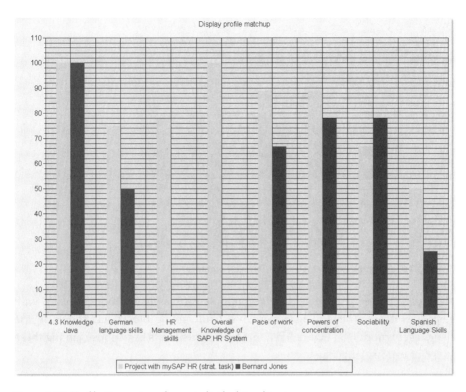

Figure 9.39 Profile Comparison for an Individual Employee

Customizing

By default, the ranking list is limited to 20 entries, which are sufficient for "real" succession planning. It can easily be larger for the process addressed here. You can adapt the limitation with the QUALI – MAXEN entry in table T77S0.

9.3.2 Trainee Program

The design of the development plan is exceptionally well suited to map trainee programs, particularly when several trainee programs in a company consist of some of the same modules. In this case, you can leverage the option to reuse development plans as an element of a superior development plan.

In the first step, identify the existing trainee programs. As far as possible, you can then detach modules used repeatedly. You can create both within the development plan catalog—in the first step without a preliminary definition of the items (see Figure 9.40).

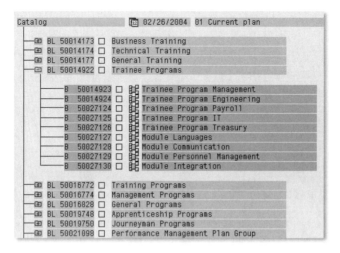

Figure 9.40 Development Plan Catalog: Trainee Programs

Next, you create the module development plans (this means: the sub-plans) with steps and items. These plans often consist of training blocks—as shown in the "languages" module in Figure 9.41, in which participants can choose among three levels of various languages.

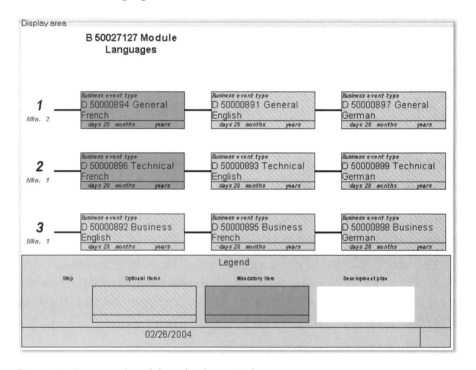

Figure 9.41 "Languages" module as development plan

Now you can define the actual trainee programs, which include the predefined modules and additional items. The items primarily involve departments in which the trainees must gain experience. You usually cannot define the sequence of departments as a reusable module. Figure 9.42 shows such a plan that contains the "languages" module described above.

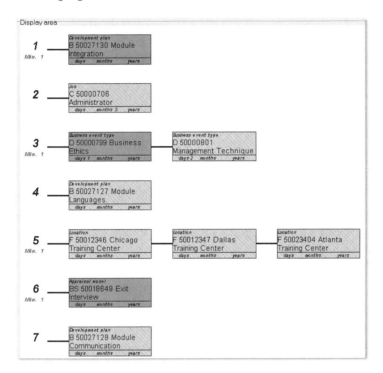

Figure 9.42 "Management" Trainee Program (Excerpt)

In principle, you can define the development plans in any sequence once you have created them as a "torso" in the catalog. You can also change the module later on. Additional customizing or even programming is not required to create this design.

9.3.3 Goldfish Bowl

The "goldfish bowl" is a favorite concept in personnel development planning. With this approach, central personnel planning limits itself to a selected area during the documentation and tracing of potentials. The form of system-supported documentation also remains quite simple. The limitation of the area occurs in two dimensions:

▶ Only the positions of higher levels of the hierarchy and strategically important expert positions are considered.

▶ Only the *high potentials* that you believe can be developed into one of the potential positions are considered.

You then maintain potentials only for the employees selected as above. You can also use the concepts of designation and dislikes, where a designation is viewed as an "increase" of the potential. The goldfish bowl is then cared for as best as possible—no matter what the actual present-day vacancies are: the employees in the bowl are developed and bound to the company. However, you should regularly check to see if expectations have been fulfilled thus far. If you plan on staffing a vacant position in a strategically important area, you will be able to find a suitable employee quickly.

To further simplify reporting, you can also assign the same job as a potential to all the *high potentials*. The job therefore is a "dummy" job: it's never actually used and serves only for reporting. That's why you can call it a "goldfish bowl." The number of employees produced by a report on this job is a simple, but informative indicator of succession problems in the high potentials area: Your bowl must always contain enough "goldfish."

Figure 9.43 illustrates the procedure in broad strokes. The essential part of the model is the limitation to important positions and to a few entries in the system. This approach makes the procedure very efficient as a centralized instrument. It leaves the planning of employee development and succession in other areas to decentralized areas. Group-wide and cross-country development of high potentials should be controlled centrally.

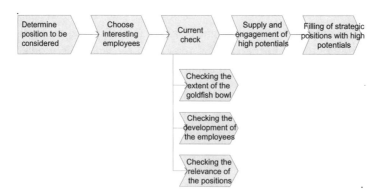

Figure 9.43 Procedure Model for the "goldfish bowl"

9.3.4 Succession Planning as Risk Management

Along with the process described in Section 9.3.1, traditional succession planning also belongs to the essential elements of risk management. In Sections 9.1.5 and 9.2.5, the process of succession planning has already been described in detail. In order to build stable risk management on that foundation, you must provide only a few organizational points:

▶ The relevant jobs and positions must be documented.

▶ The age structure must be considered carefully. It is not enough to know that you have 10 employees who possess the vital engineering skills for your business. Even if this number of skilled employees is adequate, it is vital that you develop other employees at this time, if 9 of these 10 employees are less than two years away from retirement.

▶ A key figure must be defined that indicates the number of potential successors for each position. Such a definition is required to ensure succession in light of typical fluctuations.

▶ You must also consider other aspects, in particular, motivation.

9.4 Critical Success Factors

The following aspects are significant for the effective support of development planning processes:

▶ The area to be considered must be defined exactly:
  ▷ Does it include all tasks or only strategically important tasks?
  ▷ What hierarchy levels does it cover?
  ▷ Which employees does it include?

▶ Maintenance conventions and their consequences for reporting must be clarified.

▶ You should limit yourself to a few of the tools offered.

▶ You should also reduce the number of object types used in development planning. In particular, you should avoid using positions in development plans, potentials, preferences, and dislikes; whenever possible, use jobs instead of positions.

▶ Insofar as possible, decentralized maintenance of preferences and dislikes is preferable to employees.

▶ Development planning must be part of the staff dialog. The system must provide input for the discussion, and the results must be documented in the system. It's completely conceivable to work with the system during the meeting (at defined portions of the conversation, but not constantly).

▶ You must weigh the use of careers carefully; they are usually inflexible and reveal little information that is significant.

▶ When designing skill management, you should consider the use of development planning.

▶ You can also derive requirements for Organizational Management from development planning. The granularity of organizational units, jobs, and positions must be suitable for the maintenance of potentials, preferences, and dislikes.

▶ The authorization concept can become very complex with a decentralized approach. You must schedule enough time for design—and especially for testing.

▶ When using preferences and dislikes, maintenance by ESS is very important. You must prepare a suitable user interface for this task.

▶ Development planning should be used at least in those areas that are relevant to personnel risk management. Its use must then be fine-tuned to reflect the cross-process risk management of the entire company. Because purely financial considerations strongly characterize this field so far, you should not unquestioningly accept specifications that do not lead to the target according to the view of personnel management. The structure of personnel risk management primarily requires knowledge of the various processes of personnel management. An examination by traditional auditors or financial experts is therefore ineffective, almost by definition.

▶ Customizing for this process is very simple. It involves only several special settings and perhaps the adjustment of links or, creating customer-specific object and relationship types. The focus here—as with skill management—is on the definition of processes, the creation of easily manageable structures in the system, and the creation of suitable conventions. If the adaptation options of Customizing are insufficient, greater development effort can easily be required in the user interfaces intended for decentralized use and in the reports. Accordingly, you should ensure that you don't underestimate the effort involved because there are far fewer Customizing points here when compared with processes such as time management and payroll. A realistic estimate of the effort involved is possible only after an inspection of the specific requirements.

10   Appraisals and Setting Objectives

mySAP HR covers a wide range of personnel appraisals. Because of the broad scope of functionality inherent in mySAP HR, there is support for a multitude of personnel appraisal processes and many options for customization as well.

10.1   The Design in mySAP HR

The personnel assessment system contains many of the elements that we addressed in the previous two chapters. Therefore, in this chapter, we will not delve into all these elements with the same level of detail. This application defines the process more strictly than do the screens in development planning; therefore, the presentation on working with the system is less involved. However, system configuration, particularly in the area of the appraisal model, is somewhat more complex and therefore requires a bit more attention.

Please note that in this chapter we describe the functionality of Release 4.6C. In Release 4.7 (R/3 Enterprise), this functionality can be replaced by a new component, which we describe in Chapter 12.

10.1.1   Scope of Functionality

In principle, mySAP HR can map almost every type of personnel appraisal. Some possible applications include the following:

▶ Performance review of individual employees

▶ Performance review of groups

▶ Potential appraisal

▶ Bottom-up appraisal

▶ 360-degree feedback

▶ Reference

▶ General employee survey

▶ Survey on satisfaction with the cafeteria

▶ Documentation of test results

▶ Business event appraisal

▶ Attendee appraisal

The last two bullets are actually better suited to the subject addressed in Chapter 11, namely, *Training and Event Management*; however, the basic system of assessment and the setup of Customizing are also relevant here. To avoid redundancies, in Chapter 11, we therefore briefly discuss *assessments* only in the context of the specific application. You can also store test results as an attendee appraisal in Training and Event Management if the test belongs to an event maintained there or, if it is created as an individual event (such as an assessment center (AC), for example). The option for anonymous assessment is a particularly important characteristic, because it is required in most practical cases.

The system supports not only the simple entry of assessment, but also the entire assessment process from preparation to approval—so that the status of the assessment procedure is always known. As a follow-up, you have access to follow-up tools that cover integration issues and various assessments. If the process in its entirety is not conducted on the system, you can print assessment forms and later enter the data from the forms centrally.

10.1.2 Terminology and Structure

In the area of appraisals, SAP uses terms that might not be intuitive. Therefore, we have provided the following clarification of the terms and in what context they are used.

Appraisal model The central term in the configuration of the assessment system. Forms the basis for every assessment. In particular, it sets the criteria that an assessment uses and defines other characteristics of the assessments.

▶ Appraisals catalog
   Summarizes all the appraisal models in the system.

▶ Criteria group
   Combines various appraisal criteria, that is, criteria can be linked to an appraisal model directly or as a group.

▶ Criteria and qualifications
   The individual basic elements within an appraisal model can be both criteria (created within the criteria catalog) and qualifications (from the qualifications catalog). Common usage refers to "criteria" in both cases. To distinguish between "criteria" and "qualifications," we will use SAP terminology. When no special considerations are involved, the following examples will be based on criteria. The same applies to qualifications.

▶ Result
   You can enter or calculate a result for individual criteria, criteria groups, or an entire appraisal.

▶ Form of appraisal
   Defines the distribution of roles within an appraisal. It sets which object types are used as appraisers or the appraised within an appraisal and how (by which relationship) they must be linked to each other.

▶ **Appraisal type**

Appraisal types are distinguished as follows:

▷ An *individual appraisal* is an appraisal that stores exactly one appraisal. Of course, several objects can be involved as appraisers and the appraised.

▷ An *anonymous individual appraisal* does not store any information about the appraiser.

▷ A *multisource appraisal* contains several appraisals, each of which creates a *subappraisal*. The total of the subappraisals is also called an *overall appraisal*.

▷ An *anonymous multisource appraisal* stores no information on the individual appraisers.

▶ **Appraisal scale**

Determines how the result of a criterion, a criteria group, or an appraisal is expressed. Essentially, this scale corresponds to the scale used in Skill Management to assess qualifications (see Chapter 8, *Skill Management*)

▶ **Calculation method**

Defines how a result is to be calculated. It is used when the result in question is not solely to be created manually. You can define the calculation based upon the subordinate results or freely.

▶ **Functions**

Describes the modules used in the customizing of the personnel assessment system for calculating results or, for the further processing of appraisals.

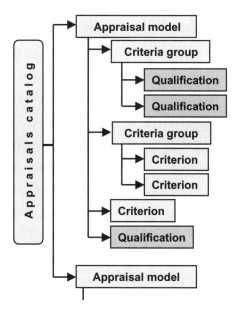

Figure 10.1 Structure of the Assessment Catalog

Figure 10.1 illustrates the structure of the appraisals catalog with appraisal models, criteria groups, criteria, and qualifications. You can assign criteria and qualifications to an appraisal model directly and indirectly. The hierarchy does not support the insertion of additional levels. Of course, you can reuse criteria, qualifications, and criteria groups, which allows for a modular structure of the catalog. You must define criteria groups in general use only once; you can combine them with various specific criteria groups in various appraisal models.

A form of appraisal primarily links appraisers with the appraised (see Figure 10.2), but only by the allowed combinations of object types. You can also use additional criteria: you can use an existing relationship or a selection ID to determine the appraised who belong to the appraiser and vice versa. This feature enables the system to create a "to-do" list of objects to be appraised for each appraiser. The objects can include those employees for whom the appraiser is responsible or, training events that have been attended. The form of appraisal also determines the descriptions to be used for the appraised and appraisers (supervisor and employee, for example).

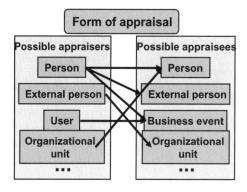

Figure 10.2 Structure of a Form of Appraisal

10.1.3 Phases of the Appraisal Process

The flow of this process varies somewhat depending on the form of appraisal, the type of appraisal, and the actual application. Figure 10.3 illustrates clearly the essential parts of the phases of the appraisal process.

Preparation for the appraisal can be done expediently or, take a longer duration (especially with multisource appraisals). This phase includes the following tasks:

▶ Selection of the objects to be appraised (the system can perform this task, depending upon the definition of the form of appraisal)

▶ Selection of the appraiser or the appraised

- Selection of the appraisal model, if the parameters in effect permit more than one possibility
- Setting the appraisal period, which need not be the same for all appraisers with multisource appraisals
- Setting the anonymity options for non-anonymous appraisal models (see Section 10.2.1 for an explanation of this rather unusual statement)
- Setting the weighting of individual subappraisals for multisource appraisals

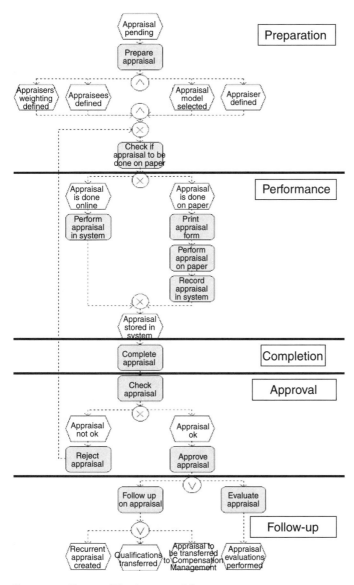

Figure 10.3 Phases of the Assessment Process

The process of performing the actual appraisal is very simple. Even if the flow of the appraisal deviates from the system when the appraisal is done on paper, you can still capture the information centrally. As soon as appraisers are satisfied with their work, they can close the appraisal, after which it is no longer possible to change the results. In many scenarios, the appraised has a right to object to it. If the employee does not accept the appraisal, its status is reset and it can once again be maintained. If the appraisal is approved, the appraisal process is closed. Follow-up activities include the following tasks:

▶ If the appraisal occurs regularly in this form, you can start to plan the next appraisal (e.g., annual performance review for the next year).

▶ If the appraisal model also contains qualifications, you can transfer the results into the employee's qualifications profile.

▶ If Compensation Management includes guidelines that build on the appraisal results, you can now make the results available to Compensation Management.

10.1.4 The Structure of Appraisal Models

Figure 10.1 displays the rough structure of appraisal models in the context of qualifications catalogs. An appraisal model consists of criteria, criteria groups, and the following elements:

▶ The possible appraisers and the appraised are set by assigning the form of appraisal to the model.

▶ The form of appraisal.

▶ The scale used for appraisal results and as a proposal for the results at lower levels. You can override the proficiency texts for this scale much like you can in a qualifications catalog. However, proficiencies and proficiency texts are relevant only for quality scales.

▶ An explanation that specifies the purposes of the model and any special considerations to be observed.

▶ The form of enumeration for individual criteria (affects only the appearance).

▶ Various entries that determine the layout if the appraisal is called from an HTML interface.

▶ Possible follow-up functions, such as transfer to Compensation Management.

▶ A flag that indicates which actions are still permitted after a closed appraisal. In particular, the flag can indicate if a reset is possible because of a missing approval.

▶ The calculation guidelines for the result.

▶ A weighting for the directly subordinate results, which can come from criteria or criteria groups. The weighting then becomes part of the calculation guidelines.

▶ A flag that indicates if the result can be maintained manually or if an entry is required. If an automatically calculated result is flagged as allowing manual maintenance, automatic calculation produces only a proposed value. Given this feature, it's possible that the appraisal is calculated from the results of the individual criteria, but that the appraiser nonetheless decides on another result. Figure 10.4 shows the interplay between the results of various levels.

▶ Additional subordinate elements such as the permissibility of notes or sorting the elements in the display

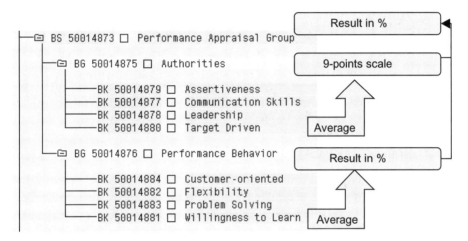

Figure 10.4 Aggregation of Results

Some of the elements of appraisal models listed here also apply to criteria groups and criteria. The most important are the results and their calculation, the scales, and (for criteria groups) the weighting.

10.1.5 Integration

The primary integration aspects have already been addressed in the context of the process. The following offers a more detailed description:

▶ In addition to specifically created criteria, qualifications from the qualifications catalog are also used as elements of an appraisal. Doing so is a good idea whenever the contents of the appraisal criteria and qualifications are identical. You can then transfer the appraisal into the qualifications after you have approved it. This approach avoids redundancy and ensures consistency.

▶ In Compensation Management, *compensation guidelines* control the proposals for adjusting remuneration (see Chapter 15, *Compensation Management*). The proposals can also use the results of appraisals as the basis of calculation. If this occurs, we recommend that you automate the availability of thbasis of this calculation, which you can accomplish during the follow-up processing of the appraisal.

▶ Because both persons and most of the object types involved in organizational management can participate as appraisers and, above all, as the appraised, integration with several additional HR components results. For example, you can use them to appraise a vendor based upon the quality. You should then fine-tune this approach to reflect the process of Training and Event Management because companies are maintained as organizers there.

▶ Integration with Training and Event Management also arises because Training and Event Management also uses appraisals with models that are maintained in the same catalog and that use the same scales as the appraisal components.

▶ Scales must be fine-tuned to reflect the processes of Skill Management.

▶ Because an appraisal model is often used as a career item in development plans, integration with development planning arises.

10.2 Realization in mySAP HR

This section focuses on an explanation of Customizing activities, including the maintenance of the appraisal catalog. Work in the application is addressed only at critical points and to clarify the opportunities for a solution. You can best understand the relationships based on Customizing, which we address in the following section.

10.2.1 Basic Customizing Settings

The basic settings primarily affect the creation of elements that are in turn required to define appraisal models. The following describes the details of these elements.

Forms of Appraisal

You maintain forms of appraisal with the IMG path **Personnel Management · Personnel Development · Appraisal Systems · Edit Form of Appraisal.**

At the upper level of the dialog structure, the form of appraisal is created only with an ID and a long text; it is also given a description for the appraiser and the appraised. As shown in Figure 10.5, the core of the configuration occurs at the second level. You store all allowed combinations of appraisers and the appraised there. You should limit yourself to combinations that actually occur. You can also use an evaluation path or a selection ID to determine how persons to be appraised are to be derived from the appraiser and vice versa. Doing so also simplifies the creation of a "to-do" list in preparation for an appraisal. You can create specific evaluation paths and selection IDs for this purpose. The effort involved pays for itself as it results in a more efficient maintenance of forms of appraisal.

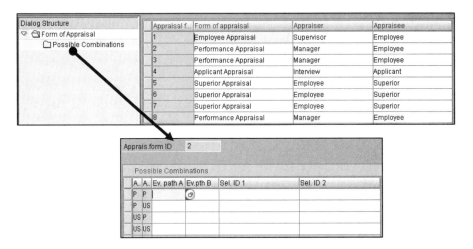

Figure 10.5 Maintaining Forms of Appraisal

Keep the number of forms of appraisal low and limit the forms to those that meet the requirements of assignments between the appraisers and the appraised. There is often a tendency to create one form for each appraisal model here. However, this approach is not feasible: you can use forms of appraisal in various appraisal models—even with different appraisal types. Accordingly, questions of anonymity and the number of appraisers are not criteria for building new forms of appraisal.

The key for the form of appraisal is given here without leading zeros. However, if you assign the forms of appraisal in Customizing of Training and Event Management to attendee appraisals or business event appraisals, you must use leading zeros.

Scales

See Section 8.2.2 on maintaining scales. The area of appraisals adds only quantity scales: Figure 10.6 illustrates the maintenance of quantity scales. Because you must maintain only a proficiency interval with a quantity scale and there are no proficiency texts, the setup of a proficiency interval is less complex than that of a quantity scale. To design maintenance efficiently, keep the number of decimal places as low as possible. Only the rarest of cases requires more than 1,000 grades.

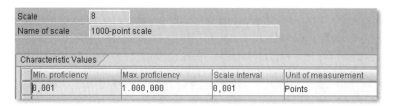

Scale	8		
Name of scale	1000-point scale		

Characteristic Values

Min. proficiency	Max. proficiency	Scale interval	Unit of measurement
0,001	1.000,000	0,001	Points

Figure 10.6 Creating a Quantity Scale

In the customizing of the personnel appraisal system, you must navigate to scale maintenance via the IMG path **Personnel Management · Personnel Development · Appraisal Systems · Edit Scales**.

Functions

You store the functions available for follow-up processing, further processing, and calculation over the IMG path **Personnel Management · Personnel Development · Appraisal Systems** · Define Permissible Functions. The effort required for customizing is less than that required in programming customer-specific function modules.

If needed, you can also use standard SAP function modules as templates. Possible applications of new functions include the following:

▶ Calculating a result based on revenue numbers determined in SAP Sales & Distribution (SAP SD).

▶ Calculating a result based on a fluctuation number for the department led by the appraised. You can calculate the number from HR data, but doing so requires rather extensive programming.

▶ Triggering a workflow that informs HR personnel of an especially poor appraisal.

If the programming effort seems frightening at first, remember that you should not underestimate the possibilities opened by the installation of your own functions, which does not create a "modification" and therefore is not critical for updates.

Assigning Appraisal Models to Personnel Administration Structures

The assignment of models to structures in Personnel Administration enables the system to propose the correct model. Assignment occurs via the IMG path **Personnel Management · Personnel Development · Appraisal Systems · Assigning**

Appraisal Models to Personnel. However, you must have already assigned the combinations of personnel area/personnel subarea and employee group/employee subgroup in maintenance views V_001P_L and V_503_F to a grouping for appraisals. Then, you can use the IMG path noted above to assign the appraisal model to the possible combinations of both groupings.

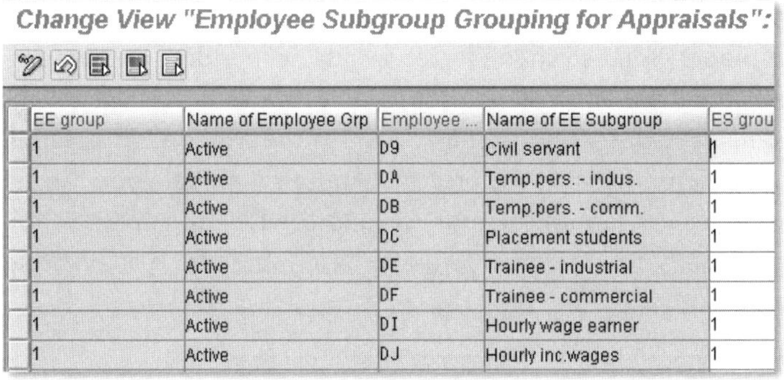
Change View "Employee Subgroup Grouping for Appraisals":

EE group	Name of Employee Grp	Employee ...	Name of EE Subgroup	ES grou
1	Active	D9	Civil servant	1
1	Active	DA	Temp.pers. - indus.	1
1	Active	DB	Temp.pers. - comm.	1
1	Active	DC	Placement students	1
1	Active	DE	Trainee - industrial	1
1	Active	DF	Trainee - commercial	1
1	Active	DI	Hourly wage earner	1
1	Active	DJ	Hourly inc.wages	1

Figure 10.7 Grouping Employee Groups and Subgroups

The differentiation of appraisal models according to employee subgroups (see Figure 10.7) is often a good idea because appraisals of managers usually contain criteria on their leadership quality and appraisals of sales people are based on the revenue.

Profile Views

In the section on Skill Management, we addressed the configuration of the profile view (see Figure 8.8). You can use the IMG path **Personnel Management • Personnel Development • Appraisal Systems • Define Profile View** to record appraisals in other profile views (particularly in the personnel development profile). You can also use this menu path to supplement the views used in the appraisal (AE and AM) with further subprofiles as additional information. For example, we recommend that you insert qualifications profiles here if the appraisal also contains qualifications.

Automatic Default Period

If a special rule requires that the system propose an appraisal period, you can have it do so by programming a simple Business Add-In (BAdI). Follow the IMG path **Personnel Management • Personnel Development • Appraisal Systems • Enhancements • BAdI: Default Period...** and program customer-specific logic to propose a period based upon plan variants and the appraisal model. Because the period can be based on the model in use (annual appraisal, quarterly appraisal, and so on), this option is recommended.

10.2.2 Creating an Appraisal Model

In Section 10.1.4, we described the structure of the appraisal model. You maintain appraisal models via the IMG path **Personnel Management · Personnel Development · Appraisal Systems · Edit Appraisals Catalog**. Now, we will show you the procedures with a series of figures.

Because you cannot create a hierarchy for appraisals, position the cursor on the catalog to create a model. You can then create various header data and properties. You should assign criteria and criteria groups only afterward to take advantage of inheriting default values. Maintenance occurs in the window displayed in Figure 10.8 over five different tabs. In the first tab (**Appraisal model**), you can set some essential properties in the form of appraisal and the type of appraisal. You should use this opportunity to enter an additional description, such as one that names the recipient group.

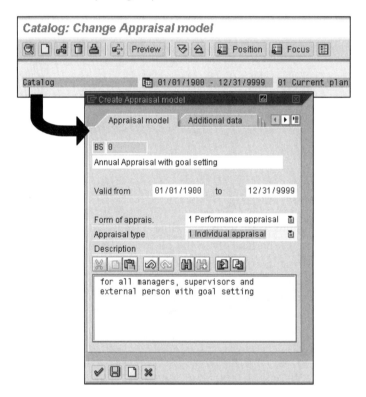

Figure 10.8 Creating an Appraisal Model in the Catalog

The following tabs, as shown in Figure 10.9 are less important; however, you should maintain them for an optimal process design. The **Additional data** tab pertains only to the appearance of the appraisal in the application:

- ▶ You can determine whether and how individual criteria and groups are to be numbered.
- ▶ You can define the following formatting options for a display in HTML:
    - ▶ The number of lines available for notes is limited.
    - ▶ You can determine if the descriptions of proficiencies should be displayed. Activate this option if you plan on using HTML output. Comparability is guaranteed only when the meaning of the proficiencies can be read directly.
    - ▶ The option of displaying checkboxes instead of entry fields for proficiencies is also recommended. Doing so greatly simplifies work with the browser interface. Here, you specify the upper limit of proficiencies for which a checkbox should be generated because too many proficiencies would make the display unmanageable. Therefore, this option does not exist for quantity scales.

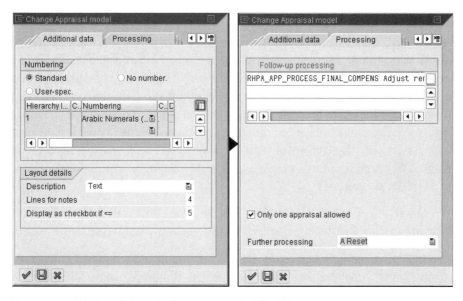

Figure 10.9 Additional Data and Editing an Appraisal Model

The **Processing** tab regulates the functions to be performed during follow-up processing of the appraisal. The example in Figure 10.9 transfers the results of an appraisal to Compensation Management. Follow-up processing regulates whether a closed appraisal may be reset to "in process" or deleted.

If allowed here, you should protect both actions with authorizations. You should allow a reset in any case, but grant the corresponding authorization very restrictively. Without this option, you have no way of correcting errors if an employee contests the appraisal. The resulting workflow works correctly only when a reset is allowed. For non-anonymous appraisal types, the indicator "Only one appraisal allowed" is important. It prevents the same person from issuing several appraisals for one object.

The **Result** tab (see Figure 10.10) is very significant. Here, you select the scale used for the result of the appraisal. Although the system proposes a scale for the following criteria and groups, you don't have to accept the proposal. Note this feature well, particularly when selecting the calculation method. You should always calculate the results of appraisals and of criteria groups from the results of the subordinate elements. Only when all elements use the same scale does using an average make sense. The calculation of a percentage with a percentage scale is offered here. This approach first converts each subordinate result into a percentage value based on each maximum value. Then, it uses that figure as a weighted average to determine the percentage result of the superior level. Special calculation methods based on a user-specific function module are usually recommended only at the level of criteria, where they prove to be enormously useful.

The field attribute for data entry is also very important. You can use it to define results as mandatory. But, above all, it regulates whether calculated results can be overwritten. If you don't want to enable overwriting, select the option for **No entry**, which makes sense only for results with automatic calculation. You can also prevent appending a note to the result. In general, we recommend that you allow the maintenance of a note to indicate the justification for the appraisal. However, you should also regulate notes with a convention that limits the texts to be entered to justifications, for example, and makes them mandatory for very poor and for very good values.

You can enter specific comments for the scale values, just as you did in the qualifications catalog. This feature does not apply to quantity scales (see Figure 10.10).

Inserting criteria groups (see Figure 10.11) and criteria into the model differs only slightly from the maintenance of the model itself. You simply have a little less data to maintain. One essential difference, however, is that you don't have to create new criteria and groups repeatedly. You can use the corresponding button to include existing elements.

If you reuse criteria or groups, you must be very careful when changing them because any changes affect several locations. This caution applies to attributes maintained in the tabs (see Figures 10.8-10.10) and to sorting and weighting (see Figure 10.12). You should use the where-used list to determine the exact location where a modification will have an effect. You must define a weighting to calculate results from several subordinate elements. The weighting is maintained along with sorting; use the menu entry "Entry." All weightings are set to "1" by default.

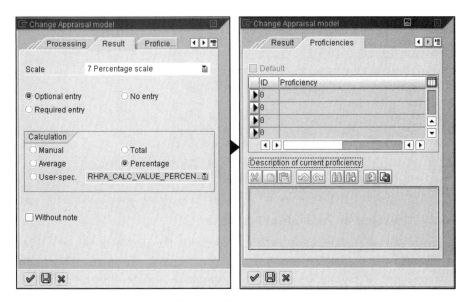

Figure 10.10 Displaying Results and Scale Attributes

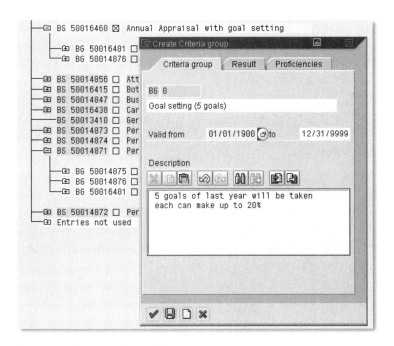

Figure 10.11 Inserting Criteria Groups

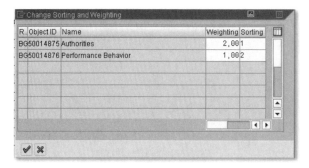

Figure 10.12 Modifying Weighting and Sorting

10.2.3 Creating an Individual Appraisal

You can create individual appraisals directly with the profile of the employee involved (for one appraiser and one appraised) or with menu path **Personnel Management · Personnel Development · Appraisal · Create**. The process runs as described in Figure 10.3. You can select several appraisers, all of whom then create one appraisal. Consequently, you can select the anonymity option only for all of them as a group.

Figure 10.13 shows how the system automatically creates a "to-do" list with a normal individual appraisal. In this case, the standard evaluation path, BOSSORG, is stored in the Customizing of the form.

Figure 10.13 "To-do" List from Preparation for Appraisal

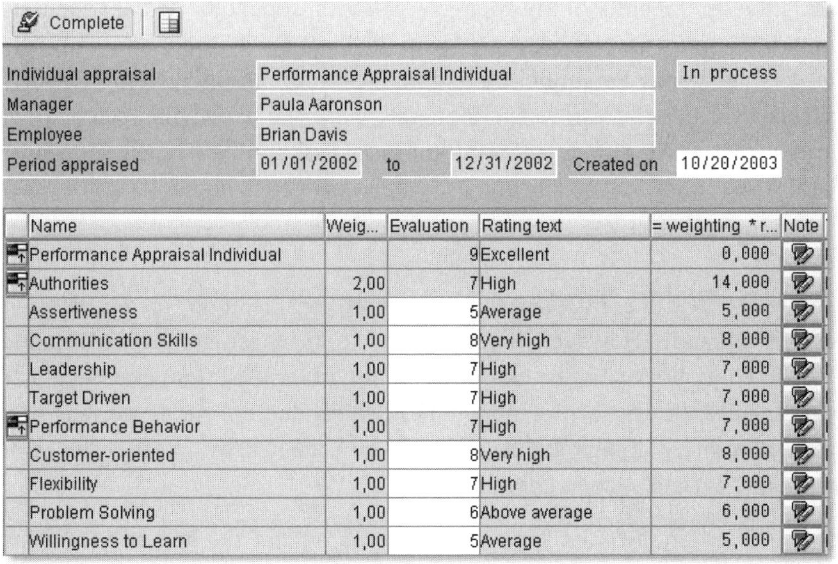

Figure 10.14 Performing an Individual Appraisal

After having completed the preparations, you maintain the data as shown in Figure 10.14. Then, you can close maintenance immediately. As an alternative, you can save the data and complete it later. Use the menu path **Personnel Management · Personnel Development · Appraisal · Edit** for each appraiser, and select all the appraisals with a status of "**in process**" or "**in preparation**."

Once you have completed this task, you can use follow-up processing to begin to plan the appraisal for the following year. The appraised can approve or reject the appraisals only by using a workflow (see Section 10.2.7). However, you can design the process without an approval step.

Who Creates the Appraisal in the System?

When an individual appraisal involves several appraisers, it's apparent that users represent others when they create a result in the system. In all other cases—and especially with multisource appraisals—the question of whether appraisers enter the data in the system themselves or, have a third party maintain it is a question that always arises. If managers appraise their employees, it's always preferable for them to use the Manager's Desktop. If all or a large number of employees are involved (as might be the case with a bottom-up appraisal, 360-degree feedback, or employee surveys, online entry becomes more complicated. You would usually need Employee Self-Service (ESS) scenarios in this case, which the standard system does not include to be complete in the required form.

To enable the central entry of the appraisal, you must supply the actual appraisers with a form. To print several appraisal forms, it's best to use the menu path **Personnel Management · Personnel Development · Information System · Reports · Appraisals**. There, you can select appraisals that have already been prepared. You can use the list display to print the appraisal form for each individual appraisal. You can also set how many lines are available for notes.

Anonymity

The anonymity of the appraisers is an important consideration, for example, in bottom-up appraisals. However, direct feedback for management can significantly foster open communication and prevent a culture of mistrust from emerging. For most companies, however, the anonymity is demanded by the employees. If a company guarantees anonymity, it must also be provided technically. The term "anonymous" is used twice in appraisals:

▶ The use of an anonymous appraisal type ensures that the appraiser remains anonymous to the system. The system does not store the appraiser as a relationship. The only weakness here is the logging of the name of the user who performed the last change to an Infotype record. You can use a simple, customer-specific program to provide enhanced anonymity.

▶ If you select another appraisal type and set the "anonymous" flag at creation, the appraiser is indeed saved in the relationship. However, the standard screens of the application don't display the appraiser's name. Saving the name of the appraiser is often required to prevent one person from creating several appraisals. Therefore, there is always at least one user in the HR department who can determine the appraiser. When the logged-on user is proposed as the appraiser during the initial creation of an appraisal, no option for anonymity is visible. To select the option, you must click on the **Additional Appraisers** button—even when you want to retain the proposed appraiser.

You often face the dilemma of being able to ensure only partial anonymity or, risk a loss of ensuring anonymity all together due to the need for multiple appraisals, and thus incurring anger and mistrust from your employees. In ESS scenarios, you can solve the problem as follows:

▶ Every employee who participates in the appraisal (such as an employee survey) receives a key code. You can organize the distribution of the codes so that no one knows what code each specific employee has received.

▶ An employee can perform an appraisal without having the entry screen perform a check.

- ▶ A Java application requests the code only when the appraisal is to be closed. The application checks the validity of the key entered and then removes it from the list of valid codes.

- ▶ The employee cannot enter additional appraisals—or at least cannot close an additional appraisal.

This kind of scenario is fairly secure; however, the realization of this scenario does demand a considerable effort.

10.2.4 Setting Objectives

In general, the standard delivery of SAP R/3 4.6C does not support setting objectives. Only the new component, *Management by Objectives*, supports this process (see Chapter 12). With some restrictions, however, you can also map the setting of objectives with typical appraisal models. The basic approach is to define an appraisal criterion for an objective and then name it "objective number n." Because the number and, above all, the weighting of individual criteria is fixed, you must adhere to some conventions.

Various objectives are typically weighted differently when setting objectives. To extrapolate this approach to appraisal criteria with fixed weights, you must set a specific granularity. When the weighting of a single objective may be only a multiple of 20%, an appraisal model as shown in Figure 10.15 will suffice. In this example, the employee has two objectives (goals), weighed with 40% and 60%. Because the employee has fulfilled the first objective (100%) and the second objective (50%), both values must be assigned to two or three criteria. To simplify this approach, imagine that all objectives must be weighted at exactly 20% and that many objectives appear repeatedly: you can then still reach a weighting of 40% or 60%. A granularity of 10% might represent a good compromise between flexibility and manageability.

If you use this procedure, we recommend that you use a note to describe the relationship between the appraisal criterion and the true objective. Even if the mapping does not appear to be particularly elegant in the system, you can still accomplish this task with very little effort.

individual appraisal	Annual Appraisal with goal setting			In process	
Supervisor	Paula Aaronson				
Employee	Brian Davis				
Period appraised	01/01/2002 to 12/31/2002 Created on 10/20/2003				

Name	Weig...	Evaluation	Rating text	= weighting * r...	Note
Annual Appraisal with goal setting		79	Percent	0,000	
1. Goal setting (5 goals)	1,00	70	Percent	70,000	
1.1. 1st Goal	1,00	100	Percent	100,000	
1.2. 2nd Goal	1,00	100	Percent	100,000	
1.3. 3rd Goal	1,00	50	Percent	50,000	
1.4. 4th Goal	1,00	50	Percent	50,000	
1.5. 5th Goal	1,00	50	Percent	50,000	
2. Performance Behavior	1,00	8	Very high	8,000	
2.1. Customer-oriented	1,00	7	High	7,000	
2.2. Flexibility	1,00	6	Above average	6,000	
2.3. Problem Solving	1,00	9	Excellent	9,000	
2.4. Willingness to Learn	1,00	8	Very high	8,000	

Figure 10.15 Mapping the Setting of Objectives

10.2.5 Multisource Appraisals

In principle, the creation of a multisource appraisal, a bottom-up appraisal, for example, occurs much like that of an individual appraisal. The preparation phase differs only with regard to selecting the appraisers, because you must enter the number of appraisers for anonymous appraisals and you might have to specify a weighting for individual appraisers in a non-anonymous appraisal. The latter can be a good idea when appraising a department head and you want to give team leaders a heavier weight than employees. Figure 10.16 illustrates the creation of an anonymous bottom-up appraisal.

▱ Complete	Overall appraisal	Subappraisals	Appraisal view	▤

Anonymous multisource appra...	Bottom-Up Appraisal			In process	
Employee	N.N.				
Manager	Jonathan Tyler				
Period appraised	01/01/2002 to 12/31/2002 Created on 10/20/2003				

Name	Weig...	Evaluation	Rating text	= weighting * r...	Note
Bottom-Up Appraisal		⊙		0,000	
1. Performance Behavior	1,00			0,000	
1.1. Customer-oriented	1,00			0,000	
1.2. Flexibility	1,00			0,000	
1.3. Problem Solving	1,00			0,000	
1.4. Willingness to Learn	1,00			0,000	

Figure 10.16 Anonymous Bottom-Up Appraisal as Multisource Appraisal

You then use the **Subappraisals** button to create the appraisals of the individual appraisers. Typically, you won't use this method for non-anonymous appraisals. Once you have closed the preparation phase, it's far better to create subappraisals via the menu path **Personnel Management · Personnel Development · Appraisal · Edit**, where subappraisers can select and maintain their open subappraisals. Figure 10.17 illustrates the central maintenance of anonymous subappraisals.

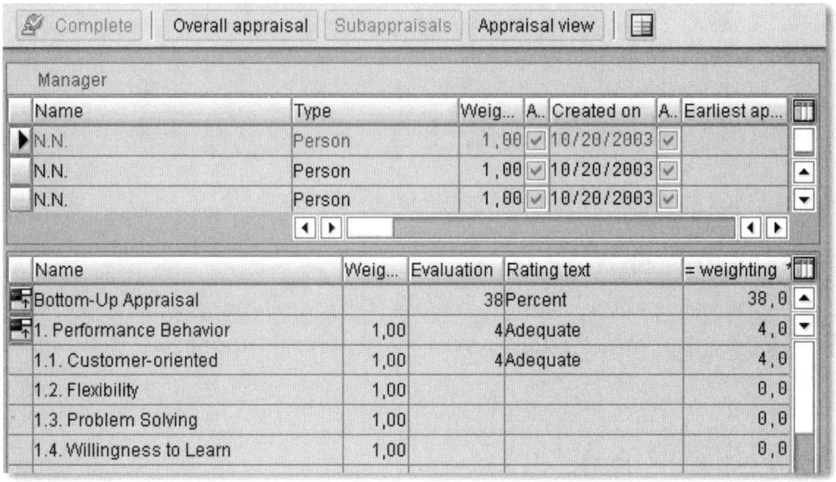

Figure 10.17 Maintenance of Anonymous Subappraisals

The **Overall appraisal** button provides an overview of all subappraisals (see Figure 10.18).

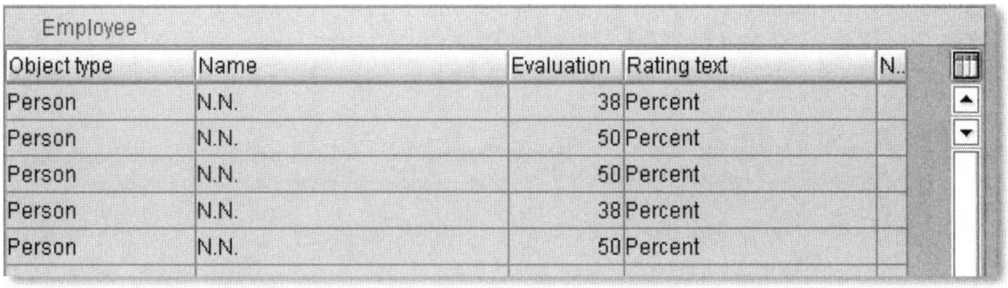

Figure 10.18 Overview of Subappraisals

Once you close all subappraisals, you can close the overall appraisal and, if necessary, perform any follow-up work (see Figure 10.19).

The organization of the group is important with a multisource appraisal. You must organize the process differently, depending on whether you perform it in SAP R/3, online with a customer-specific scenario, or offline on an appraisal form.

Name	Evaluation	Rating text	= weighting *r...	Note	Ty...	O
Bottom-Up Appraisal	38 percent		8,000		BS	5(
1. Performance Behavior	4	Adequate	4,000		BG	5(
1.1. Customer-oriented	5	Average	5,000		BK	5(
1.2. Flexibility	4	Adequate	4,000		BK	5(
1.3. Problem Solving	5	Average	5,000		BK	5(
1.4. Willingness to Learn	3	Rudimentary	3,000		BK	5(

Figure 10.19 Result of an Anonymous Multisource Appraisal

10.2.6 Reporting on Appraisals

You can report on appraisals via the menu path **Personnel Management · Personnel Development · Information System · Reports · Appraisals** (see Figure 10.20).

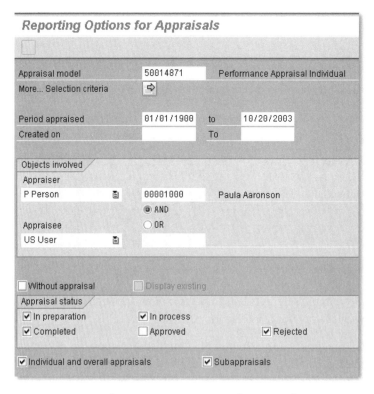

Figure 10.20 Comprehensive Reporting Options for Appraisals

You have access to various useful reports:

▶ Various overview lists with selection (by status, for example)

▶ Ranking lists

▶ Average values

▶ List of employees with an appraisal

▶ Comparison of several appraisals based on the overall results, the criteria groups, and individual criteria (see Figure 10.21)

▶ Printing the results on the appraisal form for individual employees

▶ Printing a blank appraisal form

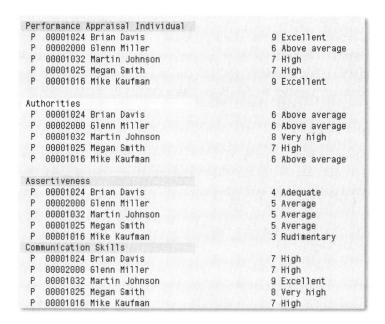

```
Performance Appraisal Individual
  P   00001024 Brian Davis            9 Excellent
  P   00002000 Glenn Miller           6 Above average
  P   00001032 Martin Johnson         7 High
  P   00001025 Megan Smith            7 High
  P   00001016 Mike Kaufman           9 Excellent

Authorities
  P   00001024 Brian Davis            6 Above average
  P   00002000 Glenn Miller           6 Above average
  P   00001032 Martin Johnson         8 Very high
  P   00001025 Megan Smith            7 High
  P   00001016 Mike Kaufman           6 Above average

Assertiveness
  P   00001024 Brian Davis            4 Adequate
  P   00002000 Glenn Miller           5 Average
  P   00001032 Martin Johnson         5 Average
  P   00001025 Megan Smith            5 Average
  P   00001016 Mike Kaufman           3 Rudimentary
Communication Skills
  P   00001024 Brian Davis            7 High
  P   00002000 Glenn Miller           7 High
  P   00001032 Martin Johnson         9 Excellent
  P   00001025 Megan Smith            8 Very high
  P   00001016 Mike Kaufman           7 High
```

Figure 10.21 Comparison of Several Appraisals

10.2.7 Process Support

Employee Self-Service (ESS)

The standard system includes the MY_APP_CREATE service for installation in mySAP Workplace or Enterprise Portal: you can use it to perform an individual appraisal with one appraiser. You can also use it as a template for the creation of more complex, customer-specific templates. We recommend that you supplement user prompts with the service. In particular, you might have to use customer-specific development to avoid multiple appraisals with anonymous appraisal models.

Manager's Desktop (MDT)

The MDT is predestined to perform and report on top-down appraisals. The standard system provides the function codes APPRAISAL_CREATE and APPRAISAL_DISPLAY, which you can easily link into customer-specific scenarios. They cover almost the entire spectrum of the assessment system.

Workflow

We recommend that you use a workflow because it noticeably improves the quality and user-friendliness of the processes. The standard workflow model, *Appraisal* (1000105, PdvAppraisal), supports the process of an employee examining an appraisal and then accepting or rejecting it. Only the use of a workflow maps the complete flow of the appraisal process, including its status, in the system. Without the workflow, it's still unclear after closing the appraisal if it has its final form or, if it must be reworked because of an employee's objection to it. However, if you still don't' want to use a workflow, you can create a convention whereby an appraisal may be closed only after an employee has accepted it.

10.3   Sample Process

Because the basic process flow is similar to that illustrated in Figure 10.3, the following example does not present a comprehensive illustration of the process. The designs are described only in text, and, where helpful, with the mapping of processes.

10.3.1   Canteen Survey

A survey on the employees' satisfaction with the company canteen (i.e., cafeteria) is one example of an employee survey that aims to evaluate the opinion of staff towards specific aspects of their employment or, towards the overall quality of the company as an employer. If the information in a survey is generally not critical (as is the case with the canteen example), you don't have to work with an anonymous appraisal model and can use standard functions to ensure that multiple appraisals do not occur. As you will see from the following, we use figures to illustrate the required system configuration of the canteen survey example.

You should combine the employees as appraisers with the canteen as the "object" being appraised. You could use object type VE ("service") from Training and Event Management to do so; however, although this approach is allowed, we have learned from experience that it leads to undesirable system behavior. Therefore, you must select a different object type. We have decided to use object type H ("external person"). The external Persons are given names such as "Main Building Canteen." Figure 10.22 shows the customizing of the appraisal form.

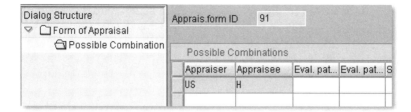

Figure 10.22 Form of Appraisal: "Canteen Appraisal"

To keep the process simple, you should handle it with an individual appraisal rather than a multisource appraisal. You can then use standard reports to calculate the average of the individual appraisals. Since we're not using an anonymous appraisal (but employees still have an option for anonymity), the result is the configuration of the appraisal model shown in Figure 10.23. Because an ESS scenario should be used whenever possible, the settings for the HTML layout are also important.

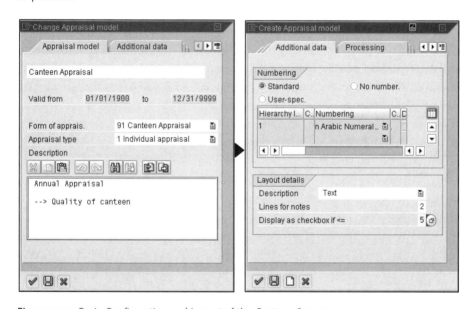

Figure 10.23 Basic Configuration and Layout of the Canteen Survey

The process should run simply and not take a lot of time, so we'll exclude options to reset and delete appraisals (see Figure 10.24). The flag "Only one appraisal allowed" must remain empty because from the view of the appraised, several appraisals will be created for each period. You can choose the scale to reflect your personal taste.

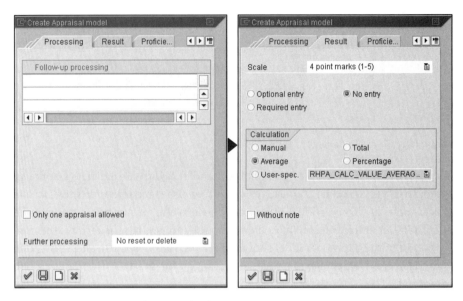

Figure 10.24 Additional Configuration for the Canteen Survey

Figure 10.25 shows the result of the configuration. The appraisal is quite simple and can be closed quickly, which makes it particularly well suited for use as a Web scenario. You can use the model provided in MY_APP_CREATE without incurring any significant changes.

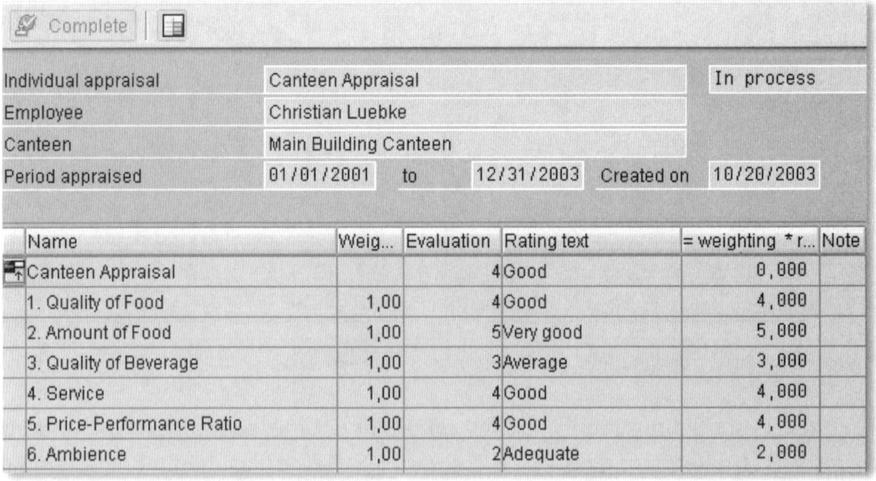

Name	Weig...	Evaluation	Rating text	= weighting * r...	Note
Canteen Appraisal		4	Good	0,000	
1. Quality of Food	1,00	4	Good	4,000	
2. Amount of Food	1,00	5	Very good	5,000	
3. Quality of Beverage	1,00	3	Average	3,000	
4. Service	1,00	4	Good	4,000	
5. Price-Performance Ratio	1,00	4	Good	4,000	
6. Ambience	1,00	2	Adequate	2,000	

Figure 10.25 Maintaining the Canteen Survey with the SAP R/3 Interface

10.3.2 Better Involvement of Employees

In practice, employees must frequently first produce a self-appraisal in preparation for an appraisal meeting. You can map this approach in mySAP HR by using a multisource appraisal. During the preparation phase, you select both the employee and the manager as appraisers, and therefore enable both to produce an appraisal. When you configure the appraisal models (multisource appraisal, non-anonymous), you must make a setting to ensure that only the last appraiser, the manager, decides on the overall appraisal. The system documents the employee's self-appraisal so that the manager can refer to it.

10.4 Critical Success Factors

In the Personnel Development processes considered so far, the critical success factors resided primarily at the level of the processes. In this chapter, the technical level involves considerations that are just as critical:

▶ Authorizations are extremely important for this kind of critical data. The following factors make an already difficult topic even more problematic (although the problems can be solved by maintaining an awareness of them):

  ▶ Many of those involved in the process work directly with the system

  ▶ Use of workflow

  ▶ Multisource appraisals

  ▶ Use of ESS

▶ A credible ability to guarantee anonymity is an important consideration with appraisals that are to be maintained with a decentralized approach (bottom-up appraisals and employee surveys). Employees also generally want to remain anonymous to the personnel department as well.

▶ The process is to be defined and communicated exactly—especially when using multisource appraisals. The preparation for appraisals should occur from a central point (HR department).

▶ Particularly when anonymity is to be ensured, it's difficult to ignore the problems that can arise when employees are asked to participate in a survey or a bottom-up appraisal more than once. The problem exists not only with decentralized online entry, but also when you use anonymous paper forms. One possible solution is to use paper forms that require the employee's name to be entered. An external service provider could then enter the data anonymously. The service provider can certainly enter the data into your own SAP R/3 system so that the anonymous data remains available at all times. In this case, the trust that employees have in the service provider is critical.

▶ As shown, problems arise most often with surveys and multisource appraisals. Typical top-down appraisals by managers aren't problematic and should therefore be used as the first appraisal type.

11   Training and Event Management

In this chapter, we describe the structure of a training catalog, the management of training participants, and the planning of resources, such as training materials and instructors. From the process view, Training and Event Management represents the completion of Personnel Development.

11.1   The Design in mySAP HR

The design of mySAP HR Training and Event Management is the foundation for understanding the structure and interplay of the individual components that constitute this design. Basic terms are explained; later, chapters build on these terms. We assume that you are already familiar with terms such as *objects* and *infotypes*. You can understand the design here best if you have already read Chapter 2, *Organizational Management*.

Training and Event Management supports the following business processes:

▶ **Preparation for business events**

  ▷ Determining the demand for business events

  ▷ Creating the business event catalog

  ▷ Planning the schedule of business events

  ▷ Planning resources

  ▷ Entering business event costs

  ▷ Budgeting training expenses

  ▷ Marketing business events

▶ **Execution of business events**

  ▷ Booking, rebooking, and canceling attendees

  ▷ Printing (or e-mailing) the required correspondence

  ▷ External invoices

  ▷ Activity allocation

  ▷ Cost transfer posting

▶ **Follow-up work for training and events**

  ▷ Appraisals of business events, instructors, and attendees

  ▷ Automatic transfer of qualifications

  ▷ Reports on business events, attendance, and resources

Figure 11.1 illustrates the essential business processes and their sequence based on an event cycle.

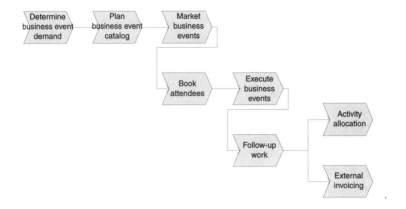

Figure 11.1 Business Processes of the Business Event Cycle

11.1.1 The Training and Event Management Structure

Training and Event Management consists of individual object types and the infotypes related to them, as is also true of Organizational Management. You use relationships within a structure—the *business event catalog*—to link the object types to each other.

In the following section, we address the object types and relationships in detail and highlight additional information as infotypes. Similar to Organizational Management, Training and Event Management also uses plan variants and number ranges. The flexibility of Training and Event Management for creating new, customer-specific object types, relationships, and infotypes is also comparable to that of Organizational Management. For more information, see Chapter 2, *Organizational Management*.

Business Event Groups

The object types of the business event group represent the highest level in the business event catalog. You structure business event groups by summarizing business event types into topically related groups such as language courses, IT training, and business courses. You can also use business event types as search terms for events in the context of Employee Self-Service (ESS).

Business Event Types

Business event types are located directly under the business event groups in the hierarchy. Business event types describe a business event, but without specifying the schedule and location. Business event types store the characteristics that will apply to all the business events that are derived from them. The result is similar to jobs in Organizational Management: the work is easier because the data in the business event types serves as proposed values for the business events that result from them. You can override the proposed value for a specific business event if desired. In detail, the proposed values can include prices, descriptions of the contents of the business event, the number of places available in a seminar, or information on the required resources. In addition, business event types provide a manageable overview of the business event catalog and form the business event hierarchy, together with business event groups and the actual business events.

Business Events

Business events are real examples of a business event type: they occur on a specific date and at a particular location. You can book attendees only for a business event, not for a business event type. You can use business event types only for prebooking possible attendees. See Section 11.2.3 for more details.

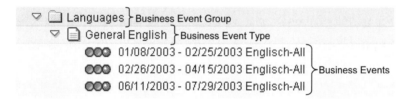

Figure 11.2 Business Event Hierarchy

Resources

First, we will explain the term *resource type*. mySAP HR Training and Event Management recognizes four resource types: *room, instructor, material* (from the material master data in logistics), and *other resources*. Resource types describe the type and specific characteristics of resources; they help to create a better overview of the resources available to enable easy manageability. You can assign resource types to business event types and therefore define the required tools. Then, you can assign the operative tools used for execution—namely, the resources—to the business events created from the business event types. If you want, you can also create additional resource types in Customizing.

Business Event Catalog

The *business event catalog* aggregates business event groups, business event types, and business events into a central tool for maintaining events. You can also make the business event catalog available to ESS users. This catalog is the basis for booking, canceling, and rebooking attendees.

11.1.2 Dynamic Menus

Training and Event Management has a total of seven dynamic menus. What makes the menus dynamic is that changes in one menu simultaneously affect all the other menus. For example, if a new business event date is set up in a business event menu, the data is displayed immediately in the **Attendance** menu.

The dynamic menus are tailored for specialized tasks that must be performed: each important functional area has its own menu. This approach enables the dynamic menus to cover the processes shown in Figure 11.1. You can store user-specific settings in the system for each of the menus. Doing so can improve performance when calling the menus; it also provides you with a better overview of the menus.

Use the SAP menu **Personnel · Training and Event Management · Settings · User-Specific Settings** to perform all settings for the dynamic menus. You can also reach the entry settings from every dynamic menu from the **Settings** menu. In this section, we will address only the control options for the dynamic menus. You can select the desired plan variant here (see Chapter 2, *Organizational Management*, for more information on plan variants). The **Dynamic Menus** tab contains an additional tab for each menu and two general tabs for filtering and sorting.

You can use the **Filter** tab to limit the display of business event groups, business event types, and business events according to specific criteria. The criteria might include the language, location, or status of the business events. Depending on how strong the division of labor is within a company, we recommend that you set up a filter for each employee, so that employees' dynamic menus show only those business events that require them to perform specific actions; for example, internal business events (see Figure 11.3). However, because the filter settings affect the view of all employees' dynamic menus, you must exercise caution when undertaking this task. Given the dynamic nature of the menus, this situation is unavoidable. Users can switch between menus quite easily; however, the structure must always remain the same.

If the default sorting performed in the menus does not satisfy the requirements of users, they can simply change the sorting criteria with user-specific settings on the **Sort order** tab (see Figure 11.4). Users can select sorting criteria based on business event groups and business event types; they can also select criteria for attendees and arrange the criteria into any sequence.

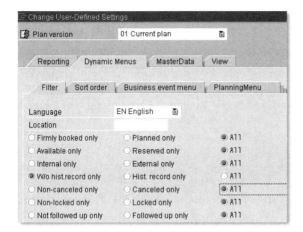

Figure 11.3 User-Specific Settings on the Filter Tab

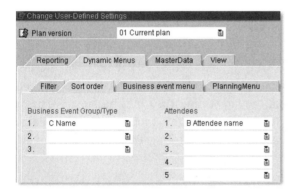

Figure 11.4 User-Specific Settings on the Sort Order Tab

These settings also apply globally to all dynamic menus for each user. You can also make the following settings for individual menus:

▶ **Initial access period in the menu**
Displays all the objects of a menu that are valid in this period.

▶ **Initial access by a specific business event group or type**
You can make this setting for the **Business Event**, **Planning**, and **Tool** menus.

▶ **Initial access by specific resources (and types)**
You can make this setting only for the **Resource** menu.

Business Event Menu

You create and change business events and manage business events in the **Business Event** menu. You can create, book, cancel, lock, unlock, and perform follow-up work for business events. From the **Business Event** menu, you can perform all the activities required for the Billing and Clearing of business event fees and costs. Using the **Business Event** menu, you can branch directly to the **Attendance** menu because the activities for both of these menus are closely related. The attendees booked for a business event are displayed for informational purposes. For more information on the individual features of the **Business Event** menu, see Section 11.2.1.

Attendance Menu

The **Attendance** menu enables you to access the business events previously created in the **Business Event** menu. It books attendees for the business events, adds them to waiting lists, prebooks attendance (for event types), cancels reservations, rebooks attendees, and so on. From this menu, you can also generate correspondence and display a correspondence history, an overview of the letters (or e-mails or faxes) already sent in relation to a business event. You can also start an attendee appraisal of a seminar from the **Attendance** menu.

Information Menu

In some ways, the **Information** menu is the reporting system for Training and Event Management. Starting from the target object (such as business events or attendees), you can generate specific reports. You can report on individual attendees, resources, and business events. The following list contains some of the available options :

▶ Attendances

  ▶ Attendee list

  ▶ Attendance list

  ▶ Bookings per attendee

  ▶ Attendee's training history

▶ Resources

  ▶ Resource reservation

  ▶ Resource equipment

▶ Business events

  ▶ Business event appraisals

  ▶ Attendance statistics

  ▶ Material requirements per business event

  ▶ Business event brochure

Planning Menu

Unlike the **Business Event** menu, the **Planning** menu enables you to create simultaneously several business events of one type based on supporting information from the system. Planning can involve the various criteria to determine the quantity and dates of the business events being planned:

▶ Determine demand from prebookings

▶ Determine demand from bookings in the previous year

▶ Transfer demand from the previous year's planning

See Section 11.2.2 for additional information on the **Planning** menu.

Tool Menu

You can display and change several infotypes of objects in Training and Event Management (business event groups, business event types, and business events) from the **Tool** menu. However, you cannot create new objects from the **Tool** menu: you must use the Master Data catalog instead. The Tool menu's special feature is its marking function, which enables you to mark several objects and edit their data simultaneously. With this feature, you can enter specific facts (such as a price increase) that affect several business event types immediately. The **Tool** menu is also the only menu from which you can translate language-dependent objects of Training and Event Management. This capability lets you use a business event catalog for several national offices and display the catalog in the local language.

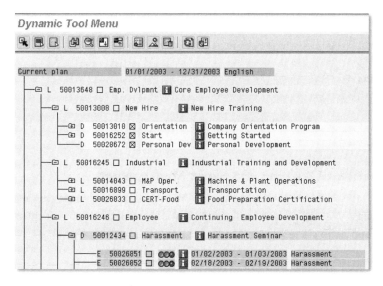

Figure 11.5 Dynamic Tool Menu

Resource Menu and Room Reservation Management

Because rooms are a resource type, we will discuss **Room Reservation Management** and the **Resource** menu here. When you use the same plan variant for Room Reservation Management that you use for Training and Event Management, you can simultaneously use the resources of resource type "room" that you have created in both areas. The **Resource** menu initially structures the resources beneath the corresponding resource types. From the **Resource** menu, you can create new resources and change or block existing resources. Users can also create an overview of reservations or, the availability of a resource. See Section 11.2.2 for more information on the **Resource** menu.

Master Data Catalog

You create the structure of business event groups and business event types in the *master data catalog*. You can create business event groups, business event types, and the relationships between both objects efficiently only in this menu. Just as you created the organizational structure in Organizational Management, you create the structure of the master data catalog so that subsequent objects are created from a root object. The system proposes the possible objects and automatically creates the relationships between the objects. For more information on the structure of the master data catalog, see Section 11.2.1.

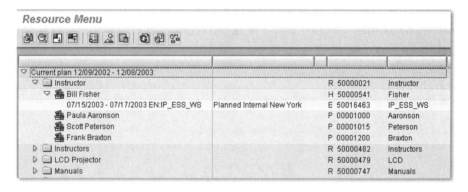

Figure 11.6 Resource Menu

11.1.3 Integration of Training and Event Management

Figure 11.7 illustrates just how tightly integrated Training and Event Management is with other areas. We will now discuss individual aspects and what you must keep in mind when setting them up.

Figure 11.7 Integration Aspects in Training and Event Management

Sales & Distribution

Integration with Sales & Distribution (SD) allows you to use a report to generate invoices for attendance at a business event. In addition to activating integration in Customizing, a precondition requires setting a flag that indicates that the bookings are to be invoiced. To do so, you use the function book + fee when booking an attendee. The attendee must be created as an external person in the system and have an address. SD must also have a corresponding record for customer master data. After you call a report from Training and Event Management, you use an invoicing interface in SD to create invoices and then transfer the invoice to Financials (FI) if it is present. You can also activate integration in Customizing via the IMG path **Training and Event Management · Integration · Billing and Clearing · Invoicing · Wizard**. The Wizard guides you through the required settings step-by-step.

Knowledge Warehouse

You can use infotype 1062, "Knowledge Link," to create a link between business event types and business events to InfoObjects in the SAP Knowledge Warehouse

(SAP KW). For example, you can also store the training materials for a business event type and make them available to prepare for the actual course. From the dynamic **Business Event** menu, you can begin with a business event or a business event type and use the context menu (right mouse button) entry **Knowledge Link** to call the corresponding InfoObject. Doing so presupposes that you are already using SAP KW.

Personnel Administration

When you book internal attendees, you also create a relationship between the business event as an object type of Training and Event Management and the external object of the person. Depending on the authorizations in force, you can access the employee's master data from the dynamic menus. You can also link internal persons listed in Personnel Administration to a business event as an "instructor" resource.

Organizational Management

In addition to specifying persons, you can use Training and Event Management to specify organizational units as attendees and instructors. When you book an entire organizational unit for a business event, you also indirectly book the persons assigned to the organizational unit because of inheritance.

Time Management

When integration with Time Management is active and you book an internal attendee, the system verifies if an employee is available during the training period. You can activate integration with Time Management in Customizing via the IMG path **Training and Event Management · Integration · Time Management · Integration yes or no?** Set the Group switch PLOGI (**Group**) and TIME (**Sem. abbr.**) to "X" (see Figure 11.8).

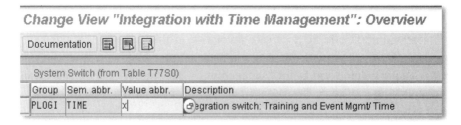

Figure 11.8 Activating Integration with Time Management

You use the next Customizing activity to define incompatible attendances and absences. In this context, *incompatible* means that when these attendances and absences are present, you cannot book an attendee for this period. Here, you set the attendance types and absence types from Time Management that are incompatible with bookings from Training and Event Management (A = attendance as an instructor; B = attendance at a business event (see Figure 11.9). The default setting, $$$$, stands for days off according to the employee's schedule. In other words, if the employee's schedule indicates a day off (Saturday, for example), an incompatible absence results: the employee is unavailable for the day on which the business event is scheduled. This feature requires full maintenance of the Time Management settings in master data.

You can also override the setting for each business event type. You can use infotype 1029, "Info Business Event Type" (see the remarks on Figure 11.30) to turn off the check for days off and therefore enable the booking of an employee for a business event that occurs over the weekend.

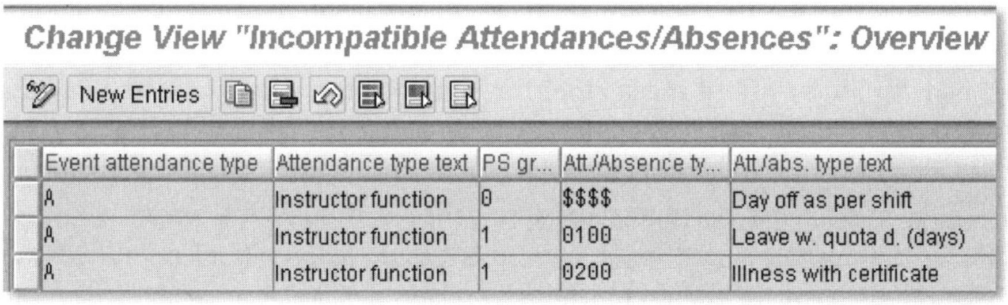

Change View "Incompatible Attendances/Absences": Overview

New Entries

Event attendance type	Attendance type text	PS gr...	Att./Absence ty...	Att./abs. type text
A	Instructor function	0	$$$$	Day off as per shift
A	Instructor function	1	0100	Leave w. quota d. (days)
A	Instructor function	1	0200	Illness with certificate

Figure 11.9 Defining Incompatible Attendances and Absences

In addition to checking for conflicting attendances and absences, you can use the booking to have the system automatically generate an entry in the master data of Time Management for the internal instructor or attendee. Because attendance at training events is maintained in mySAP HR Time Management as attendance (infotype 2002), the system can also create an attendance when you perform a booking.

You make the appropriate settings via the Customizing (IMG) path **Training and Event Management · Integration · Time Management · Specify Attendance Types**. For a business event, the table can specify an attendance type for instructors and another attendance type for attendees: (**Group** SEMIN, **Sem. abbr.** AINST or APART). From the viewpoint of master data in Time Management, note that an attendance record is created for every day of the business event—not just one record for the entire period. This approach is required for an automatic cancellation should the employee break off his or her attendance early, for example, because of illness.

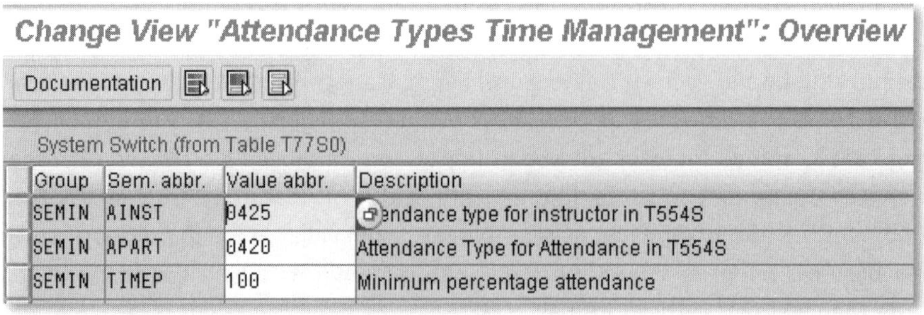

Figure 11.10 Generating Activation of Attendances

If you have already booked an employee successfully and generated the attendances for the period and the employee becomes ill, which requires entry of an absence via infotype 2001, you can specify a percentage for the semantic abbreviation that sets whether and when the attendance should be automatically cancelled. Example: an employee is booked for a business event that occurs from Monday to Friday, which means that the system automatically creates five data records of infotype 2002, "Attendances." The employee takes a vacation day for the first day of training, Monday, which deletes one attendance record. If the value for the minimal percentage of attendance is at 80%, the system does not cancel the employee's participation because the employee will still attend 80% of the business event. If the employee also takes Tuesday as a vacation day, the booking is automatically cancelled in Training and Event Management. An important note: recreating the previously deleted attendances in time management does not annul the cancellation in event management.

If you want to use this type of automation in your company, the department responsible for entering attendances and absences must be notified that the entry of an absence and the deletion of an attendance can effect a cancellation in Training and Event Management. Messages and plausibility checks should also be used in the maintenance of master data to ensure that the cancellations are not triggered inadvertently.

Materials Management

Integration also enables you to access materials from the material master data in SAP Materials Management from within Training and Event Management. Doing so requires use of a dialog-controlled tool, a Wizard. You can navigate to the Wizard in Customizing via the IMG path **Training and Event Management · Integration · Materials Management · Wizard** and then make all the necessary settings to integrate Training and Event Management with Materials Management.

Personnel Development

As we explained in Chapter 8, *Skill Management*, you can define specific qualifications as requirements for participation in a business event. You can also specify the qualifications imparted by attending each business event.

To enable the first of those aspects, you can store the qualifications required for a business event, with relationship A 029 "presupposes" (see Figure 11.11). This relationship links all the qualifications and the required characteristics that a potential attendee must fulfill to be allowed to attend the training. You can either initiate the relationship directly, by using the master data catalog when you create a business event type, or initiate the relationship later on.

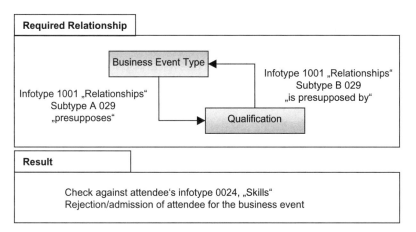

Figure 11.11 Checking the Required Qualifications of an Attendee

After a business event is completed, you can use *follow-up actions* to transfer the qualifications with their proficiency values stored in the business event to the attendees. You must have already made Customizing settings via the IMG path **Training and Event Management · Recurring activities · Follow-Up Processing** (see Figure 11.12). Here you set the actions to be performed during the follow-up processing of a business event. The settings depend on the "Attendee type" (Organizational unit, Person, External person, and so on).

By default, the decisive column for transferring qualifications is active only for attendee type "Person." If you want to transfer qualifications for other types of attendees, make the appropriate settings in this table. Transfer of qualifications occurs with the creation of data records of infotype 0024, "Skills," in the personnel master data record of the attendee. All the qualifications created with relationship A 028, "imparts"—between the business event types and the qualifications (see Figure 11.13) that are selected in the follow-up processing—are transferred.

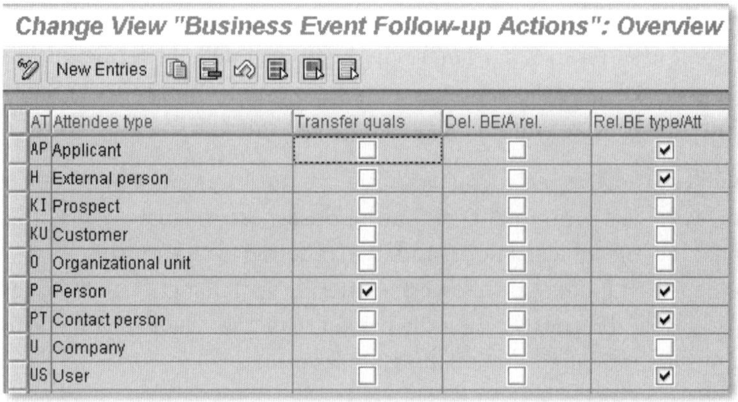

Change View "Business Event Follow-up Actions": Overview

AT	Attendee type	Transfer quals	Del. BE/A rel.	Rel.BE type/Att
AP	Applicant	☐	☐	☑
H	External person	☐	☐	☑
KI	Prospect	☐	☐	☐
KU	Customer	☐	☐	☐
O	Organizational unit	☐	☐	☐
P	Person	☑	☐	☑
PT	Contact person	☐	☐	☑
U	Company	☐	☐	☐
US	User	☐	☐	☑

Figure 11.12 Business Event Follow-Up Actions

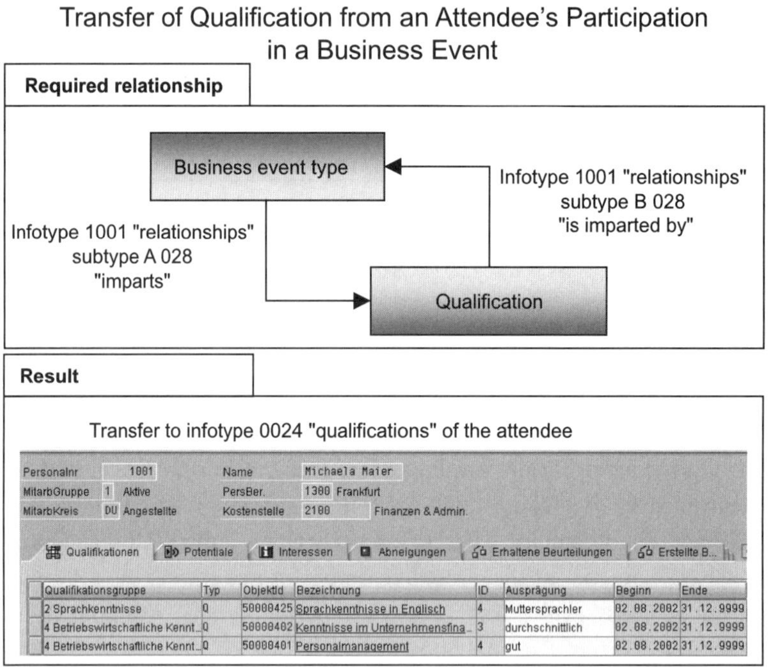

Figure 11.13 Transfer of Qualifications from an Attendee's Participation in a Business Event

If a profile comparison in *Skill Management* (see Chapter 8, *Skill Management*), reveals gaps between the required qualifications (such as from a position) and the available qualifications, the system can automatically generate proposals for training events. This also occurs on the basis of the qualifications to be imparted, as stored in Training and Event Management (see the required relationship in Figure 11.13).

Controlling

Integration between SAP Controlling (SAP CO) and Training and Event Management enables you to allocate the costs of business events and instructors internally with Training and Event Management. The attendance fees are posted to the cost centers of the attendees, and the cost center of personnel development is credited. However, activity allocation for instructional activity debits the cost center of personnel development and credits the cost center of the internal instructor. You can find all the settings for activating integration with controlling with Customizing (IMG path) **Training and Event Management · Integration · Billing and Activity Allocation · Activity Allocation · Wizard**:

▶ Activity allocation switch
  Simply check "yes" or "no" here.

▶ Define number range
  You must create a number range interval for the reference documents of internal activity allocation in Training and Event Management. You can use the reference document number in Controlling to find the original document for this procedure. The number range for HRTEM reference documents is valid not only for internal activity allocation, but also for invoicing, cost-transfer posting, and material orders in Training and Event Management.

▶ Controlling area selection
  Internal activity allocation must occur within a controlling area because all internal allocations refer only to the accounting objects of that controlling area.

▶ Select cost center
  You can use a specific evaluation path to determine the cost center of the cost objects for internal activity allocation and for cost-transfer posting. The cost center of the organizer, such as an organizational unit, is selected by default (generally the cost center of personnel development). If the evaluation path does not find a cost center, the default cost center is used.

▶ Define cost elements
  Cost elements document which kind of (and at which level) costs have been incurred within a Billing period. A secondary cost element must be stored with the activity type to capture costs with activity allocation. Verify if a suitable cost element is available. You must also assign an appropriate cost element type to the cost element. Cost element Type 43 must be maintained as a precondition for internal activity allocation (see Figure 11.14).

▶ Define activity type
  Internal activity allocation uses activity types for allocation. When you specify the evaluation path, you can also define the activity types for attendees and

instructors. If an evaluation path fails to find any activity types, the system uses the activity types stored here. In Training and Event Management, planning the price of the sender cost center with the activity type will suffice. The activity type sets the activity unit used to capture quantity and the price used to valuate the activity quantities. Note: The activity type for activities in Training and Event Management must always be set to "1." Remember that the evaluation path specified here is also used for invoicing because the data that is relevant to the invoice is also stored in infotype 1037, "Billing/allocation info" (see Figure 11.15).

CO Area	Cost Ele...	Name	Long Text
1000	611000	DAA Setup	Dir. Int. Act. Alloc. Setup producti
1000	612000	Internal acty alloc.	Internal activity allocation
1000	613000	DAA Setup Auxilary	Dir. Int. Act. Alloc. Setup Auxilary
1000	614000	DAA Intern. Transp.	Dir. Int. Act. Alloc. Internal Transp
1000	614500	Internal travel	Internal travel services
1000	615000	DAA Repair Hours	Dir.Int.Activity Alloc. Repair Hours
1000	615500	Dir.ActyAll.:Quality	Direct activity allocation: quality
1000	616000	DAA Inspection	Dir. Int. Act. Alloc. Inspection

Back   Continue   Cancel

Figure 11.14 Cost Elements for Activity Allocation

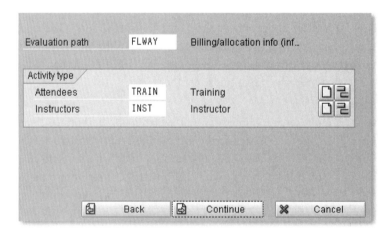

Figure 11.15 Defining the Entry of Activity Types

In addition to internal activity allocation, you can also perform cost-transfer postings to determine the costs of a business event and transfer them to Controlling. The costs determined are based on cost items assigned to the business event type or the business event and to the resource types or the resources. Cost-transfer posting credits the cost centers of the resources and debits the cost centers of the organizer (e.g., personnel development).

If you want to use both internal activity allocation and cost-transfer posting, some settings will overlap—the settings were already entered for internal activity allocation. Accordingly, the following settings address only the peculiarities of cost-transfer postings. The settings for transfers are made with a Wizard found at **Training and Event Management · Integration · Billing and Activity Allocation · Cost Transfer Posting · Wizard**.

You can create a cost item as shown in Figure 11.16 via the IMG path **Training and Event Management · Business Event Preparation · Define Cost Items**.

The costs of the business event are identified by cost items and transferred to Controlling based on the cost elements stored in the cost items. A transfer of costs requires that the cost items be defined as relevant to transfers and assigned to a primary cost element.

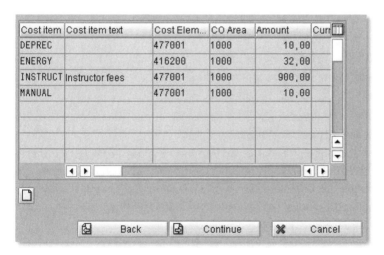

Cost item	Cost item text	Cost Elem...	CO Area	Amount	Curr
DEPREC		477001	1000	10,00	
ENERGY		416200	1000	32,00	
INSTRUCT	Instructor fees	477001	1000	900,00	
MANUAL		477001	1000	10,00	

Back   Continue   Cancel

Figure 11.16 Creating a Cost Item

Workflow

In Training and Event Management, you should always consider the use of workflow. Even mapping an approval process in the system can lighten the load on the HR department because the process has to cycle through the departments until it leads to a result. Furthermore, workflow can also significantly improve communication between attendees and the training department, especially regarding cancellations or rebookings. Chapter 5, *The SAP Business Workflow*, describes the technical preconditions for starting a workflow for mySAP HR Training and Event Management. The standard delivery of mySAP HR includes some sample workflows for Training and Event Management. The samples are intended for Employee Self-Service (ESS) because it allows employees to access the business event catalog online and select the business events they want. The following workflows are available as standard:

Correspondence Error Handling

You can use the Correspondence Error Handling workflow (ERROR PD-SCM) to inform employees that the automatic output of correspondence did not run without any errors. The employees responsible receive a message in their inboxes and can then output the correspondence manually. The WORKF ACTIV switch in table T77S0 must be activated (value "X").

The workflow is started when one of the following problems occurs:

▶ Missing authorization

▶ Missing parameters (plan variant, notification abbreviation, and so on)

▶ Missing form

▶ Form not permitted for the user (user group)

▶ Incorrect recipient

▶ Missing address/Name of the output medium

▶ Missing data of mandatory text variables

Approve Employee's Attendance Booking

You can approve and book attendance that employees may not book for themselves with this workflow. You can use this workflow for the "training center" in ESS. This ESS enables employees to display their Training Center and book themselves or, apply for a booking for a business event. See Chapter 4, *Portals in mySAP HR*, for more information on ESS.

The workflow is triggered when an employee—who does not have booking authorization—attempts to book attendance with ESS. Figure 11.17 illustrates the default workflow steps that result.

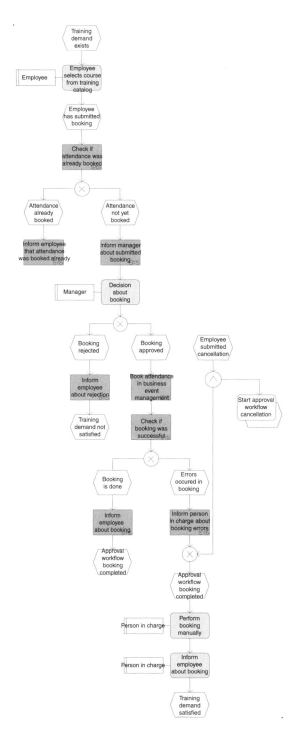

Figure 11.17 Approval Workflow: Booking 1

A work item for the employee's manager is generated; the manager can use it to approve or reject attendance at the business event:

▶ If the manager approves attendance, the attendance is automatically booked. The system then checks to see if the booking was successful. If it was, it sends the employee an e-mail to that effect. However, if an error occurs, a work item is generated for the employee responsible. Attendance can be booked manually from the work item.

▶ If the manager rejects attendance, the system sends the employee an e-mail stating that the manager has not approved the attendance.

Cancellation of a booking in the "Approve employee's attendance cancellation" workflow is similar to the approval of a booking. You can also stop an approval workflow for the booking by triggering an approval workflow for cancellation (see Figure 11.17).

Approve employee's attendance cancellation

This workflow is also triggered if an employee attempts to perform a cancellation in ESS without the required authorization. The workflow first checks to see if the attendance to be cancelled has actually been booked or merely requested. If the attendance should have been requested, it is deleted without requiring the approval of a manager (see Figure 11.17). The attendee receives a notification that the requested attendance was cancelled. The approval workflow that was previously started for the requested booking ends at the same time.

Bookings that require approval also require approval for cancellation. The system reads the cancellation data on the attendee and generates a work item for the employee's manager. The manager can the use the work item to approve or reject the cancellation:

▶ If the manager approves the cancellation, the attendance is automatically deleted; an e-mail informs the employee of the deletion.

▶ If the manager rejects the cancellation, an e-mail informs the employee of the decision.

To determine the cancellation fees, the system checks the availability of a customer enhancement (business add-in HRTEM00NET_WEBST), which it uses to determine the valid reasons for a cancellation. If no such customer enhancement is present, the system uses the cancellation reason set with Customizing (IMG path) **Training and Event Management · Employee Self-Service (ESS) · Set Up Control Element for ESS** with the switch: SEMIN (**Group**) WEBST (**Sem. abbr.**) (see Figure 11.18).

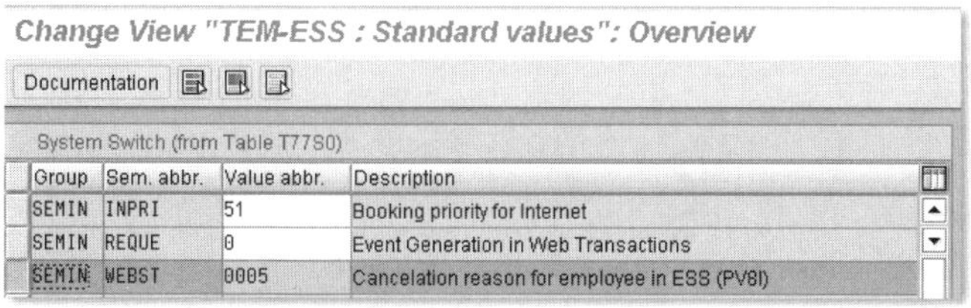
Change View "TEM-ESS : Standard values": Overview

Documentation

System Switch (from Table T77S0)

Group	Sem. abbr.	Value abbr.	Description
SEMIN	INPRI	51	Booking priority for Internet
SEMIN	REQUE	0	Event Generation in Web Transactions
SEMIN	WEBST	0005	Cancelation reason for employee in ESS (PV8I)

Figure 11.18 Default Cancellation Reason for ESS

If no reason for a cancellation exists, the system uses switch SEMIN CCDEL (proposed value for cancellation fees), which you can call with Customizing (IMG path) **Training and Event Management · Day-to-Day Activities · Canceling Attendance · Control data**.

That location, however, does not store a reason for cancellation; it stores a percentage that defines the portion of the overall fee that is to be charged as a cancellation fee. For more information on creating a reason for cancellation, see Section 11.2.3. The approval workflow for the cancellation ends prematurely when the attendee reuses "training center" in ESS to request attendance at the business event for which a cancellation was requested.

R/3 Appointment Calendar

The last integration consideration is that of Training and Event Management with the R/3 appointment calendar: follow the **SAP menu Office · Appointment Calendar · Owner**. If the internal mail system and internal calendar or, ESS for Training and Event Management and the ESS calendar are used, you can automatically enter the appointments for attendees and instructors into the R/3 appointment calendar.

You activate integration with Customizing via the IMG path **Training and Event Management · Integration · Appointment Calendar · Integration yes or no?**. To switch on integration, enter a "1" in the **Value abbr.** field for group PLOGI and semantic abbreviation APPNT. To be able to create appointments, you must first create appointment types for instructors and attendees with Customizing via the IMG path **Basis · Basis Services · Generic Business Tools · Appointment Calendar · Maintain Appointment Types** (**SAP Web Application Server · Basis-Services ·** ... in SAP R/3 4.7).

When defining the appointment types, you must adhere to the customer name space of Y* or Z*. You can require the entry of a title when an appointment is created. You can also define actions that the user may not perform when using the appointment calendar within and outside of SAP R/3 (in ESS, for example: see Figure 11.19).

Figure 11.19 Defining Appointment Type "Training Attendance"

You then use **Training and Event Management · Integration · Appointment Calendar · Specify Appointment Types** to assign the appropriate appointment types to the attendance and instructor activities (see Figure 11.20).

Group	Sem. abbr.	Value abbr.	Description
SEMIN	TINST	ZINSTRUCT	Date type for instructor function
SEMIN	TPART	ZATTENDANC	Date type for business event attendance

Figure 11.20 Assigning the Appointment Types

So that the system can assign SAP or ESS users to the booked attendee (usually a person from personnel master data) and enhance the users with their appointment calendars, you must create a link between the personnel master data and the users. You do this with infotype 0105, "Communication" (subtype 0001) in the master data (see Figure 11.21).

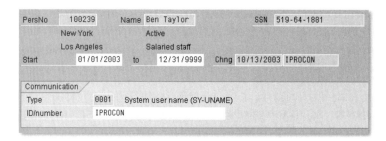

Figure 11.21 Infotype 0105: "Communication"

Once all the preconditions have been fulfilled, the system can enter the corresponding appointment in the personal appointment calendars of an attendee or instructor (see Figure 11.27). If the training event is cancelled, the appointment that was entered automatically in the appointment calendar disappears.

In actual practice, most companies do *not* use the mySAP mailing system and mySAP appointment calendar as their default mail system; the use of automatic appointment maintenance is only recommended when the appointments from the SAP tools are immediately loaded or transferred into the mail software that the company actually uses. You can synchronize the entries in the SAP tools with the calendar in Microsoft Outlook, for example, with less effort than is required to implement the solution on its own in mySAP HR.

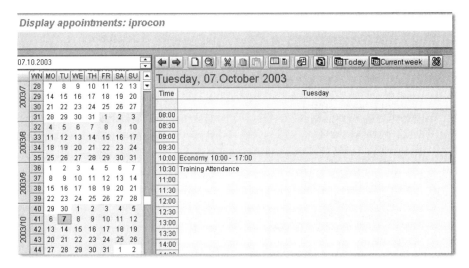

Figure 11.22 Automatic Entry in the Appointment Calendar

11.2 Realization in mySAP HR

11.2.1 Setting Up the Training Catalog

Before you can set up the training catalog in the system, you must consider the structure of training in the company. Typically, the objects that you use to structure the training catalog (business event groups and business event types) should suffice—particularly because you can group several business event groups one under the other.

You maintain the training catalog with the master data catalog of mySAP HR Training and Event Management: follow the SAP menu **Personnel · Training and Event Management · Settings · Current Settings · Master Data Catalog**. To understand the structure of the training catalog, you must understand terms such as object types, relationships, and infotypes. See Chapter 2, *Organizational Management*, for detailed information on these terms.

The creation of many business event groups and types on the highest level can lead to poor performance when calling dynamic menus, because they always directly display the highest level. Therefore, to improve performance, you can link all the business event types at the highest level to a virtual business event group.

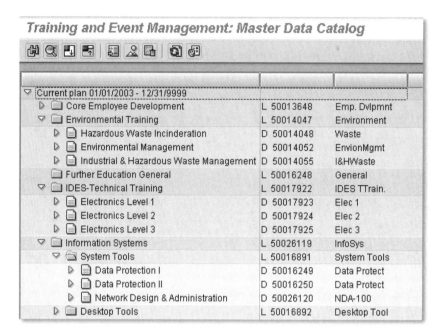

Training and Event Management: Master Data Catalog

▽ Current plan 01/01/2003 - 12/31/9999		
▷ ☐ Core Employee Development	L 50013648	Emp. Dvlpmnt
▽ ☐ Environmental Training	L 50014047	Environment
▷ 🗎 Hazardous Waste Incinderation	D 50014048	Waste
▷ 🗎 Environmental Management	D 50014052	EnvionMgmt
▷ 🗎 Industrial & Hazardous Waste Management	D 50014055	I&HWaste
☐ Further Education General	L 50016248	General
▽ ☐ IDES-Technical Training	L 50017922	IDES TTrain.
▷ 🗎 Electronics Level 1	D 50017923	Elec 1
▷ 🗎 Electronics Level 2	D 50017924	Elec 2
▷ 🗎 Electronics Level 3	D 50017925	Elec 3
▽ ☐ Information Systems	L 50026119	InfoSys
▽ 🗀 System Tools	L 50016891	System Tools
▷ 🗎 Data Protection I	D 50016249	Data Protect
▷ 🗎 Data Protection II	D 50016250	Data Protect
▷ 🗎 Network Design & Administration	D 50026120	NDA-100
▷ ☐ Desktop Tools	L 50016892	Desktop Tool

Figure 11.23 Master Data Catalog

Navigate through Customizing (IMG path) **Training and Event Management ·
Basic Settings · Dialog Control · Technical Settings · Dynamic Menus** to arrive
at table T77S0, which specifies a switch for the ID of a virtual business event
group created specifically for such a link (entry SEMIN – LROOT). The business
event hierarchy of the dynamic menus does not display this business event group.

You then link all the business event groups and types of the highest level with
relationship B003, "belongs to," to the virtual business event group. If the relationship is not created, the unlinked business event groups and types are invisible
in the hierarchy. When you use the virtual business event group, its ID is automatically considered as a proposed value when you create new business event groups
and types for the "belongs to" relationship.

Creating Business Event Groups

You first create business event groups, starting with the plan variant, "current
plan." Whenever you create an object in Training and Event Management from a
dynamic menu, the system starts a personnel action in the background. *Personnel
actions* are combinations of logically connected infotypes that are used for processing in an exactly defined sequence. Consider the creation of a business event
group as an example—it executes personnel action "L" by default.

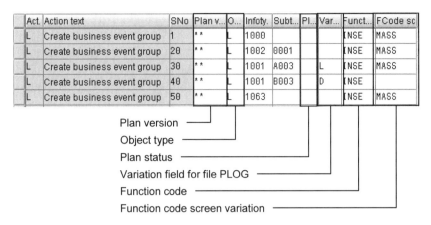

Act.	Action text	SNo	Plan v...	O...	Infoty.	Subt...	Pl...	Var...	Funct...	FCode sc
L	Create business event group	1	* *	L	1000				INSE	MASS
L	Create business event group	20	* *	L	1002	0001			INSE	MASS
L	Create business event group	30	* *	L	1001	A003		L	INSE	MASS
L	Create business event group	40	* *	L	1001	B003		D	INSE	
L	Create business event group	50	* *	L	1063				INSE	MASS

Plan version
Object type
Plan status
Variation field for file PLOG
Function code
Function code screen variation

Figure 11.24 Personnel Action "Create Business Event Group"

The settings shown in Figure 11.24 ensure that when you create a business event group from the master data catalog, the system offers infotypes for creation (see Figure 11.25). You can also change the setting if you wish to create an additional infotype when creating a business event group or with another object, for example. Remember that infotype 1000, "Object," must be the first infotype available in the personnel action.

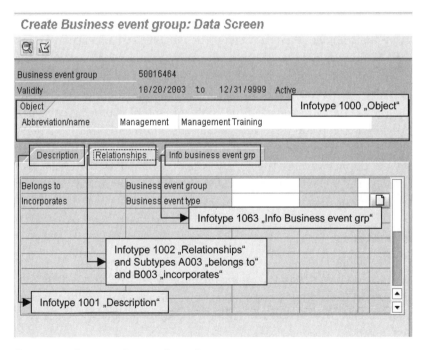

Figure 11.25 Creating a Business Event Group

When you create objects from the master data catalog, it's important to know that their starting date is automatically set to the starting date for the plan variant that you have selected. An ending date of December 31, 9999 always appears by default. The default includes infotype 1000, "Object," and a "Description," infotype 1002, that can also be called in Employee Self-Service. This text should be a short description of the business event types contained in the business event group. A good description makes things easier for attendees when they search for a business event later on. As a rule, the system automatically populates infotype 1002, "Relationships": as soon as you create a business event type, the system creates relationship B 0003, "incorporates."

As noted briefly in Section 11.1.1, the training catalog and the entire business event catalog can be made available to ESS users. If you want to do so for a business event group, you must check the "subject area" in infotype 1063, "Info Business event grp." After defining your event groups, you must subdivide them by creating business event types because you can only create actual business events under the event types.

Creating Business Event Types

To create business event types within the master data catalog, you must begin at a business event group. Open the **context** menu and select **Create Lower Level**. You then can select a business event group or a business event type. This option lets you store the complete training catalog. The default personnel action for the creation of a business event type supports the infotypes described below. In the following, we highlight the infotypes and their peculiarities, unless earlier sections have already done so. If you don't choose to use an existing business event type as a template ("Create by Copying" in the context menu of another event type), all the infotypes are empty at first. Note that all the information that has already been specified for a business event type is transferred as proposed values when you create the business events later on. This feature simplifies the creation of business events. The following descriptions of infotypes relates to the creation of business events in the dynamic business event menu.

Selected Infotypes

Infotype 1000: "Object"

This is the short and long description of the business event type. The system notifies you if the short description is not unique; however, you can override the notification. Nevertheless, you should avoid using a short description twice because it is displayed in various lists and in ESS.

Infotype 1001: "Description"

Maintenance of the description is particularly relevant in the context of using ESS with Training and Event Management. The data stored here can be used later by users of ESS to help locate the correct business event. Moreover, it is used to create the "Business Event Brochure" (menu path **Training and Event Management · Information System · Reports · Business Events · Business Event Brochure**.

Infotype 1042: "Schedule Model"

When you create business event types, you must also create a main schedule model, a subtype of infotype 1042. The schedule model describes the time associated with a business event: its duration in days, the start day, and the times it begins and ends each day. You have three options when storing the schedule:

1. **Schedule with pattern**

   In Customizing, follow the IMG path **Training and Event Management · Business Event Preparation · Define Schedule** to Create a Schedule Pattern. The schedule pattern is then assigned to the business event type, which means that it therefore determines the schedule model of the business event type (see Figure 11.26). You can also select a preferred start day if you don't want the business event to start on just any day. To determine that the course is split into several parts that occur at a certain interval, you can check the **Multiple dates** checkbox. For example, you can use this option to map language courses that run for a long time (perhaps as long as a year) and meet once a week.

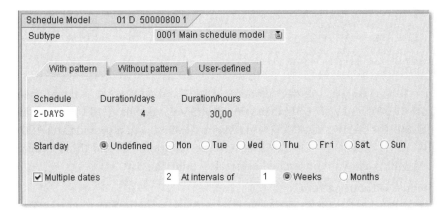

Figure 11.26 Schedule with Pattern (Business Event Type)

The following explains how you compose such a schedule pattern. At first, a schedule model consists of individual day schedules (see Figure 11.27). The number of day schedules determines the number of days within a schedule. You also define a *day segment* for each individual day schedule. You set starting and ending times for each day in the day segments. A simple example provides the most clarity. The day number sets how many days the schedule comprises: two days in Figure 11.27. Detailed information on the day's schedule is hidden behind the day segments assigned here. For the schedule 2-DAYS, the day segment of the first day is defined as SPAET and the day segment of the second day is defined as NORMAL.

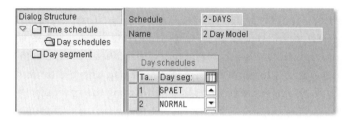

Figure 11.27 Day Schedules: 2-DAYS

Day segment	Start 1	End TB 1	Start 2	End TB 2	Start 3	End TB 3	Dauer
08001300	08:00:00	13:00:00	00:00:00	00:00:00	00:00:00	00:00:00	05:00:00
ABEND	17:00:00	19:00:00	00:00:00	00:00:00	00:00:00	00:00:00	02:00:00
FIRST	09:30:00	12:00:00	13:00:00	16:30:00	00:00:00	00:00:00	06:00:00
FRUEH	08:00:00	09:00:00	00:00:00	00:00:00	00:00:00	00:00:00	01:00:00
LAST	08:30:00	12:00:00	13:00:00	14:30:00	00:00:00	00:00:00	05:00:00
MIDDLE	08:30:00	12:00:00	13:00:00	16:30:00	00:00:00	00:00:00	07:00:00
NACHMITT	13:00:00	17:00:00	00:00:00	00:00:00	00:00:00	00:00:00	04:00:00
NORMAL	09:00:00	17:00:00	00:00:00	00:00:00	00:00:00	00:00:00	08:00:00
SPAET	10:00:00	17:00:00	00:00:00	00:00:00	00:00:00	00:00:00	07:00:00
SPMITTAG	15:00:00	19:00:00	00:00:00	00:00:00	00:00:00	00:00:00	04:00:00
VORMITT	09:00:00	12:00:00	00:00:00	00:00:00	00:00:00	00:00:00	03:00:00

Figure 11.28 Day Segment: NORMAL and SPAET

If you look closely at the day segments, SPAET and NORMAL, in detail, (see Figure 11.28), you will see that the first day (SPAET) begins at 10:00 and ends at 17:00. The second day (NORMAL) begins at 09:00 and also ends at 17:00. Within a day segment, you can specify three starting times and three ending times, which allows you to schedule breaks during the day.

2. **Schedule without pattern**
   Here you specify only the duration in days and hours, along with the day of the week on which the business event begins. This option is not appropriate for business events that consist of several dates on given intervals.

3. **User-defined schedule**
   Similar to specifications in a schedule pattern, you can enter day types and day segments here. Use this option when you need an unusual schedule, but don't want to expend the effort required to create a schedule pattern in Customizing.

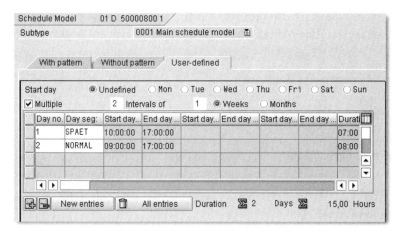

Schedule Model	01 D 50000800 1									
Subtype	0001 Main schedule model 🖹									

With pattern | Without pattern | User-defined

Start day ⦿ Undefined ○ Mon ○ Tue ○ Wed ○ Thu ○ Fri ○ Sat ○ Sun
☑ Multiple 2 Intervals of 1 ⦿ Weeks ○ Months

Day no.	Day seg:	Start day...	End day...	Start day...	End day...	Start day...	End day...	Durati
1	SPAET	10:00:00	17:00:00					07:00
2	NORMAL	09:00:00	17:00:00					08:00

New entries 🗑 All entries | Duration ∑ 2 | Days ∑ | 15,00 Hours

Figure 11.29 User-Defined Schedule

Infotype 1024: "Capacity"

You can use the capacity to set how many attendees can participate in a business event. You can also specify a minimum capacity (number of participants) if you would like to be able to cancel a business event because of low attendance. You can also use a field for the optimum and maximum capacity. The maximum capacity is used to determine when a course is full. Once the maximum capacity is reached, the system proposes booking the user to the waiting list.

Infotype 1021: "Prices"

You can specify both an internal price and an external price. The internal price is used for internal activity allocation and the external price is used for invoicing. You can use the **Propose price** button to propose a price based on the following information:

▶ Infotype 1036: "Costs"

  ▷ Internal currency

  ▷ Cost from cost items

▶ Infotype 1024: "Capacity" (value in **Optimum** field)

▶ Infotype 1042: "Schedule Model" (number of days and hours)

  The system proposes a price based on the cost entries given in Figure 11.33. Of course, you must maintain the information that is provided here.

Infotype 1029: "Business Event Type Info"

Select fields in the "Business Event Type Info" infotype to determine how you want to handle the business event type in marketing activities, such as including the business event type in a brochure. You can also use this infotype to override Customizing settings in Time Management. The following fields are available (see Figure 11.30):

▶ **Include in business event brochure**
If this field is checked, the business event is considered when creating a brochure on the business event types offered.

▶ **Convention**
Check this field if the business event type involves the combination of several individual events that occur in parallel. Additional information on handling conventions and multipart business events is provided later in this chapter.

▶ **No display in Intranet**
Check this field if you don't want to offer the business event type and the business events created beneath it to ESS employees.

▶ **No integration**
Check the appropriate field if you don't want to have integration with Time Management active for the business event type. A check means that attendances will not be created and that the availability of attendees or instructors will not be checked during a booking.

▶ **Time off allowed**
This field overrides the Customizing settings for integration with Time Management that make employees unavailable for training on their days off (see the comments on Figure 11.9).

▶ **Minimum percentage attendance**
The entries that you make to set a percentage rate—in order to define the point at which employees' absences (from a business event) mean that they have not completed the business event—are also relevant to the Customizing settings for integration with Time Management. In other words, the attendance is cancelled (see the comments on Figure 11.10).

```
Business Event Type Info 01 D 50000800 1
  ☑ Include in business event brochure
  ☐ Convention
  ☐ No display in Intranet
  Settings for Time Management integration
     ☐ No integration for instructors
     ☐ No integration for attendees
     ☑ Allowed in instructor's time off
     ☑ Allowed in attendee's time off
  Minimum percentage attendance          [      ]
```

Figure 11.30 Infotype: "Business Event Type Info"

Infotype 1002: "Relationships"

Infotype 1002, "Relationships," plays an important role in both Organizational Management and Training and Event Management when you create structures, link additional data to an object, or link objects to one another. In the following sections, we'll discuss some selected relationships and how they can be used as additional functions in Training and Event Management. If you want to use Training and Event Management together with the management of resources, you must create the "requires" relationship between the business event type and one or more resources. You must also specify the number of required resource types. For example, you can use this relationship to define that a business event type requires two instructors. You can make enough refinements to requirements to specify how many instructors are needed for each day. Figure 11.31 defines that two instructors are required for the first day and that one instructor only is required for the second day.

Search term	Name	A	Unit	Per	Busine...	Attendee	Pr	Day number	Day segm...
50000482	Instructors	☐	2,00	1	◉	○		001	SPAET
50000482	Instructors	☐	1,00	1	◉	○		002	NORMAL
		✔	0,00	0	◉	○		000	
		✔	0,00	0	◉	○		000	

Figure 11.31 Setting the Requirements for Resource Type "Instructor"

You must also further refine the required resource types by specifying the related resources. Here, you can use relationships "Uses (for attendee)" and "Uses (for bus. event)" in the context of resource type "material." You can also use relationship "Is held by" in the context of resource types "instructor." Figure 11.32 shows the relationship to each instructor with a business event type.

Figure 11.32 Instructor Relationships

Here you create the relationship "Is held by" between the "Business event type" object and a "Person," a "User," an "External person," or a "Contact person." You can relate several objects of type "Person" as instructors to one business event type. When you create business events, you can select one or more persons from the list of instructors. The priority sets the sequence in which instructors are offered. See Section 11.2.2 for more information on the topic of resources.

The following additional relationships are also available:

▶ **"Presupposes"**
You can create a relationship to a business event type (for courses that build on each other: training plans) or, to qualifications.

▶ **"Imparts"**
This relationship to qualifications that can be transferred to employee master data applies to integration in Personnel Development (see Section 11.1.3)

▶ **"Has attendee apprsl model"/"Has event apprsl model"**
You can use this relationship to override the default settings in Customizing for the appraisal models to be used for attendee or business event appraisals. See Section 11.2.4 for more information. Note that you can use an appraisal model to set the criteria to be used when appraising business events or attendees.

▶ **"Is planned for"**
This relationship specifies a target group (mapped with object type "job") for a business event type. You can provide the information on the target group for a business event in the business event brochure. SAP Learning Solution uses a similar relationship to offer the training catalog to users based upon their positions (see Chapter 17, *E-Learning and Learning Management*).

Infotype 1025: "Deprec. Meter/Validity"
When business event types build on each other, you can use deprec. meter/validity to set a validity period for the knowledge gained in a basic course and thus when an employee is authorized to take a follow-up course. Once the validity period expires, the system treats attendees as new beginners, i.e., as if they had not taken the basic course.

Infotype 1060: "Business Event Demand"
This infotype helps you store the demand for business events by quarter, language, and location. Nonetheless, we recommend that you plan the demand for business events with the dynamic planning menu.

Infotype 1030: "Procedure"
When an attendee is booked for a business event, the system can perform specific checks, such as a check to determine if an employee is already booked for a busi-

ness event of the same type. You can activate these checks in Customizing (IMG path) with **Training and Event Management · Day-To-Day Activities · Booking · Attendee Checks**, and depending on the attendee type (person, external person, applicant, and so on). Infotype "Procedure" overrides these default settings.

In addition, you can also override the activities defined for follow-up processing in Customizing (IMG path) **Training and Event Management · Recurring Activities**. For more information on recurring activities, see Section 11.2.4.

Infotype 1036: "Costs"

You can use infotype "Costs" (see Figure 11.33) to enable the automatic calculation of a proposed price for a business event type (see infotype 1021: "Prices"). The cost items also help distribute business event costs across the appropriate cost centers.

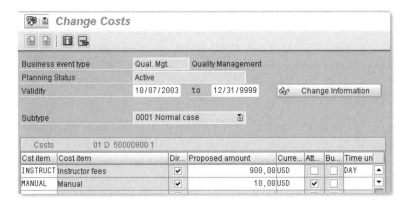

Figure 11.33 Infotype: "Costs"

Infotype 1037: "Billing/Allocation Info"

You can use this infotype to assign a sales area to a business event type for the activity allocations and invoicing addressed in Section 11.1.3; the sales area is required for invoicing business events. Here, you can also enter the controlling area and the activity type for internal activity allocation of attendee and instructor activities.

All the information created on business event types is optional. Except for the short and long descriptions, you aren't required to populate any of the infotypes. However, we highly recommend that you enter as much information as possible for similar business events that are held frequently (if not, the various default values set in Customizing, as described in this chapter, can be applied). Doing so accelerates the generation of business events.

Special Aspects of Individual Business Events

As we indicated in Chapter 7, *The Process of Personnel Development*, the concept of using business event types as a template for business events is advantageous as long as you work with the planning and organization of training events that are frequently repeated. However, dealing with events that occur less frequently (e.g., the attendance of individual employees at special business events of various external training providers, which occurs rather rarely) is somewhat cumbersome. The difficulty with this latter scenario is that you would always have to create a business event type for every single business event when working with external, dissimilar business events.

For such cases, which do occur often enough, you can use the structure of Training and Event Management differently. To do so, create a business event group, possibly named "external business events." Then, use business event types instead of lower level "groups" for external business events, such as "external IT training" and "external language course." Next, maintain only the description and a dummy schedule for these business event types. The description, the actual schedule, and additional data would always be created on the single business event. By using this approach, you wouldn't have to create a business event type for every external business event.

Note: Although this variation significantly simplifies maintenance, it hinders certain plausibility checks; for example, the warning "is already booked for a business event of the same type" no longer has any significance when external courses are mapped in this manner.

Creating Business Events

You use the **Business Event** menu to create the selection of business events, based on the existing structure in the Master Data Catalog. To plan many business events at one time, please refer to the **Planning** menu for creating business event data that will be required in the future, as described in Section 11.2.2.

If you don't use the planning components (because you don't yet have a reasonable basis for planning), you can create business events in the **Business Event** menu, always starting from a business event type. You can navigate to the Business Event menu from the SAP menu path **Training and Event Management · Business Events · Business Event Menu**. When you create a business event, you decide if you want to create it with or without resources. If you decide to create it "with resources," you can create the business event only if you have already stored the "requires resource type" relationship for the corresponding business event type (see the comments on Figure 11.31).

When creating business event dates, you must distinguish between internal and external business events. You cannot plan an external business event with resource reservations: external business events can be created only without resources. Using the **Planning** button always automatically generates internal business event dates. You can create business events with the following statuses: "planned" or "firmly booked" (corresponding with the object-status "active" that was discussed in Chapter 2). If you create a business event with the status of "planned," you can issue temporary attendance confirmations when booking an attendee. Once the status changes to "firmly booked," you can transmit final attendance confirmations. This procedure is helpful when you plan business events far from their business event dates. If needed, the dates can be cancelled before you publish the final confirmations of attendance. You can also identify business events as "locked." You cannot book attendees to a business event with the "locked"-flag set. When you create a business event with resources, you can branch directly to the availability check of the required resources (see the **Resource selection** button in Figure 11.36). From there, you can also temporarily set and cover additional resource requirements for the individual business event to be created—exceeding those stored in the event type.

Figure 11.34 Creating a Business Event with Resources

Figure 11.35 illustrates recording resource type "instructor" from the definition of the business event type and a temporary resource type requirement, "overhead projector." The Availability (**Avail. %**) column shows the percentage of the required resource's availability. The Remaining Requirements (**Remain %**) column shows the requirements that have not yet been covered for an availability percentage other than 100%.

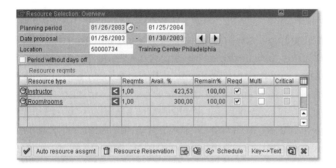

Figure 11.35 Resource Requirement

You can use the **Select Resources** button (icon) on the left side of each resource type to branch to the available resources (see Figure 11.36). There, you can select and reserve one or more resources for the business event. When selecting a resource, you can temporarily insert an additional resource, for example, when considering additional instructors in addition to the assigned instructors for the business event type.

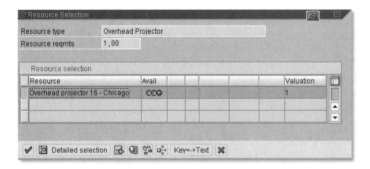

Figure 11.36 Resource Selection: "Overhead Projector"

Note: Resources that are indirectly available as part of a room's equipment (such as computers with fixed installations) are considered for resource coverage after the room has been assigned, but are not displayed in the **Avail. %** column (see Figure 11.35). Accordingly, when you work with "equipment," you should always assign the room first. The best evaluation of rooms with optimal equipment occurs with the system proposal for selecting resources.

Multisession Business Events and Conventions

In addition to "normal" business events (with or without the resource reservations), mySAP HR Training and Event Management can also map *multisession business events and conventions*. By definition, multisession business events involve sessions that run in parallel. The precondition for a convention is checking the **Convention** field on the business event type (see the comments on Figure 11.30). Conventions cannot be planned with the **Planning** menu or in the **Business Event** menu with a status of "planned." They must be defined individually with the corresponding business event type. Each session is assigned its own schedule. Unlike one-session business events, for which you can transfer the schedule of the corresponding business event type, multisession business events require you to define the daily schedule of the individual sessions separately, with time intervals.

As we already noted, mySAP HR Training and Event Management supports users in planning business events as long as the business events aren't excluded a priori, which is the case with conventions and external business events.

11.2.2 Planning in Training and Event Management

The support offered by Training and Event Management for planning is not limited to the quantitative planning of business events. It also includes tools to plan and control training budgets and to plan resources and materials.

Budgeting

To monitor education and training budgets, you can create education and training budgets for organizational units and compare them to the attendance fees of the business events that have been booked. Because budgets are assigned to organizational units, the organizational structure must be maintained and Organizational Management must operate in the same plan variant as Training and Event Management.

You set integration with budget management with Customizing (IMG path) **Training and Event Management · Integration · Budget Management**. After you define the currency for the budget, you must set up a budget structure element type. Similar to Compensation Management (see Chapter 15, *Compensation Management*), here, too, you must flag the budget structure element type as addressable if funds are to flow from it (see Figure 11.37). You define the availability of a budget with its budget period: make the required settings in Customizing via IMG **Training and Event Management · Integration · Budget Management · Specify Budget Period**.

Figure 11.37 Budget Structure Element Type: "Training"

Now you can begin to set up the budget structure. Follow SAP menu **Personnel · Training and Event Management · Business Events · Budget · Budgeting**. The structure is composed of individual budgets that are linked to each other. If the budget structure corresponds closely to the organizational structure, you can generate the budget structure from the organizational structure. Follow the SAP menu path mentioned above to branch to the initial budgeting screen, from which you can start to generate the budget structure. The system then displays a selection screen (see Figure 11.38).

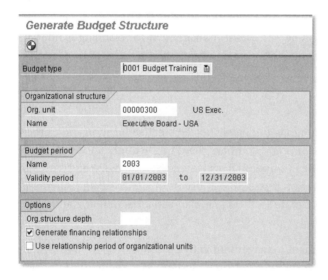

Figure 11.38 Generating a Budget from the Organizational Structure

To set the scope of the budget structure, you must specify the root organizational unit from which the budget is generated and outline the depth of the organizational structure ("blank" means all levels). If you check the **Generate financing relationships** field (which is recommended), links are created immediately between the organizational units and the budgets derived from them (see Figure 11.39). You can modify and add to a budget structure that is created in this way until it meets your requirements. You must also supply the budgets with financial resources. You can distribute the financial resources either top down or bottom up.

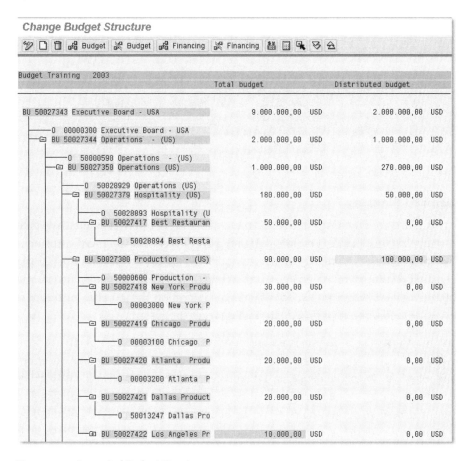

Figure 11.39 Generated Budget Structure

Depending on the method you select, the system shows a budget that is still missing or that is still to be distributed (see Figure 11.39). The budget can be released when all financial resources have been distributed. You cannot edit a structure with a status of "released." If you need to edit the structure after it has been released, you must reset it to a status of "planned."

Budgets are reduced accordingly during the internal activity allocation of attendance and cancellation fees. You can see previous deductions from a budget—as of a specific key date—by starting a budget comparison. The budget comparison lists actual values opposite the original budget (see Figure 11.40).

Budget Comparison

Selection period   01/01/2003 - 08/10/2003

Object ID	Valid From	End Date	Object name	Budget value	Actual value	Currency
300	01/01/2003	08/10/2003	US Exec.	900,000.00	6,900.00	USD
50000590	01/01/2003	08/10/2003	.Oper. -US	90,000.00	2,350.00	USD
50028929	01/01/2003	08/10/2003	..Operation-US	90,000.00	1,750.00	USD
50028893	01/01/2003	08/10/2003	...Hospital-US	60,000.00	0.00	USD
50028894	01/01/2003	08/10/2003	...Best Rest	60,000.00	1,750.00	USD
50000600	01/01/2003	08/10/2003	...Prod. -US	6,900.00	100.00	USD
3000	01/01/2003	08/10/2003	....New York	6,900.00	100.00	USD
3100	01/01/2003	08/10/2003	....Chicago	6,900.00	0.00	USD

Figure 11.40 Budget Comparison

Demand Planning

You can use the **Planning** menu to plan the demand for business events. Navigate through the SAP menu **Personnel · Training and Event Management · Business Events · Dates · Planning Menu**. As indicated briefly in Section 11.1.2, the **Dynamic Planning** menu enables you to create several business events of one business event type simultaneously and to determine the number of business events, based upon supporting information from the system.

You must first start at the selected business event type to create a plan. After you select the planning period by quarters, you must specify the language, location, and schedule. With Planning Options, you can also specify if planning is to cover all the obligatory resources. This setting compares the available resources and uses that basis to set up the dates. In addition to the resource types required by the business event type, you can also add additional resource types and resources with the **Selection: resource types/resources** button. However, this option is also available after creating the business events for each individual date. Another planning option involves the distribution of dates. You can space the business events evenly throughout the planning period or space them at predefined intervals of days or weeks (see Figure 11.41).

Starting planning displays the options available to select the basis for determining the number of business events. You can use the following data to determine demand:

▶ **Determine demand using prebookings**

You can use prebookings (see Section 11.2.3), indications of interest in a business event type, and the capacity of a business event to determine the number of business events required.

▶ **Determine demand using previous year's bookings**
You can assume that the number of bookings and the number of required business events for the planning year will agree with the figures from the previous year.

▶ **Demand taken from previous year**
If planning occurred for the previous year, you can transfer the results to the current year.

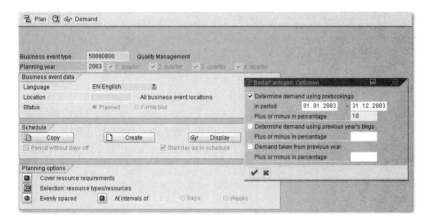

Figure 11.41 Planning Business Events

If the demand is stored directly on the business event types, the **Planning** menu can display demand. All three options noted here let you specify a plus or minus percentage change to the data used in the determination. If you choose not to use any of these options to determine demand, you can enter the demand yourself manually, in which case you may not select any options for determining demand.

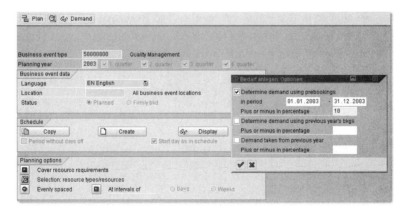

Figure 11.42 Planning Business Events from the Planning Menu

You can adjust or directly transfer the demand calculated by the system (see Figure 11.43) as you want. If no data is available to determine the demand, you must enter the dates manually.

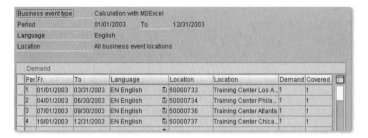

Figure 11.43 Creating the Demand for Business Events

If the generated dates cover the demand for business events, an appropriate traffic light icon is displayed with the business event type (see Figure 11.44).

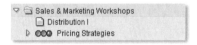

Figure 11.44 Displaying Coverage of Demand for Business Events

Resource Planning

The planning and management of the resources required by business events is closely related to planning the business events themselves. Internal business events usually require internal resources, such as instructors, overhead projectors, training binders, or rooms. You can use resource planning in Training and Event Management to manage existing resources and to ensure that the required resources meet the demand.

Resource types are allocated at the highest level of the **Resource** menu and are assigned to one of the resource categories in mySAP HR Training and Event Management. Four categories of resource types are available:

▶ Room

▶ Instructor (person, external instructor, and so on)

▶ Material from Materials Management

▶ Other resources (flipcharts, manuals, and so on)

For every resource category, the system contains a resource type of the same name as an example. Figure 11.46 shows the relationships between resource category, resource type, and resource, and how they are used with business event types and business events.

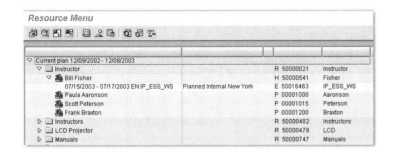

▽	Current plan 12/09/2002 - 12/08/2003				
	▽ ☐ Instructor			R 50000021	Instructor
	▽ ⬚ Bill Fisher			H 50000541	Fisher
	07/15/2003 - 07/17/2003 EN:IP_ESS_WS	Planned Internal New York		E 50016463	IP_ESS_WS
	⬚ Paula Aaronson			P 00001000	Aaronson
	⬚ Scott Peterson			P 00001015	Peterson
	⬚ Frank Braxton			P 00001200	Braxton
	▷ ☐ Instructors			R 50000482	Instructors
	▷ ☐ LCD Projector			R 50000479	LCD
	▷ ☐ Manuals			R 50000747	Manuals

Figure 11.45 The Resource Menu

If the default resource types prove insufficient, you can create new ones, such as overhead projector, training binders, and so on. Use Customizing (IMG path) **Training and Event Management · Business Event Preparation · Resource Management · Create Resource Type** to refine the structure of resource types.

As illustrated in Figure 11.46, resource types are required to determine scheduling for the resource requirements of business events. However, to equip the business events themselves with the required materials, instructors, and so on, resources are required. Therefore, the business events actually use the resources. You can create resources in Customizing of Training and Event Management or with the **Resource** menu.

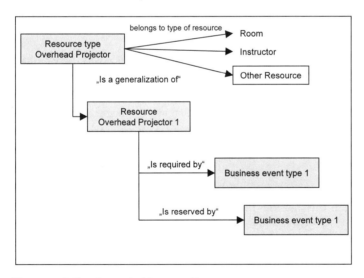

Figure 11.46 The Concept of Resource Types

When you create resources, you must specify the relationship to the resource type whose data, such as cost center assignment, can be transferred or overridden (see Figure 11.47). If you create a room, you must also specify the room's capacity and the building's address for this location-dependant resource.

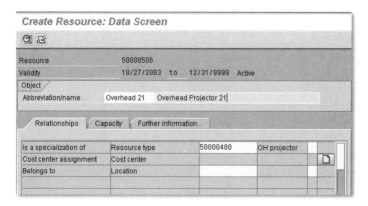

Figure 11.47 Creating a Resource

When creating training rooms, please note that the system does not do a good job of mapping rooms that can be broken up into a number of smaller rooms. If a room had a normal capacity of 100 attendees but can be broken up into two rooms, each with a capacity of 50 attendees, the system would have to map three rooms: one with a capacity of 100 and two with a capacity of 50. This approach would enable you to book the entire room and the two smaller rooms. However, one problem still remains: both rooms with a capacity of 50 would have to be blocked if a business event required the large room with its complete capacity (100) and vice versa. You could manually block the resources or set up a rather involved workflow to block them automatically.

You can block a resource from the Resource menu. Figure 11.45 uses the example of resource type "instructor," to highlight that the resource assignments are displayed based on the business event that is affiliated with the resource. For example, you can use this feature to determine which rooms are occupied and when. You also can use the **Resource** menu to link business events to resources that are still lacking.

Material Planning

To make material from the material master available in the **Resource** menu, you must create one or more resource types. When you do so, note that the **Resource** menu does not display materials as resources, because materials are managed in mySAP Materials Management. The assignment of resource type "material" to a business event type is quite typical and just like an assignment to other resource types, it uses the "Is required by" relationship (see the comments on Figure 11.35). You can also assign the relationship "Uses (for attendee)" to the actual materials on the business event type or on the business event. Afterward, you must call a report from the **Business Event** menu (**Business Event · Materials**

Procurement) to display the material requirements by business event. Select a business event, and you can transmit a materials request to Materials Management directly from the list of material requirements (**Reserve Material** button in Figure 11.48). If the materials are to be reserved for each attendee, you must decide—before the final reservation—if you want to reserve the material based on the number of attendees already booked or, upon the optimal capacity of a business event.

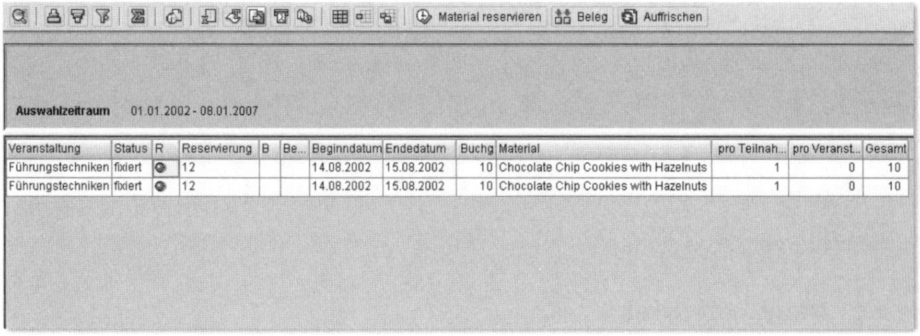

Figure 11.48 Material Requirements for Each Business Event

A traffic-light icon and the reservation number are displayed to indicate a successful reservation. If the material is not available in the warehouse, a purchase request is created automatically and displayed in the report with an order ID. You can double-click on the reservation or order ID to branch directly to the original document in Materials Management (reservation) or purchasing (purchase request).

Calculation

As described briefly in the comments on Figure 11.33, you can use infotype 1036 "Costs," to calculate a price for a business event automatically. You can then enter that figure into infotype 1021, "Prices" and use it for internal activity allocation or invoicing. Maintenance of the "costs" infotype requires a previous definition of cost items in Customizing via the IMG path **Training and Event Management · Business Event Preparation · Define Cost Items**. From the **Business Event** menu, you can call a corresponding calculation with **Business Event · Price Proposal**. The result is a price for an individual attendance that covers the costs. You can transfer the price for the business event (infotype 1021: "Prices").

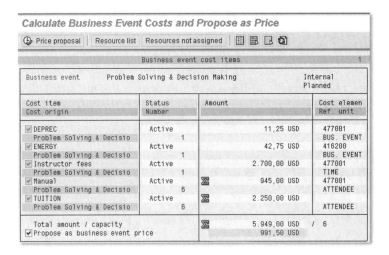

Figure 11.49 Price Calculation

11.2.3 Daily Activities

Daily (day-to-day activities) contain the bulk of activities that must be performed in Training and Event Management: processing booking requests, cancellations, and rebookings based on scheduling conflicts and so on. Section 11.1.3 has already indicated that the bulk of the work can be performed by the attendees themselves. The use of ESS for Training and Event Management with workflow support (for the approval of bookings and cancellations, for example) can save the HR department a great deal of work and allow it to concentrate on other tasks. The following section highlights the activities and options of centralized processing of daily activities.

Book, Rebook, and Cancel

As Section 11.2.1 indicated, you can perform certain checks when booking an attendee, depending on the attendee type (person, external person, and so on). The checks consider the cases listed below; you define the checks in Customizing via the IMG path **Training and Event Management · Day-to-Day Activities · Booking · Attendee Checks**. When the checks prove positive, you can assign various types of notifications to them. A blank stands for no check, "I" for information, "W" for warning (meaning that the data record can still be saved), and "E" for an error, which means that the user is not allowed to save the action (booking or prebooking).

▶ Check for bookings for the same business event type

▶ Check for a prebooking for the same business event type

► Check for a prerequisite business event

► Check for an attendee's qualifications

You can also control system messages for the cases that conflict one another, defined in the system with **Training and Event Management · Day-to-Day Activities · Book · Conflict Reaction**. The types of notifications described above are also possible:

► Check to see if an attendee is also simultaneously an instructor

► Check to see if an attendee is also simultaneously an attendee (on another event)

To ensure the consistency of data when booking business events, you should use the options available in the checks. However, we suggest that you don't use too many error messages. Doing so will make it impossible for users to save their entries. In most cases, a warning will suffice.

In typical cases, bookings are performed from the **Attendance** menu. You start with a business event and then select a booking type in the context menu. You can book individual persons, group attendees (such as companies and organizational units), and entire lists. Before you perform a booking, you can use the traffic-light icons in the **Attendance** menu to determine the capacity of a business event.

With individual bookings, you must first select the attendee type desired: a person, a customer, an external person, or an organizational unit, for example. If the optimal capacity of a business event has not yet been reached, you would generally perform a *normal booking*.

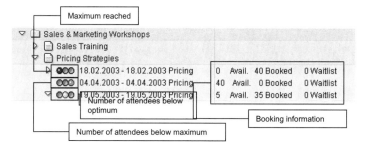

Figure 11.50 Traffic Light Icons for a Business Event

Once the optimum has been reached, the system accepts only essential bookings or booking to a waiting list. This approach avoids booking a business event without any inquiry right up to the maximum when booking a complete list of employees. You can also perform an essential booking at the outset (see Figure

11.51) by selecting a booking priority: attendance at a business event is guaranteed for an essential booking. Unlike a normal booking, an essential booking cannot be removed from the attendee list when firmly booking a business event. When you book organizational units, you can specify the number of attendees. In this case, you would use an N.N. (no name) booking. In actual practice, this option is used when a specific number of employees in a department are to attend training, but the identities of the individual attendees are not yet known.

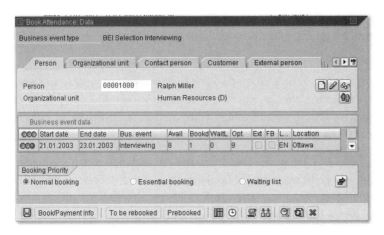

Figure 11.51 Entering an Individual Booking

During booking, you can also accept or override the payment information stored with the attendee type (see Figure 11.69). Use the **Book/Payment Info** button to override or display the payment information. If necessary, you can then override the information displayed, such as the Billing for an attendance and the cost distribution information for internal activity allocation (see Figure 11.52).

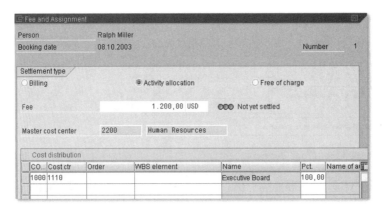

Figure 11.52 Display of Payment Information

You can control attendee types for Training and Event Management and also determine if an attendee type must pay for attending a business event or, if the employee's cost center is responsible for the attendance fees. Use Customizing (IMG path) **Training and Event Management · Day-to-Day Activities · Booking · Specify Attendee Type Control**. Figure 11.53 illustrates the appropriate Customizing settings.

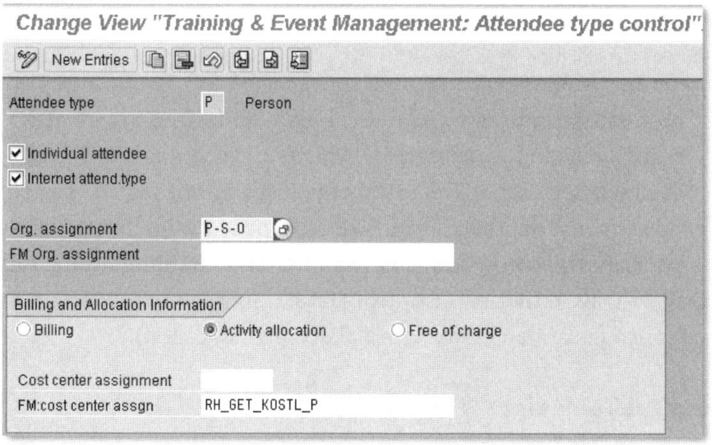

Figure 11.53 Attendee Type Control

You can book a list to book many employees for a business event simultaneously. Here you can access entries on the attendee list of another business event and a list of employees from one or more organizational units. For business events that build on each other, you can access the attendee list of the previous business event. If you want to book an employee to an entire series of business events, use the SAP menu path **Personnel · Training and Event Management · Attendances · Book: Attendee to Business Event List**. When you need to rebook an employee from one business event to another, a list offers you the relevant alternative dates. For group attendees (organizational units and firms), you can also decide to rebook all or only individual attendees.

Training and Event Management handles cancellation fees with cancellation reasons. You use cancellation reasons to set how much (if any) of the attendance fee an attendee must pay for a cancellation or what amount (if any) is used for internal activity allocation.

You maintain reasons and other additional data in Customizing (IMG path) **Training and Event Management · Day-to-Day Activities · Canceling Attendance · Reasons for Attendance Cancellation** (see Figure 11.54). You can enter percentages for the standard entries and add new reasons.

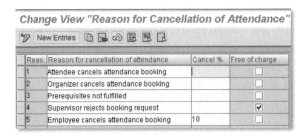

Figure 11.54 Definition of Cancellation Reasons

In the event that no cancellation reason was selected when canceling an attendance, or if a cancellation reason was chosen for which no percentage for the cancellation fee was maintained, or if the Free of Charge flag was not set, the system uses the value of the semantic abbreviation CCDEL (proposed value for cancellation fees). You can specify this in Customizing via IMG path **Training and Event Management · Day-to-Day Activities · Control Data**. Cancellation fees are handled just like attendance fees (invoices or internal activity allocation).

Waiting List and Prebook List

The mode for moving an attendee off the waiting list is an additional control element indirectly related to canceling attendees that you can set in Customizing. Note the difference between the *waiting list* and the *prebook list*. Waiting lists are maintained in business events and waiting-list candidates can be booked as attendees when places open up. Prebook lists are stored on business event types and express the interest of candidates on the list. They are not related to an actual business event, but rather to the content of a business event. You can use prebook lists as a basis for planning future business event dates (see Section 11.2.2.)

Use Customizing (IMG path) **Training and Event Management · Day-to-Day Activities · Prebooking** to control the settings for reading the business event catalog and highlight a notification that informs the user that dates are available for the selected business event type. You can set the mode mentioned above for moving potential attendees off the waiting list (via the IMG path **Training and Event Management · Day-to-Day Activities · Canceling Attendance · Control Data**) as follows:

▶ *I = interactive*: the user selects candidates to move off the waiting list based on a proposal from the system.

▶ *D = direct*: candidates are selected automatically as follows to move off the waiting list. The waiting list for the business event is sorted in ascending order according to priority and booking date. The system starts at the beginning of the sorted list and selects the first attendee; it continues to select attendees until it reaches the permissible number of candidates. If "N.N. bookings" of companies or organizational units appear among the first bookings in the list and contain a greater number of bookings than is permitted, the system ignores these bookings.

▶ *N = none*: no movement off the waiting list occurs.

Only when the optimal number of attendees is reached can candidates move off the waiting list. You can book attendees for business events that have already reached their optimum capacity only as essential bookings (see the comments on Figure 11.51). To handle attendees' questions about bookings, rebookings, cancellations, and so on, you can use the **Information** menu to start various reports from the business event structure.

Sharing Information

You call the information menu via the SAP menu **Personnel · Training and Event Management · Information System · Information Menu**. The menu allows reporting from all levels of the displayed structure that affect attendance, business events, and resources. The scope of the reports always depends on the object type from which the report was started.

For example, if you call a formatted attendance list from a business event, the report lists only the attendees of the business event. However, if you start the report from a business event type, the report contains an attendance list for each of the business events created under the business event type. If you don't select an object from the business event structure, the report is called with an empty selection screen that you must fill out.

You can also call reports in Training and Event Management via the SAP menu **Personnel · Training and Event Management · Information System · Reports**. Should the standard reports on the Information menu prove to be insufficient, you can integrate customer-specific reports via the maintenance interface of the **Dynamic Information** menu. Use Customizing via the IMG path **Training and Event Management · Information System · Integrate Customer-Specific Reports** to display a report tree; you can add your own reports to the tree.

Attendances

The following sample reports on "attendances" provide an insight into reports:

▶ **Attendee's Training History**
The report (see Figure 11.55) lists all the business events that an employee has already attended and those for which the employee is booked. In other words, the report contains current and historical bookings. The output displays business event data such as a description and a date, information on the number of hours,

and the attendance fees. This report will enable you to quickly determine how much has been invested in an employee's training thus far. If fees are listed in various currencies, the sums are provided in all occurring currencies. You can start this report for all attendee types. This report is not suited to reporting on the training history of an organizational unit because selecting an organizational unit displays only the N.N. bookings for the organizational unit, rather than the individual attendees belonging to the unit. To solve this problem, you can select attendee type "person" based on its organizational assignment. Unfortunately, the report's output cannot show the organizational assignment.

Training History

Selection period 01.01.1900 - 31.12.9999

Abbr.	Attendee name	Event	Event type	Bus. event	Start date	End date	Σ Days	Σ Hours	Σ Fee	Crcy	Σ Bookings	BP
Hughes	Miss JoAnn Hughes	✓	☐	Leadership	09.04.2001	10.04.2001	2	15,00	550,00	USD	1	50
Jackson	Kate-Lynne Jackson	✓	☐	Bus Ethics	26.11.2001	26.11.2001	1	8,00	250,00	USD	1	50
Jones	Mr Andrew Jones	✓	☐	Orientation	26.06.2002	26.06.2002	1	2,00			1	50
Jones	Mr Andrew Jones	✓	☐	Leadership	09.04.2001	10.04.2001	2	15,00	550,00	USD	1	50
Perry	Michael Perry	✓	☐	IBI	04.11.2002	05.11.2002	2	15,00	750,00	EUR	1	50
Peterson	Tom Peterson	✓	☐	Economics	29.07.2000	14.08.2000	9	54,00	850,00	USD	1	50
Smith	James Smith	✓	☐	Qual. Mgt.	30.11.2001	09.12.2001	6	40,00	800,00	USD	1	50
Smith	James Smith	✓	☐	Bus Ethics	26.11.2001	26.11.2001	1	8,00	250,00	USD	1	50
							▪ 24	▪ 157,00	▪ 750,00 EUR 3.250,00 USD		▪ 8	

Figure 11.55 Training History

▶ **Attendance Prerequisites**
This report (see Figure 11.56) lists the prerequisite business events and qualifications for business event types or groups. If you have maintained alternative qualifications for the required qualifications (see Chapter 8, *Skill Management*), the report can also display them. The checkmarks in the "Event type" and "Qual." columns indicate if the prerequisite is a business event type or a qualification. The report on prerequisites matchup is closely related to attendance prerequisites.

▶ **Prerequisites Matchup**
You must specify both objects for the matchup: an attendee and a business event type or business event group (see Figure 11.57). The report lists the objects opposite each other and matches them up.

▶ The system reads the required qualifications and prerequisite business event types and groups for the business event group, and it reads the existing qualifications in infotype 0024 and the business events previously attended for the attendee types. The result shows which business event types and qualifications are required and whether the employee has fulfilled the prerequisites by displaying a traffic-light icon.

Attendance Prerequisites

Selection period   08.10.2003 - 08.10.2003

Business event type	Event type	Qual.	Prerequisite	Qual.start	End date
Management Techniques	✓	☐	Business Ethics	01.01.1995	31.12.9999
Business English	✓	☐	General English	01.01.1995	31.12.9999
Technical English	✓	☐	General English	01.01.1995	31.12.9999
Business French	☐	✓	French Language	01.01.1994	31.12.9999
Business French	✓	☐	General French	01.01.1995	31.12.9999
Technical French	☐	✓	French Language	01.01.1994	31.12.9999
Technical French	✓	☐	General French	01.01.1995	31.12.9999
Business German	✓	☐	General German	01.01.1995	31.12.9999
Technical German	✓	☐	General German	01.01.1995	31.12.9999
Communication	✓	☐	Business Ethics	01.01.1995	31.12.9999
Organization Planning	✓	☐	Business Ethics	01.01.1995	31.12.9999
H2S Instructor	☐	✓	Certificate, H2S Alive	01.01.1997	31.12.9999
Data Protection II	✓	☐	Data Protection I	01.01.2001	31.12.9999
Electronics Level 2	✓	☐	Electronics Level 1	01.01.2001	31.12.9999
Electronics Level 3	✓	☐	Electronics Level 1	01.01.2001	31.12.9999

Figure 11.56   Attendance Prerequisites

Prerequisites Matchup

Selection period   01.01.2003 - 31.12.2003

Business event type name	Name Attendee	Object type Prerequisite	Name Prerequisite	Analysis
Management Techniques	Ralph Miller	Business event type	Business Ethics	●●●
Management Techniques	Pamela Floyd	Business event type	Business Ethics	●●●
Management Techniques	John Jefferson	Business event type	Business Ethics	●●●
Management Techniques	Tom Peterson	Business event type	Business Ethics	●●●
Management Techniques	Debbie Davis	Business event type	Business Ethics	●●●
Management Techniques	Jeff Larsen	Business event type	Business Ethics	●●●
Management Techniques	Karen Johnson	Business event type	Business Ethics	●●●
Management Techniques	Michael Houseman	Business event type	Business Ethics	●●●
Management Techniques	James White	Business event type	Business Ethics	●●●

Figure 11.57   Prerequisites Matchup

Figure 11.58 lists additional reports on business events, attendances, and resources.

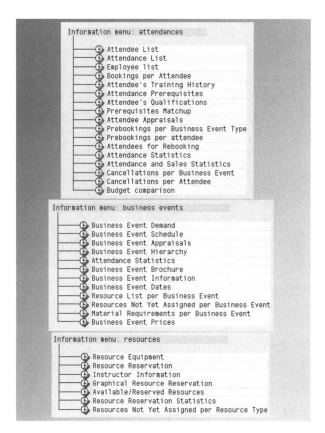

```
Information menu: attendances

        ⊕ Attendee List
        ⊕ Attendance List
        ⊕ Employee list
        ⊕ Bookings per Attendee
        ⊕ Attendee's Training History
        ⊕ Attendance Prerequisites
        ⊕ Attendee's Qualifications
        ⊕ Prerequisites Matchup
        ⊕ Attendee Appraisals
        ⊕ Prebookings per Business Event Type
        ⊕ Prebookings per attendee
        ⊕ Attendees for Rebooking
        ⊕ Attendance Statistics
        ⊕ Attendance and Sales Statistics
        ⊕ Cancellations per Business Event
        ⊕ Cancellations per Attendee
        ⊕ Budget comparison

Information menu: business events

        ⊕ Business Event Demand
        ⊕ Business Event Schedule
        ⊕ Business Event Appraisals
        ⊕ Business Event Hierarchy
        ⊕ Attendance Statistics
        ⊕ Business Event Brochure
        ⊕ Business Event Information
        ⊕ Business Event Dates
        ⊕ Resource List per Business Event
        ⊕ Resources Not Yet Assigned per Business Event
        ⊕ Material Requirements per Business Event
        ⊕ Business Event Prices

Information menu: resources

        ⊕ Resource Equipment
        ⊕ Resource Reservation
        ⊕ Instructor Information
        ⊕ Graphical Resource Reservation
        ⊕ Available/Reserved Resources
        ⊕ Resource Reservation Statistics
        ⊕ Resources Not Yet Assigned per Resource Type
```

Figure 11.58 Reports from the Information Menu

Correspondence

Correspondence in Training and Event Management is based on SAPscript forms. A *notification abbreviation* is associated with every event in Training and Event Management (canceling, booking, rebooking,…). A SAPscript form is behind every notification abbreviation. You can find utilities to help you with corresponding in Customizing (via the IMG path) **Training and Event Management · Day-to-Day Activities · Correspondence · Wizards**. The following Wizards are available:

▶ **Correspondence Setup**
Select the required notification abbreviations and copy SAPscript forms to the customer namespace. Examples of notification abbreviations include: BOOK = booking, CANC = cancellation, and CONF = confirmation.

▶ **Form**
Use the Wizard to adjust an existing form; however, the Wizard directs the user into the maintenance of SAPscript forms, therefore, users must know how to use SAPscript.

▶ **Text Variable**

If the available text variables—which offer dynamic information from the master data of Training and Event Management—should prove insufficient, you must create and provide new text variables. In order to generate the program to populate text variables, you must have programming knowledge of ABAP/4.

▶ **Notification Abbreviations**

If Training and Event Management does not offer a notification abbreviation for an event, you can use this Wizard to create a customer-specific abbreviation. You must consider the function codes and data views that mirror a specific action in the system. If new functions have been implemented in Training and Event Management, you must undertake more significant modifications in the system.

You aren't limited to SAPscript forms when outputting correspondence; you can also export the letters into Microsoft Word as form letters. However, then you must start the output of the correspondence manually. Using SAPscript for output, you can define automatic output of correspondence with Customizing via the IMG path **Training and Event Management · Day-to-Day Activities · Correspondence · Output Control**. For example, you can automatically send letters to a printer (or as a fax or an e-mail) as soon as an action (such as booking an attendee to a planned business event) has occurred. You can design different correspondence for users and attendee types.

If the correspondence is not output automatically after an event in the system, you can trigger output manually from the **Dynamic Attendance** menu. The scope of the letters depends on the object (attendee, business event, or business event type) from which correspondence was started.

11.2.4 Follow-Up Processing of Business Events

Once business events have taken place, you must perform a series of follow-up activities. Follow-up processing requires that business events have been frozen by the status "firmly booked", and that the event has taken place. All the functions to be performed here can be called and started from the **Business Event** menu.

You can automate some of the actions to be carried out in Customizing. The following actions can be activated per attendee type in Customizing via the IMG path **Training and Event Management · Recurring Activities · Follow-Up Processing**:

▶ **Transfer objectives to an attendee's qualifications**

You can automatically transfer the qualifications stored on a business event type and imparted by a business event to employee master data in infotype 0024, "Qualifications," respectively to skill management.

► **Delete the relationships between business event and attendee once the business event has ended**

To reduce data volume, you can delete the relationship between an attendee and the business event attended by the attendee after the attendance has ended. But you must also create a relationship between the attendee and the business event type so that you can map the attendance history and perform checks. This option is rarely used.

► **Create a relationship between a business event type and an attendee after the attendance has ended**

Activate this setting if you want to check for prerequisite business event types.

You can override these settings per event type with infotype 1030, "Procedure." If you want to automate correspondence (the output of attendance confirmation) in addition to the default settings, you can use Customizing (via the IMG path) **Training and Event Management · Day-to-Day Activities · Correspondence · Output Control · Specify User-Specific Output Control** to set automatic output of notification abbreviation CERT and define an appropriate output medium.

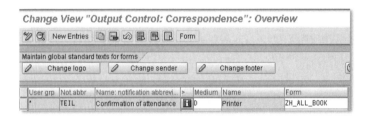

Figure 11.59 Output Control for Correspondence

From the **Business Event** menu, you can start the actions you have defined by starting at a business event or a business event type and select the menu path **Business Event · Follow-Up Processing**. In the screen that appears, you can make entries under additional data to track the history of a business event. When you do this, the business event is removed from the Business Event Catalog—provided that your filter criteria exclude tracked events as we recommend. Note: once you track the history of a business event, you cannot change the business event data: the action is irrevocable.

Before qualifications can be transferred into personnel master data or default relationships can be deleted or created, an overview list displays all the actions. You can still make adjustments to the actions before they are performed for the final time. Figure 11.60 shows the options for adjustments.

In the following section, we address in detail one action that does appear in the overview: namely, appraisals.

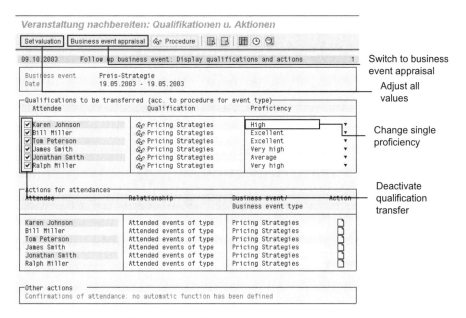

Figure 11.60 Overview of Activities in Follow-Up Processing

Appraisals

Chapter 10, *Appraisals and Setting Objectives,* already mentions business event and attendee appraisals. These types of appraisals are intended specifically for Training and Event Management; however, the basic approach to personnel appraisals and the setup of Customizing are identical to other types of appraisals. Accordingly, this section examines appraisals only briefly and solely from the viewpoint of the specific application. You can also store test results as attendee appraisals in Training and Event Management, as long as the test belongs to a business event maintained there or, has been created as its own business event (such as an assessment center). For more detailed information on personnel appraisals and the creation of appraisal models, see Chapter 10.

You can call appraisals for business events or attendees from the **Business Events** menu or from the **Attendance** menu. To do so, select the object that you want to appraise (i.e., select it with your mouse). Then, call the appraisals by following the menu path **Business Event/Attendance · Appraisal · Create**. After you select the appraisal model that you want, a template for appraisal that contains appraisal criteria and characteristics, you can generate a *to-do list* (see Figure 11.61).

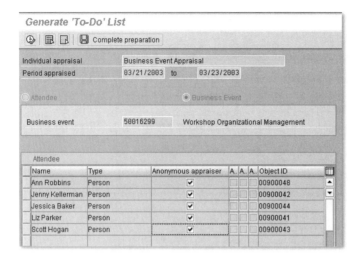

Figure 11.61 Generating the To-Do List

To generate the to-do list, select the individual attendees who have turned in a business event appraisal. The individual appraisal forms are generated from this information and can then be filled out in the system (see Figure 11.62). You can also specify if the appraisal is to occur anonymously or not. You make this setting in the **Anonymous Appraiser** field. To avoid having an employee submit two appraisals, the database stores a relationship between the person and the appraisal, despite the anonymity option; however, it does not display the relationship in the application. You can complete an appraisal according to the proper criteria with the simple selection of characteristics previously defined in the appraisal model. You can also create a note for each criterion.

Name	Weig...	Evaluation	Rating text	= weighting * r...	Note	Ty...	Object ID
Business Event Appraisal				0,000		BS	50014847
Contents: Practical Relev.	0,00	1	Very good	0,000		BK	50014848
Contents: Subject Matter	0,00	2	Good	0,000		BK	50014849
Materials: Contents	0,00	2	Good	0,000		BK	50014850
Materials: Scope	0,00	2	Good	0,000		BK	50014851
Instructor:Teaching Style	0,00	3	Satisfactory	0,000		BK	50014852
Instructor: Preparation	0,00	1	Very good	0,000		BK	50014853
Instructor: Manner	0,00	1	Very good	0,000		BK	50014854
Total: Qualititive Eval.	0,00	2	Good	0,000		BK	50014855

Individual appraisal — Business Event Appraisal — Completed
Attendee — N.N.
Business Event — Workshop Organizational Management
Period appraised — 03/21/2003 to 03/23/2003 Created on 11/21/2003

Figure 11.62 Business Event Appraisal

Billing and Allocation of Business Event Costs

Whether for invoicing or internal activity allocation, the following preconditions must be met to settle business event costs :

▶ **Allocation of attendances**

  ▷ Attendance may not be free-of-charge.

  ▷ The attendee is not on the waiting list.

▶ **Allocation of instructors**

  ▷ Cost items are maintained on resource type "instructor."

▶ **Allocation of attendance and instructor activities**

  ▷ The cost center assignment must be maintained.

  ▷ The receiving cost center is maintained.

  ▷ The sending cost center is maintained.

  ▷ The sending and receiving cost centers must lie in the same controlling area.

  ▷ When booking and canceling an attendee, you must populate the display of payment information with the appropriate data and select internal activity allocation or billing as the Billing type (see Figure 11.52). You can do so in the attendee type that depends on the Billing type or as a default in Customizing (see Figure 11.53).

  ▷ Follow the **Business Event** menu path **Business Event · Activity Allocation · Attendance/Instructor Function** or billing to call Billing or Allocation. The result provides an overview of the data found (see Figure 11.62) before the Billing or Allocation was created.

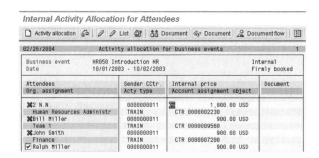

Figure 11.63 Internal Activity Allocation

11.3 Sample Process

11.3.1 Paperless Training and Event Management

Practical realization of the process of "Paperless Training and Event Management" in mySAP HR Training and Event Management (see Figures 11.64 and Figure

11.65) used some of the Customizing settings that have been discussed. Automatic correspondence with e-mail output was set up with **Training and Event Management · Day-to-Day Activities · Correspondence · Output Control · Specify User-Specific Output Control**. The medium "I" (Internet mail) was stored there for notification abbreviation BUCH so that when an employee is booked to a planned business event, a confirmation e-mail can be sent to the employee.

The standard workflows "approve employee's attendance booking" and "approve employee's attendance cancellation" were also modified slightly, because both approvals are normally sent to the manager, which was not the intention in this case. Here, the HR department issues the approvals. In addition, some e-mails sent within the workflow were deactivated because the recipient received two e-mails for certain actions: one from workflow and one from output control in Training and Event Management.

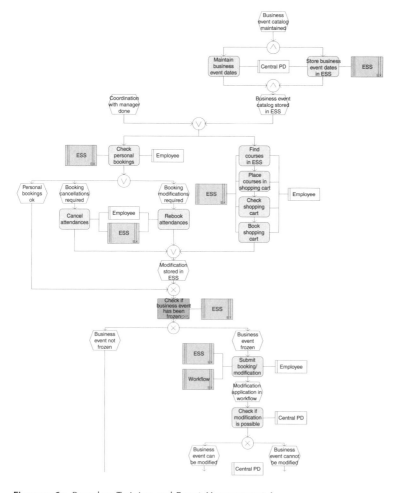

Figure 11.64 Paperless Training and Event Management 1

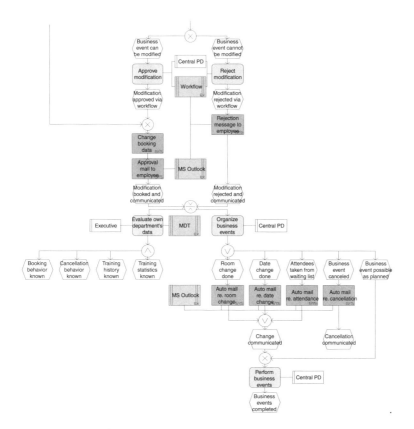

Figure 11.65 Paperless Training and Event Management 2

To make the Outlook e-mail addresses of employees known to the system, sub-type "E-Mail Address" was maintained in infotype 0105, "Communication." To guarantee that the e-mail address remains current (in the event of name changes, new hires, and so on), a *dynamic e-mail* can inform the Outlook administrator of any changes to infotype 0105, "Communication," assuming that mySAP HR is the leading system for the definition of e-mail addresses.

11.4 Critical Success Factors

Consider the following success factors when implementing Training and Event Management:

▸ Processes, particularly the approval of bookings, cancellations, and so on, and the structure of the training catalog must be clarified.

▸ Because of the many options for integration with Training and Event Management, clarify the objective early and determine which integration options should be activated. In particular, don't be overly optimistic about the benefit from integration with Time Management and Materials Management.

▶ Those affected by the ramifications caused by integration must be informed: for example, deletion of attendances with active integration into Time Management.

▶ Because of the many options to store data on business event types, there's a danger in entering more data than you really need. You should always check to ensure that the data being entered can be used intelligently for business purposes.

▶ The processes for maintaining data must be clarified early on. Definition of the processes should be supported by employees or consultants with a great deal of experience with mySAP HR Training and Event Management.

▶ Strive for the standardization of correspondence, because adaptation and, in particular, enhancement (new text variables) demand a relatively great deal of time.

▶ Many processes in Training and Event Management are suitable for decentralized use. Take advantage of these options: Employee Self-Service, for example.

▶ If you want to activate integration into Personnel Development, especially into Skill Management (qualifications), you must involve those teams in the implementation early on.

12 R/3 Enterprise and Enterprise Portal

In the area of personnel development, SAP provides some completely new applications. Moreover, the portal technology allows much more decentralized processes, and therefore creates an enormous potential for improved efficiency.

12.1 Overview

With the concept of extension sets, new functions will be available in shorter intervals and are no longer dependent on a new release of the R/3 core. In this chapter, we provide you with an overview of the relevant applications that are presently available.

The following innovations are significant improvements for the process of personnel development:

▶ SAP Learning Solution (SAP LS) is not only a complete e-learning platform, it also has a portal that enables you to access the entire area of education. It is integrated into the training and event management, skill management, and development planning. You should note that the installation of the SAP LS structure does modify the configuration and application of training and event management in some places. The solution is discussed in Chapter 17.

▶ The new solution, *Appraisals and Setting Objectives* (see Chapter 10), closes the gap in the area of objectives. The whole process of participative management by objectives is well supported and integrated in other HR-processes and in Strategic Enterprise Management (SEM) (see Chapter 19).

▶ The Expert Finder can be viewed as a knowledge management tool. It not only documents the knowledge, it also provides a portal that is designed to help you search for experts in any area.

▶ The *management of global employees* function makes personnel development in an international context much easier to address. Because the transfer of an employee to another country typically leads to a new personnel number, it was very difficult to present an overview of the development data for those employees. Therefore, the new *Personal ID*, which is introduced with this function, significantly reduces the complexity of working with development data for global employees.

▶ The new e-recruiting solution is a powerful tool for recruiting the best applicants, whether hiring from insidor outside one's company. It's also an important part of personnel development that fosters a stronger bond among staff members. The so-called *Talent Warehouse* allows applicants to look for interesting jobs in the company anonymously. Therefore, employees who are dissatisfied with their current position are encouraged to look for a better job internally—without leaving the company. Because recruiting is not an integral part of this book, we won't describe this solution in detail; however, you should consider e-recruiting as a useful tool for tapping into internal and external talent alike.

▶ Strategic Enterprise Management (SEM) is a part of the Business Intelligence package and belongs to the area of controlling. Because of its link to the objective setting in HR and because of its ability to describe an HR-Scorecard, it has a significant impact on HR and therefore, it is fully addressed in Chapter 19 of this book.

12.2 New Possibilities through Portals

Users in personnel development benefit from portal technology, for example, Employee Self-Service (ESS) and Manager's Self-Service (MSS), in the following processes:

▶ Maintanance of skill profiles

▶ Searching for employees well suited for special tasks or positions

▶ Succession planning

▶ Appraisal

▶ Web Surveys

▶ Booking of courses

In the last chapters, we learned that decentralized processes can boost efficiency, and sometimes are even essential for effectiveness in personnel development. Therefore, web-based scenarios are very important in this context. As most users use ESS and MSS only occasionally, a simple user interface is vital. With the enterprise portal and the growing number of Web applications, we have been able to significantly improve most processes of personnel development.

12.3 Objective Setting and Appraisals

12.3.1 Business Process

Management by objectives is not supported in Release 4.6C. Therefore, many companies did invest substantial amounts in developing solutions of their own. The new solution that is available from extension set 1.10 provides not only a more flexible user interface for appraisals, but also supports the process of management by objectives as shown in Figure 12.1.

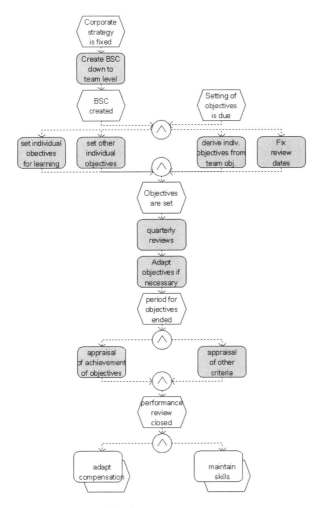

Figure 12.1 Process of Performance Review

The process shows that the individual objectives are derived from the objectives of the team and of the higher levels of the organization. The system supports this hierarchical process via the integration of HR and SEM.

12.3.2 Application

A critical difference between the new appraisal and the old appraisal is the appraisal form itself. With the new version, you have a lot more flexibility and therefore, it's much easier to use. Even if you work with the *normal* user interface via SAP GUI, you can see the difference (see Figure 12.2).

Document Status	In Process					
Surveyor	Michaela Maier					
Employee	Michaela Maier					
Validity Period	01/01/2004 to 12/31/2004				Additional Data	
Objective Setting Date	02/27/2004					
Appraisal Date	02/27/2004					

Number...	Element Name	Ad...	Del...	Obj...	Final Appraisal	Final Appraisal (V...	Fin...
	Customer / Employee Surv...				80	Percent	
1	Survey Statements						
1.1	Objective 1			🕎	3	Rudimentary	🕎
1.2	Objective 2			🕎	1	Very low	🕎
1.3	Objective 3			🕎	8	Very high	🕎

Figure 12.2 Appraisal Form via SAP GUI

Using the Web interface, any manager can easily fill in the form (see Figure 12.3). By comparing the content of the two figures, you can see that in Figure 12.3 the whole process of the performance review is displayed by the self-appraisal, the manager's appraisal, and the final appraisal. The appearance of the web-based appraisal form depends on the customization of the appraisal template.

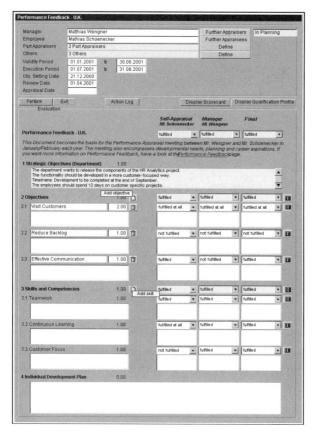

Figure 12.3 Web-Based Appraisal Form

Also in Figure 12.3, you'll note that there are different types of criteria, which are structured by so-called *criteria groups*. In this example, four groups are used:

▶ Strategic objectives

▶ Objectives (individual)

▶ Skills and competencies

▶ Individual development plans

Besides the standard criteria, a criteria group can contain external elements that are implemented via Business Add-ins (BAdIs).

12.3.3 Customizing

The first thing that you must do in customizing is to activate the new appraisal system. This is controlled by the entry *HAP00 – REPLA* in table T77S0, which you reach via the IMG-path **Personnel Management · Personnel Development · Objective setting and appraisals · maintain basic settings**. Here, you can activate the new system for personnel appraisals, for training and event appraisals, or for both. In most cases, we recommend that you activate the new system only for personnel appraisals, that is, you must enter an *X*. Only if you want the participants of events to maintain their appraisal online, would it be appropriate to activate the system for both personnel appraisals and training and event appraisals.

Via the same IMG-path, you also reach the field where you can enter the Remote Function Call (RFC) destination of your SEM system. This is necessary to look into the Balanced Scorecard (BSC) while doing a performance review. Note that additional configuration for the SEM integration must be done on the SEM system. First, you must ensure that the SEM system can locate the appropriate R/3 system with which to communicate. Secondly, and perhaps most importantly, you must define the structure of the BSC in the SEM system.

The appraisal templates are grouped in categories, which, in turn, are grouped in so-called *category groups*. These two elements are simply used to structure the catalog of appraisal templates.

Defining the template catalog, down to the level of criteria, is the primary task that you must do in customizing. Before you start customizing, however, you should ensure that the business concept for your appraisal system is fixed. You'll find this customizing activity via the IMG-path **Personnel Management · Personnel Development · Objective setting and appraisals · Maintain templates**. There, you're prompted by a wizard to maintain the attributes of:

- ▶ Groups and categories (see Figure 12.4)
- ▶ Templates (see Figure 12.5)
- ▶ The criteria group and criteria (see Figure 12.6)

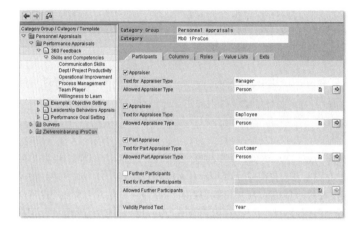

Figure 12.4 Maintenance of a Template Category

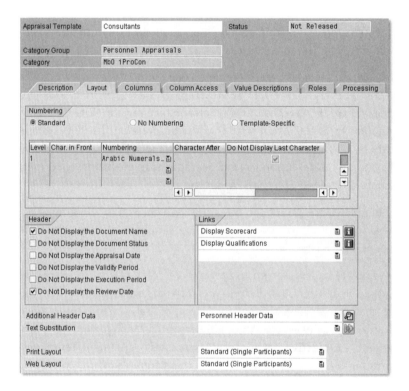

Figure 12.5 Maintenance of a Template

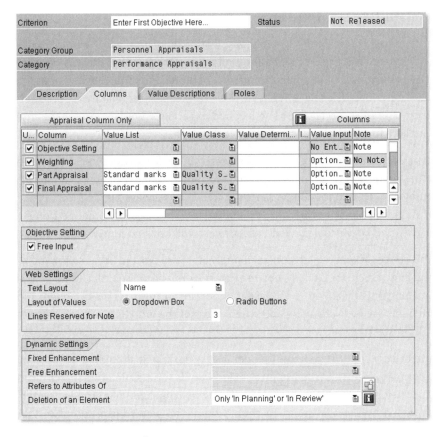

Criterion	Enter First Objective Here...				Status		Not Released

Category Group	Personnel Appraisals
Category	Performance Appraisals

Description / Columns / Value Descriptions / Roles

Appraisal Column Only   ℹ️   Columns

U...	Column	Value List		Value Class		Value Determi...	I...	Value Input	Note	
✔	Objective Setting		🗐		🗐			No Ent..🗐	Note	
✔	Weighting		🗐		🗐			Option..🗐	No Note	
✔	Part Appraisal	Standard marks	🗐	Quality S..🗐				Option..🗐	Note	
✔	Final Appraisal	Standard marks	🗐	Quality S..🗐				Option..🗐	Note	▲
			🗐		🗐				🗐		▼

◀ ▶ [   ]   ◀ ▶

Objective Setting
✔ Free Input

Web Settings

Text Layout	Name 🗐	
Layout of Values	⦿ Dropdown Box	○ Radio Buttons
Lines Reserved for Note	3	

Dynamic Settings

Fixed Enhancement		🗐
Free Enhancement		🗐
Refers to Attributes Of		🖼️
Deletion of an Element	Only 'In Planning' or 'In Review'	🗐 ℹ️

Figure 12.6 Maintenance of a Criterion

After you have completed the customization, you must do the following steps:

1. Conduct an automatic consistency check.

2. Translate the templates to other languages, if necessary.

3. Release the templates.

As you can see in the figures, there is a great deal of detailed customizing to do in order to define precisely the layout and functionality of the appraisal forms. However, this is not as complex as it may appear, once you have defined your business concept. Therefore, we won't explain every single field that you see here, but merely give you an overview of the task at hand.

Note this very important hint: the three-level structure (group, category, and template) may suggest that you should create many different templates. This, however, is not recommended in most instances. Rather, our best advice is to keep it simple and ensure that the results of different employees are comparable.

12.4 The Expert Finder

The core of the Expert Finder is a database with expert profiles. The primary difference between the Expert Finder and skill management is that there is no catalog of qualifications that you need to maintain beforehand. The knowledge of the experts is described by using a free text. There, any expert can maintain, for example, what kind of projects he or she has had experience working on. Then, anybody looking for an expert can do a keyword search.

It is apparent, however, that this kind of search is not well structured and therefore, does not ensure that an expert will be found, even if the data is maintained. The problem is that conducting a search in free text is always difficult (e.g., if the expert describes himself or herself as a *human resources expert*, someone doing a search with the keyword *personnel management* will not find him or her).

Still, this concept has a big advantage, namely, it is very flexible because the maintanance and search for skills is not restricted to qualifications that belong to a fixed catalog This flexibility is especially important in business areas, where the requirements are ever-changing and where most of the work is based on projects (e.g., IT consulting).

Because the concept of the Expert Finder is very flexible, it should be adapted by every company. Thus, it is feasible to include fields for a structured search from the skill catalogue. The best example here may be language skills. The user interface provided by the SAP standard should simply be viewed as a template that must be adapted.

The following data about experts is maintanied and shown:

▶ Name
▶ Communication data
▶ Knowledgas free-form texts (e.g., project experience)
▶ Special knowledgwithin a fixed structur(e.g., languages)
▶ Membership in expert communities
▶ Company-specific data

Any expert can be a member of different communities. These communities can then be used to foster communication within a community (e.g., the SAP HR community). Any member can deduce who else belongs to the community and ask community-specific questions. Furthermore, any member can maintain a more community-specific detailed expert profile (e.g., quote his or her experience in SAP HR). Community members can still be found by other employees because of their normal expert profiles, but not because of the community-specific profile.

The expert search based on keywords and other filters is done by a search engine that can process large quantities of data.

The result of the search is a hitlist that contains the names of the appropriate experts. Now, you can contact these experts and ask questions or enlist them to join your project team.

This concept can be used as being complementary to the skill management or, it can be used instead of it. However, it can only provide the functionality necessary to search for individual experts for special tasks. The Expert Finder is not the appropriate tool to use to support strategic skill management or risk management.

Part 3
Personnel Planning

13 The Personnel Planning Process

Personnel planning affects all areas of work in Human Resources. The core processes in personnel planning are the medium- and long-term planning of personnel costs and capacity. Both quantitative and qualitative aspects of personnel planning are integral to personnel capacity planning.

13.1 The Objectives of This Chapter

Planning is carried out in all areas of HR work; however, the extent to which this planning is carried out systematically, addressed among different departments, and appropriately documented varies from one enterprise to another. Planning in individual subprocesses is often done only in the context of an isolated solution. ERP-system support is frequently limited to a very simple documentation of planning results using Office products. The involvement of participants who are not central to the process, above all, the management, also is accomplished to very different degrees.

In this chapter, our goal is to provide you with an integrated approach to planning. Particular attention is paid to the division of tasks between central and local process steps. In Section 13.2, we'll introduce the basic elements of personnel planning; elements that must also be provided by an integrated information system. In doing so, we will focus on the core processes of personnel planning, which include planning capacity demands, available capacity, and personnel costs. By focusing on these core processes, you will see that it is difficult to separate *personnel planning* from *personnel development*. On the one hand, both personnel planning and personnel development are closely linked in the enterprise strategy. On the other hand, the Balanced Scorecard (BSC)—the qualitative aspect of personnel planning—forms part of personnel development. We have already touched on these areas in which planning and development overlap in Part 2 of this book; we will discuss them further in Part 4. Section 13.3 shows an overview of the planning process as the result. Section 13.4 draws a brief conclusion, in which the most important requirements made on IT support in the area of personnel planning are summarized, and the possibilities offered by mySAP HR are weighed against them.

13.2　An Approach to Integrated Personnel Planning

13.2.1　Elements of Personnel Planning

The main elements in personnel planning are capacity planning, compensation planning, and personnel cost planning. We shall now present each of these elements in greater detail.

Capacity planning

Capacity planning refers to the medium- and long-term planning of personnel capacity (a planning period of at least one year). It does not refer to the short-term planning of individual employees and their specific assignment to individual activities and times. This detailed planning is known as *short-term manpower planning* or—to use the SAP term—*shift planning*.

The objective of capacity planning is to plan the capacity demand for the overall future work at the company and its various departments, and to define suitable measures to ensure that these demands can be met in an optimal way. Even if the data used is derived in part from the employee level, the actual planning is completely removed from the individual employees. Therefore, the following three steps are necessary to constitute planning:

▶ Determine the demand in personnel capacity over the entire planning period.

▶ Estimate the available capacity and consider any changes that have been identified.

▶ Deduce what actions need to be carried out, in particular, new recruitment and redundancy (both internal and external).

Capacity must also be viewed from a qualitative standpoint throughout the entire planning process, although, here, it can be viewed with less detail than was necessary in skills management. In general, employees are classified according to quality; for example, on a level that corresponds to the SAP concept of the job. A possible basis for this level can include such common classifications as the "International Standard Classification of Occupations" (ISCO). Due to the constant changes in job descriptions, you will probably need to adapt the ISCO to reflect the current standard operating procedures (SOPs) and job descriptions in your enterprise.

Determining demands is usually done according to management estimates based on the current volume of tasks and the capacity available. You can also use various different methods or models, such as:

- Simple key figure procedures, i.e., productivity key figures, which constantly measure work volumes against the number of employees and can therefore derive the necessary number of workers from demand planning

- Span of supervision model

The following methods are available for forecasting capacity available in the future, for example:

- The Markoff analysis (Using transition probabilities between groups of employees and the "outside world")

- System dynamics model

Compensation planning

The objective of *compensation planning* is to set the *Total Compensation* and how it is divided among individual employees within a given overall framework. The following criteria are factored into this equation:

- Market-driven compensation (benchmarking)

- Comparability within the enterprise (job evaluation)

- In line with a compensation policy, which can make compensation dependent on certain parameters (appraisal results, length of time with the company, and so on)

- Compliance with budgets

- Optimal compensation packages (from the employees' point of view) with the given total expenditure

Compensation planning is therefore primarily done from the employee's point of view. It provides perhaps the most important input for personnel cost planning, which is done from the vantage point of the enterprise.

Personnel cost planning

Personnel cost planning is the result of considering all the cost-related implications of all personnel actions both currently and in the future. The goal of personnel cost planning is to estimate the total personnel costs for a defined period of time. It also reports on how changes to certain general conditions will affect personnel costs as well as provide a forecast of future personnel costs. To get a planned value for the coming year, it isn't enough to simply consider the current personnel costs of employees and multiply that by twelve. Rather, you must first identify and evaluate certain determining factors, which are enumerated below.

▶ **Factors that influence personnel cost planning, related to salary changes**
Statutory changes
There are many statutory changes that can influence the personnel costs of an employee (such as changes to tax or social security).

▷ **Non-payscale salary adjustment**
This refers to a freely negotiated change in remuneration.

▷ **Level increase**
With a level increase, employees automatically receive more money when they have been with the company for a certain number of years or have reached a certain age.

▷ **Collective wage agreement**
Employers tied by collective agreements must pass on wage adjustments to employees that arise from annual negotiations with the employee union.

▷ **Reassignment to wage group**
Employees continue to learn and gain additional qualifications. If, due to a promotion, they carry out more upper-level tasks, their salary is adjusted accordingly by reassigning them to a wage group or level. If employees are not paid by the pay scale, their individual payments are adjusted.

▶ **Influencing factors arising from organizational changes Labor turnover**
Employees retire or leave the company; new employees join the company. All of these measures have a certain time frame and can therefore be considered in planning. Retirement depends on the age and health of employees. Employees who choose to leave the company are bound by law to give an adequate period of notice. New employees are hired after the recruitment process has run its course.

▷ **Reorganization/restructuring**
Successful business units constantly verify if their processes still receive optimal support from the existing organization structure. If the support is less than optimal, the company is restructured in order that its continued success be ensured. In large enterprises, the profitability of different enterprise areas is also checked. Consequently, entire areas of business can be sold off and other areas can be purchased if necessary.

▶ **Additional influencing factors**
In addition to remuneration, there are other costs that can also be considered in the context of personnel cost planning. In many enterprises, these costs are planned in the area of material costs, outside of personnel planning. You should, however, not forget that these costs are directly influenced by the hiring or firing of employees.

- Costs of the working place and its equipment
- Education and training costs
- Recruitment costs
- Redundancy costs (such as severance pay)
- Travel expenses

Additional elements of personnel planning

In addition to these core elements, which generally have a significant effect on all other elements of personnel planning, for each subprocess in personnel work, you can—in principle—define a *planning process.* The following are the main processes:

- Shift planning
- Personnel development planning (this is dealt with in greater detail in Part 2 of this book)
- Recruitment planning (derived directly from capacity planning)
- Travel planning (generally, this is planning at a very low level)

13.2.2 Dividing Tasks Between Central and Local Planning Steps

As with personnel development, personnel planning is also divided into local and central tasks. Managers of the individual organizational units provide the main information and forecasts from current business ("from the front," as it were) and implement agreed-on planning guidelines. The central planning instance contributes information regarding enterprise strategy. It is also responsible for consolidating planning and drawing up guidelines.

With a diagram of the planning process, Figure 13.1 shows roughly how tasks are divided between central and local participants. In this example, central responsibility lies with the department of personnel controlling. In practice, planning tasks are often done in other departments because personnel controlling is only responsible for monitoring compliance with guidelines and the derivation of measures in the event of irregularities. Basically, however, planning coordination is in good hands in personnel controlling, since that is where one would normally expect control instruments to be found.

In the example process, the area managers are referred to as local process participants. As a rule, direct reconciliation with personnel controlling is also done on a higher hierarchy level. Nevertheless, lower levels are also involved in the process. Here, however, the manager in question is responsible for the coordination of the personnel planning process and provides a consolidated result for their area. This process, in which guidelines are broken down for lower organizational units and the sub-plans are then put back together again, already makes significant demands on IT support.

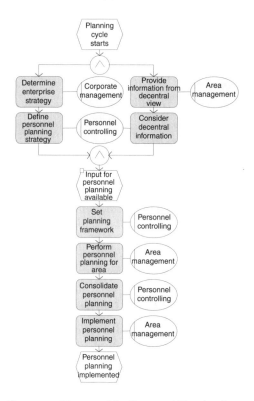

Figure 13.1 Diagram of the Personnel Planning Process

In practice, the process is not as straightforward or linear as shown in Figure 13.1. Often, several iterative steps are required, in which area managers submit plans and personnel controlling sends back guidelines for planning adjustment either before or after consolidation. In addition, changes can often be made to the strategic guidelines during the planning process. Furthermore, local planning does not usually occur without the support of central authorities. Personnel controlling or other staff departments, separate from the HR department, offer support with issues at the department level, for example. Planning at the employee level is often supported by personnel administrators who have a detailed knowledge of compensation rules.

13.2.3 Integrating Central and Local Planning Steps

If non-integrated planning media are used (for example, paper or individual MS Excel files), consolidation will prove to be very difficult. Deriving consolidated figures is very labor-intensive and requires manual access each time a change is made to local sub-plans. In addition, there is a high risk of errors when transferring data. Consequently, all participants should work in an integrated data basis to ensure that processes are more efficient. Such a system must enable planning changes from local departments to either be included before approval or not, as required, in the drawing up of consolidated results. This would allow for the effect of the change to be estimated in advance. On principle, only central approval can then include this change in the basis for planning. This integration is a difficult but vital requirement for the implementation in an information system.

In the next section, we will differentiate between the central tasks and the local tasks. In so doing, we shall once again focus on the core processes of capacity planning and cost planning.

13.2.4 Local Tasks

Those persons addressed here constitute the management in charge of planning or, their assistants who are responsible for entering the planning into the system. Also involved in the local planning are the individual employees who can access or even provide information (for example, regarding their own availability) using an Employee Self-Service (ESS) solution. However, their involvement in the IT-supported process is nowhere near as critical here as it is in personnel development. Apart from IT support, the role of the individual employees is instrumental because, for example, in performance reviews, compensation planning is done on an individual level. Furthermore, the information that is amassed from consultations with employees is also used as input for various sub-plans.

The following tasks are included in local planning:

▶ Conduct performance reviews with employees for planning on an individual level. This can include the following aspects, for example:

  ▷ A pay raise

  ▷ The contents of the compensation package

  ▷ Working time and available capacity

  ▷ Transfer

  ▷ Retirement provision

  ▷ Time off (parental leave, sabbatical, and so on).

▶ Determine capacity demands.

▶ Forecast available capacity.

▶ Break down guidelines/budgets for subordinate levels.

▶ Agree on targets at department level.

▶ Consolidate sub-plans from subordinate levels.

- Monitor guidelines, and reconciliation and consultation for subordinate levels.
- Oversee maintenance of relevant information in the information system.
- Manage the reconciliation of guidelines with higher levels.
- Oversee the hiring or transfer of employees from other departments.
- Oversee the release or transfer of employees to other departments.
- Perform other types of capacity adjustment.
- Ensure the reconciliation of budgets for personnel costs with budgets for material costs and, if necessary, oversee cross-budget balancing.

13.2.5 Central Tasks

The following tasks are undertaken by central personnel controlling—in partial collaboration with other (staff) departments:

- Derive a personnel strategy.
- Prepare planning and evaluation tools for decentralized locations.
- Consider trends in enterprise strategy and in the environment that may have an effect on the strategy and process of personnel planning.
- Define the organizational and content framework of the decentralized planning process.
- Set the budget at the highest levels.
- Draw up a compensation policy.
- Provide methods for those involved in local processes.
- Train/coach those involved in decentralized processes.
- Ensure that results are comparable via the quality assurance of processes.
- Verify whether guidelines have been adhered to.

13.3 An Overview of the Personnel Planning Process

13.3.1 The Foundations of Personnel Planning

The most important data for the planning process considered here (see Figure 13.2) includes:

- The organizational structure
- The job index
- Compensation data
- Additional cost data
- General HR master data

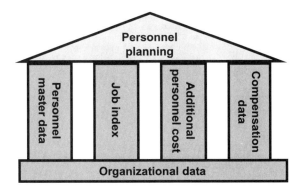

Figure 13.2 The Foundations of Personnel Planning

13.3.2 Personnel Planning Process Outline

Given the various different iterative steps in reconciliation between central and local units and the different planning subjects, it is difficult to present one generally applicable personnel planning process outline. The process in Figure 13.3, however, can serve as a model for your enterprise-specific planning process.

Input for the planning process is provided by personnel controlling and company management. The following areas are included:

▶ Enterprise strategy

▶ Planning the business development

▶ The current job index and staffing assignments

▶ A projection of personnel costs based on the current status
This projection can be rather difficult. It is not enough to simply multiply the costs for the month of October by twelve to get the value for next year. Agreements on special payments and previously agreed-on changes must also be included in calculations.

This input can be carried out in several different variants, if different development scenarios need to be planned for the enterprise. Because this will not change the elements inherent in the process, we will use only one scenario as an example. The budgets are then defined based on the objectives of the individual areas (or departments, sections, and so on); for example, they may be:

▶ Budgets for changing basic pay

▶ Budgets for bonuses or other special payments

▶ Budgets for adjusting employee capacity (measured in what are known as full-time equivalences (FTEs), whereby two employees working at 50% count as one capacity)

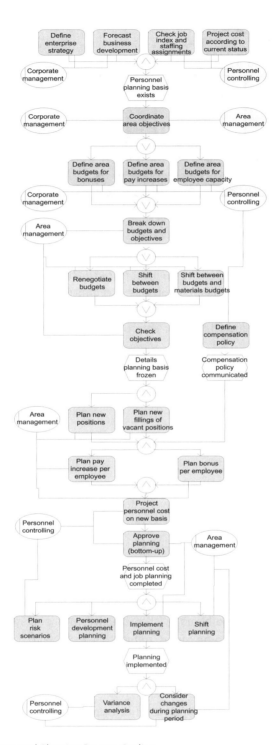

Figure 13.3 Personnel Planning Process Outline

Both objectives and budgets are then broken down along the organizational hierarchy. This part of the process is the responsibility of the area managers and the respective subordinate heads of department. In general, there will then be shifts between different budgets (for example, instead of increasing basic pay, there may be more bonus payments). Moreover, based on the capital that is ultimately available, the objectives will once again be checked with regard to their attainability. The first local planning phase deals with capacity:

▶ Will new positions be created or will existing ones be cut?

▶ Which vacant positions will be filled at what time, and so on?

The result of this planning phase is the target *capacity plan* with vacancies for the planning period. Based on this, you can plan changes to compensation, wage-level or wage-group reassignment, bonus payments, and so on. This planning is done in the context of guidelines from the compensation policy, for example, calculating the bonus based on the appraisal results.

Planning, which is first done at the lowest level, then goes through an approval process from the bottom up. In this way, the adjusted compensation is included in a new projection of costs. This projection then becomes the final plan—so long as approval is not denied at a higher level—thus ensuring a new process with new guidelines. In addition to various sub-plans already addressed, what now follows is the planning of particular risk scenarios, which we will discuss in the next section.

The planning that has been agreed upon is checked throughout the entire planning period for changed circumstances and, if necessary, is adjusted. Variance analysis is not only done at the end of the planning period; it is ongoing. In this way, variances can be identified from an early stage and counter measures can be initiated if they're required.

13.3.3 Risk Management

Elements of risk management also form an important output of personnel planning. The following relevant risks can be identified in the planning processes that we have addressed here:

▶ **Cost risk**
  With a simple cost planning, personnel costs can be forecast to such an extent that there is hardly any serious risk of a surprise. One special aspect of this is the company pension plan.

▶ **Capacity risk**
Over-capacity in certain areas can quickly lead to a cost risk. Under-capacity can lead to a significant loss of market share.

▶ **Compensation risk**
Compensation that does not reflect the current market can lead to a lack of motivation and therefore to a drop in employee performance. A similar situation can arise if compensation for many employees is subjectively considered to be unfair. If this occurs, the compensation risk can become a motivation risk.

13.4 Conclusion for Implementation in an Information System

The demands made on IT support can be divided into two areas: Content requirements describe which functions are provided by the system; requirements related to role-specific access describe how different groups of users can use the system. The latter is a determining criterion in the planning process.

13.4.1 Role-Specific Access

We can differentiate between three different groups of users:

▶ Management, who not only executes reports, but also enters planning into the system. The personnel planning period is possibly the only time during the entire year in which this target group maintains data—to any significant extent—in the HR system.

▶ Employees who are involved in the planning process from the central HR-department. These employees primarily include those working in personnel controlling and also personnel administrators.

▶ Lastly, there is the group of individual employees who want to access their own data (for example, to display appraisals, total compensation, summaries, and so on).

Access to individual employees is therefore not essential in this process and is far less critical here than it is in personnel development.

The products of SAP basically fulfill these requirements with their role concept together with the portals Employee Self-Service (ESS) and Manager Self Service (MSS). With R/3 Release 4.6C, however, if you're not using the Enterprise Portal 5.0 or higher, you will find that MSS—in the form of the Manager's Desktop (MDT)—is not yet available as a Web portal. In addition, decentralized access for management still has some gaps; therefore, they cannot be linked to the process completely via the system.

13.4.2 Content Requirements

In principle, an EDP system must support the following block of tasks:

▶ Integration into strategic enterprise planning

▶ Capacity planning

▶ Cost and compensation planning

▶ Support for decentralized processes

Now, we shall present a brief preliminary assessment of the possibilities offered by mySAP HR.

Integration into Strategic Enterprise Planning

Personnel planning should be integrated into strategic planning for the entire enterprise. The technical representation of this integration, however, is rarely a very high priority requirement. In general, integration at this high level can be very well arranged via organizational measures. In the standard Release 4.6C of R/3, integration is still not very efficiently developed. It is only possible to transfer completed cost planning to the controlling component (with many more possibilities in R/3 Enterprise than were available in Release 4.6C). A look at the market, however, shows that technical support for this integration is only provided in a very limited way by other ERP products too. By using Strategic Enterprise Management (SEM), however, integration can be greatly improved.

Functions of Capacity Planning

The results of capacity planning can be well integrated into the system in different ways. Integration into Recruitment, Personnel Development, Remuneration Accounting, Time Management, and Cost Planning are particularly well developed. Reports in this area also meet the most important requirements. Long-term requirement planning methods—as mentioned in Section 13.2.1—are not supported. However, you can derive requirements from short-term capacity planning, i.e., from the shift planning component.

Functions of Cost and Compensation Planning

Cost planning offers multifaceted calculation scenarios. Because most enterprises have special requirements in this area, enhancements are often necessary. There are many so-called business-add-ins (BAdIs) available for this which enable you to make adjustments quite easily with your own programming of specific requirements. Overall, the functions of central cost planning meet the most important requirements. The new Cost Planning component, supplied as an enhancement to R/3 Enterprise, is a marked improvement.

Compensation planning primarily includes the areas of compensation policy, (for example, benchmarking and job pricing), budgeting, and the approval process. Planning at the employee level is also possible; however, it is still lacking in the area of payscale changes and in ergonomics. The integration with cost planning is only achieved with the new solution in cost planning (R/3 Enterprise/Release 4.7).

Support for Decentralized Processes

The interfaces for managers are available in the MDT and the MSS. Unfortunately, these functions are limited to compensation management and capacity planning in Release 4.6C. Cost planning is only supported locally with the Line Manager tool of the new solution. Employee information requirements can be covered by ESS.

13.4.3 Summary

The individual functions offered by mySAP HR cover most requirements. There are only a few gaps which, fortunately, are not critical. The biggest shortcoming is the lack of integration of the three aspects considered regarding local processes. The gap between cost planning (overall costs) and compensation management (employee view) still frequently forces the user to switch over to Office products. (The need for the user to switch to Office products exists only up to Release 4.6C. As of Release 4.7, it is no longer necessary.) Decentralized cost planning is also supported by the new solution in R/3 Enterprise and this closes the main gaps.

14 Position and Quota Planning

Organizational management provides a good basis for planning personnel capacity. The quota planning component within it and the great degree of flexibility for defining any structures offer further planning possibilities.

14.1 The Design in mySAP HR

14.1.1 Planning at Position Level

The term *position* is a key element in Organizational Management. If correctly maintained, positions can provide information on the required capacity while the staffing of positions describes the actual available capacity. By integrating positions into the organizational structure, associated evaluations are possible on different levels.

The following attributes of a position serve as a basis for planning:

▶ **Working time**
Indicates the actual capacity needed at a particular work center.

▶ **Validity period**
States the period during which (i.e., from when to when) the capacity is needed.

▶ **Vacancy status**
Determines whether a position is to be filled.

▶ **The "obsolete" indicator**
Indicates that a position is no longer needed. It is only continued because the current holder is still in the position. Because this indicator is also considered to be an "ejector seat" indicator, it is often used with great discretion. Nevertheless, it is necessary to ensure a clear planning basis if the planning is not done on a quota planning level (see Section 14.1.2).

▶ In new screens, the combined information from the vacancy status and the "obsolete"-indicator is referred to as the "staffing status."

▶ In addition, special data on positions or the jobs that describe them is used for the optimal planning of staff assignment; for example, this includes:

   ▶ Restrictions that limit the circle of possible position holders to specific people (for example, in terms of height, age, or disability)

- ▶ Competencies that are affiliated with the position (such as the power of procuration) and for which the position holder must also be qualified
- ▶ Additional information that can also be created in user-defined infotypes without much extra work

▶ Data from personnel development, and in particular, requirement profiles, can also be used.

Therefore, it is possible to clearly determine where capacity is still required and where there may be over-capacity. An important prerequisite here is that the working time recorded in the positions also corresponds to the actual requirement. It should neither be left at a flat rate working time, or be adjusted to fit the contractual working time of the position holder. If, for example, a full-time worker is needed for a specific activity, but there is currently only one part-time employee working 50% of the time, then the outstanding capacity requirement must also be reflected in the reports. This type of position can then be filled by two job holders (*Job sharing,* see Figure 14.1). On the other hand, a full-time employee can also hold two part-time positions. A common occurrence is that a full-time employee partially occupies two full-time positions. This type of situation can occur particularly at management level if a manager acts as provisional manager of a second department over an extended period until a successor has been found. Figures 14.1, 14.2, and 14.3 show the interrelationships between an employee's working time and the working time associated with a position. The other data addressed in Organizational Management also supports planning and can be evaluated accordingly.

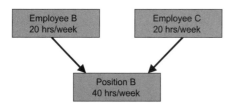

Figure 14.1 Job sharing – No Over- or Under-Occupation

Figure 14.2 Part-Time with Slight Under-Occupancy

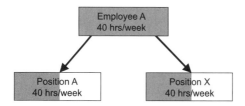

Figure 14.3 Two Positions for One Employee with 50 % Under-Occupancy

14.1.2 Quota Planning

Quota planning is not done on the basis of evaluating individual positions; rather, planning is done on a job level instead of on a position level. If, for example, the number of assembly operators in a department needs to be increased from eight to eleven, you don't have to create three new positions in the system for the job "assembly operator." Rather, you only have to record the target number "11" for the job in question. The number of employees and positions (both can be part-time) that are actually used to meet the capacity is not relevant here.

Specifications are given in so-called *Full-Time Equivalents* (FTE). This makes maintenance much simpler and faster. In particular, when reducing the number of employees, this procedure is also more practical. If three out of eleven positions must be cut, it isn't necessary to select three specific positions and set them as "obsolete." It is sufficient to simply set the target value to 8. Furthermore, in reality, it is often not known which positions will ultimately be closed or eliminated.

Quota planning is usually carried out directly on the Manager's Desktop (MDT) by the managers of the individual departments. Planning approval can then be done at the next level up in the hierarchy or, via a central instance (for example, Personnel Controlling). The timeframes for which planning is created are determined in Customizing. Typically, quarterly plans are a good compromise between clarity and exactitude. Integration in Personnel Cost Planning is a very important aspect of quota planning. The quotas can be incorporated into the calculation, based on the Cost Planning information at the corresponding jobs in infotype 1015.

14.1.3 Openness for Enhancement and New Structures

The object types, relationship types and infotypes in Organizational Management can be freely extended (see Chapter 2, *Organizational Management*). Thus, it is possible to integrate specific planning bases that aren't available in the standard release, i.e., R/3 Release 4.7.

- You can use newly defined infotypes to record additional information that is required for planning.
- With new object types and relationship types, you can map extended structures, such as the additional structuring of the job catalog (see Section 14.3.2).

14.2 Implementation in mySAP HR

14.2.1 Relevant Infotypes

In this section, we'll introduce infotypes that contain important information for planning. For specific customizing for these infotypes, use the IMG path **Personnel Management · Organizational Management · Infotype Settings**.

Vacant and obsolete identifiers

Flagging a position as "vacant" or "obsolete" is essential for planning, and in particular, for integration with recruitment:

- Infotype 1007: "Vacancy" (see Chapter 2, *Organizational Management*)
- Infotype 1014: "Obsolete" (see Figure 14.4)

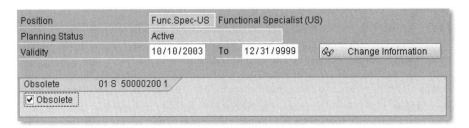

| Position | Func.Spec-US | Functional Specialist (US) |

| Planning Status | Active | |

| Validity | 10/10/2003 To 12/31/9999 | Change Information |

Obsolete   01 S 50000200 1
☑ Obsolete

Figure 14.4 Infotype 1014: Obsolete Indicator

Restrictions

By default, this infotype (1006) is only permitted for work centers. You can allow the use of this infotype, for example, for jobs or positions using the IMG path *Personnel Management · Organizational Management · Basic Settings · Data Model Enhancement · Infotype Maintenance · Maintain Infotypes*. Here, you can record if certain groups of people aren't suitable for occupying a certain position, for example, because of health reasons. The possible restrictions are stored in Customizing using **Infotype Settings** (see Figure 14.5). Similarly, you can store explanations for the restrictions.

When maintaining infotypes, you can then choose from the selection available (see Figure 14.6).

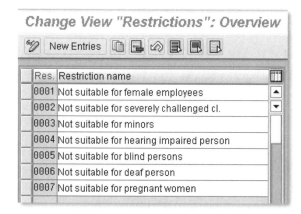

Figure 14.5 Creating Restriction Types

Res.	Restriction name
0001	Not suitable for female employees
0002	Not suitable for severely challenged cl.
0003	Not suitable for minors
0004	Not suitable for hearing impaired person
0005	Not suitable for blind persons
0006	Not suitable for deaf person
0007	Not suitable for pregnant women

Job	Welder (CA) Welder (CA)	
Planning Status	Active	
Validity	10/10/2003 to 12/31/9999	Change Information

Restrictions	01 C 5000072 3 1	
Restrictions	0007 Not suitable for pregnant women	
Reason	0001 Exposure to X-rays	

Figure 14.6 Infotype 1006: Restrictions

Authorities and Resources

Infotype 1010 is used for two separate purposes:

▶ You can record which authorities or powers of attorney the position holder has (see Figure 14.7). This is only useful if this power of attorney is linked to the position and not to the employee. If the employee automatically retains this power of attorney when leaving a position, it is preferable to maintain this authority in infotype 0030 in Personnel Administration. Use of infotype 1010 is also relevant for planning. Ultimately, a prerequisite for the employee who occupies this position is the power of procuration, i.e., having the ability to execute the authorities associated with this right.

▶ You can record resources that are required for working in the position (for example, a cell phone). This is not relevant to capacity planning.

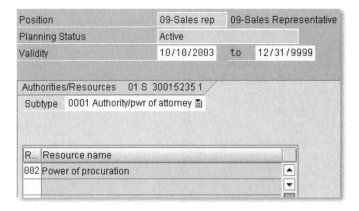

Figure 14.7 Power of Procuration as a Prerequisite for Occupying the Position

Teaching hours

Infotype 1507, which is shown in Figure 14.8, is a very special example. It is used in universities or other educational establishments to plan capacity in teaching/class time. Although it can also be considered suitable for enterprises with a corporate university, here, we shall show it primarily as an example or a suggestion of how you can record special planning data in the system without much effort.

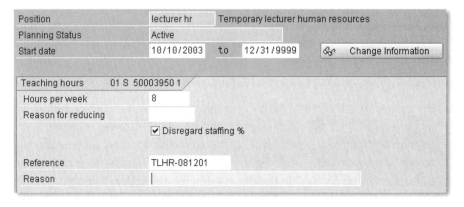

Figure 14.8 Fixed Teaching Hours

14.2.2 Reports Based on Positions

Use the menu path **Personnel · Organizational Management · Info System · Position** to access reports that can be useful for planning personnel capacities, recruitment, and personnel reduction. The most helpful reports are described below.

Staff Assignments

The *Staff Assignments report* is the most popular of these reports. It allows you to present positions and how they are staffed, in particular, with working times and staffing percentages. The presentation allows you to show or hide numerous useful columns and create totals. Using this report, you can instantly identify over- or under-staffing by comparing the target working hours with the actual working hours. Vacancies are also displayed with a date. In dialog processing, this report is a very useful tool. Figure 14.9 shows a simple form of the list in which the target and actual working hours are compared to each other.

Staff assignments

Key date 10/10/2003

Org. unit	Positions	Employee(s)	Staffing status	Actual working hours	Target working hours
Hum Res -US	Vice President of Human Resources (US)	Ben Taylor		173,33	173,60
Hum Res -US	Director, HR Initiatives (US)	Mr. Dan Young		173,33	173,60
Hum Res -US	Receptionist	Lisa Felix		173,33	173,60
Comp/Ben -US	Manager of Compensation & Benefits (US)	Joanne Pawlucky		173,33	173,60
Comp/Ben -US	Functional Specialist (US)		Vacant since 02/01/2001	0,00	173,60
Comp/Ben -US	Administrative Staff (US)		Vacant since 09/27/2001	0,00	173,60
Comp/Ben -US	Sr. Compensation Consultant	John Parker		173,34	173,60
Comp/Ben -US	Sr. Benefits Advisor (US)	Megan Young	Vacant since 10/31/2000	173,34	173,60
Comp/Ben -US	Functional Specialist (US)	Liam Morton	Vacant since 12/14/1999	173,34	173,60
Lab.Rel. -US	Manager of Labor Relations (US)	Ann Takahashi		173,33	173,60
Lab.Rel. -US	Functional Specialist (US)	Richard Jones		173,34	173,60
Lab.Rel. -US	Supervisor of Labor staff (US)		Vacant since 09/27/2001	0,00	173,60
Lab.Rel. -US	Legal Advisor	Michael Houseman		173,34	173,60
Lab.Rel. -US	Administration Staff (US)	Jennifer Esposito		173,34	173,60
Lab.Rel. -US	Functional Specialist (US)	Michael Davis		173,33	173,60
HR Adm. -US	Manager of Human Resources (US)	Tom Peterson		173,33	173,60
HR Adm. -US	Functional Specialist (US)		Vacant since 09/27/2001	0,00	173,60
HR Adm. -US	Administrative Staff (US)		Vacant since 03/03/2001	0,00	173,60

Figure 14.9 Staff Assignments: Employment Percentages

Periods When Positions Are Unoccupied Per Organizational Unit

Using this report, you can quickly get an overview of which positions are or were unoccupied during a particular period of time and for how long. Consequently, you can use this report not only as a tool for planning, but also to check the quality of planning and recruitment. If positions are unoccupied for a long duration, it can indicate a lengthy recruitment process or poor planning.

Authorities and Resources

The *Authorities and Resources report* lists all selected positions and shows any authorities and resources that have been assigned to these positions. It is suitable for a quick first evaluation; however, because positions are always listed and the result is shown in list form, we recommend that you create a query.

Periods when positions are unoccupied per org. unit

Selection period: 01/01/2003 - 12/31/2003

Organizational unit	Position	Unocc. from	Unocc. to	New holder	Unocc. da...
Compensation and Benefits - (US)	Administrative Staff (US)	01/01/2003	12/31/2003		365
	Functional Specialist (US)	01/01/2003	12/31/2003		365
Labor Relations - (US)	Supervisor of Labor staff (US)	01/01/2003	12/31/2003		365
Human Resources Administration - (US)	Admin. HR	01/01/2003	12/31/2003		365
	Administrative Staff (US)	01/01/2003	12/31/2003		365
	Functional Specialist (US)	01/01/2003	12/31/2003		365
Development and Training Admin - (US)	Sr. Performance Management Consultant	01/01/2003	12/31/2003		365
Payroll Administration - (US)	Functional Specialist (US)	01/01/2003	12/31/2003		365
		01/01/2003	12/31/2003		365
Workforce Planning	Administrative Staff (US)	01/01/2003	12/31/2003		365
	Sr. HR Planning Advisor	01/01/2003	12/31/2003		365
		01/01/2003	12/31/2003		365
		01/01/2003	12/31/2003		365

Figure 14.10 Periods for Unoccupied Positions

Vacant Positions

The *Vacant Positions report* (see Figure 14.11) serves as an important basis for recruitment planning. In contrast to the *Periods When Positions Are Unoccupied... report*, this report evaluates infotype 1007. A position can remain unoccupied after it has been planned, but a vacancy is not created until you want this position filled.

Vacant positions

Key date   10/10/2003

Organizational unit	Position	vacant from/to	Staffing status
Compensation and Benefits - (US)	Functional Specialist (US)	2/01/2001-12/31/9999	Unoccupied since 03/30/1996
	Administrative Staff (US)	9/27/2001-12/31/9999	Unoccupied since 09/21/2001
	Functional Specialist (US)	12/14/1999-12/31/9999	occupied until 12/31/9999
	Sr. Benefits Advisor (US)	10/31/2000-12/31/9999	occupied until 12/31/9999
Labor Relations - (US)	Supervisor of Labor staff (US)	9/27/2001-12/31/9999	Unoccupied since 06/16/2001
Human Resources Administration - (US)	Functional Specialist (US)	9/27/2001-12/31/9999	Unoccupied since 01/01/1994
	Administrative Staff (US)	3/03/2001-12/31/9999	Unoccupied since 03/02/2001
Development and Training Admin - (US)	Sr. Performance Management Consultant	11/16/2000-12/31/9999	Unoccupied since 10/16/2000
Payroll Administration - (US)	Functional Specialist (US)	3/01/2002-12/31/9999	Unoccupied since 03/01/2002
	Functional Specialist (US)	3/01/2002-12/31/9999	Unoccupied since 03/01/2002
	Administrative Staff (US)	5/30/2002-12/31/9999	occupied until 12/31/9999
Workforce Planning	Sr. HR Planning Advisor	10/02/2000-12/31/9999	Unoccupied since 10/02/2000

Figure 14.11 Evaluation of Vacancies

Obsolete Positions

The *Obsolete Positions report* enables you to identify areas in which over-capacity still exists. In particular, this report provides information on how long obsolete positions will continue to be occupied. Therefore, the latest date on which the position can be closed is made immediately apparent.

14.2.3 Quota Planning

Quota planning is maintained in infotype 1019. In general, this does not appear "directly." You usually have to call quota planning using the Manager's Desktop (MDT)—in the standard scenario—under the **Costs and Budget** view.

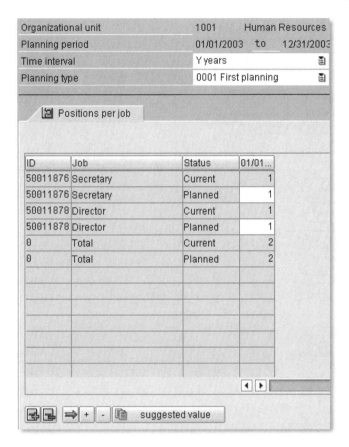

Figure 14.12 Quota Planning for a Team in the MDT

Execution of Quota Planning

The planning objects and data related to the manager's area of responsibility are directly available in the MDT. The planning interface provides the current full-time equivalents (FTEs) per job. The planned values can then be maintained in the following rows (see Figure 14.12). You can also add new rows, which enables you to plan quotas for other jobs. Figure 14.13 shows a very rough outline of such planning (on an annual basis). Planning intervals can be defined in Customizing.

You can also control the data flow via Customizing. There are often several planning rounds, whereby the first round presents local managements "preference," which is later adjusted in a second planning round following the examination by top management. A possible flowchart—including several rounds of planning—is shown in Figure 14.13.

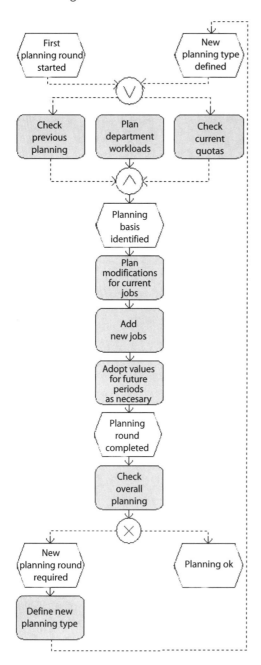

Figure 14.13 Quota Planning with MDT and Central Checking

Customizing

The planning types (such as first round, final round, and temporary planning) must be created as subtypes of infotype 1019 (see Chapter 2, *Organizational Management*). Only when you have done this can you use the IMG path **Personnel Management · Manager's Desktop · Quota Planning · Define Planning Type and Periods** to maintain the essential characteristics of the planning type on this basis. These are the planning intervals and the validity period. In the same Customizing view, you can also define which planning type (or round of planning) is currently in progress. Management can only maintain the current round in the MDT.

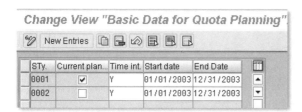

Figure 14.14 Basic Data and Current Indicator

In order for the quotas to be displayed in actual FTEs and not in positions—which is the recommended planning interface—you must activate this Customization using the IMG path **Personnel Management · Manager's Desktop · Quota Planning · Define Calculation in FTEs**. You can use the same IMG path to set the FTE calculation type.

14.3 Process Examples

14.3.1 Risk Management

If you set quota planning with a forecast period of more than one year, two critical developments, in particular, can be identified:

▶ Local management can plan a large reduction in the number of employees in many areas. Generally, this decision is based on estimates regarding the state of the market and future changes to tasks. Assuming that management estimates are correct, you must immediately plan to take steps to reduce the number of employees in the areas in question. Otherwise, the reduction will be too late to defray the costs incurred due to over-capacity. Consequently, the very competitiveness of the enterprise will be threatened.

▶ The opposite case can also be critical. If several departments plan a strong increase in capacity to cover their future tasks, you must verify the likelihood of this event and view its probability in relation to the labor market. If, for example, a significantly higher capacity of engineers is planned due to an upcoming market expansion, but engineers are in short supply, then counter measures must be found in time. A shortage of labor that is only identified at short notice can endanger the implementation of the enterprise strategy. This process is a simplified form of risk management in skill management.

Figure 14.15 shows an overview of the scenarios. In this figure, whether the requirement or surplus is of a general nature or it is only for specific jobs (for example, engineers and HTML specialists) is distinguished.

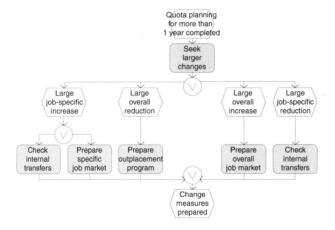

Figure 14.15 Risk Management Based on Quota Planning

14.3.2 Structuring the Job Index

As discussed in Section 14.1.3, Organizational Management offers many possibilities for user-defined enhancements. One commonly used variant is to strengthen the structure of the job plan. If you put additional hierarchy levels above the existing jobs in the system, additional selection possibilities will be available. Then, not only can jobs be selected against new criteria, but everything that is related—either directly or indirectly to the jobs, and in particular, the positions and the employees—can be selected as well. Possible additional structuring criteria are:

▶ Wage type class
▶ Departmental alignment
▶ Driving license: Yes/no criterion

In addition, the following customizing activities are essential (only a summary is provided here, since customizing has already been described in detail in Chapter 2, *Organizational Management*, and above):

▶ Create the structuring criteria as an object type (for example "job subgroup")

▶ Assign the corresponding relationship types

▶ Create evaluation paths

Figure 14.16 shows a three-level structure. Jobs are first combined to form job subgroups and job subgroups are, in turn, combined to form job groups. Both structures group jobs according to the makeup of the criteria. The jobs are then separated according to wage class.

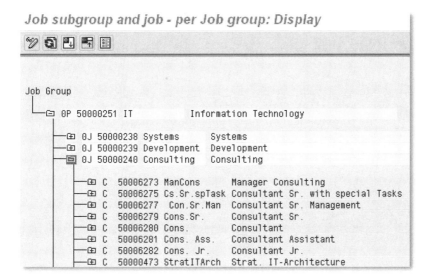

Figure 14.16 Three-Level Structured Job Index

14.4 Critical Success Factors

Because Organizational Management serves as a basis for many processes in mySAP HR, the simple Position and Quota Planning is often neglected during design. The following aspects should, however, always be considered:

▶ The possibilities offered by the standard here are generally not used very much. Before complex processes based on Office products are set in motion, you should always check the standard possibilities.

▶ Maintenance of positions is an area of weakness in most enterprises. Therefore, you must ensure that positions are created in a reasonable time and above all, are delimited again when no longer needed, and the vacancy status is correct.

- ▶ The working times of positions must be correct.
- ▶ You must ensure the integration of processes with recruitment, on the one hand, and with personnel administration on the other hand.
- ▶ The possibilities offered by new object types and evaluation methods, which can be created with little effort, are often not fully appreciated in many enterprises.
- ▶ Quota planning should be favored because it can be easily maintained by management.
- ▶ FTEs should be used for quota planning.
- ▶ It is important to define a clear and simple process for quota planning, that is, you must ensure that each round of planning is completed by a certain point in time.

15 Compensation Management

Compensation should be transparent, fair, performance-oriented, and market-oriented. It should promote employee motivation and be aligned with enterprise strategy. Compensation Management in mySAP HR helps you to meet these requirements.

15.1 The Design in mySAP HR

15.1.1 Elements and Objectives of Compensation Management

The primary focus in our discussion of *Compensation Management* will be on the basic interrelations between the numerous concepts and the customizing that is based on them. Once you understand these interrelations, applying these concepts should be quite elemental.

Compensation Management should assist both management and the HR department. It involves both the simplification of administrative procedures (for example, transferring wage planning to the actual salary master data) and the controlling, strategic, and analytical functions (for example, budget monitoring, benchmarking, and so on). Compensation Management meets these objectives with the following elements:

1. *Job Pricing* supports the creation of a compensation structure. For this creation, you can use only internal evaluation methods or external benchmarking.

2. In the *Compensation policy*, you can define guidelines that will shape the actual compensation structure. You can base these guidelines on various different foundations (for example, employee performance appraisal, see Chapter 10, *Appraisals and Setting Objectives*).

3. *Budgeting* is also a component of the compensation policy, because it determines the general conditions for the actual compensation structure. Because of the importance of budgeting in the process, it is dealt with separately. Different budgets for remuneration are supported.

4. *Compensation planning and Adjustment* forms the actual core of the process. Remuneration is planned for individual employees based on the guidelines and then, finally, specific adjustments are made.

In SAP terminology, points 2 and 3 above are grouped together under the term *Compensation administration*. Because we're looking at the different process steps here, with point 4 dependent on the results of point 2, we have chosen to present these two points separately.

Figure 15.1 shows the overall interrelations in Compensation Management. Compensation policy, budgets, and salary structure provide the framework for planning individual compensation. This is usually done locally. The appropriate functions are provided for line managers in the Manager's Desktop (MDT). After central approval or approval from an immediate superior, any planned changes can then be implemented as actual compensation adjustment. Planning—like budget distribution—can run in several cycles until it is finally agreed upon and approved. To simplify the presentation (see Figure 15.1), we shall assume that there is only one planning cycle. After first discussing integration aspects, we will present the conception of the individual elements in the following sections.

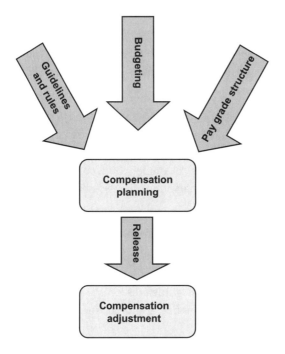

Figure 15.1 Simplified Presentation of Interrelations in Compensation Management

15.1.2 **Integration Considerations**

Compensation Management is primarily integrated in Personnel Administration:

▶ The master data on the employee's compensation to date is displayed and usually forms an important foundation for the calculation of the new compensation. After compensation adjustments have been implemented, this master data can also be changed from the Compensation Management module.

▶ Data from job pricing can be verified for plausibility checks in compensation master data.

▶ Additional employee master data can be incorporated into compensation calculation via the compensation guidelines.

▶ Compensation adjustments are stored in infotype 0380 of personnel master data. Long-term incentives are stored in infotype 0382.

In addition to master data, employee performance appraisal is another possible component of the compensation guidelines, which allows for performance-oriented remuneration to be supported. Organizational management is a very important base. It not only forms the basis for budgeting; it also defines responsibilities in decentralized planning processes. Beyond these internal R/3 aspects, you will find that integration in an external benchmarking system is also relevant. There is an interface that can be used to integrate job pricing in an external provider's system (i.e., the Hay Paynet interface). Figure 15.2 shows an overview of the integration correlations.

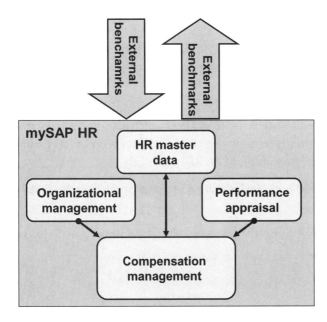

Figure 15.2 Integration in Compensation Management

In Release 4.6C, there is no default integration for Personnel Cost Planning. Results from Compensation Management can only be considered there if you carry out your own development using the user exit described in Chapter 16, *Personnel Cost Planning*. Integration with Personnel Cost Planning is available in R/3 Enterprise, but only if the "new" version of cost planning is used.

15.1.3 Job Pricing

The main purpose of job pricing is the creation of a salary structure—based on certain infotypes—and, if necessary, this structure correlates with industry sector benchmarks.

Special Infotypes

Compensation Management uses three special infotypes that are generally maintained in jobs or positions, and if necessary, also in work centers:

- The "Planned compensation" infotype (1005) contains the planned compensation for the job or position (generally as a range) in one of the following three variants:
  - By referring to the salary structure
  - By referring to the pay scale structure
  - By entering a range directly
- The "Job Evaluation Results" infotype (1050) documents the results of internal or external job evaluations. You can also store several analyses for which different subtypes are used.
- In the "Salary survey results" infotype (1051), the results of salary surveys are stored. These results present comparative salaries, which are usually generated from the results of cross-enterprise surveys. Comparability is ensured by using the job evaluation results from infotype 1050.

Together, the infotypes 1050 and 1051 allow you to participate in salary benchmarks.

To participate in the salary survey, the infotype 1028 ("Address") must also be maintained for each position.

Salary Structure

Basically, the *salary structure* is just a pay scale structure; however, it is a pay scale structure that does not reflect the content of collective agreements. Rather, it is a company-specific compensation structure based on job evaluations and market salaries. You can use the pay scale structure for pay scale employees and the salary structure for non-pay scale employees. The pay scale structure can be created in two ways:

- It can be maintained manually.
- It can be generated automatically based on infotypes 1050 and 1051.

15.1.4 Compensation Policy

In the *compensation policy*, a framework is defined that will later be used for the actual salary adjustments. The following elements are relevant to this framework.

Compensation Areas

Compensation areas are the highest structuring criterion within Compensation Management. They should be used to differentiate between different countries. Because they depend on wage type customizing, they should not contain more than one payroll country grouping (MOLGA). A one-to-one allocation is generally recommended. In the remainder of this chapter, we will always refer to Customizing and its application within a compensation area. Expansion to other compensation areas is then no longer a problem.

Compensation Packages

Compensation packages are a basic element of Compensation Management. They group together all the different types of compensation that an employee can receive. Figure 15.3 shows the interrelations associated with the compensation package concept. Employees are assigned to compensation packages using feature CMGRP for example, on the basis of the personnel area or the employee subgroup. Compensation packages consist of individual compensation components. These components, in turn, are characterized by three attributes:

▶ The compensation category, which by default can be fixed payments, a variable payment or, a long-term incentive

▶ Wage type

▶ The infotype that is adjusted when the compensation component is allocated to the individual employees

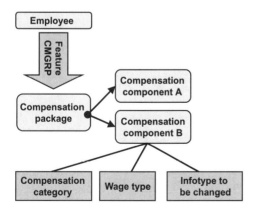

Figure 15.3 Compensation Packages and Employee Assignment

Eligibility Rules

Eligibility rules define which compensation adjustments are possible for which employee. Figure 15.4 shows the process of the eligibility check, depending on the employee. Employees are assigned to eligibility groups using feature CMELG, for example, on the basis of the personnel area or the employee subgroup. The eligibility rule together with the eligibility group then determine which checks must be run:

▶ Checking the working time (for example, "at least 16 hours/week")

▶ Checking seniority (for example, "at least 6 months")

▶ Additional criteria such as appraisal result, job, and so on, and also, in particular, customer-specific checks

Decisions reached in this way—as to whether an employee is eligible for the adjustment—can be changed on an individual level using infotype 0381.

Compensation Guidelines

The *compensation guidelines* define the calculation methods for compensation adjustments. These calculations can be very simple (such as a 5% raise) or, rather complicated with multiple dimensions (for example appraisal result, position in salary scale, and so on). The calculation basis on which, for example, the percentage is applied, is not yet defined here. We will define this calculation when we discuss adjustments in more detail.

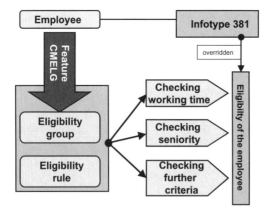

Figure 15.4 Eligibility Rules and Employee Assignment

Figure 15.5 shows how the calculation method is set based on the employee. Employees are assigned to guideline groups using feature CMGRL, for example, on the basis of the personnel area or the employee subgroup. One guideline group can contain several compensation guidelines, each of which is characterized by its attributes. The attributes determine one of three possible calculation alternatives:

▶ A simple calculation, such as a raise by a certain percentage

▶ A customer-defined calculation using a user exit

▶ A calculation using a matrix
Matrix guidelines have been defined for this calculation, and they, in turn, have been assigned multiple dimensions. Each of these dimensions has a calculation method, which, by default, has four variants:

  ▶ Calculation based on Compa-Ratio

  ▶ Calculation based on appraisal result

  ▶ Calculation based on age

  ▶ Calculation based on years of service

Each of these variants is defined using a function module. If you define a new method with its own function module, any customer-defined method is possible. For example, you might use a calculation based on turnover data from the SD (Sales and Distribution) module or based on the results from Profit Center Accounting.

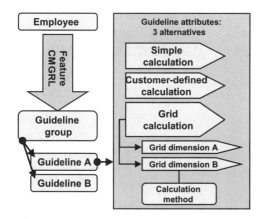

Figure 15.5 Determining Calculation Methods According to Guidelines

15.1.5 Budgeting

Budgets can be created for different aspects, which is typical in the area of Compensation Management, for example:

▶ An increase in fixed salary

▶ A one-time payment (bonus)

▶ Employee shares

The *budget type* is determined by one of the aforementioned aspects. Other budget types can be created in addition to the aforementioned three. In a hierarchy, budgets comprise so-called *budget units*. The corresponding overall budget is at the top of the hierarchy. Apart from this, the budget structure can be assembled in any way. Generally, however, the budget structure reflects the organizational structure, so that each budget unit corresponds to an organizational unit. Often, however, the budgeting structure is not divided as deeply as the organizational structure because, for example, many companies do not assign any budget responsibility on the lowest level of their hierarchy.

How budget units correspond to organizational units is represented by the special "finances" relationship. In this way, the system can identify which budget unit is used if a certain employee receives a compensation adjustment. Figure 15.6 shows the correlation between budget structure and organization structure and how budgets are spent from the bottom up.

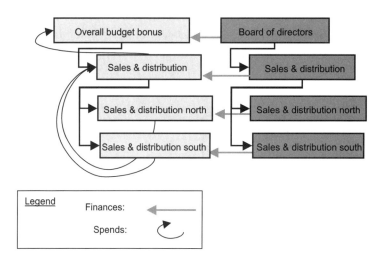

Figure 15.6 Financing and How Budgets Are Spent

The concept of budgeting is not only used in Compensation Management, but also in Training and Event Management (see Chapter 11). The technical implementation is the same in both cases.

15.1.6 Compensation Planning and Adjustment

The planning and implementation of adjustments at the employee level is, effectively, the ultimate goal of compensation management. To ensure an optimal process, compensation planning and adjustment should be done locally by management. Tools are available for this, particularly in the Manager's Desktop (MDT).

The concepts that we presented up to this point will now be integrated in our description of the compensation adjustment, which is the technical link in the system between all parts of SAP-Compensation Management. Consequently, this area is somewhat complex and therefore we strongly recommend that you have a clear understanding of all the SAP terms and their correlation to one another before reading this section.

Figure 15.7 provides an overview. The *adjustment reason*, as a higher-level element, directly defines the budget type to be deduced and the output type—in case of a budget deficit (for example, an error message). Several *adjustment types* can be assigned to the adjustment reason, each referring to a compensation component. The adjustment type—as a core element of the entire process—is characterized by the following elements:

▶ **An eligibility rule**
Indicates for which employees a particular compensation adjustment is considered.

▶ **A calculation base**
Percentage adjustments, for example, refer to a calculation base. These may be wage types, in particular, cumulating wage types or, even a customer-specific, defined calculation base (user exit).

▶ **A wage type model**
Indicates the wage types for which the adjustment type can be used. For each wage type, a guideline and a rounding rule is indicated in the model.

The business equivalent of an adjustment reason is the *adjustment round* such as "bonus round" or an "annual adjustment of fixed salary." A specific adjustment type must then be defined for each relevant compensation component.

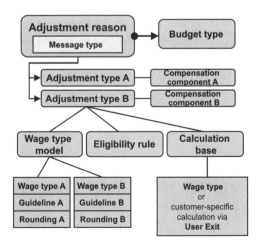

Figure 15.7 Relationships Between Adjustment Types and Reasons

15.1.7 Long-Term Incentives

Compensation management offers extensive support for the administration of *long-term incentives*. These long-term incentives are initially integrated as separate compensation categories in the overall concept, just like fixed salary and bonus payments. In addition, there are special functions available for granting and exercising awards and for representing special events (such as termination). At the employee level, the information is stored in the "Awards" infotype (0382). We shall not address the long-term incentives of the specific "Awards" infotype again in this chapter.

15.1.8 Strengths and Weaknesses

Compensation management is very flexible. Apart from the configurable set of rules, made up of guidelines, packages, calculation formulae, and so on, the numerous user exits also contribute to this flexibility. However, with this flexibility comes a high degree of complexity which, although it need not be apparent to the end user, must nevertheless be visible in the configuration. The integrated Excel interface is a particularly concise tool for the decentralized planning and approval of adjustments. In the event of complicated wage type structures in basic pay and indirectly valued wage types, planning becomes somewhat complex and laborious. The primary shortcoming is certainly the focus on non-pay scale payment. Planning pay scale group changes is not possible in this way with the tools available.

15.2 Implementation in mySAP HR

15.2.1 Basic Settings

You can set up compensation areas and planning periods using the IMG path **Personnel Management · Compensation Management · Basic Settings**. The process is sufficiently described there. You will also find the entry **Define profile view** using this path. There, you can define data to be displayed in the planning template at the employee level. The procedure for configuration is exactly the same as the definition of profile views in Personnel development (for example, see Chapter 8, *Skill Management*).

15.2.2 Job Pricing

The main basis for job pricing is the salary structure, where this is used instead of or in addition to a pay scale structure. If possible, the salary structure should not be maintained manually; rather, it should be generated automatically. In order for the salary structure to be generated automatically, the data basis must first be provided and the following infotypes must be maintained:

- ► **Infotype 1005: "Planned Compensation"**
  Figure 15.8 shows the direct recording of a salary range without reference to a pay grade or pay scale.

- ► **Infotype 1050: "Job Evaluation Results"**
  Figure 15.9 shows the maintenance of the evaluation points—here, these results pertain to the evaluation method EV01. The job shown is also a benchmark job, which means that it is included in the calculation of reference salaries by external benchmarking service providers.

- ► **Infotype 1051: "Salary Survey Results"**
  This infotype stores the data provided by benchmarking surveys. With the survey's Job field, you can create a link between jobs in your own system and jobs in benchmarking. In the example in Figure 15.10, the average values for the basic salary and the bonus are maintained.

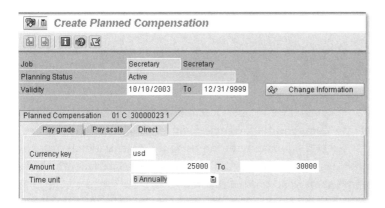

Figure 15.8 Infotype 1005: "Planned Compensation" with Range Entered Directly

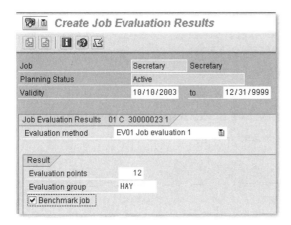

Figure 15.9 Infotype 1050: "Job Evaluation Results"

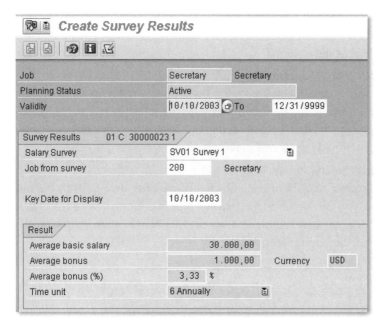

Figure 15.10 Infotype 1051: "Salary Survey Results"

The simplest way to maintain the infotypes described is to use the menu path **Personnel Management · Compensation Management · Administration · Job Pricing**. There, you can select the jobs in question using the organizational structure and you can maintain all relevant infotypes via an easy-to-use interface. The initial maintenance screen is somewhat unusual: the requested job is marked and then you click on the button that is usually used for displaying (see Figure 15.11). From the same screen, you can maintain or generate salary structures.

Customizing for job pricing is done using the IMG path **Personnel Management · Compensation Management · Job Pricing**. To customize job pricing, you need to perform the following actions:

▶ Define the relevant compensation structures

▶ Define the survey types

▶ Define jobs from the surveys and store the corresponding survey results

▶ Define job evaluations (methods and groups)

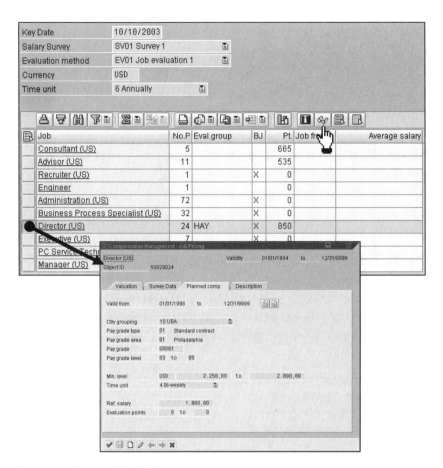

Key Date	10/10/2003
Salary Survey	SV01 Survey 1
Evaluation method	EV01 Job evaluation 1
Currency	USD
Time unit	6 Annually

Job	No.P	Eval.group	BJ	Pt.	Job fr	Average salary
Consultant (US)	5			665		
Advisor (US)	11			535		
Recruiter (US)	1		X	0		
Engineer	1			0		
Administration (US)	72		X	0		
Business Process Specialist (US)	32		X	0		
Director (US)	24	HAY	X	850		
Executive (US)	7		X	0		
PC Service Techn						
Manager (US)						

Compensation Management - Job Pricing

Director (US)   Validity   01/01/1994   to   12/31/9999
Object ID   50029024

| Valuation | Survey Data | Planned comp. | Description |

Valid from   01/01/1998   to   12/31/9999

Ctry grouping	10 USA
Pay grade type	01 Standard contract
Pay grade area	01 Philadelphia
Pay grade	GRD01
Pay grade level	03 to 05

| Min. level | USD   2.250,00   to   2.800,00 |
| Time unit | 4 Bi-weekly |

| Ref. salary | 1.800,00 |
| Evaluation points | 0 to   0 |

Figure 15.11 Carrying Out Job Pricing

15.2.3 Compensation Policy

Compensation policy is only processed in Customizing. Knowledge of the correlations described in Section 15.1.4 is important. To structure customizing in a targeted way, you must understand the overall context of compensation adjustment.
The most important vertices in the customizing process are described below using
the screens.

To define the compensation packages (IMG path **Personnel Management · Compensation Management · Planning and Administration · Compensation Packages**), you must first define the compensation components. Figure 15.12 shows a
variable component based on wage type M101 and updated by an adjustment to
infotype 0015. After defining all components, these are gathered into packages
and assigned to employees using the feature CMGRP.

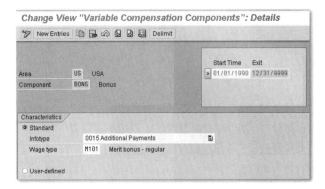

Figure 15.12 Variable Compensation Component

To customize guidelines (IMG path **Personnel Management · Compensation Management · Planning and Administration · Guidelines)**, you must first define the calculation variants (for example, by percentage). The default entries will usually suffice. The most difficult course of action is customizing with matrix guidelines, which use several different criteria for calculating compensation. The matrix can be maintained as shown in Figure 15.13. In this case, a two-dimensional matrix has been created.

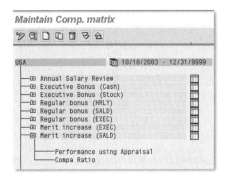

Figure 15.13 Two-Dimensional Compensation Matrix

Before customizing the matrix, you must first create the matrix dimensions, and, before this, you must create the methods to be used in them. Figure 15.14 shows a matrix dimension, which calculates compensation depending on employee appraisal. The appraisal model used for the relevant appraisal is given as a parameter in this case.

Once the definition of the compensation guideline matrix is complete, the guideline groups and the guidelines themselves are defined and equipped with the necessary attributes. In the example in Figure 15.15, the guideline matrix "MRT2" is used as a basis for calculation.

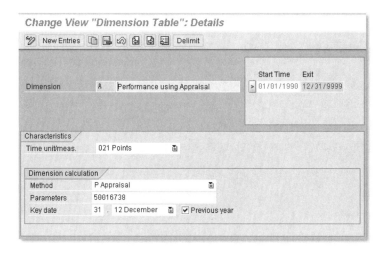

Change View "Dimension Table": Details

New Entries Delimit

			Start Time	Exit
Dimension	A	Performance using Appraisal	> 01/01/1990	12/31/9999

Characteristics
Time unit/meas.   021 Points

Dimension calculation
Method   P Appraisal
Parameters   50016738
Key date   31 . 12 December   ☑ Previous year

Figure 15.14 Matrix Dimension "Appraisal"

			Start Time	Exit
Area	US	USA	> 01/01/1990	12/31/9999
Guidelines	MERIT	Merit increase		
Guide.group	SALD	Salaried		

Characteristics
○ Fixed   Percentage
   Calculation variant   Amount
                           Number

◉ Matrix
   Guideline matrix   MRT2   Merit increase (SALD)

○ User-defined

Figure 15.15 Guideline Based on a Matrix

Customizing for eligibility (IMG path **Personnel Management · Compensation Management · Planning and Administration · Eligibility**) is structured very simply, but can be used very flexibly. Figure 15.16 shows an eligibility rule with the following criteria:

▶ The employee must have been on the payroll for at least three months by the key date of January 1st.

▶ The minimum weekly working time is ten hours.

▶ A defined minimum point score must be attained in the appraisal.

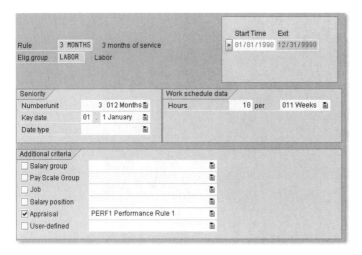

Figure 15.16 Eligibility Rule

15.2.4 Budgeting

Customizing

Customizing here is very simple. Using the IMG path **Personnel Management · Compensation Management · Budgeting**, you can, above all, define budget types (such as Bonus, Increase of fixed salary, distributing stocks/shares, and so on) and budget periods. Also, note the importance of the reference currency for international use.

Working with Budgets

Working with the budget structure is also quite elemental. If it is aligned with the organizational structure, it can be automatically generated via the menu path **Personnel Management · Compensation Management · Budgeting · Structure · Create**, using the generation function available there. Typically, we recommend that you also generate the financing relationships at the same time. First, you must select the head organizational unit that is responsible for the total budget to be created.

Finally, the individual budget values (menu path **Personnel Management · Compensation Management · Budgeting · Change**) must be maintained, that is, provided with amounts. There are basically two ways in which you can accomplish this:

▶ Maintain the budget units on the lowest level and subsequently add them up. This is easy and straightforward; however, it usually doesn't meet the requirements of the actual process.

► Maintain budget units on higher levels and manually distribute them down throughout the hierarchical levels. The system monitors the deduction of upper budget units, thereby enabling you to determine if more budget units have been distributed than are actually available.

Figure 15.17 shows this procedure in the system using a two-level budget structure. Of the $100,000 that is available at the highest level, in this example, only $72,000 has been distributed. In the "Distributed budget" column, apart from the budgets distributed to subordinate organizational units, the actual amounts used are also displayed. Once the budget values have been correctly maintained for all budget units, the budget can be released and only then will it be available for compensation adjustments.

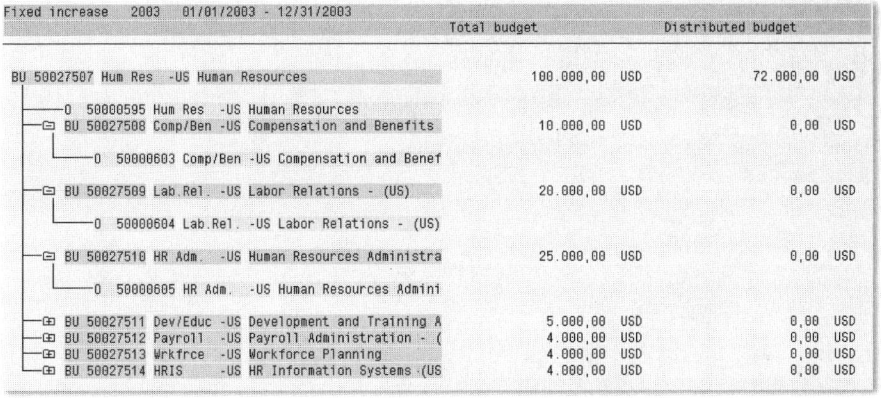

```
Fixed increase    2003    01/01/2003 - 12/31/2003
                                              Total budget              Distributed budget

BU 50027507 Hum Res   -US Human Resources              100.000,00  USD              72.000,00  USD

    ─0  50000595 Hum Res   -US Human Resources
    ─⊟ BU 50027508 Comp/Ben -US Compensation and Benefits    10.000,00  USD               0,00  USD

        ─0  50000603 Comp/Ben -US Compensation and Benef

    ─⊟ BU 50027509 Lab.Rel. -US Labor Relations - (US)        20.000,00  USD               0,00  USD

        ─0  50000604 Lab.Rel. -US Labor Relations - (US)

    ─⊟ BU 50027510 HR Adm.   -US Human Resources Administra   25.000,00  USD               0,00  USD

        ─0  50000605 HR Adm.   -US Human Resources Admini

    ─⊟ BU 50027511 Dev/Educ -US Development and Training A      5.000,00  USD               0,00  USD
    ─⊟ BU 50027512 Payroll   -US Payroll Administration - (     4.000,00  USD               0,00  USD
    ─⊟ BU 50027513 Wrkfrce   -US Workforce Planning             4.000,00  USD               0,00  USD
    ─⊟ BU 50027514 HRIS      -US HR Information Systems ·(US     4.000,00  USD               0,00  USD
```

Figure 15.17 Distribution to Sub-Budgets

If a budget structure from the previous year is to be used as a basis for the current budget round, you can simplify the generation of the budget by extending the existing budget structure (see Figure 15.18). In this way, not only is the structure copied; you can also carry forward the budget values and then adjust them manually. When updating, it is vital that you don't overlook the financing relationships. Figure 15.19 shows an overview of the budgeting process.

When working with budgets, you can always choose between the *Financing view* and the *Distribution view*. The financing view (see Figure 15.17) shows the organizational units that correspond to each budget unit and is, consequently, somewhat more complex. If the budget structure is based on the organizational structure and the budget units have the same name as do the organizational units, you don't need the financing view. In some instances, it might be useful to change financing (if, contrary to the norm, for example, a department finances the budgets for several subordinate units).

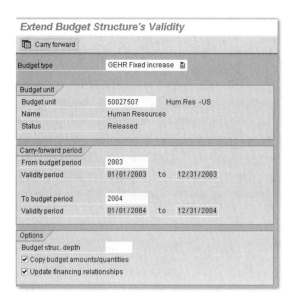

Figure 15.18 Carrying Forward the Budget Structure

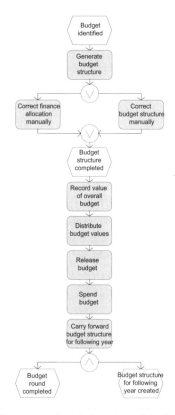

Figure 15.19 Rough Overview of the Budgeting Process

15.2.5 Compensation Planning and Adjustment

Customizing

The customizing activities described in this section are grouped together under the IMG path **Personnel Management · Compensation Management · Planning and Administration · Adjustments.** The configuration of compensation adjustment is, for the most part, reflected in Figure 15.7. We shall now present the most important customizing steps using very simple examples. At the top level is the adjustment reason. It also represents the unit that links the different compensation areas together, and therefore ensures integration in international use. The creation of the adjustment reason determines which budget will be deduced and what type of message is created by the system in the event of budget deficits (see Figure 15.20).

Adjust. reason	03	Bonus			
Type	Text		Budg. type	Name	Mess.type
BONU	Bonus plan		0002	Bonus	E

Figure 15.20 Creating an Adjustment Reason

Before creating the adjustment types, you must configure the necessary wage types and set up the wage type models. Wage types, to which the adjustment type is to be applied, will already be combined in the wage type model. Therefore, within the Wage type model, the guidelines to be applied and the Rounding type are assigned to each Wage type (see Figure 15.21). Frequently, individual wage types comprise wage type models.

Area	US	USA						
WT model	IPROCON							
N.	Valid From	End Date	Wage type	Wage Type Long Text	Guidelines	Text	Rounding type	Deg.exact.
1	01/01/2002	12/31/9999	9MRT	Merit increase	MERIT	Merit increase	K To Nearest	1

Figure 15.21 Wage Type Model with Guidelines

The adjustment types are initially only defined with very few attributes. The essential characteristics are then defined in the IMG activity **Assign adjustment types.** Here, all threads effectively come together and the Adjustment type, Calculation base, Wage type model, and Eligibility rule are all assigned (see Figure 15.22).

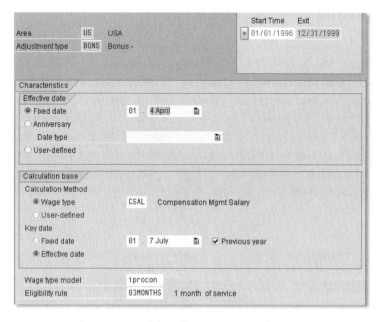

Area   US   USA

Adjustment type   BONS   Bonus -

Start Time   Exit

» 01/01/1996   12/31/1999

Characteristics

Effective date

● Fixed date   01 . 4 April

○ Anniversary

   Date type

○ User-defined

Calculation base

Calculation Method

   ● Wage type   CSAL   Compensation Mgmt Salary

   ○ User-defined

Key date

   ○ Fixed date   01 . 7 July   ☑ Previous year

   ● Effective date

Wage type model   iprocon

Eligibility rule   03MONTHS   1 month of service

Figure 15.22 Characteristics of the Adjustment Type in the Compensation Area

Planning and Executing Adjustments

The planning and execution of adjustments is generally based on an adjustment reason. Alternatively, an individual adjustment type may be selected. To illustrate the system, we shall start with an overview of the individual adjustment types, as seen in Figure 15.23. You can go to this screen, for example, via the menu path **Personnel Management · Compensation Management · Administration · Adjustments · Change.** Once there, you must carry out the following steps:

1. Select an employee.

2. Select an adjustment type (for example "increase fixed salary").

3. Check the effective date and adjust if necessary.

4. Record the change amounts using one of the following possibilities:

   ▶ Enter the amount directly.

   ▶ Enter the percentage directly. The amount will subsequently be calculated based on the calculation base. This will be displayed in the template immediately under the wage type to be changed and follows the configuration shown in Figure 15.22.

   ▶ Use a guideline in accordance with the configuration shown in Figure 15.21.

   ▶ Use the rounding rule which also comes from the customizing activity shown in Figure 15.21.

5. Check what amount of the budget is used to adjust the employees' salary. The system reduces the budget according to the configuration of the adjustment reason (see Figure 15.20) and reacts to a budget deficit by issuing the message stored there.

In accordance with the profile views configuration, additional data on the employee can be displayed under the main screen, which may provide useful information during the adjustment process.

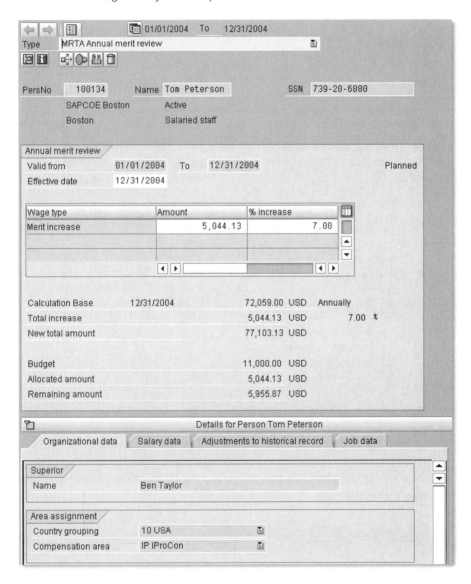

Figure 15.23 Adjustment for Individual Employee with Adjustment Type

The adjustment is then subject to an approval process. It is first created with the status "requested." Then, it can be approved or rejected by the next level of management up. Approved adjustments must still be activated in order for them to be incorporated into compensation master data. Infotype 0380 ("Compensation adjustments") documents this process.

The decentralized process flow is supported by three concepts:

▶ The workflow template "Compensation adjustment approval process" (CMPApprProc, WS1000083) controls the approval and activation of requested adjustments.

▶ The MDT offers an easy-to-use access for individual managers (see Figure 15.24).

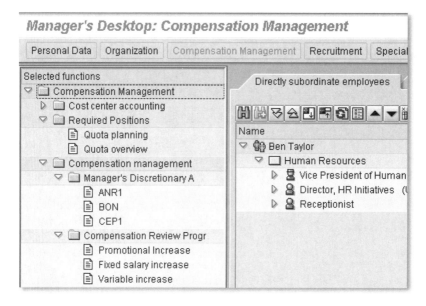

Figure 15.24 Access to Planning Using the MDT

▶ The concise presentation of an adjustment reason for all employees in a department—in the Excel presentation integrated into the R/3 interface— offers a manager optimal support for planning (see Figure 15.25). It is best accessed from the MDT.

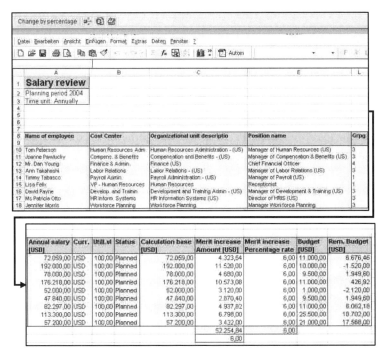

Figure 15.25 Integrated Excel Interface for Planning

15.2.6 Reports

Compensation management provides its own evaluation reports via the menu path **Personnel Management · Compensation Management · Infosystem · Reports**. Now, we shall briefly present three of these reports.

Total Compensation Statement

The *Total Compensation Statement* allows you to present all compensation components for each employee. Non-monetary elements are also included. The statement is in the form of a PDF file whose content can be configured very flexibly (IMG path **Personnel Management · Compensation Management · Reports · Total Compensation Statement**). Several user exits are also available to integrate the different compensation elements.

Compa-Ratio

The *Compa-Ratio report* allows you to show employees in a department how they compare in relation to the corresponding salary range for their job or position. The payments in master data are compared with the salary band for the position or job in infotype 1005. The employment percentage is also considered accurately.

Projected Pay

This list shows all positions in a department with the corresponding planned compensation from infotype 1005.

15.3 Process Example: Benchmarking

To participate in benchmarking (salary surveys), you must first make some basic settings in customizing (IMG path **Personnel Management · Compensation Management · Job Pricing**). The infotypes 1005 (Planned Compensation), 1028 (Address for geographical evaluation), 1050 (Results of job evaluation and benchmarking job indicator), and 1051 (Relationship to survey job number) serve as a data basis. Once this base has been completed, you can proceed with data extraction using the menu path **Personnel Management · Compensation Management · Infosystem · Reports · Salary Surveys**.

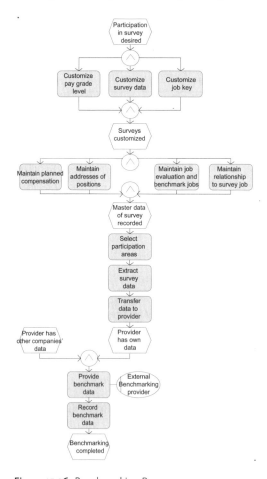

Figure 15.26 Benchmarking Process

Combined with data from other participants, the survey provider then identifies the benchmark values and returns them to the participants. These values should be stored in Customizing using the IMG path **Personnel Management · Compensation Management · Job Pricing · Survey Data · Define Survey Results** and are then displayed in infotype 1051.

15.4 Innovations in R/3 Enterprise

▶ The major innovation is the long awaited for integration between Compensation Management and Cost planning as it is described in the next chapter.

▶ R/3 Enterprise provides many new functions in the area of long-term incentives. Of special importance, it provides an integration to the Treasury component in Financials to get the price for the valuation of awards. Additionally, there are some new possibilities in reporting and in creating simulations of future provisions.

▶ Extension 2.0 will deliver a redesigned solution. In this solution, especially the benchmarking functions are considerably improved. Furthermore you can enter two adjustment reasons on the same day.

15.5 Critical Success Factors

Compensation management can be implemented in many ways; however, one constant remains—the following aspects should always be considered:

▶ The structures that must be built in Customizing are quite complicated. Before entering customizing, you should have a thorough and clear understanding of the correlations and therefore be able to work out an integrated concept. To do this, we suggest that you identify the individual concepts in Customizing with the elements of the application, as is partly the case in Section 15.2.5.

▶ The process can be viewed as efficient if it can offer optimal support for decentralized processing. Note that the system still suffers from the integration of pay scale employees and an organizational solution must be found to resolve this problem.

▶ Depending on the actual definition of the process, integration in cost planning can be very important. If R/3 Enterprise is not available, you can still achieve integration by using the user exit in cost planning.

▶ The responsibility framework for budgets and compensation adjustments must be clearly defined and mapped in the system.

▶ Building on these responsibilities, implementation in roles/authorizations is an important criterion.

16 Personnel Cost Planning

You can create a Personnel Cost Plan using master data and Organizational Management. The planning method is supported by various different scenarios.

16.1 The Design in mySAP HR

Personnel cost planning determines the personnel costs of employees, which are enhanced with changes already known and are then available as a planning basis for cost accounting. The employee is at the center of this HR view of personnel costs. Costs associated with employees are displayed separately according to cost items (for example, basic salary, non-recurring payments, and so on). Anticipated future changes to relevant data can be added at this level, because they usually affect an employee (for example, if an employee is leaving the company) or a cost item (for example, a 3% increase in the basic salary).

Personnel costs for individual employees are added together in organizational units and compressed upwards in the organization reporting structure. In this way, personnel costs can be determined in line with the organizational structure. However, this structure of personnel costs cannot generally be transferred to cost accounting. There, personnel costs must be based on cost centers and cost elements. Therefore, it is necessary to move from the HR view to the cost accounting view (see Figure 16.1).

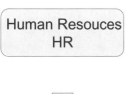
Personnel costs
based on cost items
per organizational unit
in line with the organizational
structure

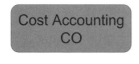
Personnel costs
per cost element and
per cost center

Figure 16.1 Different Views of Personnel Costs

16.1.1 Master Data

The data required for personnel cost planning is stored in the employee's master data. This data is presented in greater detail below.

Personnel costs

An employee's personnel costs are made up of a range of components that are stored at different locations in mySAP HR. The simplest way to determine these costs is using infotype 0008 "Basic pay." Monthly payments are stored in this infotype, separated according to wage type (see Figure 16.2).

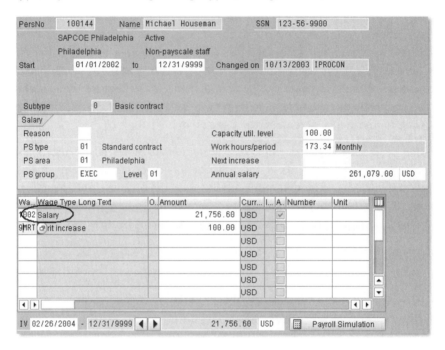

Figure 16.2 Wage Types in Infotype 0008 "Basic Pay"

Cost center

To generate the cost accounting view from the HR view (see Figure 16.1), the cost center (the target object in cost planning) must be stored. The cost accounting view is determined from infotype 0001 "Organizational Assignment" for the employee (see Figure 16.3). The cost center from infotype 0001 represents the simplest way of assigning an employee to a cost center. **Each employee is assigned to just one cost center.** Each infotype has a validity period, whereby the assigned cost centers can also change, if necessary, during the planning period.

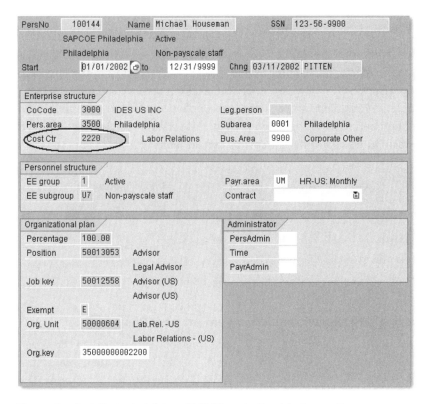

| PersNo | 100144 | Name | Michael Houseman | | SSN | 123-56-9900 | |

SAPCOE Philadelphia   Active
Philadelphia   Non-payscale staff
Start   01/01/2002 ⊕ to   12/31/9999   Chng 03/11/2002 PITTEN

Enterprise structure

CoCode	3000	IDES US INC		Leg.person		
Pers.area	3500	Philadelphia		Subarea	0001	Philadelphia
Cost Ctr	2220		Labor Relations	Bus. Area	9900	Corporate Other

Personnel structure

| EE group | 1 | Active | | Payr.area | UM | HR-US: Monthly |
| EE subgroup | U7 | Non-payscale staff | | Contract | | |

Organizational plan

Percentage	100.00	
Position	50013053	Advisor
		Legal Advisor
Job key	50012558	Advisor (US)
		Advisor (US)
Exempt	E	
Org. Unit	50000604	Lab.Rel.-US
		Labor Relations - (US)
Org.key	35000000002200	

Administrator

PersAdmin	
Time	
PayrAdmin	

Figure 16.3 Cost Center in Infotype 0001 "Organizational Assignment"

In addition to the cost center in infotype 0001, the employee can be assigned a "cost distribution" using infotype 0027 (however, infotype 0027 can only be considered since Release 4.5 of Personnel Cost Planning.) This option takes into account that some positions pass on their personnel costs to more than one cost center (for example two departments can share a secretary).

As you can see in Figure 16.4, several target cost centers can be recorded together with a percentage. The sum of the percentages may be less than 100, but it can never exceed 100. If the total is less than 100 in infotype 0027, the unused percentage is assigned to infotype 0001. For this reason, the cost center in infotype 0001 is also referred to as the master cost center.

Cost Center		
2300	50 %	0027
2100	20 %	0027
2220	30 % (…)	0001

Figure 16.4 Distribution of Costs in Infotype 0027

The rule for distributing personnel costs to cost centers is also applied if there is no infotype 0027 "Cost Distribution." Then, 0 % of the costs are distributed in accordance with infotype 0027. The remainder (100 % – 0 % = 100 %) is assigned to the master cost center from infotype 0001. Apart from the cost center, you can also specify a range of other cost accounting objects in infotype 0027 (for example: PSP element, order). For the example (Mr. Michael Houseman with personnel number 100144) depicted in Figures 16.3 and 16.4, we can see how costs are distributed over different cost centers in Table 16.1

Cost center	Percentage	Source infotype
2300	50 %	0027
2100	20 %	0027
2200	30 % (Remainder)	0001

Table 16.1 Result of the Cost Distribution in Figure 16.4

16.1.2 Using Organizational Management as a Basis

The current number of employees is stored in personnel master data; however, personnel cost planning based on personnel master data contains very little future-oriented elements. In this way, it is more like a personnel cost forecast. The personnel costs of vacant (not occupied) positions can only be considered if Organizational Management is used as a base.

Figure 16.5 shows an excerpt of staff assignments in organizational management. For occupied positions, the actual working hours are greater than zero. It shows the relationship with the holder (in this example, this is the position "Sr. Compensation Consultant," held by John Parker). Further down the list, we can see a vacant position "Functional Specialist (US)". Therefore, in Organizational Management, there are links to the employee's current master data as well as links to information about vacant positions.

Staff assignments

Key date   10/13/2003

Org. unit	Positions	Employee(s)	Chief	Staffing status	Actual working hours	Target working hours
Comp/Ben -US	Manager of Compensation & Benefits (US)	Joanne Pawlucky	Chief		173,33	173,60
Comp/Ben -US	Functional Specialist (US)			Vacant since 02/01/2001	0,00	173,60
Comp/Ben -US	Administrative Staff (US)			Vacant since 09/27/2001	0,00	173,60
Comp/Ben -US	Sr. Compensation Consultant	John Parker			173,34	173,60
Comp/Ben -US	Sr. Benefits Advisor (US)	Megan Young		Vacant since 10/31/2000	173,34	173,60
Comp/Ben -US	Functional Specialist (US)	Liam Morton		Vacant since 12/14/1999	173,34	173,60

Figure 16.5 Staff Assignments from Organizational Management

Until now, it has been assumed that a position either has a holder or is flagged as vacant. The former is the most common scenario; however, other possibilities can exist:

▶ A position can have more than one holder, for example, to train a successor.

▶ If we assume that a position can have a planned working time, just as an employee can, then part-time positions are possible. Thus, for example, a full-time employee can be linked to two part-time positions, meaning that the personnel costs for that employee are split between the two positions equally. This is done by setting the relationship between the position and the employee at 50%.

▶ The two scenarios described can also be combined. Two full-time employees can each be 50 % associated with two full-time positions.

In Section 16.1, we indicated that before you can transfer the HR view of personnel planning into cost accounting, you must first convert the target values based on the HR objects "wagetype" and "organizational unit" to the basis of the CO objects "cost element" and "cost center." In Section 16.1.1, we also described how the information on assigned cost centers for employees is determined by personnel cost planning. Now, you must determine where exactly is the link between cost centers and vacant positions.

The "Account Assignment" View

Organizational management has a great deal of varied information. The staff assignments screen shown in Figure 16.5 is only one view of the stored data. In the account assignment view (see Figure 16.6), organizational units and positions can be linked with cost centers.

▽ ☐ Compensation and Benefits - (US)	O 50000603	01/01/1994	Unlimited
🏢 Compensation and Benefits	K 2210	01/01/1994	Unlimited
▷ 🧍 Manager of Compensation & Benefits (US	S 50000199	01/01/1994	Unlimited
▽ 🧍 Sr. Compensation Consultant	S 50025723	10/01/2000	Unlimited
👥 John Parker	P 00100241	10/02/2000	Unlimited
▽ 🧍 Sr. Benefits Advisor (US)	S 50025847	10/31/2000	Unlimited
🏢 Procurement	K 2300	01/01/1994	Unlimited
👥 Megan Young	P 00100133	09/01/1996	Unlimited
🧍 Functional Specialist (US)	S 50000200	01/01/1994	Unlimited

Figure 16.6 "Account Assignment" View in Organizational Management

The concept of inheritance is used so that you don't have to individually map each organizational unit with a cost center. Therefore, the cost center assigned to an organizational unit is inherited by its subordinate organizational units, unless another cost center has been assigned to them (see Figure 16.7). By employing this concept of inheritance, you should, ideally, only have to link each cost center once.

If one or more positions contains a cost center that is different from the organizational unit, it can be assigned its own cost center, which will, in turn, override the inheritance mechanism for this level in the organizational hierarchy.

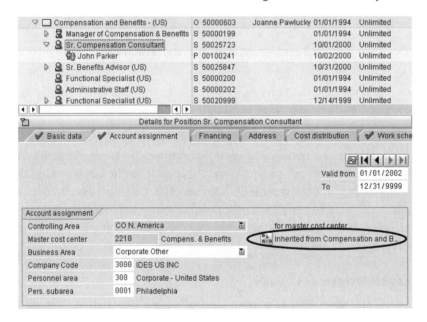

Figure 16.7 Inherited Cost Center for a Position

Using this concept, each position in organizational management is assigned a cost center and this resolves the issue of the relationship between cost center and vacant position. A vacant position is a "normal" position, but one that is not related to a holder. It may contain additional information on the nature of the vacancy (infotype 1007). If there is active integration between organizational management and personnel administration, the cost center inherited by or directly assigned to the position is automatically transferred to the infotype 0001 "Organizational Assignment" as a master cost center. It is then no longer necessary to maintain the cost center in infotype 0001 (moreover, it is no longer possible).

As you will see in Figure 16.8, since Release 4.6C, you can maintain cost distribution directly in organizational management, similar to that in infotype 0027 (see Figure 16.4). In Customizing, you can set whether cost distribution for an employee should be from organizational management or from infotype 0027.

Figure 16.8 Cost Distribution in Organizational Management

Cost distribution can also be attained if an employee is linked to two positions, each of which is, in turn, linked to different cost centers.

16.1.3 Infotype 1015 "Cost Planning"

The personnel costs of an employee are recorded in infotype 0008 "Basic pay" (see Figure 16.2). Vacant positions have no employee assigned and therefore no infotype 0008. For this reason, personnel costs for the position can be created directly in infotype 1015 "Cost planning" (see Figure 16.9). They are separated into wage elements.

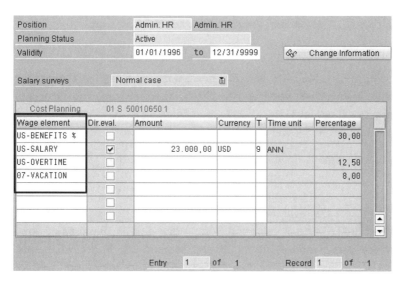

Figure 16.9 Infotype 1015 "Cost Planning"

The inheritance concept also applies here between jobs and positions so that you don't have to create the infotype 1015 "Cost Planning" for each position. Positions of the same type are usually grouped together in jobs. The infotype 1015 "Cost Planning" is maintained for the jobs. Then, it is passed on to the position, which means that if personnel cost planning finds no infotype 1015 for a position, it checks the assigned job.

Wage Elements

Wage elements are defined in Customizing under **Personnel Management · Compensation Management · Personnel Cost Planning · Maintain Wage Elements**. In their simplest form, wage elements can be evaluated directly. They are given an actual amount for a period (see Figure 16.10).

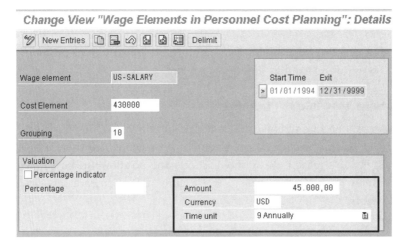

Figure 16.10 Wage Element Evaluated Directly

It may also be necessary, however, to add a percentage extra payment to existing wage elements. In this case, you need to check the **Percentage indicator** and enter a percentage (see Figure 16.11). The percentage will be calculated for all wage elements that are in a lower grouping.

The second wage element in infotype 1015 in Figure 16.9 is US-SALARY. As explained above, this wage element is assigned a specific value, which is taken from Customizing. However, if a different value is to be used, the previous value is overwritten and the **Dir. eval.** field must be checked. From the start, the logic is similar to that of the indirect valuation from infotype 0008 "Basic pay"; however, it is not nearly as complex. The third wage element, US-OVERTIME, is then calculated as a percentage of wage element US-SALARY, since the grouping 10 for US-SALARY is lower than 11 for the wage element US-OVERTIME.

Unfortunately, you cannot set a maximum limit for the percentage extras. Inaccuracies can occur if such rules exist.

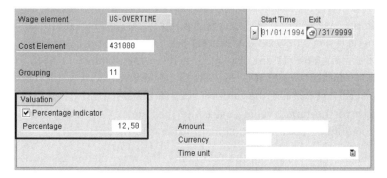

Figure 16.11 Wage Element Evaluated by Percentage

16.1.4 The "Cost Object" Concept

Organizational management serves as a basis for personnel cost planning. The objects to be considered, known as *cost objects*, are—as is typical in organizational management—generated by one or several root objects and an evaluation path. The employee associated with a position is identified as the first cost object. In the example of the vacant position, positions and the jobs as groups of positions are established as additional cost objects.

However, it can also be useful to create additional elements of personnel cost planning directly in organizational units or work centers (for example, further training costs). Thus, all cost objects from Organizational Management share the fact that their personnel costs can be described using infotype 1015 "Cost planning" (see Figure 16.12). If additional cost objects are considered, the evaluation path must be adjusted accordingly in Customizing.

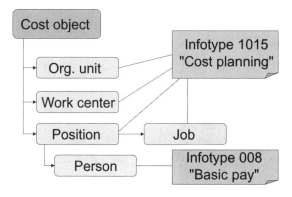

Figure 16.12 Cost Object

16.1.5 The "Cost Element" Concept

Personnel cost planning brings together the wage elements from infotype 1015 "Cost planning" (see Figure 16.9) and the wage types from the employee's infotype 0008 "Basic pay" (see Figure 16.2) under the term *Cost element*. This means that a cost element is not a new object; rather, it is a combination of concepts. Wage types and wage elements are displayed in the same column. In Section 16.1, we indicated that to transfer the HR view of personnel planning into cost accounting you must first convert the target values to the *cost element* and *cost center*. Conversion to the target value cost center has already been explained. Now, we need to address how the cost element value is formed.

The cost elements are generated from the cost items. The wage elements in Customizing are assigned to a cost element (see Figure 16.10). Assignment for wage types is a little more complicated. They are assigned to a cost type using account assignment customizing in Payroll. Figure 16.13 illustrates this relationship.

To ensure that personnel planning is clearly arranged, an important property of cost items is that there should be a high aggregation to the lowest possible number of cost items. This can only influence the wage items in infotype 1015 "Cost planning," since these items are only used in personnel cost planning. Wage types are provided by personnel administration or payroll accounting and are usually much too detailed for planning purposes. A possible structuring of cost items could look like this:

▶ Basic salary

▶ Employer's contribution social insurance

▶ Employer's contribution company pension scheme

▶ Non-recurring payments

▶ Time variables (for example, night work bonus, overtime pay)

▶ Incentive variable (for example, piecework wage)

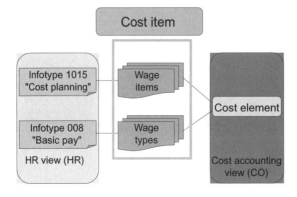

Figure 16.13 Cost Item

16.1.6 Scenarios in Personnel Cost Planning

Both the position and the employee are cost objects. For personnel cost planning, it must be clarified which cost elements are to be used. SAP deals with the different possibilities by offering three different scenarios.

Personnel Cost Planning on the Basis of "Basic pay""

In this scenario, emphasis is placed on master data. The cost elements of the employee (that is to say, those from infotype 0008 "Basic pay") are used. The infotype 1015 "Cost planning" maintained at the position is consulted only if the position is vacant. If this is not the case, that is, if the position is not vacant, assigned jobs are checked for vacancies. The disadvantage of this procedure lies in the fact that important cost items are missing. Only the employee's basic pay is stored in infotype 0008 "Basic pay." The infotypes 0015 "Additional payments," 0014 "Recurring payments/deductions," and so on, are not considered. Moreover, no benefits are reflected. Future changes made to master data will, however, be included correctly.

Personnel Cost Planning on the Basis of "Payroll results"

This scenario on the basis of "Payroll results" tries to compensate for these restrictions. Instead of infotype 0008 "Basic pay," the results of payroll accounting are read for a definable period, averaged, and used as a basis for planning. All wage types, which are assigned to an expense account in cost accounting, are included in personnel cost planning. Filtering or grouping is not possible. Furthermore, the additional account assignment that was determined from payroll accounting is also admitted from wage types (for example, cost center, order, WBS element).

Before you can use this scenario, you must transfer payroll results to the personnel cost planning database (Table PCL5). To initiate this transfer in the posting run, you select the option **Cost planning data,** as can be seen in Figure 16.14. (In R/3 release versions earlier than 4.0, you must activate some inactive cells for this transfer in Schema D500). The transfer of payroll results to the personnel cost planning database can therefore be done at any time before personnel cost planning is carried out. To trigger the transfer, all you have to do is execute the posting run with option **T – Test run; no document creation**.

With the **Simulate payroll run** option, you can calculate future periods and transfer the results to the database of personnel cost planning. In this case, the payroll results are not saved. They only exist as an intermediate result.

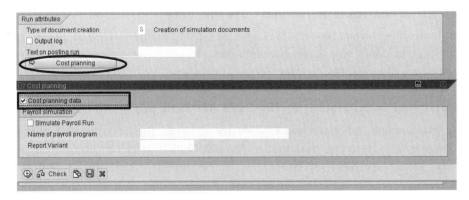

Figure 16.14 Extract from Posting Run Selection Screen (RPCIPE00)

This planning should be based on an entire year, that is to say, twelve payroll periods, so that periods with non-recurring payments (such as Christmas bonus) are not forgotten. Nevertheless, periods with individual non-recurring periods—that are only recorded promptly before payroll accounting (such as bonuses, premiums, participation in sales)—must be taken from real payroll results instead of simulations so that they are not overlooked in personnel cost planning. Another restriction regarding the use of simulation for the future are time bonuses and overtime. If these restrictions are to be included correctly, only past results can be used as a basis for planning. These elements do not yet exist for future payroll periods.

Personnel Cost Planning on the Basis of "Projected pay"

The scenarios outlined above try to generate personnel cost planning from the current position. They are more like forecasting than planning. Therefore, it would be preferable and far more interesting to focus on the planning aspect and to evaluate alternative organizational structures (reporting structures). You can generate almost any number of copies of the current plan versions in Organizational Management. The copied plan variants can then be adjusted using the same tools as the current plan variant. Typically, however, any reference to actual employees is lost. For this reason, this scenario is completely based on the infotype 1015 "Cost planning." This is the only scenario in which infotype 1015 "Cost planning" is used for all cost objects and not only for the evaluation of vacancies. It is difficult to determine the projected pay correctly and therefore equally difficult to estimate the cost items.

Infotype 1015 "Cost planning" has a subtype that is evaluated from personnel cost planning. It is called "survey" (see Figure 16.9). With it, you can generate additional scenarios within this scenario (for example, with/without overtime, with/without variables, with/without further education and training costs).

	Pros	Cons
Basic pay	•View of the future	•Important cost items are missing
Payroll results		•View of the past •Cost items are too detailed •Poor perfomance
Projected pay	•Structural changes can be evaluated	•Projected pay must be correctly calculated

Figure 16.15 Evaluating the Planning Scenarios

Figure 16.15 shows a summary of the evaluation of the three scenarios. On closer inspection of this table, you'll see that there does not appear to be any one ideal scenario. Using the user exits provided since Release version 4.0, however, you can create almost any combination of scenarios. The user exit is called for each cost object with all the cost items determined by standard logic. The newly established or adjusted cost items are returned. In this way, all levels of autonomy are available to adjust existing scenarios or, to combine scenarios with each other.

16.2 Implementation in mySAP HR

16.2.1 The Personnel Cost Planning Process in mySAP HR

The process of personnel cost planning in mySAP HR is done in three steps (see Figure 16.16):

1. Create a personnel cost plan.

2. Manually rework the planning and identify any changes.

3. Release the personnel cost plan to cost accounting.

Until now, we have only looked at the first step (creating the plan). In order for personnel cost planning to be reworked, you must save the personnel cost plan generated by the system (Step 1). It is saved as a planning group in a plan scenario. The plan scenario is the superordinate concept here. The valid plan version and planning period for the subordinate planning groups is defined here. The plan version is identified with a two-character alphanumeric key and a descriptive text.

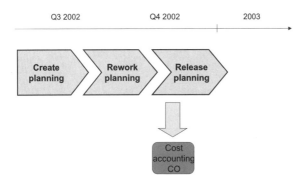

Figure 16.16 The Personnel Cost Planning Process in mySAP HR

A plan scenario must always have at least one planning group. In a decentralized scenario, you can create a planning group for each enterprise area. Each planning group is identified by name and can be protected with a password. This means that local groups can only process the planning groups for which they know the password. Planning groups in a plan scenario cannot be brought together for processing, that is, each planning group must be processed individually. You can only generate an overall view, in display mode, of all program groups in a plan scenario.

Executing personnel cost planning

You can access personnel cost planning in the menu under **Personnel · Personnel Management · Personnel Cost Planning · Planning Group · Create**. Once a plan has been started in dialog mode—in order to be able to process it later—you must save it in a planning group belonging to a plan scenario.

For voluminous planning runs, however, it is recommended that you use report RHPP25SL to calculate personnel cost planning instead and save it on the database. The entries found using the menu via the path above, however, only present views on the selection screen of the report. For this reason, in Figure 16.17, only the selection screen of the report is shown. It contains all scenarios and all selectable options.

When calculating personnel cost planning, you may encounter a problem with the cost items, that is, it cannot be determined—either because no infotype 0008 has been maintained, there are no payroll results or, there is no infotype 1015. In this case, a list of errors is generated, as seen in Figure 16.18. You can ignore this list by using the **Continue without correction** button or, you can correct it interactively by marking the relevant row and selecting **Extras · Maintain cost data**.

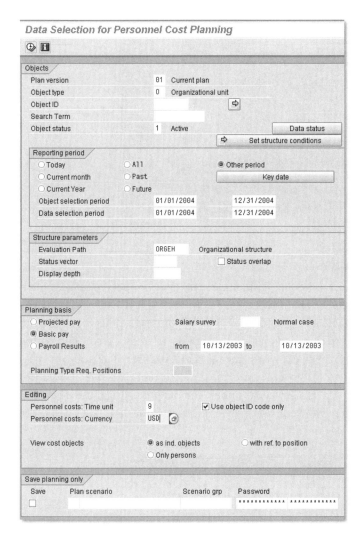

Figure 16.17 Selection Screen RHPP25SL – Personnel Cost Planning

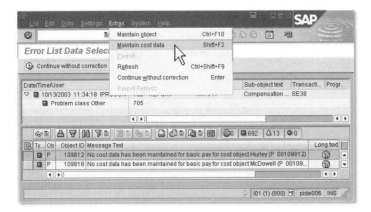

Figure 16.18 Errors in Personnel Cost Planning

Planning Presentation

As shown in Figure 16.1, different views are calculated from personnel cost planning. The standard view is the HR view (see Figure 16.19). It is displayed using the **Organizational unit** tab. Here, you can see the organizational units together with the costs determined from personnel cost planning. The costs are added to the base of the organizational chart, which means that the costs of all sub-organization units are contained in those of an organizational unit. The overall total for personnel cost planning is displayed under the fictitious organizational unit "Total." You can switch between the presentation of names and keys using the menu option **View · Key on/off**.

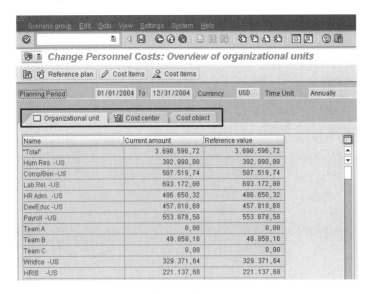

Figure 16.19 Views in Personnel Cost Planning

By selecting the **Cost center** tab, you can branch to the cost accounting view. With the **Cost object** tab, you can get an overview of all the cost objects that are incorporated in personnel cost planning, together with their costs.

Double-click on an organizational unit to call up additional detailed information, as illustrated in Figure 16.20. Two additional views are available with detailed information. One view shows a list of the cost objects incorporated, while the other view shows the costs grouped according to cost elements. You can retrieve the same information in the views **Cost centers** and **Cost objects**.

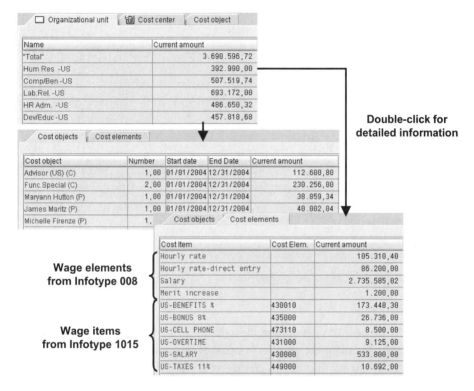

Figure 16.20 Detailed Information on Organizational Units

You can transfer all of the data shown here directly to Excel by using **Go to. TabCalculation PC**. The results of personnel cost planning saved in the database can also be analyzed using reports RHPP25L2 and RHPP25LI (see Figure 16.21). These reports can be particularly useful if the result of personnel cost planning is not to be transferred to SAP cost accounting.

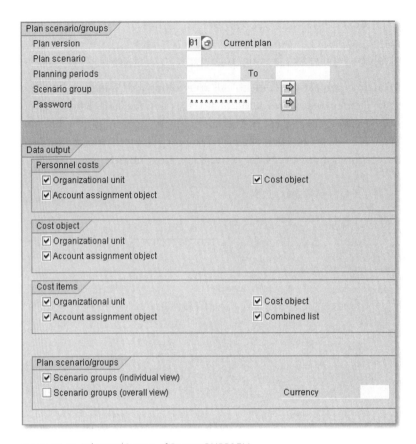

Figure 16.21 Selection Screen of Report RHPP25LI

Editing the Plan

Step 2 in the process of plan editing, described in Figure 16.16, can be executed for not yet released planning groups. The cost objects can be adjusted or cost elements can be changed. In order to change cost objects, you must branch to the Cost objects view. The following actions can be carried out here, as can be seen in Figure 16.22:

▶ Add cost objects

▶ Delete cost objects

▶ Change cost object quantities

▶ Adjust cost object periods

In addition, cost elements can be changed by percentages, for example, to general wage settlements (see Figure 16.23).

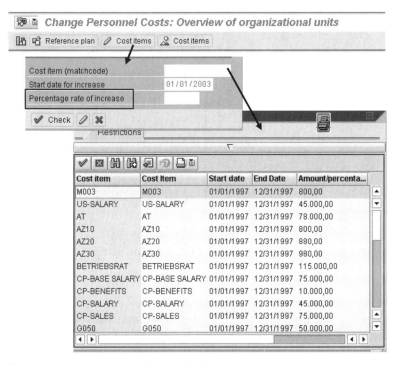

Cost object	Number	Start date	End Date	Current amount
Manager (C)	14,00	01/01/1997	12/31/1997	462.763,28
Administratn (C)	14,00	01/01/1997	06/30/1997	181.799,80
Administratn (C)	15,00	07/01/1997	12/31/1997	194.785,49
Engineer (C)	8,00	01/01/1997	12/31/1997	509.983,84
Executive (C)	5,00	01/01/1997	12/31/1997	495.817,60
Director (C)	5,00	01/01/1997	12/31/1997	212.493,30
Sales Reps. (C)	20,00	01/01/1997	12/31/1997	755.531,60

Figure 16.22 Change Cost Objects

Change Personnel Costs: Overview of organizational units

Reference plan   Cost items   Cost items

Cost item (matchcode)	
Start date for increase	01/01/2003
Percentage rate of increase	

Check

Restrictions

Cost item	Cost Item	Start date	End Date	Amount/percenta...
M003	M003	01/01/1997	12/31/1997	800,00
US-SALARY	US-SALARY	01/01/1997	12/31/1997	45.000,00
AT	AT	01/01/1997	12/31/1997	78.000,00
AZ10	AZ10	01/01/1997	12/31/1997	800,00
AZ20	AZ20	01/01/1997	12/31/1997	880,00
AZ30	AZ30	01/01/1997	12/31/1997	980,00
BETRIEBSRAT	BETRIEBSRAT	01/01/1997	12/31/1997	115.000,00
CP-BASE SALARY	CP-BASE SALARY	01/01/1997	12/31/1997	75.000,00
CP-BENEFITS	CP-BENEFITS	01/01/1997	12/31/1997	10.000,00
CP-SALARY	CP-SALARY	01/01/1997	12/31/1997	45.000,00
CP-SALES	CP-SALES	01/01/1997	12/31/1997	75.000,00
G050	G050	01/01/1997	12/31/1997	50.000,00

Figure 16.23 Adjusting Cost Elements by Percentage

The adjustments carried out are immediately included in personnel cost planning. If large planning groups with a lot of cost objects are processed, then performance problems may arise here. For this reason, the immediate calculation of the effect of each individual input can be switched on or off using **Settings · Calculation on/off**. Under **Planning Group · Manage**, for certain planning groups, you can use **Edit · Recalculate** to reverse all manual adjustments.

Comparing Planning Groups

If planning groups with different plan scenarios are generated for the same organizational units or, if planning groups are edited locally, it might prove useful to compare these groups with each other to identify any deviations. You can use the *reference plan* for this exercise. As shown in Figure 16.24, you can add one or more planning groups to each other. You can then analyze the variations in the different views using the mechanisms we described previously. The reference plan can be presented as a value or as a percentage variation.

🔲 🔳 Reference plan	🖉 Cost items	👤 Cost items

Planning Period   01/01/1997 To 12/31/1997   Currency   USD   Tim

Scenario group   MATTHEWS

🔲 Organizational unit   📋 Cost center   Cost object

Name	Current amount	Reference value
"Total"	3.833.943,82	3.833.943,82
US Subsid.	586.717,49	586.717,49
New York	155.958,32	155.958,32
Chicago	509.983,84	509.983,84
Atlanta	136.463,53	136.463,53
Los Angeles	230.168,50	230.168,50
Corp.Svc -US	33.054,52	33.054,52

Figure 16.24 Comparing Two Planning Groups

Transferring Personnel Cost Planning to Cost Accounting

A planning version, together with all assigned planning groups, is transferred to cost accounting in two steps:

1. When phases 1 and 2 from Figure 16.16 have been completed, the planning version is released. A check is then run for the cost accounting view in personnel cost planning. All cost objects must have cost centers, all cost items must have cost types, and all cost centers and cost types must exist. If the check is successful, then the plan is released, and the release cannot be reversed. The check can also be run independently of the release.

2. Released plan scenarios can be transferred to cost accounting. If necessary, the transfer can be reversed (Cancellation run).

This procedure is very similar to posting the payroll. Similar to payroll accounting, the transfer of personnel cost planning is an ALE scenario, which means that the HR and cost accounting applications can run on physically separate systems with different releases.

One important restriction is the fact that only costs without headcount and without employee capacities, that is, Full-Time Equivalents (FTEs), are moved over to cost accounting. By default, the costs are then distributed evenly to all periods. This can, however, be controlled in cost accounting. If there are twelve monthly paychecks plus an additional paycheck for Christmas during November, then $^1/_{13}$ of the costs should be posted for all months except November and $^2/_{13}$ for November.

16.2.2 Considering Vacant Positions

In Customizing, you can decide when a position should be considered as "vacant." (This allows for the possibility that a position without a holder is not necessarily a vacancy.) In some cases, a decision has not yet been made as to whether the position will be eliminated or, whether it should be filled with a new holder. The PPVAC PPVAC switch in table T77SO can be used to set whether a position without a holder should be considered as vacant for personnel cost planning or, if a position should only be considered vacant if it has the infotype 1007 "Vacancy."

Quota Planning

To avoid having to create vacant positions on a grand scale, for correct personnel cost planning, you can maintain the headcount or FTEs in infotype 1019 "Quota planning" as can be seen in Figure16.25. However, this infotype can only be recorded for organizational units. The "planned" values entered are saved. All "current" values are determined from current data and made available at the time of display. Infotype 1019 "Quota planning" must be activated in Customizing for personnel cost planning. If this is not done, the value entered will be ignored. Quota planning is described in detail in Chapter 14, *Position and Quota Planning*.

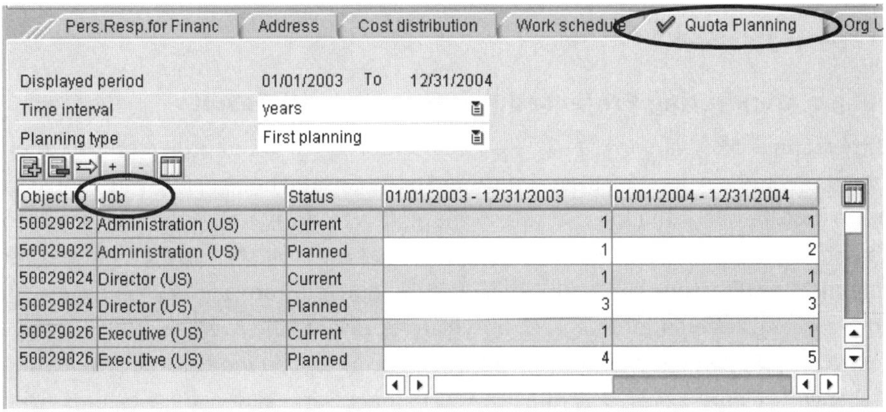

| Pers.Resp.for Financ | Address | Cost distribution | Work schedule | ✓ Quota Planning | Org U |

Object I Job		Status	01/01/2003 - 12/31/2003	01/01/2004 - 12/31/2004	
50029022	Administration (US)	Current		1	1
50029022	Administration (US)	Planned		1	2
50029024	Director (US)	Current		1	1
50029024	Director (US)	Planned		3	3
50029026	Executive (US)	Current		1	1
50029026	Executive (US)	Planned		4	5

Displayed period 01/01/2003 To 12/31/2004
Time interval years
Planning type First planning

Figure 16.25 Infotype 1019 "Quota Planning"

16.2.3 Customizing Personnel Cost Planning

As with most planning components in mySAP HR, the concepts and processes are the main focus here. Customizing is usually set quickly (not considering the programming of user-exits), if you use the "old" version of cost planning from Release 4.6C. SAP has prepared a customizing wizard for personnel cost planning that guides you through all relevant points, asks for facts, and generates customizing settings based on personnel cost planning (see Figure 16.26). You can find the customizing wizard in Customizing (IMG) under **Personnel Management · Compensation Management · Personnel Cost Planning · Wizard**.

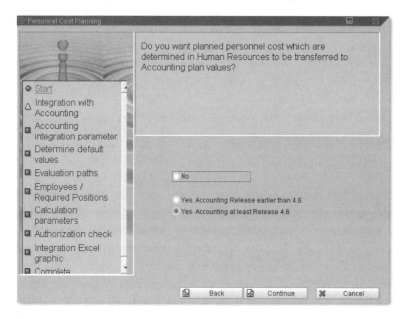

Figure 16.26 Customizing Wizard for Personnel Cost Planning

16.3 Process Examples

16.3.1 Generating Projected Pay from Payroll Results

If personnel cost planning is to be carried out on the basis of projected pay, then the projected pay (that is to say, infotype 1015 "Cost planning") must be prepared with cost items for the jobs. If, furthermore, it is to be assumed that the scenario based on payroll results and the scenario based on projected pay should deliver identical results, then the cost items must be derived from the payroll results. In the end, we have an Infotype 1015, which represents the average of all employees doing the same job and therefore can serve as a good indicator for evaluating vacancies. Figure 16.27 describes the steps necessary to derive cost items from the payroll results:

1. Infotype 1015 "Cost planning" must be created for jobs, which means that all employees must be grouped by job. To generate infotype 1015 at a job, you must select all employees in this job.

2. You must then read the payroll results for these employees.

3. Infotype 1015 is made up of wage elements. Payroll results are recorded in the form of wage types. Wage types are usually presented with more details than are required at the level of wage elements. There must, therefore, be some way to convert wage types to wage elements. This could, for example, be resolved with a special processing class for wage types. The specifications in the processing class represent the wage elements. If all wage types are now allotted in terms of this processing class, then wage elements can be generated from the payroll result. It is also necessary to generate a midpoint value by dividing the total for the wage elements—generated from the payroll results added together—by the number of payroll results.

4. The wage elements-per-job calculated in this way are recorded as infotype 1015.

The steps described here can be carried out as a report program in the customer name range.

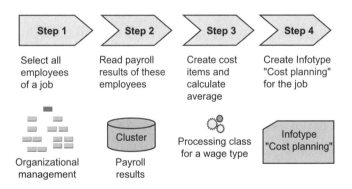

Figure 16.27 Generating Projected Pay from Payroll Results

16.3.2 Deriving an Ideal Scenario

We described the process of planning personnel costs in mySAP HR in Section 16.2.1; however, we omitted one important step in the process. The personnel cost plan created should have been compared with the actual results and a monthly plan/actual variance analysis should have been carried out. This is usually carried out in cost accounting. On closer examination, it is apparent that a more detailed analysis is possible in mySAP HR (see the reference plan and the different views). All data that is required for the analysis is available in the system. The planned values are stored in personnel cost planning, while the "actual" values can be found in payroll accounting in the form of the payroll result. From there, they are posted to financial accounting and cost accounting. This results in an extended process (see Figure 16.28).

Because the "actual" values in the variance analysis are based on payroll results, a range of questions emerge:

▶ On which scenarios should the original planning be based (comparability of results)?

▶ Is a variance analysis possible if the original planning is not based on payroll results?

▶ When can a variance analysis be generated? Is one payroll run enough?

The existing scenarios cannot resolve these problems. A composite scenario is required, with the following properties:

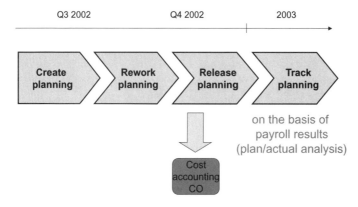

Figure 16.28 Process of Personnel Cost Planning and Tracking

▶ To achieve comparability, the cost elements must be standardized. This may involve actions to convert wage types into wage elements, for example, as described in Section 16.3.1, Step 3.

▶ If payroll results from payroll accounting are available for a period in the personnel cost plan, then these results can be used in the plan (actual).

▶ If no results from payroll are available for a period in the personnel costs plan, then a qualified estimate is carried out on the basis of the master data recorded for employees (planned).

► Optionally, the qualified estimate can be derived from the original planning to eliminate additional disruptive factors for the variance analysis.

Therefore, the same composite scenario can be used for planning and for variance analysis (see Figure 16.29). This ensures that the plans will be comparable. After payroll accounting has been carried out, the personnel cost plan should be repeated with the composite scenario. Subsequently, the original plan that was transferred to cost accounting is placed alongside it as a reference plan. You can analyze variances by using different views.

Planning on 10/01/02

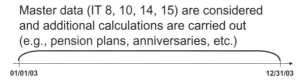

Planning on 02/01/03

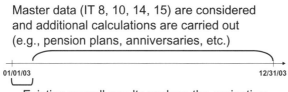

Figure 16.29 Composite Scenario for Variance Analysis

16.3.3 Local Scenarios

You may not always want personnel cost planning to be carried out just centrally from the HR department. Rather, the area and department managers should be involved as well to carry out detailed planning and therefore improve accuracy. The result may be, for example, a process like that shown in Figure 16.30.

If the area or department managers have access to mySAP HR, it is possible to work with planning groups (see Section 16.2.1). For every area or department, a separate planning group can be set up in the planning scenario with personnel cost planning for this particular area. Each planning group is protected with its own password, which is known only to the HR department and the area/department manager in question. After all detail planning has been completed and checked by the HR department, the planning scenario is forwarded to cost accounting.

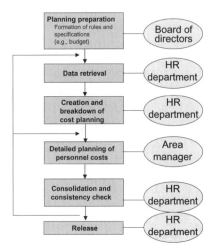

Figure 16.30 Possible Decentralized Local Planning Process

However, the personnel cost planning component of mySAP HR is not always the most appropriate planning tool. It may be that the advantages of integrated planning in a planning tool, together with other components, such as turnover and profit margin, prevail, with the result that the planning process in mySAP HR personnel cost planning is only used as a data source. The results of a planning run can, for example, be transferred from the system into another planning tool using reports RHPP25LI and RHPP25L2.

16.3.4 Risk Management

In addition to personnel cost planning, a risk analysis of remuneration elements should be conducted. Many companies, for example, offer their employees a company pension scheme. In general, annual provisions are set up for this, which are allocated on the basis of an actuarial appraisal report. These provisions, however, are usually not reflected in personnel cost planning, and must therefore be considered separately. If, for example, the company has made a total commitment, by which it is obliged to supplement the employees' retirement payments to a certain percentage of their last salary, the reserves would increase disproportionately if the retirement payments were to decrease (because, for example, statutory pensions were reduced). You may encounter such problems particularly in your subsidiaries in European countries such as Germany.

There may also be compensation elements that may indicate that different scenarios would be processed in personnel cost planning. If the enterprise pays the sales force a sales-related premium, for example, then sales volume would become an influencing variable in personnel cost planning. The larger the compensation element, the greater the influence. If, for example, the premium is set at 30% of sales, then this compensation element may account for 15% of overall personnel costs. Consequently, the company turnover would be a key planning factor in personnel cost planning.

16.4 Critical Success Factors

In addition to integrating cost planning into Personnel Administration, Payroll, Organizational Management, and Compensation Management, you should also consider the following aspects:

▶ The first point in personnel cost planning should be to clarify the target values and target objects. Are we only interested in personnel costs, or do headcount and employee capacity also play a role? What objects need to be planned? Are cost centers sufficient or should, for example, project costs also be planned?

▶ After you have decided what needs to be planned, next comes the question of "how," that is, how are the processes to be defined and how is the plan to be orchestrated. There is also the question of "who," and whether planning should be carried out locally or centrally (see Section 16.3.3).

▶ Only after establishing what needs to be planned and how to implement the plan is a check run for the appropriate planning scenario.

▶ In most cases, it is necessary to use MS Office or other third-party products to integrate managers.

▶ For more complex scenarios, you should consider the possibilities offered by a user exit.

16.5 Cost Planning and Simulation in R/3 Enterprise

16.5.1 Presentation in R/3 Enterprise

The new component, "Personnel Cost Planning and Simulation," is the successor to personnel cost planning (hereinafter called "old cost planning"), which we have addressed-up to this point-in this chapter. Although some concepts of the previous solution have been inherited, the new solution should nevertheless be regarded as a new development.

The old cost planning can still be used. It is delivered in the R/3 Enterprise Core. To use the new cost planning, however, you must install and activate the extension set 1.1 at least. In addition, in Customizing, you must activate the preparation of payroll results for the new cost planning. The system switch HCP00 – VERSN in table T77S0 must be set to the value "2".

This switch setting selects the use of the new solution over the old one.

Figure 16.31 shows an overview of how the new cost planning is integrated into the overall system. Whereas some HR components are only used as data sources, Compensation Management and Training and Event Management get input from the linked cost planning in the form of budgets. Furthermore, the results of cost planning can also be used in cost accounting and in SAP Business Information Warehouse (SAP BW).

Figure 16.31 Integration of the New Cost Planning

16.5.2 Significant Process Changes

The following are the most important changes and options for the personnel cost planning process using the new solution:

▶ The participation of local, decentralized managers receives much better support. Particularly during the detailed planning phase, they can influence the planning results online. Thauthorization concept makes it possiblfor each manager to havaccess to thpart of planning that is relevant to them.

▶ The data basis for thsimulation of personnel costs is now much broader. It is, in general, no longer necessary to uspayroll results or payroll simulations from remuneration accounting as a planning basis.

▶ In particular, theris bidirectional integration in Compensation Management and in Training and Event Management.

▶ The data basis to bconsidered can badjusted very well to meet threquirements of each enterprisusing Business Add-Ins (BAdIs).

▶ The transfer of results to thCO (Cost Accounting) modulis now morflexibland in particular, it also allows thtransfer of statistical key figures (for example, number of employees).

16.5.3 Clarification of Terms

First, we would like to explain some concepts and correlations that are new to this cost planning.

Planning Context and Scenario

The *planning context* describes a self-contained planning world. Several planning contexts may be used if multiple sections of the corporate group both carry out their own specific plans (in accordance with corporate group rules) and are also involved in group-wide planning. The planning context is also a control element for customizing the planning run.

You can have any number of scenarios in a planning context. These scenarios can represent certain assumptions about the general conditions or possible variants of compensation policy (for example, worst case scenario; possible changes to the legal conditions, etc.).

Data Collection

Data collection forms the basis of cost planning. Here, data is read from the different possible sources and is stored in infotype 0666. Because data collection is the most obvious difference between the new cost planning and the old cost planning, and given that it forms the basis for the enhanced possibilities, we will address it in greater detail now.

Methods and Parameters

The methods used for data collection determine which data will actually be considered and how it will be evaluated. The methods are divided into three groups:

▶ Data collection of employee data (for example, infotype 0008 or business event bookings)

▶ Data collection of organizational objects (for example, infotype 1005 or nn (unnamed) bookings in Training and Event Management)

▶ Manual changand derivation (changes from detailed planning)

Parameters can be assigned to each method that will influence data collection in detail (for example, planning variants for Training and Event Management)

Data Selection Period and Data Collection Period

By *data collection period*, we mean the period during which plans are being made (for example, the following year)-frequently referred to as a "planning period." The *data selection period* refers to the period from which the planning basis is read. Often, the data selection period is the same as the data collection period (in general, for example when reading infotype 0008 "Basic pay"). Another possibility is that the data selection period and the data collection period are not the same. Thus, for example, planning for bonus payments can also use the amounts paid in the current year as a basis. Then you plan for the following year, but the planning is based on data from the current year.

Cost Planning Run

The *cost planning run* creates the actual plan on the basis of data collection and customizing.

Detail Planning

Detail planning enables line managers and central cost planning experts the ability to further modify their plans in individual cases.

Types of Cost Items

The term *cost item*, by itself, was also used in the previous solution, that is, the old cost planning. Now, however, we can differentiate between three types of cost items:

▶ *Direct cost items* comdirectly from data collection and are usually already evaluated in monetary terms.

▶ *Additional cost items are only evaluated during the planning run on the basis of customizing settings*; for example, a $1,000 Christmas bonus for each employee in December.

▶ *Dependent cost items* aralso evaluated during the planning run and they are dependent on other cost items (basic cost items); for example, the employer's allowance for a retirement pension of 5% of his or her annual basic salary.

16.5.4 The Cost Planning Process

Figure 16.32 shows an overview of the cost planning process.

Planning Preparation

Planning preparation is mostly done in Customizing, as described below.

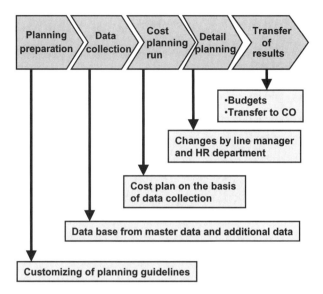

Figure 16.32 The Cost Planning Process

Data Collection

Data collection can be accessed using the following menu path: **Personnel management · Personnel cost planning · Data collection.** There are three menu options to choose from:

▶ Data collection for employees

▶ Data collection for organizational objects

▶ Editing collected data

We shall present the process here using the example of data collection at the employee level. Generally, both procedures are required so that the planning run is ultimately carried out using a mixed data basis with both employee data and data on organizational objects.

Figure 16.33 shows a selection screen for data collection for employees. Apart from the typical possibilities for selecting people, you must enter the following:

▶ The parameters for the methods used

▶ The data collection period

▶ The subtype of infotype 0666 in which the data basis is to be recorded (this subtype can be selected again later during the planning run)

▶ The Test indicator

▶ The indicator conveying whether a log should be saved or not

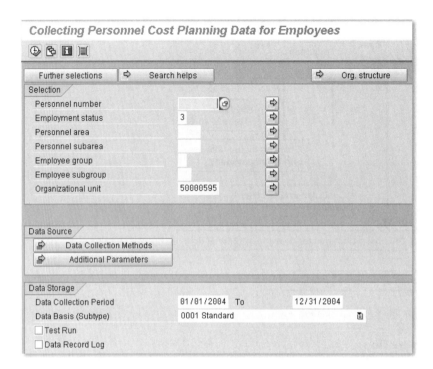

Figure 16.33 Selection Screen at the Start of Data Collection

Figure 16.34 shows the selection of data collection methods. In this example, the infotypes 0008, 0014, and 0015, the compensation guidelines, and (not visible in the illustration) data from Training and Event Management should all be considered. The selection also shows some other standard methods. There are no customer-defined methods available for selection here; however, they can be implemented individually.

Method	Data Sel. From	To	Info	
Infotype: Basic Pay (0008)	01/01/04	12/31/04	🛈	
Infotype: Capital Formation (0010)	01/01/04	12/31/04	🛈	
Infotype: Rec.Payments/Deductions (0014)	01/01/04	12/31/04	🛈	
Infotype: Additional Payments (0015)	01/01/04	12/31/04	🛈	
Infotype:1-Time Payments Off-Cycle(0267)	01/01/04	12/31/04	🛈	
Difference betw. Act. and Planned Comp.	01/01/04	12/31/04	🛈	
Compensation Guidelines	01/01/04	12/31/04	🛈	
Data from Payroll	01/01/04	12/31/04	🛈	
Simulated Payscale Reclassification	01/01/04	12/31/04	🛈	

Figure 16.34 Selecting Methods for Data Collection

Figure 16.35 shows how the parameters are set for some of the selected methods. In this case, the parameters on reading and evaluating data from Training and Event Management are filled (cost items must be filled and plan variants read).

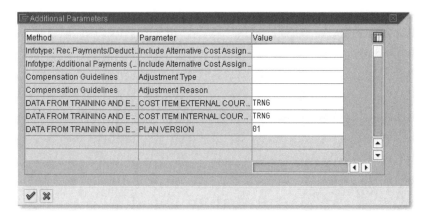

Figure 16.35 Maintaining Parameters for Data Collection

The data collection output first displays warnings and messages (see Figure 16.36). These error messages are based on the data collection method for Compensation Management. Reasons for error may be, among other things:

▶ Missing or inconsistent method parameters

▶ Missing or inconsistent customizing in the data source to be considered (in particular, Compensation Management)

▶ Missing or inconsistent data on individual methods

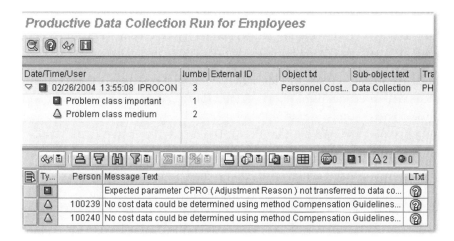

Figure 16.36 Errors and Warnings on Data Collection

After successful data collection, the data basis can be checked and also manually changed. This step is not to be confused with detail planning, which provides an easy-to-use Web interface (as Business Server Pages, BSPs).

Figure 16.37 shows the maintenance screen for changing data for a single employee. Here, for example, you can make a change to the basic pay or you can add further cost items. After you have made changes, you must activate the **Re-Calculation** button. Once the changes have been saved, they are considered in subsequent planning runs.

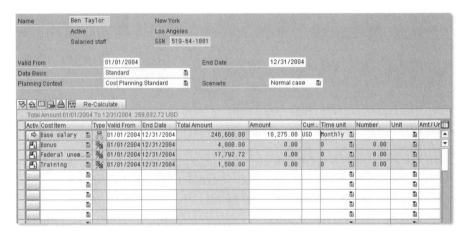

Figure 16.37 Changing the Data Basis Generated

Cost Planning Run

The planning run itself does not provide the user with that many additional possibilities for selection. Creating and processing planning runs is done in cost planning management (via the menu path **Personnel management · Personnel cost planning · Cost plans · Manage**) (see Figure 16.38) following these steps:

1. Create plan (via menu path **Plan data · Personnel cost plan · Create plan**). Some parameters need to be maintained for this, in particular, context and scenario and the details on the data basis (sub-types in data collection and quota planning (compare Chapter 14). The result of this step is an "empty" cost plan (see Figure 16.39).

2. Only when you have achieved this base, can a planning run be executed using the menu path **Plan data · Execute Planning Run**. Each planning run is given a unique name. At the start of a planning run, you also must select the organizational units and people for which the plan will be made. Figure 16.40 shows the output of the planning run: a detailed itemization of all cost objects and cost items.

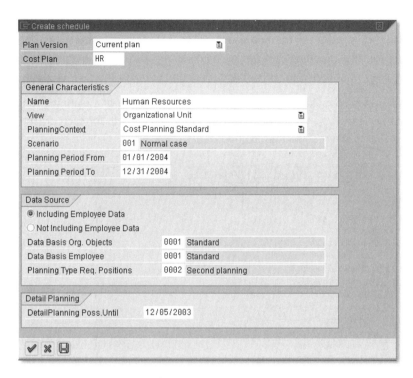

Figure 16.38 Creating a Cost Plan

PlVer./Plan/Run/Package	Start date	End Date	Planning Context	Scenario
▽ 🗁 Current plan				
📄 Human Resources	01/01/2004	12/31/2004	Cost Planning Standard	Normal case

Figure 16.39 "Empty" Cost Plan

Cost Items per Cost Object

Plan: Human Resources (01 HR)
Planning Period: 01/01/2004-12/31/2004

Cost Unit	Text	Cost Object	Cost Item Text	Crcy	Σ Amount Qu 1 / 2004	Σ Amount Qu 2 / 2004	Σ Amount Qu 3 / 2004	Σ Amount Qu 4 / 2004	Σ Total Amou
Human Resources	🗊	Mr. Dan Young	Bonus	USD	5,000.00				5,000.00
			Federal unemployment tax	USD	355.00				355.00
			Federal social security/Medicare	USD	382.50				382.50
			Training	USD	375.00	375.00	375.00	375.00	1,500.00
		Ben Taylor	Base salary	USD	30,825.00	30,825.00	30,825.00	30,825.00	123,300.00
			Bonus	USD	4,000.00				4,000.00
			Federal unemployment tax	USD	2,472.59	2,188.59	2,188.59	2,188.59	9,038.36
			Federal social security/Medicare	USD	2,664.12	2,358.12	2,358.12	2,358.12	9,738.48
			Training	USD	375.00	375.00	375.00	375.00	1,500.00
		Lisa Felix	Base salary	USD	11,960.00	11,960.00	12,091.43	12,091.43	48,102.86
			Bonus	USD	3,000.00				3,000.00
			Federal unemployment tax	USD	1,062.18	849.16	858.49	858.49	3,628.30
			Federal social security/Medicare	USD	1,144.44	914.94	924.99	924.99	3,909.36
			Training	USD	375.00	375.00	375.00	375.00	1,500.00
Compensation and Benefits - (US)		Megan Young	Bonus	USD	4,000.00				4,000.00

Figure 16.40 Result of Planning Run

Caution! In this example we have executed the planning run for a single department. In practice, with the new solution, this is no longer necessary (and generally not even advisable). With detail planning and in evaluation, line managers can

then also access the sub-plans relevant to them (and only those plans that are relevant) if planning is done for the entire enterprise in a single planning run. The prerequisites for this planning run are as follows: organizational management must be correctly maintained and a suitable reporting concept must be in place.

Figure 16.41 shows cost plan management after the execution of a planning run. It is particularly clear that an individual package has been created for each organizational unit that is assigned to the planned department.

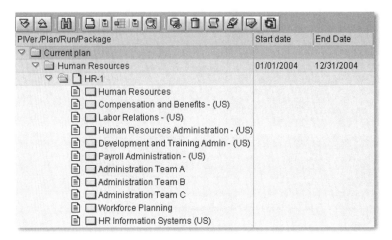

Figure 16.41 Cost Plan Management After a Planning Run

Within cost plan management, you can perform the following actions:

Displaying the results

▶ Display results of data

▶ Delete data

▶ Change attributes

▶ Release a planning run (after which no more changes can be made)

▶ Post a transfer into accounting

Detail Planning

Detail planning now allows for changes to be made to planning data. This can be done either by the line manager or centrally by those responsible for personnel cost planning in the HR department.

The possibilities of detail planning are limited by two restrictions:

▶ When a cost plan is created, a date is set after which time no detail planning is allowed. No more changes can be made after this datas well.

▶ In Customizing, it is defined whether each cost item can be changed, added, or deleted in detail planning.

Within these restrictions, you can perform the following actions:

▶ Change cost items
▶ Delete cost items
▶ Add cost items
▶ Change the capacity utilization level

Change requirements planning

Detail planning is not done via the normal interface of the SAP GUI; rather, it is done using a Business Server Page (BSP) in a browser interface. This means that the layout can be adjusted to meet the needs of the enterprise.

Transfer of Results

The results of cost planning can be transferred in three ways:

1. Post the results to accounting
2. Generate budgets for Compensation Management
3. Generate budgets for Training and Event Management

Reports

SAP BW is the main evaluation tool (see Chapter 18). A very extensive standard content is available in it.

Within R/3, some evaluations are available under the menu path **Personnel management · Personnel cost planning · Infosystem · Reports**. The "Task list changes" and "original documents" reports can be used, first, to trace the planning processes and then, to look for errors.

The "plan data" evaluation is a very flexible instrument and by itself, offers more possibilities than were available with the old cost planning. As you can see in Figure 16.42, there are various views for displaying the overall costs per cost item, per cost object or per organizational object as well as a detailed itemization. In addition, you can display the costs per month, per quarter or per year.

Figure 16.43 shows the result of the report in the view "Total Costs per Cost Item."

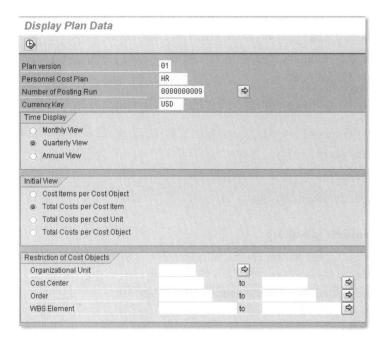

Figure 16.42 Evaluating Plan Data

Total Costs per Cost Item

Plan	Human Resources (01 HR)
Planning Period	01/01/2004-12/31/2004

Cost Item Text	Crcy	Σ Amount Qu 1 / 2004	Σ Amount Qu 2 / 2004	Σ Amount Qu 3 / 2004	Σ Amount Qu 4 / 2004	Σ Total Amou
Base salary	USD	42,785.00	42,785.00	42,916.43	42,916.43	171,402.86
Bonus	USD	172,000.00				172,000.00
Federal unemployment tax	USD	15,249.75	3,037.75	3,047.08	3,047.08	24,381.66
Federal social security/Medicare	USD	16,431.06	3,273.06	3,283.11	3,283.11	26,270.34
Training	USD	16,500.00	16,500.00	16,500.00	16,500.00	66,000.00
	USD ▪	262,965.81 ▪	65,595.81 ▪	65,746.62 ▪	65,746.62 ▪	460,054.86

Figure 16.43 Total Costs per Cost Item

16.5.5 Customizing

Currency Conversion

The "Basic settings" section is very simple. Here, only the retention period for logs and the exchange rate type for currency conversion need to be maintained. This is done via the IMG path **Personnel Management · Personnel Cost Planning and Simulation · Edit Basic Settings**. The exchange rate type for currency conversion is very important in an international planning context. To plan the results of cost accounting consistently, the same exchange rate type should be used as in cost accounting. In distributed systems (HR system and FI/CO system are linked via ALE), particular attention should be paid so that the exchange rates for the corresponding exchange rate type are current in the HR system. However, typically, you should not put the rate of the day here; otherwise, the planning results would change daily. Instead, you should set a base rate that will be realistic for the planning period.

Below, when describing the IMG path, the first two steps will be omitted because all actions come under **Personnel Management · Personnel Cost Planning and Simulation**.

Planning Context and Planning Scenario

You can access Customizing for the planning context and planning scenario via the IMG path **Planning Preparation**. There, the planning contexts and scenarios, together with a descriptive text, are created. It is important to keep the circumstances in mind, and to decide which contexts and scenarios are actually necessary. In particular, Customizing is used to control the cost planning run depending on the planning context (see Figure 16.44).

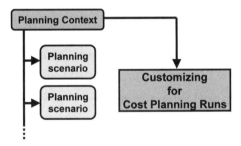

Figure 16.44 Planning Context and Scenario

General Customizing for Data Collection

Under *Data Collection,* we find general customizing for cost items and symbolic accounts, which is familiar from the old cost planning and posting the remuneration accounting. What is new here is the ability to define a cost item as a statistical key figure. The activity *Create data basis* determines the subtypes for infotype 0666 (and 5010), which can be used to store different databases alongside each other (see also Section 16.1.3).

Methods and Parameters

The data collection methods and their parameters are provided in the standard. You can use the IMG path **Data Collection · Data Collection Methods and Parameters · Define Attributes of Data Collection Methods and Parameters** to initialize specifications for the different parameters.

Then, you can use the BAdIs to create additional enterprise-specific methods (and parameters). This can be useful in many cases to take advantage of the flexibility of new cost planning (for example, to factor in the customer-defined infotypes or the company pension scheme). BAdIs are also listed and described in IMG under **Data collection**.

Controlling the Planning Runs

In addition to some general parameters, three main points should be considered here:

1. The definition of dependent and additional cost items (see Section 16.1.5). The definition of the dependent items is of particular interest. Each dependent item can be generated from one or more basis items. Each base item can, in turn, serve as a basis for one or more dependent items. The time-related component is particularly noteworthy. The values of the base items can be drawn from the planning year or the previous year, and from any month. The dependent item can then be generated for any number of months of the planning year. Figure 16.45 shows the simple case in which both items have the same time base. The monetary valuation of the cost items generated in this way is defined in the next step.

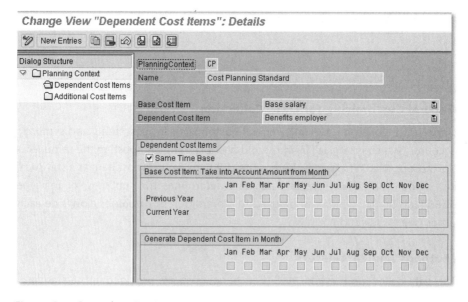

Figure 16.45 Dependent Cost Item

2. The definition of scenario-specific values includes the valuation of cost items that have not yet been evaluated (dependent and additional). This can be done

as an absolute value or as a percentage. Figure 16.46 shows the valuation of the cost item "Benefits" at 28% of the value of the underlying basis item. In addition, the scenario-specific values are also given capping limits. For example, you can specify that the cost item "Benefits" can reach a maximum value of $20,000.

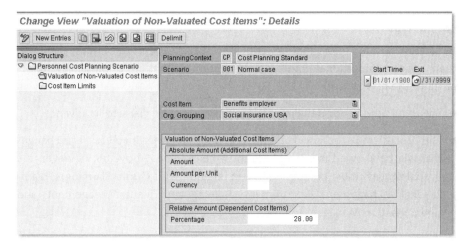

Figure 16.46 Valuation of a Dependent Cost Item

3. Grouping the cost objects using the features HCP01 and HCP02 sorts employees and other cost objects into groups, which will be handled equally in terms of admissibility, valuation, and capping.

Aside from this, there are some BAdIs that can be used to adjust the planning run in almost any way to meet the specific needs of an enterprise. Here, you can easily overshoot the target and create a disproportionately high amount of work, where the SAP standard would work almost as well.

Controlling detail planning

Customizing for detail planning is very limited. In the first place, it is important that the correct evaluation path is given using the IMG path **Detail Planning · Specify Control Parameters...** which links the line managers responsible for planning with their organizational units.

You can also use the available BAdI to add information to the detail planning interface, which is often necessary to improve acceptance. Detail planning is done using the BSP (Business Server Page) HRHCP_PLANNING.

Controlling the Posting to Accounting

Controlling the posting to accounting is very similar to the corresponding customizing for remuneration accounting. Some of the activities must be done in Customizing for accounting, which means, in particular, that if there is a separate HR system, these activities must be done in the accounting system.

16.5.6 Tips

In addition to the factors that are critical to success with the old cost planning, there are some additional points worth mentioning that are of particular importance to the new solution:

▶ The requirements for detailing and valuation must be clarified in advance.

▶ The process must be checked with the line managers involved. The changes that will be allowed in each phase must be defined. Above all, however, the overall process must be defined in combination with Quota Planning, Organizational Management, Recruitment, Training and Event Management, and Compensation Management.

▶ When making settings in Customizing, you should expand the functionality step-by-step. This means, for example, that you should first configure and test the simpler data collection methods, and then add the others bit-by-bit, and only add the company-specific programmed methods at the end.

▶ Given the multiple possibilities, process definition and customizing involve a lot more work than was needed with the old cost planning. Therefore, you should allow for a sufficient amount of time to implement the new cost planning. Optimally, you should start the project after you complete the last round of planning. In this way, those involved will still recall the actual processes and problem fields and there will be adequate time before the next planning round to set up an optimized process.

▶ Before creating your own methods, check the methods in the standard delivery closely. You may be able to change processes by maintaining the master data and therefore avoid having to create additional methods.

Part 4
Additional Solutions

17 E-Learning and Learning Management Systems

The key features in any e-learning program are the content, the actual course, and the learning. There are also systems with which you can, for example, track who uses which training course, what progress is made, what costs arise, and so on. This type of system is known as an LMS-a Learning Management System.

17.1 E-Learning: A New Class of Learning?

In the information society of the 21st century, technical progress is always changing. To stay abreast of these changes and to ensure that the enterprises they work for can remain competitive, there is a constant need for people to continuously update and expand their knowledge and skills. Buzzwords such as *Lifelong Learning*, *Learning on Demand*, and *E-learning* have been around for awhile now. These buzzwords are like an historical record of the methods and means of communication used by companies to meet their objectives. The classic resume of School · Learning → Studies → Career → Retirement has long been out-of-date; anyone who wants to survive in today's labor market must continue with their education in a purposeful manner. Therefore, furthering one's education has become a basic requirement of modern life; however, the necessary training is rather expensive, time-consuming, limiting, that is, tied to a certain place and time and, overall, rarely provides one with more than rough insights into the subject at hand. Unfortunately, conventional education offerings cannot be optimally adjusted to meet the needs of each individual, because these offerings must consider the overall interests of all course participants. This is where e-learning comes in.

By definition, *e-learning* refers to all specific forms of self-directed learning using new media and technical resources. By *self-directed*, we mean that the learner, with or without help, molds previously established learning objectives into his or her own learning objectives and tasks, and achieves them *successfully*, according to his or her own learning requirements.

17.1.1 Forms of E-Learning

In keeping with the aforementioned definition, the following forms of e-learning are possible:

▶ **Computer-Based Training (CBT) (offline)**
  This is almost the classical form of e-learning, in which the content is on CDs, such as are currently available for language courses, math learning programs,

programs for children, and other learning programs for imparting specific knowledge.

▶ **Web-Based Training (WBT) (online)**
In contrast to the offline version of e-learning, the content of this material is more dynamic and the level of integration is higher than it is with CBT. A variety of media and communication channels are used, such as chats with other learners and forums on certain content. With web-based training, it is easier for the content provider to prepare new tests and provide new information, thereby constantly adding to the knowledge base and keeping it as current as possible.

▶ **Combination of Web-Based and Computer-Based Training (WBT and CBT)**
In the early days of Internet usage, training material on CDs was often combined with the possibilities of online learning. This form is still widely used today. Interaction between participants and the updating of content and tests via the Internet are the main features that differentiate combined training from the classical CBT. The main reason for the combined use of learning media is that subject areas presented with a lot of multimedia content run faster on home PCs from a CD, thus avoiding long wait times. With the increase in the availability of access bandwidths for faster access to the Internet, this advantage is becoming less important.

▶ **Combination with Other Forms of Learning (Blended Learning)**
E-learning can also be combined with other forms of learning, such as classic classroom training. To prepare for classroom training, e-learning offers the advantage that all participants will arrive with the same standard of knowledge. Consequently, the training course can take place without interruption and without any unnecessary requests.

17.1.2 When Can E-Learning Be Used Effectively?

Many enterprises are interested in e-learning and the possibilities and advantages that it can offer. In conferences and trade fairs, there is a keen interest in the subject of learning; however, many enterprises still shrink away from actually using it.

In the following list are some prerequisites that would make the use of e-learning seem plausible (see also, Figure 17.1). Not all of these prerequisites have to be met.

▶ **Suitable conditions**
Apart from organizational and technical conditions, the existing processes in the enterprise should be considered, as well as whether e-learning should be integrated into these existing processes (see also Section 17.6).

▶ **Organizational**

Without the determined will of company management and a readiness to convincingly transfer responsibility for learning to employees, the best technology in the world will be of no use. It is the task of company management to develop a clear e-learning strategy or vision and to communicate this vision throughout the company. Management must arouse the employees' willingness and curiosity in all areas.

▶ **Technical**

There is an entire range of technical requirements that must be met in order to implement e-learning in the enterprise. Technical investment depends on the planned development of e-learning in the enterprise. It covers everything—from the configuration of PCs in the workplace to the necessary bandwidths for the company-wide dissemination of content, through the technical operator concept for a complete learning platform. There is also the question of whether the company will create its own training material or purchase it.

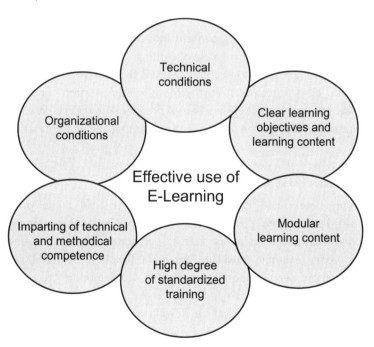

Figure 17.1 Criteria for the Practical Use of E-Learning

▶ **A high degree of standardized training**

An enterprise that, in the most extreme case, needs special training for each individual employee and thus offers a very heterogeneous and diversified training with a lot of company-specific content, will not typically look to an e-learning solution. Since the market does not have any company-specific learning content ready and available, the company would have to produce it themselves. Furthermore, this type of production is only viable in the long run if enough learners can develop skills from it.

▶ **The imparting of technical and methodical competence is the main focus**
It is certainly easier to impart established methods and technical knowledge via e-learning than it is to teach, for example, the area of so-called *soft skills*.
E-learning is suitable for training in soft skills if it is used to bring the participants in a soft skills seminar up to speed—hopefully having attained a standard level of knowledge. Despite this possibility, the focus should be on imparting technical knowledge and methodical skills.

▶ **The learning content, learning objectives, and learning tasks to be defined must be clear**
Whether learning content will be brought in or produced in-house requires a precise idea of which courses will be needed and, above all, used, in the company.

▶ **It is possible to translate the learning content into modules**
To allow learners to take charge of their own learning, the content should be broken down into modules, thereby enabling learners to focus on certain parts of the training and omit other parts. Furthermore, modularization considers the fact that learners may have different levels of previous knowledge. In addition, the individual modules can be used as both a learning *and* an information system.

Assessing the Practical Use of E-Learning

How can an enterprise determine the relevant key figures that will argue for or against the use of e-learning and can support its decision? First, the company should identify their own processes in the area of personnel development and analyze them. The process example shown in Figure 17.2 (booking an attendance course) shows that you can derive important key figures—to determine the advisability of using e-learning—from the As-Is processes. As a prerequisite for this, you should create a key figure system that provides information as to which figures will be consulted for decision-making. In Figure 17.2, you can see an excerpt of this process.

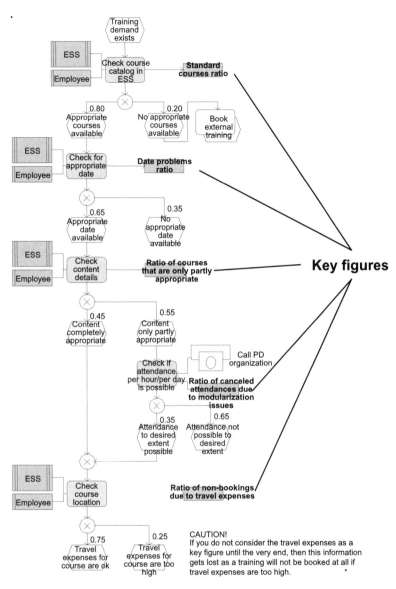

Figure 17.2 Determining Key Figures Using an As-Is Process

17.1.3 Advantages of E-Learning

The use of e-learning is advantageous to both the enterprise and the individual employees:

Advantages for the Enterprise	Advantages for Employees
▶ Cost-saving	▶ Allows for self-directed, personalized learning
▶ Time-saving: lower periods of absence from work, no travel time	▶ Flexibility of time and location
▶ Up-to-date content: adjustments can be made centrally and quickly	▶ Continuous, personal development of skills
▶ Speed: many participants can access content simultaneously	▶ Possibility of training in areas that were otherwise reserved for certain hierarchical levels
▶ Minimizes the redundant preparation of training content	▶ No previous knowledge necessary Training offered on an as-needed basis
▶ Immediate training of employees if necessary	▶ Allowance made for different learning curves
▶ Employee satisfaction, resulting in lower labor turnover	▶ Individual support possible
▶ Use as a marketing instrument: communication of processes and product information also for third parties (such as customers)	▶ Greater transparency of learning possibilities
▶ Training courses can be sold externally	▶ No redundancy due to the correspondence between the individual learning path and the existing level of knowledge
▶ Simplifies central personnel development: due to the worldwide comparability of training and the uniform quality standards of courses	▶ Reduction of extraneous knowledge
▶ Relieves personnel development of administrative tasks	▶ More opportunities for learners to practice and do exercises
▶ Improves knowledge management	▶ Exchange of know-how using new communication options
▶ Reduces the number of attendance courses	

The Cost-Saving Advantage

Let us look at the cost-saving advantage in greater detail. Despite the relatively high initial investment, the cost savings achieved in the long-term can be enormous if producing in-house e-learning content. In particular, the proportion of travel costs is generally high, as "training tourism" often accounts for a large piece of training budgets. The greater the international bias of the company, the greater the quota of flights and hotel expenses. Apart from travel costs, the enterprise saves, among other things, on employee lost time. These costs can be considerable and are often overlooked. For large enterprises in particular, the reduction of costs per participant can be alluring.

17.1.4 The Strategic Importance of E-Learning

Our intent in this book is not to provide an overview of the e-learning market; however, we do hope that the advantages and possibilities of e-learning discussed will assist some companies in their decision-making process. Until now, those who requested fully developed solutions tended to be the larger enterprises with several thousand employees and the corresponding room to negotiate. However, now, an ever-increasing number of branches or subsidiaries of large- and medium-sized enterprises are looking for e-learning.

Just like many developing markets, the e-learning market for business training and advanced training remains, to a large extent, unknown. Among vendors, there is uncertainty as to where development will lead over the next few years, what investments would be wise, and what sectors will be most attractive in the future. Enterprises who want to introduce e-learning see a multitude of suppliers and wonder what aspects they should pay particular attention to when planning and implementing their projects.

17.2 Learning Management Systems

Apart from pure content providers, more and more companies are offering what are known as *Full service services*. In addition to content, these companies also provide, for example, a platform known as a *Learning Management System*. The Learning Management System (LMS) presents the content and also fulfills the following functions:

▶ Tracks learning objectives, course progress, and costs

▶ Provides support in the selection of the best content, for example, by preparing additional information, demo versions, grading tests, course ratings, top-10 lists (lists of the most frequently booked courses)

▶ Aligns the system with the specific roles of employees by preparing content that is precisely adjusted for the role or roles of an employee in the company

▶ Offers the possibility of booking attendance training courses via the portal

▶ Supports international standards for the simple implementation of purchased content (for example, the Shareable Content Object Reference Model (SCORM)

▶ Supports authorization procedures, for example, workflow connection to automatic support for booking procedures

▶ Helps learners prepare for tests and certificates; usually both entry-level tests and tests within the learning software in question

▶ Enables people to connect to an Enterprise Portal (EP): most learning management systems offered to date can be linked up to the existing company portal based on their technical structure

▶ Provides interfaces to (Human Resource Management Systems) HRMS: the transfer of learning data, such as qualifications obtained and training history, to employee master data

- ► Provides tools for structuring courses for the rapid preparation of online content

- ► Provides the option of creating curricula, for example, the development of learning and training plans, safety training, risk management

- ► Offers evaluation possibilities for tutors, for example, storage period within a learning unit, learning progress, and so on

- ► Offers evaluation possibilities for learners, such as a personal training record, to-do lists, an overview of obligatory courses (mandatory qualifications), profile matchups, deficits, overview of personal qualifications, and the development of all the above

- ► Offers interaction and communication possibilities: expert chats, video conferencing, virtual classroom, and so on

- ► Offers the possibility to choose from different learning strategies: provides an overview of a subject; example-oriented learning, objective-oriented learning, and so on

17.3   The SAP Learning Solution

SAP has developed an LMS aligned with the criteria mentioned above: the *Learning Solution*.

17.3.1   The SAP Research Project in the Area of Learning

The SAP Learning Solution is a product that emerged as a result of SAP's position as consortium manager for the project L^3 *Lifelong Learning*, which was initiated by the German Federal Ministry of Education and Research (BMBF). This project was one of five mission projects on e-learning conducted in Germany and was carried out by a consortium of 20 companies, which included content providers, centers of learning, and technology partners. The objective of this project was to set up an organizational and technical infrastructure that would provide all citizens with the option of constantly adding to their professional training. It was, therefore, necessary to bring together all those people directly and indirectly involved in the training process (for example, teachers, students, and course designers) and the various techniques (for example, didactic methods, new media, media archives, communication networks) in an integrated service concept for education and training. Consequently, L^3 is composed of a cooperation of tried and tested learning methods—such as conventional group teaching in the classroom—and new learning techniques that arose from the possibilities of modern information and communication technologies (virtual learning groups, remote tutoring, TeleLearning, individually adjusted course configuration, and so on).

17.3.2 Features of the Service

The results of the L^3 project have been incorporated into the *SAP Learning Solution*. You should note that the Learning Solution is available for R/3 Release 4.6C in the form of a plug-in (2001.2) and in R/3 Release *Enterprise* as an add-on. For the Learning Solution, SAP uses the approach of an integrated LMS, that is, all functions are offered in an aggregate solution (see Figure 17.3). The Learning Solution supports the very different roles in the context of
e-learning. In doing so, the individual roles are currently available in the functions presented below.

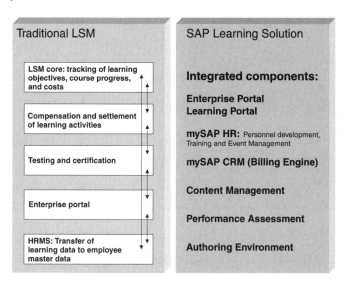

Figure 17.3 Traditional LMS Versus the SAP Learning Solution

Learner

With an individual, personalized learning environment and integration into mySAP HR (jobs, development plans), learners can call up e-learning content. They get an overview of courses that they have already taken (see Figure 17.4), an overview of mandatory courses, and a list of their qualifications and/or shortcomings (see Figure 17.5).

Learning employees can compare the requirement profile for a role and their personal qualifications profile. Any gaps revealed can be addressed by their taking the appropriate course required (see Figure 17.6).

Authors

In the *Authoring Environment,* you'll discover tools for structuring the course for the expedient preparation of online content (SCORM). The content is arranged in a logical sequence and each section is related to the others. In this way, for example, you can collocate courses that build on each other. What are known as *learning objects* are arranged within a course in a specific sequence. Courses are also divided into individual blocks.

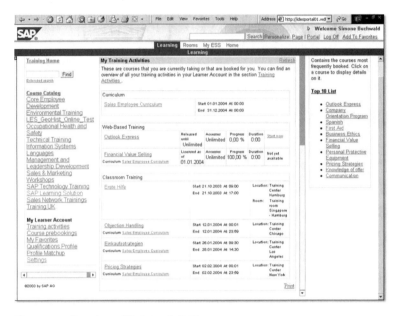

Figure 17.4 Overview of Training Activities

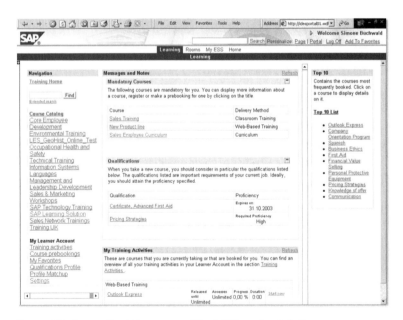

Figure 17.5 Personalized Homepage of the SAP Learning Solution

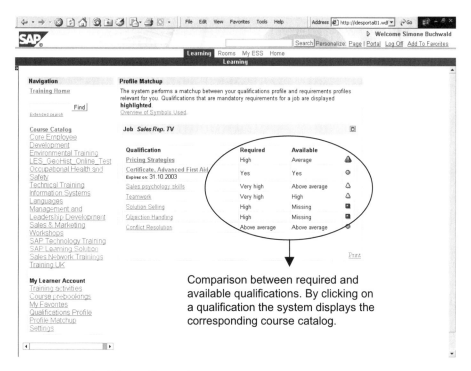

Navigation

Training Home

Find

Extended search

Course Catalog
Core Employee
Development
Environmental Training
LES_GeoHist_Online_Test
Occupational Health and
Safety
Technical Training
Information Systems
Languages
Management and
Leadership Development
Sales & Marketing
Workshops
SAP Technology Training
SAP Learning Solution
Sales N-lwork Trainings
Training UK

My Learner Account
Training activities
Course pre-bookings
My Favorites
Qualifications Profile
Profile Matchup
Settings

Profile Matchup

The system performs a matchup between your qualifications profile and requirements profiles relevant for you. Qualifications that are mandatory requirements for a job are displayed **highlighted**.
Overview of Symbols Used.

Job *Sales Rep. TV*

Qualification	Required	Available	
Pricing Strategies	High	Average	⚠
Certificate, Advanced First Aid Expires on: 31.10.2003	Yes	Yes	◉
Sales psychology skills	Very high	Above average	△
Teamwork	Very high	High	△
Solution Selling	High	Missing	■
Objection Handling	High	Missing	■
Conflict Resolution	Above average	Above average	◉

Print

Comparison between required and available qualifications. By clicking on a qualification the system displays the corresponding course catalog.

Figure 17.6 Result of the Profile Matchup

This is illustrated with an online training course on Outlook Express in Figure 17.7. Note that on the uppermost level, there is the main block of online training courses: the *learning object references*. Behind each reference object, there are one or more learning objects, which are linked to each other via different relation types. In the example, the learning object "Write e-mails" is linked to the learning object "add attachments" with a "precedes" relationship. You can access this dialog window via the menu path **Learning Object reference · Learning Object · Instructional Element.**

Under the learning object, you will find the actual content—the *instructional elements.* These elements consist of the content in different forms, such as HTML files or files in the SCORM format (see Figure 17.8). The instructional elements can be subdivided into different knowledge transfer types: these types include, for example, "explanations," "examples," "exercise," "overview," "scenario," "summary," "facts," "history," or "orientation" (see Figure 17.8). On the basis of this classification, depending on the learning strategy selected by the learner (for example, example-oriented or overview-oriented), the system can prepare the appropriate course elements.

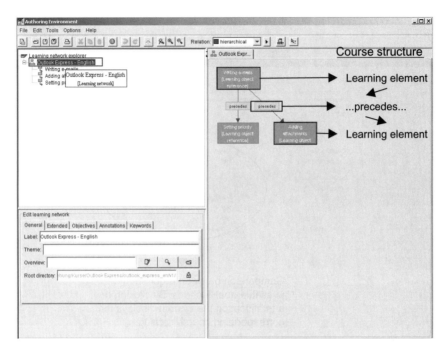

Figure 17.7 Online Training Course Structure in Outlook Express

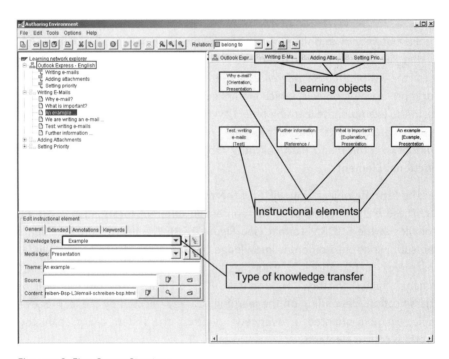

Figure 17.8 Fine Course Structure

The authoring environment is not only for structuring learning content; however, it is also for creating content or for integrating existing online training. By looking at an example, we can see how easy it is to integrate company-specific learning content into this type of structure. First, we shall create a new learning object without a template (see Figure 17.9). Next, we shall create an initial instructional element that will later be linked with the actual content (see Figure 17.10).

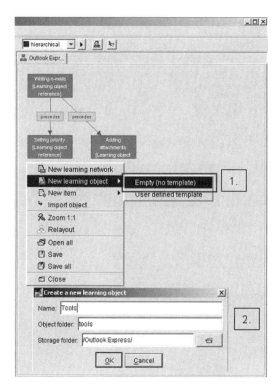

Figure 17.9 Creating a New Learning Object

The type of knowledge transfer must be defined for the new instructional element. This is necessary for the automatic allocation of the instructional element to a selected learning strategy. In the example shown, "Overview" is set as the knowledge type.

To insert the content belonging to the instructional element, you can use existing source files or create a new file directly from the authoring environment. In the example shown, a PowerPoint file is created and then saved in HTML format. The source file, therefore, exists in *.ppt format and the content, that is to be linked, is an *.htm file (see Figure 17.11).

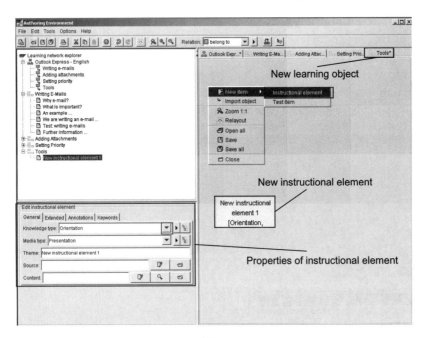

Figure 17.10 Creating a New Instructional Element

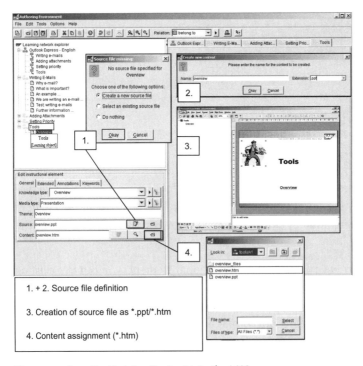

1. + 2. Source file definition

3. Creation of source file as *.ppt/*.htm

4. Content assignment (*.htm)

Figure 17.11 Inserting Training Content into the LMS

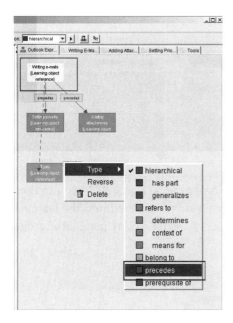

Figure 17.12 Relationship Types

Before the changes made are available in an online course, the learning objects and instructional elements added must be linked into the existing course structure. This is done using the relationship methods offered. In our example, the learning object "tools" is integrated into the existing Outlook Express tutorial. To link the learning object, you must select the relationship type. In this example, a "precedes" relationship has been created (see Figure 17.12). Here are some examples of other possible relationship types:

▶ "...has part..."
▶ "...generalizes..."
▶ "...refers to..."
▶ "...determines..."
▶ "...belong to..."
▶ "...prerequisite of..."

The changes made can be tested directly from the authoring environment. Before the test run, however, you must devise the learning strategy. Here, you can also set whether the learners can select their own learning path at the start of the course. In the example, the micro strategy "orientation first" has been selected, which means that the instructional elements assigned to the "orientation first" strategy will be shown first.

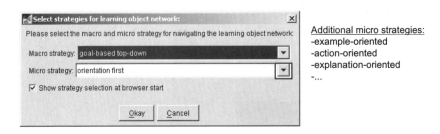

Figure 17.13 Setting the Learning Strategy

To allow you to follow the result of the settings made, in Figure 17.14 you can see how the newly created "Tools" learning object is incorporated into the learning path. The instructional element, the previously created HTML page, is also displayed.

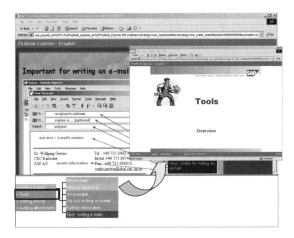

Figure 17.14 The Inserted Learning Object

Training Administrators

The Learning Solution also includes tools for the training administrators, offering them support and help with the execution of their daily work.

▶ **Simple Catalog Administration**
All functions of Training and Event Management (see Chapter 11, *Training and Event Management*) are used for the Learning Solution. Consequently, experienced users of Training and Event Management will not require any additional training.

▶ **Web Reporting**
Training administrators can *report* on the learning account of participants and implement appropriate measures in the event of any discrepancy.

Managers

Managers can be integrated into the training process via the following possibilities:

▶ **SAP Workflow Integration**
For instance, in the authorization procedure for booking, rebooking, and canceling

▶ **Preparation of reports**
This includes, for example, the attainment of learning targets and qualifications

Administrators

The screen areas of the Learning Solution can be adjusted to meet the requirements of the enterprise. Therefore, for example, the top-10 list of most frequently booked courses—as shown in Figure 17.5 on the right-hand side of the screen—can be replaced by other information. The partitioning of screen elements and the company-specific corporate design can also be set to suit each customer's preference.

17.3.3 Integration of the Learning Solution into mySAP HR

The Learning Solution is based on the classic Training and Event Management in mySAP HR and uses the technologies available there. The business event catalog—presented inside the Learning Solution—is also created in this form in mySAP HR. The necessary new objects and customizing settings are delivered with the new R/3 Release *Enterprise*. The creation of this type of online business event is carried out similarly to a "traditional" event. The Training and Event Management structures presented in Chapter 11, with business event groups, business event types, and business events, are also used here. In addition, there is a new object for e-learning "events," that is, events without location and time specification.

You can access the master data catalog of Training and Event Management via the IMG path **Training and Event Management · Business Event Preparation · Maintain Master Data via Catalog**. You must create the business event group here. If you want to allow for a business event group to be selected as a subject area, you must indicate that here as well. First, define that the business event group is also available in the Learning Solution. Next, create a new business event type and assign a training method (see Figure 17.15). If it is an online course, you can link the business event type with the training method WBT (web-based training).

The *course type content* is then assigned to the *business event type* (see Figure 17.16) to determine which WBT lies behind the business event type.

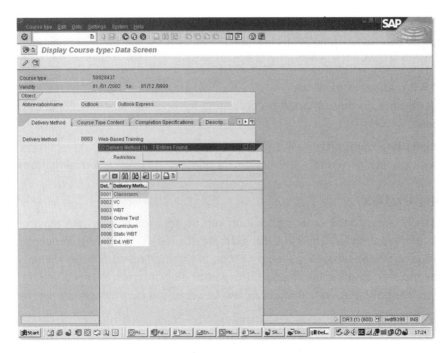

Figure 17.15 Assigning the Business Event Type to the Training Method

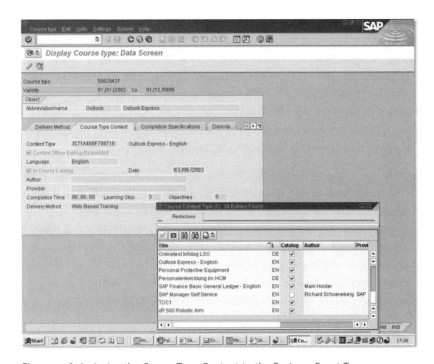

Figure 17.16 Assigning the Course Type Content to the Business Event Type

Another attribute for business event types is the **Completion time** (see Figure 17.17). Here, you can define the maximum time during which an online course can be run and the minimum time for which it must be run. This data is useful, partly, to help students choose a course, as it gives them an indication of the average duration of the course. On the other hand, this data can be used to analyze how many participants are above or below the optimal completion time for the course. The maximum availability of the online course per participant determines how much time the employees have to complete the course. You can then establish a date in which to end the general availability of the course. The course will then automatically be removed from the online offering; this can prove useful if, for example, certain courses need to be periodically updated.

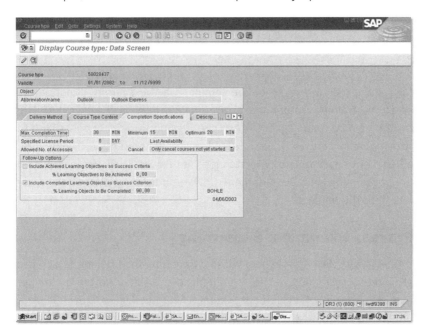

Figure 17.17 Setting the Completion Time of the Online Course

By assigning the business event type to individual roles within the enterprise and defining the *required business events*, a role is defined for the "Mandatory Courses" shown in Figure 17.5. This assignment is done using the relationship type "is planned for" (A 033). In this way, the objects "business event type" and "job" or "person" are linked to each other. The business event type is now effectively defined as a mandatory business event for the position/job holder (see Figure 17.18).

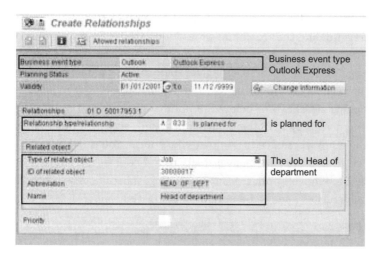

Figure 17.18 Linking the Business Event Type to a Job

The booking and execution of an online seminar via the Learning Solution are transferred to the training history and to the qualification profile in mySAP HR; from there, they can be called again via the Learning Solution. This applies both to online and attendance courses. There is no redundant data retention. The requirement profiles mentioned for profile matchups (see Figure 17.6) also come from the Personnel Planning and Development (PD) module in mySAP HR and are stored there with the *positions*.

17.4 Process Examples: E-Learning

The first process example we show here will illustrate how the booking of a course (in our case, an online training course) is influenced and/or supported by the use of e-learning or a Learning Management System (LMS) (see Figure 17.3 and Figure 17.20). The booking process then leads into the execution of the booked online training course. The execution process is presented in Figure 17.21 and it shows, once again, how and where an LMS can support the learners and the other people involved in the personnel development process. The idea of integration into the existing HRMS is also considered in this process, to the extent that the qualifications gained and the training history are transferred to the HR system.

17.4.1 Process Example: Booking an Online Seminar

If we look at the example process for booking an online course in Figures 17.19 and 17.20, we can see that a procedure can change as a result of introducing e-learning into the company. Many tasks are transferred from the personnel development department to the employee. The personnel developers act more like mentors, tutors, and internal service providers, and are relieved of many administrative tasks. With technical support in the form of tests to check required previous knowledge, for example, the employee can put together the necessary courses. Thanks to workflow integration, the person in charge of making the necessary decisions is informed of booking, rebooking, and cancellations and can process the corresponding request online.

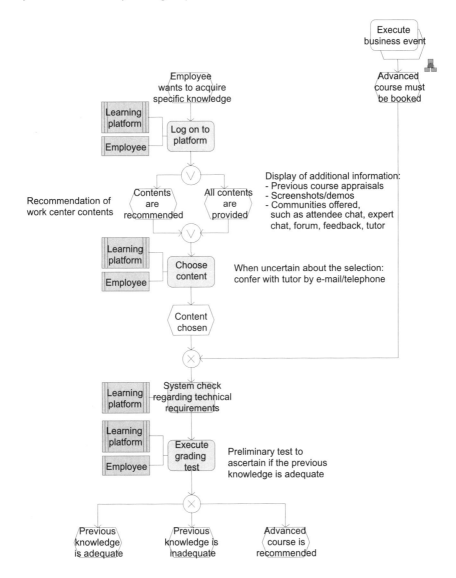

Figure 17.19 Booking an Online Course 1

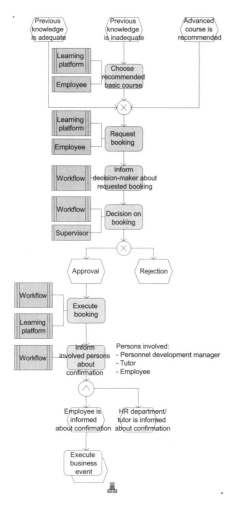

Figure 17.20 Booking an Online Course 2

17.4.2 Process Example: Completing an Online Seminar

From the process shown in Figure 17.21, we can see how an online course is completed and how technical support (such as recommendations or options for a learning path) can help to improve the process. Furthermore, learning checks are included by verifying if learning targets have been achieved. Development courses can be offered immediately after a course has been successfully completed. The automatic transfer of qualifications—that are arranged through an event—can be added to the employee's master data in mySAP HR Training and Event Management via a standard function (see also Chapter 11, *Training and Event Management).*

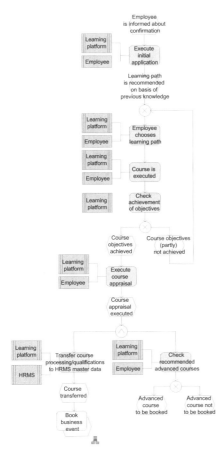

Figure 17.21 Completion of an Online Course

In addition to the process changes mentioned, there are other examples of how a process can change because of e-learning, or how new processes can be added:

▶ **Content sourcing process**
With an integrated media and method mix, the phases "content production," "content maintenance," "securing compliance with conventions," and "production monitoring" are added.

▶ **Service processes**
The service functions of the personnel development department and other departments include, among other things, the preparation of newsletters, management news, literature services, and knowledge data services.

▶ **Tutoring processes**
Changes in this area particularly affect the supervision of virtual seminar rooms, technical support, and the initiation and moderation of communication between participants.

17.5 Project Development

Despite perfect technology, high-performance servers and networks, reliable software, and intranet integration, many enterprises are not really "ready to learn." In order for e-learning to be used successfully, you need more than just technical implementation. Even with perfect technology, people still can loose sight of the importance of being open and accepting of the new methods and process flows; otherwise, the processes and technology cannot be properly coordinated.

To operate e-learning successfully, the enterprise must integrate the new methods and technologies into the existing systems and processes. Only then can the possibilities of e-learning be leveraged to optimize the personnel development process to its full extent.

You can see the complexity of implementing e-learning, and therefore the need for process definitions, in Figure 17.22, which shows all areas that must be considered when implementing e-learning. The underlying meaning of each of these points are processes that may be structured in various different ways and this depends on each individual enterprise.

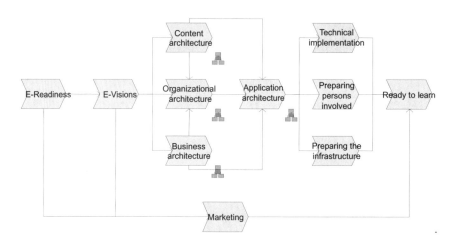

Figure 17.22 Procedure for Implementing the LMS

▶ **E-Readiness**
You must determine if e-learning is suitable for the company. You do this by evaluating the individual utility-potential and by examining the enterprise-specific personnel development processes.

▶ **E-Visions**
The enterprise must develop a vision that is supported from the top-level down in the company.

► **Content Architecture**

Questions that pertain to content types must be resolved regarding professional, media, and didactic criteria or designs, that is, the relevant information that influences how a course should be taught or structured. The content structure (for example, content catalogs, curricula) should also be determined as early as possible during the implementation, as should the selection of one or more content providers.

► **Organizational Architecture**

This architecture maps, for example, the access and utilization of the e-learning or learning platform. This includes resolving questions such as: Who has access to the system? What pull/push content is there? What roles/tasks are there? How is e-learning integrated into the work process?

► **Business Architecture**

This is where questions pertaining to the structure of the operator model, from a technical and professional point of view, and the rollout strategy must be addressed.

► **Application Architecture**

The results of the content, organizational, and business architecture lead into the application architecture, which then brings together the prepared professional concepts, IT concepts, integration concepts, and change management concepts for the consideration of technical and organizational changes.

► **Technical Realization**

Implementing the concepts

► **Preparing Participants**

Because all participants will be given new tasks, for example, content sourcing processes, service processes, or tutoring processes, providing these employees with some sort of basic training is mandatory.

► **Preparing the Infrastructure**

You must keep in mind the future use of e-learning when preparing the technical and organizational infrastructure of the learning management system. There is nothing more discouraging for a student than an online course that does not work (see also Section 17.6).

► **Marketing**

Even the best LMS will be of no use if the users stay away. Consequently, interest should be aroused as early as possible and if it can be arranged, a pilot group should be involved right from the start. The e-vision developed must be made public and the marketing of certain incentive systems, such as premium points, can be most useful at the conception of the LMS.

17.6 Critical Success Factors

When you implement e-learning or complete an LMS, apart from technical aspects, what determines the real success of the implementation and usability of the Learning Management System are the organizational and process-oriented factors (see Figure 17.23).

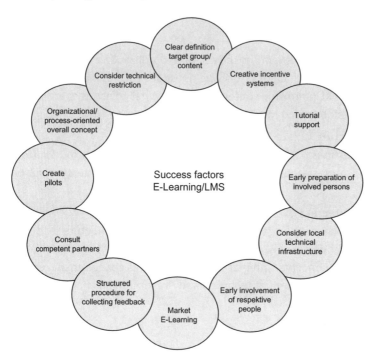

Figure 17.23 Factors of Success for E-Learning/LMS

▶ The first success factor is the involvement of the process organization right at the beginning of the project. Because this type of project affects many different areas of the enterprise (Personnel Development department, superiors, mentors, tutors, employees, IT, and so on), it is imperative that you consider the effects of the implementation on processes. If certain technical and organizational structures are constructed without attention to process and process integration, this can lead to a disproportionate amount of work towards the end of the project. Therefore, efforts should be made to integrate the project into the overall organizational or process-oriented concept right from its inception. By including all relevant processes, the relevant implementation target groups are automatically involved at the very beginning of the project.

▶ It is generally advisable to first pursue a pilot group by singling out a certain target group for e-learning and including them in the process from an early stage.

There is no better marketing tool than a successful pilot project, which will quickly arouse the curiosity of other target groups. By creating a specific incentive system, you can boost the willingness of target groups to use e-learning. There are examples of how target groups can make the initial contact with the learning platform through games (online games). In addition, the enterprise can introduce a bonus system to encourage the use of e-learning. Employees can receive points for successfully completing an online course, and upon achieving a certain number of points, they can exchange these points for a bonus. To use the experiences of the pilot group with e-learning, you will need a structured procedure for collecting and evaluating their feedback.

▶ Marketing within an enterprise is a task that should be carried out at practically every phase of the project. It not only arouses the employees' interest, but also fosters their willingness to use the learning platform.

▶ In addition to considering the overall organizational/process-oriented concept, the technical side of things must also be considered. For example, the necessary technical equipment must also be available at the work centers where the learning is to take place. Nothing does more to discourage employees and reduce their motivation than an inoperative LMS. In general, employee motivation is high with regard to e-learning, but it wanes with time and is particularly vulnerable to technical failure. As a result, it is necessary to impart information on the local technical infrastructure as early as possible. In an international corporate group, this can involve a lot of work. The aspect of a local technical infrastructure produces technical restrictions when creating content and should therefore be considered from the beginning.

▶ Didactically speaking, tutorial support for learners is mandatory because many employees will have to get acclimated to this new form of learning and will also need to have a competent contact person (i.e., a mentor) in the company. Tutors should be adequately prepared for their new tasks well in advance.

18 The SAP Business Information Warehouse

The SAP Business Information Warehouse is a standalone system that has been developed and optimized to help you to efficiently gather and analyze key figures. SAP provides the business themes in the form of Business Content.

The objective of this chapter is to provide you with a brief overview of the structure of Business Information Warehouse (BW) and how it is integrated and used in connection with mySAP HR. For additional information, see the book *SAP BW Professional* from SAP PRESS[1].

SAP BW is SAP's data warehouse solution. It forms part of the mySAP solution *Business Intelligence* (mySAP BI) and also functions as a data supplier for *SAP Strategic Enterprise Management* (SEM). The BW is an independent SAP system with its own database and a specific, role-based authorization concept. This means that there is less load on the operative SAP systems because evaluations and analyses run in a system especially optimized for this purpose.

The purpose of BW is to provide key-figure related reporting with extensive analysis possibilities. In general, there is only a small amount of employee-related data in BW reports. Employee-related reporting still falls within the scope of mySAP HR. The BW aggregates this data to key figures, and through its special design, allows views of these key figures (facts) according to different criteria (dimensions).

18.1 Architecture

The BW is, roughly speaking, divided into three levels (see Figure 18.1), which will be explained in greater detail below.

---

1 Norbert Egger, SAP BW 3.1 Professional, SAP PRESS 2003.

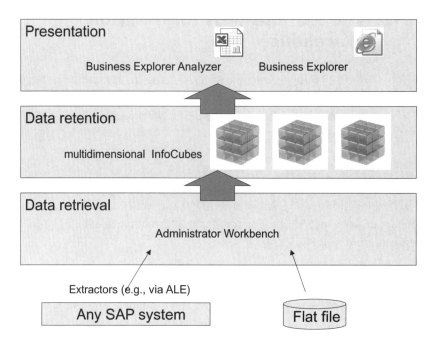

Presentation

Business Explorer Analyzer   Business Explorer

Data retention

multidimensional InfoCubes

Data retrieval

Administrator Workbench

Extractors (e.g., via ALE)

Any SAP system   Flat file

Figure 18.1 Architecture of BW

Reporting/Presentation

This is the top level, which is generally seen by users. Tools are provided for executing and defining reports or queries in the form of the *Business Explorer* and the *Business Explorer Analyzer*. Both use *Excel* for their front-end display. Queries can also be called in the intranet using the *Business Explorer Browser*, whereby the intranet is used as a possible interface for the BW user and can also be integrated into the Workplace or portals.

Data Retention

What are known as *InfoCubes* are used for data retention. The reports or queries are defined on the InfoCubes using the *Business Explorer Analyzer* The data is stored in an extended star schema to ensure high-performance analysis. The BW has many tools for monitoring the database, because the latter determines the performance of the BW.

Preparing the Data

Because the BW has its own database, the data to be evaluated must be transferred to this database. In contrast to familiar legacy data transfer in other areas, here, it is not done with a single data transfer at the start of production operation:

the BW database must be constantly updated with the latest data. For this reason, a special *Administrator Workbench* has been provided for data transfer, the purpose of which is to optimally support and automate this constant process. By means of customizing, the administrator workbench makes it possible to define transfer rules and implementation rules. Here also, new key figures can be calculated from the data provided and then stored in the BW. There are practically no limits on complexity, because if necessary, the ABAP programming language is also still available.

The time base, however, is problematic with relation to mySAP HR. Due to its design with its own database, snapshots (frozen data) are continuously sent to the BW. In mySAP HR, however, many data changes occur in the background. If BW evaluations require that these changes be considered, then the entire mySAP HR dataset must be regularly (perhaps even daily) loaded into the BW. In some circumstances, however, the concept of frozen data is welcome. In this way, you can ensure that, for example, evaluations for the same selection conditions will always produce or yield the same results.

18.2   Business Content

With Business Content, SAP provides BW users with a predefined *database metaschema* (InfoCubes) together with numerous evaluations (Queries) and the associated roles for a business theme, which ensures that the technical infrastructure provided by BW can immediately be used for the application in question. Also included in the Business Content are the necessary *extractors* for filling the BW database. The extractors can, for example, transfer data directly to BW using ALE, without the need for you to start it manually. The extractors can also be adjusted, if necessary, to transfer customer-specific data (such as data from customer-defined infotypes) to the BW.

The Business Content should be regarded as a reference that can be used optionally. It is therefore also possible to adjust the evaluations given or even to add your own data to InfoCubes. However, the BW's full effectiveness is only realized if data from various different applications is stored in it. This data can then be considered for generating new key figures (for example, number of services per number of customers" or "Turnover per sales employee"). Given the architecture of the BW, it is then irrelevant from which system the data comes and in what format it is saved.

18.3 User Types in BW

We can differentiate between the following three user types in SAP BW (see Figure 18.2):

▶ **Consumers**

The consumers call the ready-defined evaluations and can view the enterprise-wide integrated calculated key figures. Users are senior management who can call periodic reports, which they need for running their department, locally via the intranet.

▶ **Analysts**

Analysts examine certain contexts. For their evaluations, they need to be able to separate and analyze facts according to different criteria (dimensions). For this, they use the Excel front-end of Business Explorer.

▶ **Authors**

The authors are responsible for preparing the reports. They use the Business Explorer Analyzer to create new reports and make them available.

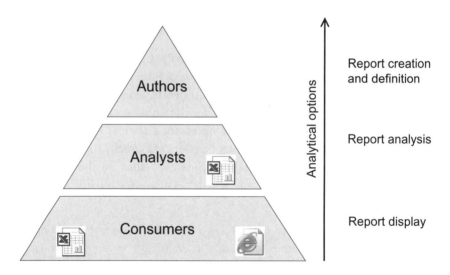

Figure 18.2 The Different User Types in BW

19 SAP Strategic Enterprise Management

The Strategic Enterprise Management component supports the control and management of the enterprise. It provides an entire range of instruments that link strategic and operative enterprise management. This component comprises several system modules and is integrated into the SAP Business Information Warehouse (BW).

19.1 Business Foundations and Problem Areas

19.1.1 Business Foundations

The goal of Strategic Enterprise Management (SEM) is the long-term development of the enterprise: an overall strategy is developed for the enterprise, based on a management vision. This strategy determines the manner and direction of planned enterprise development. Typically, it is made up of several sub-strategies, which are listed below. Various analysis methods are available for developing these strategies.

▶ **Enterprise strategy**
Determining the product-market concept

▶ **Business area strategy**
Market behavior of the business unit

▶ **Competition strategy**
Market behavior compared with the competition, which is aimed at achieving competitive advantages

▶ **Functional strategy**
Realization of the aforementioned strategies on the level of business application areas

In recent times, additional business instruments have been developed (such as *Value-based management, Target costing,* and so on) to support strategic enterprise management. These new instruments require a considerably more intensive data exchange with the operative EDP systems, which many software products cannot offer.

19.1.2 Problem Areas

Until a few years ago, the development of an overall strategy that was consistent and could guarantee success was the greatest challenge to the area of strategic enterprise management. However, development shows that although an overall strategy is indeed important, the real problems can be found in the lack of a common strategy. This can be traced back to the inadequate or nonexistent relationship between strategic and operative enterprise management. Therefore, it can be deduced that although many employees in middle management are aware of the strategy of their enterprise, they often do not understand it. What is needed is a clear and unambiguous implementation of the strategy.

Business EDP systems can be split between operative systems (for example, SAP R/3) and systems for enterprise management. In many cases, these systems are completely separate from each other and do not allow for an exchange of data. Data from the operative systems is therefore carefully extracted and then integrated into the management systems. The current requirements on a strategic level, however, require the best possible integration of operative and enterprise management systems to prepare management information quickly and consistently.

The organization structures of today, characterized by their complexity and dynamic, also require integrated application systems, as a result of the increasing decentralization of decision-making authority in enterprises.

19.2 SEM System Modules

SAP SEM is divided into the following five system modules, which we will address in the following sections:

▶ Business Planning and Simulation (SEM-BPS)
▶ Business Consolidation (SEM-BCS)
▶ Strategy Management (SEM-SM)
▶ Performance Measurement (SEM-PM)
▶ Stakeholder Relationship Management (SEM-SRM)

19.2.1 Business Planning and Simulation (SEM-BPS)

Business Planning and Simulation (BPS) offers closed and consistent enterprise planning, in which planning can be done on both strategic and operative levels. This is made possible by the following options:

▶ Modeling the planning structures on a freely defined data basis
▶ Flexible adjustment of degrees of detail to meet enterprise requirements, without having to factor restrictions of the operative system
▶ The use of similar planning functions in all business areas

Update Actual Data Current Year

| Quantity Planning | Rolling Sales Revenue Planning | Plan Prices Current Year | Planning Following Year | Plan P |

| Copy: Actual -> Plan | Copy: Forecast -> Plan | Copy: Target -> Plan | Calculate Contribution Margin |

Datei Bearbeiten Ansicht Einfügen Format Extras Daten Fenster ?

Sales Planning

| Sales Organisation | USA East | | Product Category | Hardware |
| Sales Office | Mid-Atlantic | | Product Group | Devices |

	Actual 2000	YTD/YTG 2001	Forecast 2002	Target 2002	Plan 2002
Sales quantity	7.914 ST	4.191 ST	7.241 ST	8.750 ST	8.500 ST
Average Price	4.000 USD	4.000 USD	3.997 USD	4.000 USD	4.000 USD
					34.000.000 USD
Discount 1	184.660 USD	97.790 USD	168.912 USD	184.660 USD	184.660 USD
Discount 2	21.104 USD	11.176 USD	19.322 USD	21.104 USD	21.104 USD
Discount 3	11.080 USD	5.867 USD	10.144 USD	11.080 USD	11.080 USD
					33.783.156 USD
Cost of Sales	3.033.700 USD	0 USD	2.528.083 USD	3.033.700 USD	3.033.700 USD
					30.749.456 USD
Direct Cost of Sales	3.033.700 USD	0 USD	2.528.083 USD	3.033.700 USD	3.033.700 USD
					27.715.756 USD
Indirect Sales Costs	1.055.200 USD	0 USD	879.333 USD	1.055.200 USD	1.055.200 USD
Campaign Costs	2.638.000 USD	0 USD	2.198.333 USD	2.638.000 USD	2.638.000 USD
Other Marketing Costs	527.600 USD	0 USD	439.667 USD	527.600 USD	527.600 USD
Service Costs	105.520 USD	0 USD	87.933 USD	105.520 USD	105.520 USD

◄ ► ►| \ SEM-BPS 1 ⟨ Chart ⟨ ◄

Figure 19.1 Sales Planning

Figure 19.1 shows sales planning at the *Sales Manager* level. Planning processes can be controlled according to a workflow management system type, because all planning structures, data, and functions are integrated into one system and the consistency of the data throughout the company is thus ensured. In addition, there is the possibility of using SEM BPS to simulate pending business decisions.

19.2.2 Business Consolidation (SEM-BCS)

The content of *Business Consolidation (BCS)* is, on the one hand, the preparation of external group accounting in accordance with legal guidelines, such as IAS or US GAAP. On the other hand, there can also be consolidation in accordance with internal enterprise requirements (for example, the business units), which serves as information for company management.

With regard to external group accounting, corrections from goods and services and mergers between enterprises to be integrated into the consolidated financial statements are of vital importance. These corrections can be automated to a large extent.

19.2.3 Strategy Management (SEM-SM)

The core of the *Strategy Management (SM)* module is formed by the *Balanced Scorecard* (BSC), which supports the implementation of strategies. There are also modules and business content for value-oriented enterprise management. Finally, SM also contains risk management tools.

The BSC is a management system characterized by the following factors:

▶ Consistent key figure-orientation

▶ Focus on measures and actions

▶ Well-adjusted weighting of the objectives of different business areas

▶ Linking of strategic and operative control

▶ Comprehensive and intensive communication at all levels of the hierarchy

Not only is the financial perspective of an enterprise taken into account. Customers, internal processes, and learning and growth are other perspectives that should be considered. Figure 19.2 shows a presentation of the different perspectives and criteria for defining objectives. For BSC development, the cause-effect chains—also called a *Strategy Map,* which depict relations between the individual targets—are equally important.

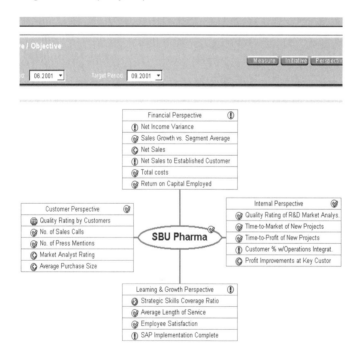

Figure 19.2 BSC Perspectives

Figure 19.3 shows a strategy map. It allows for the control of the enterprise, taking into account the interdependencies between the different perspectives.

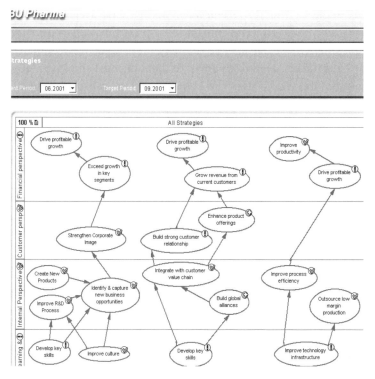

Figure 19.3 Strategy Map

19.2.4 Performance Measurement (SEM-PM)

The *Performance Measurement (PM)* module consists of the *Measure Builder*, which helps to define complex measurement categories—for evaluating enterprise performance—and develop comprehensive business key figure systems (for example, EVA, ROI).

The *Management Cockpit* is primarily used to present management information for the upper hierarchies of the enterprise and is therefore very easy to use and view.

19.2.5 Stakeholder Relationship Management (SEM-SRM)

The *Stakeholder Relationship Management (SRM)* module supports the efficient communication with the stakeholders in the company and works to maintain this relationship. It includes contact management, a stakeholder portal, functions for individual communication with entitlement groups, and options for analyzing and displaying data pertinent to the stakeholders.

19.3 Relevance to Personnel Management

SEM also, of course, influences the processes and activities in the area of HR. The influences of SEM apply to *Strategy Management (SM)* in particular, which is directly integrated into mySAP HR. This integration affects the *Management by Objectives* and *Compensation Management* components. The objectives defined in the context of BSC creation can be broken down to the individual employee level and the achievement of these objectives can be negotiated with each individual. Chapter 10, *Appraisals and Setting Objectives*, contains a more detailed description of the procedure. Once the business year is over, the level of target achievement and its effect can be developed in Compensation Management. For example, the level of target achievement can directly influence the amount of a bonus payment. Chapter 15, *Compensation Management,* includes additional notes on setting up this type of rule.

In addition, the function of risk management within SM also offers the option of defining personnel risks, such as risk of leaving, motivation, adjustment, or bottleneck risks and—where possible—of quantifying them. There is also the option of accessing HR Business Content in SAP BW from SEM and of using this data for the various modules in SEM. Thus, in the annual business planning process, you can use the data acquired to plan personnel costs and allocations locally with the Business Planning and Simulation (BPS) module and to consolidate these allocations for enterprise management.

Appendix

A   Cross-Process Customizing Tools

The most important customizing tools used in the various components of mySAP HR are briefly presented below. This presentation cannot hope to replace practical experience or training on the system. Since the IMG, in particular, has a considerable range of customer-defined functions, this would scarcely even be possible.

View maintenance

Most customizing settings are made in what is known as *View maintenance.* This offers a particular view of one or more tables which are then used to control system performance. You can access view maintenance using Transaction SM31 or with the menu path **System · Services · Table Maintenance · Extended Table Maintenance**.

In addition to directly maintaining the settings, the system also allows you to branch to IMG using the **Customizing** button (see Figure A.1). This is generally useful because it offers the possibility of using or adjusting the documentation of a project IMG.

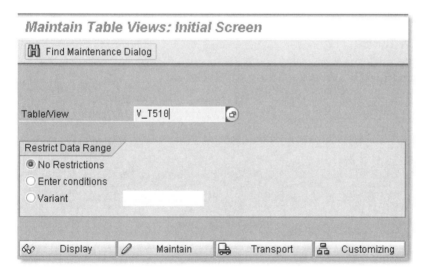

Figure A.1 Initial Screen of View Maintenance

In the actual maintenance (see Figure A.2) the following options, in particular, are available:

▶ Change existing entries (Note: the grayed key fields cannot be changed. In order to do this, you would have to copy the entry.)

▶ Copy existing entries

▶ Create new entries

▶ Delete existing entries

▶ Admit entries in a transport request

If you have to process very extensive tables, the following functions are particularly helpful:

▶ You can use the menu path **Selection · By Contents** to select specific table rows, for example, all those with an end date before December 31, 2003.

▶ You can use the menu path **Edit · Change Field Contents** to effect batch changes. You must have previously flagged all the entries to be changed prior to making these batch changes. Then you can change a certain field in all the marked entries in just one step. For example, you might use this option if you want to change working times. You could select all the work schedule rules with 38.5 hours per week and in one step change them all to 36 hours per week.

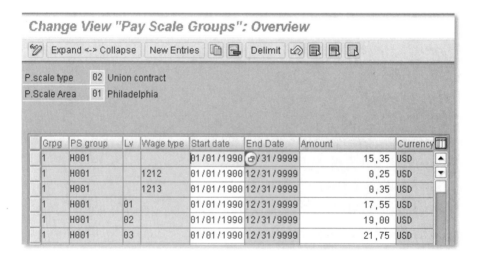

Figure A.2 Maintaining a Table View

The Implementation Guide (IMG)

The IMG (*Implementation Management Guide*) contains all customizing activities, organized according to component. In addition to the Reference IMG, which contains all activities, you can also create any number of project IMGs to support specific projects (for example, "Implementation of mySAP HR in France and Switzerland").

The use of the IMG in general, and the project IMGs in particular, offers the following advantages:

▶ It is easier to find the required activities because of clear structuring.

▶ You can use the documentation prepared by SAP for the individual steps.

▶ You can store enterprise-specific documentation for the individual steps.

▶ Project management is supported by status administration, time scheduling, and resource allocation.

Figure A.3 shows an example of a project IMG. In the left-hand side of the screen, you can see the component structure. The status, schedule, and resource allocation are maintained at the top right of the screen, and customer-specific documentation is stored below that in the form of notes.

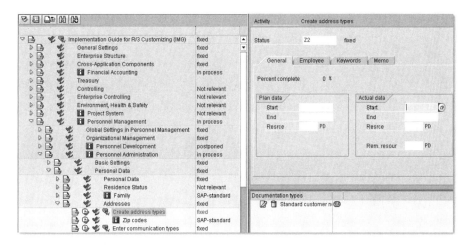

Figure A.3 Example Project IMG

B   Infotypes in Personnel Planning and Development

In the following table, you will find a list of all infotypes used in personnel planning and development, and also the object types for which they can be recorded. The abbreviations for the object types are then explained.

Infotypes

No.	Name	Object Types
1000	Object	*
1001	Relationships	*
1002	Description	*
1003	Department/Staff	O, S
1004	Character	T
1005	Planned Compensation	A, C, S
1006	Restrictions	A
1007	Vacancy	S
1008	Account Assignment Features	O, S
1009	Health Examinations	A
1010	Authorities/Resources	A, S
1011	Work Schedule	A, O, S
1013	Employee Group/Subgroup	A, BU, S
1014	Obsolete	A, S
1015	Cost Planning	A, C, O, S
1016	Standard Profiles	C, O, S, T, *
1017	PD Profiles	C, O, S, T, *
1018	Cost Distribution	A, O, S
1019	Quota Planning	O
1020	Demand (obsolete)	D
1021	Prices	D, E
1022	Schedule (obsolete)	D
1023	Availability Indicators	R

No.	Name	Object Types
1024	Capacity	D, E, G, R
1025	Depreciation Meter/Validity	Q
1026	Business Event Info	E
1027	Site-Dependent Info	F, O
1028	Address	A, G, O, S, *
1029	Business Event Type Info	D
1030	Procedure	D
1031	Room Reservation Info	E
1032	Mail Address	A, H, O, S, *
1033	Scale	QK
1034	Name Format	H
1035	Schedule	E
1036	Costs	D, E, G, R
1037	Billing/Allocation Info	D, O
1038	External Key	Q
1039	Shift Group	A, O
1041	Business Event Blocks	E
1042	Schedule Model	D
1043	Appraisal Model Info	BS
1044	Results Specification	BG, BK, BS, Q
1045	Valuation	BA
1046	Requirement Attributes	SR
1047	Processing Modules	BA, BS
1048	Proficiency Description	BK, BS, Q, QK, *
1049	Requirement Attributes	SR
1050	Job Evaluation Results	C, S
1051	Survey Results	C, S
1060	Business Event Demand	D
1061	Web Link	D, E, F
1062	Knowledge Link	D, E

No.	Name	Object Types
1063	Info Business Event Group	L
1201	WF Object Method	T
1205	WF Workflow Definition	WF
1206	WF Work Item Text	T, WF
1207	Customer Task, replaces TS	-
1208	SAP Organizational Objects	O, S, XO
1209	Cost Data	T, TS, WF, WS
1210	WF Container Definition	T, WF
1211	WF Container Texts	T, WF
1212	WF Event Binding	T, WF
1213	WF Role Binding	T, WF
1214	WF Other Binding	T, WF
1216	Function Area Assigned	T, WF, XF
1217	Classification/Lock Ind.	T, TS, WF, WS
1218	WF Def. Responsibility	RY
1220	Activity Profiles	T
1221	Excluded Activities	T
1222	General Attribute Maintenance	O, S
1240	Existence Dependency	RY
1250	Prof. Gen.: Authorizations	RY, T
1251	Prof. Gen.: Specifications	RY, T
1252	Prof. Gen.: Org. Levels	RY, T
1253	Prof. Gen.: Variants	RY, T
1254	User Variables/Activ. Grps.	*, RY, T
1260	CIC Profile	C, O, S
1270	CO Group Assignment	O
1403	Exposure: Long-Term Average	C, EG, S, T
1404	Exposure: Task	C, EG, S, T
1500	Budget Structure Element Management	BU
1501	Pay Scale Valuation	BU, S

No.	Name	Object Types
1502	Allowance Valuation	BU, S
1503	Service Type/Category	S
1504	Budget Updates	BU
1505	Budgeting Rule	BU
1506	Reclassification Rule	BU
1507	Teaching Hours	S
1516	Funding Status	S
1517	Excel Communication	BU
1518	Assignment FM designation	BU
1519	Integration FM	BU
1518	Assignment FM Designation	BU
1519	Integration FM	BU
1520	Original Budget	BU
1600	Organizer ID (F)	D
1601	Statutory Specifications	D
1620	Job Attributes (D)	C
1652	Occupational categories	C

Object Type Abbreviations

* – if all, or more than four
A – Work center
BA – Appraisal
BG – Criteria group
BK – Criterion
BS – Appraisal model
BU – Budget structure element
C – Job
CP – Central Person
D – Business event type
E – Business event
EE – Online Business Event
 (only with Learning Solution)
EG – Exposure group
F – Location
G – Resource

H – External person
L – Business event group
O – Organizational unit
P – Person
Q – Qualification
QK – Qualification group
R – Resource type
RY – Responsibility
S – Position
SR – Planned staff requirement
T – Task
TS – Standard task
WF – Workflow task
WS – Workflow template
XF – ALE split function
XO – ALE filter object

C Reports in Organizational Management

Some useful reports used in organizational management are listed in the following table. Most of these reports can also be used outside of the realm of organizational management for reporting on structures of other object types and relationship types.

Report	Description
RHDESC20	This report gives a description of a position with holders.
RHFILLPOS/ RHXFILLPOS	This report gives the total periods for which positions are unoccupied, per organizational unit. You can also choose to specify several specific organizational units for the report.
RHINFAW0	This report evaluates infotypes (including user-defined ones). Evaluations can be either sequential or structural (i.e., along a structure using an evaluation path).
RHINFAW1	This report also evaluates the infotypes or fields of an infotype that accesses text tables.
RHPAPSUB	On the basis of the specified selections, this report passes over the PD database and collects applicant numbers if objects of the type AP are included in the selected object volume. The applicant master data evaluation specified in the parameter "Applicant reporting" is then started with these applicant numbers.
RHPNPSUB	On the basis of the specified selection, this report passes over the PD database and collects personnel numbers if objects of type P are contained in the selected object volume. The personnel master data evaluation indicated in the parameter "PA reporting" is then started with these personnel numbers.
RHPREL20	This report shows the existing data on a selected personnel number in the areas of organizational structure, education and training, or general planning data.
RHRPPL00	This report gives a time-based list-in line with the organizational structure if necessary-of all positions and work centers assigned to a person. The job, organizational unit, and cost center related to these positions are also displayed.
RHSBES00/ RHSBES10	This report displays staffing assignments. It is executed in line with the organizational structure and according to the selection criteria entered. The list contains all selected positions and persons from one or more organizational units with staffing percentage and approval and employment hours.
RHXSBES0	This report displays the same staffing assignments as report RHSBES00, however, here, only the most important selection parameters are offered for selection.
RHSCRP00/ RHSCRP10	This report gives a description of all jobs or positions in accordance with entered selection criteria.

Report	Description
RHSTAB00	This report displays all objects with staff function in accordance with the entered selection criteria. The infotype 1003 ("Department/Staff") must be maintained for the objects.
RHSTEL00/RHX STEL0	This report gives a list of all jobs and assigned positions, including the holder, in accordance with the selection criteria entered.
RHXTCAT0	This report displays the task catalog. Tasks can also be maintained.
RHVOPOS0	In accordance with the selection criteria entered, this report displays a list of positions that are flagged as being vacant or obsolete.
RHVOPOS1	In accordance with the selection criteria entered, this report displays a list of positions that are flagged as being obsolete.
RHXDESC0	This report displays a description for one or more jobs. A key date or period evaluation is possible. You can list both active and planned information.
RHXDESC1	This report displays a description for one or more positions. A key date or period evaluation is possible. You can list both active and planned information.
RHXIAW00/ RHXIAW01	This report gives an overview of all work centers that can only be occupied "with restrictions." The restrictions are defined in infotype 1006.
RHXIAW02	This report gives an overview of all work centers that either have health exclusions imposed or that are subject to the health examinations in accordance with infotype 1006.
RHXIAW04/ RHXIAW05	This report gives an overview of the characterization of tasks based on hierarchy level, phase, and purpose. It analyzes the settings in infotype 1004.
RHXSCRP0	This report gives a description of one or more jobs. The description includes a descriptive text on a job (infotype 1002), the requirement profile, the activity profile and, as appropriate, authorities/resources.
RHXSCRP1	This report gives a complete description of one or more positions.
RHXSTAB0	This report shows all organizational units with staff functions.
RHXSTAB1	This report shows all positions with staff functions.
RHHFMT00	Depending on the selection criteria entered, this report shows the authorities and/or resources of the positions/work centers.
RHTPOOL0	According to the selection criteria entered, this report displays the task descriptions for positions and jobs.
RHXHFMT0	This report displays the desired resources and authorities for work centers and/or positions along the organizational structure.

D   Authorization Objects

The following table contains a listing of those authorization objects in HR that are relevant to the area of planning and development. In practice, there are other objects that have cross-process action. The most important customizing tables that affect the authorization check in HR are also listed here. They should be considered as critical in customizing for all written authorization concepts and therefore should be specially protected.

Authorization Objects in the "Human Resources" Class

Authorization Object	Description
P_ABAP	Reporting: simplifies the authorization check
P_APPL	Applicant data
P_BEN	Benefits data
P_HRF_INFO	Authorization check: infodata maintenance for HR forms
P_HRF_META	Authorization check: metadata maintenance for HR forms
P_NNNNN	User-defined authorization check
P_NNNNNCON	User-defined authorization check (R/3 Enterprise)
P_ORGIN	Master data
P_ORGINCON	Master data with structural profile (R/3 Enterprise)
P_ORGXX	Master data-extended check for administrators
P_ORGXXCON	Master data-extended check with structural profile (R/3 Enterprise)
P_PCLX	Cluster (Payroll, time management, and so on)
P_PERNR	Master data-authorization for personnel number
P_TCODE	Transaction code (S_TCODE is required in addition to this)
PLOG	PD objects
PLOG_CON	PD objects with context
S_MWB_FCOD	Valid function codes for Manager's Desktop

HR Customizing Critical to the Authorization Check

Table	IMG Path	Purpose
T582A	Personnel Management • Personnel Administration • Customizing Procedures • Infotypes • Infotypes	Controls the time dependency of access to an infotype with the "access authorization" indicator
T591A	Personnel Management • Personnel Administration • Tools • Authorization Management • (Special authorizations in personnel administration) • Test Procedures • Create Test Procedures	Defines test procedures for infotypes
T77PR	Personnel Management • Organizational Management • Basic Settings • Authorization Management • Structural Authorization • Maintain Structural Profiles	Defines a structural authorization profile
T77S0	Personnel Management • Personnel Administration • Tools • Authorization Management • Maintain Authorization Main Switches	Activates the authorization object that will be used to control access to personnel master data
T77UA	Personnel Management • Organizational Management • Basic Settings • Authorization Management • Structural Authorization • Assign Structural Authorization	Assigns a user to the structural authorization profile

E   Explanations for Process Models

In order to read process examples, you should know the meaning of the following symbols:

Events

Events (see Figure E.1) are starting points for processes, i.e., a process is started because of an event "something has happened": in Recruitment, for example, there is the event "applicant to be hired." For the hiring process, this means that a trigger event occurs and the process is started. Events can also be the results of decision-making processes. Example: after an interview, a decision must be made as to whether the candidate will be hired or not. Possible results of this decision-making process can be "applicant to be hired" or "applicant to be rejected."

Figure E.1 ARIS© Symbol: Event

Business Process Transactions/Functions

Functions (see Figure E.2) present activities, for example "interview." In accordance with general ARIS convention, an event must be set after each function (see Figure E.3). Due to the lack of space in process models, the use of this "trivial event" is waived. The relationships between functions, events, and the connectors are called *Connections*.

Figure E.2 ARIS© Symbol: Function

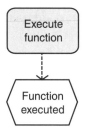

Figure E.3 ARIS© Symbol: Function → Event

System Functions

Actions carried out by the system-SAP in this case-are presented in *system functions* (see Figure E.4). These are actions that are run from the system without any user intervention.

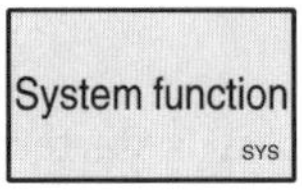

Figure E.4 ARIS© Symbol: System Function

Process Interfaces

Process interfaces (see Figure E.5) create a connection between two processes. Example: The training planning process ends with the event "Training catalog created" and then branches to the process "Book training."

Figure E.5 ARIS© Symbol: Process Interface

Jobs and Organizational Units

Jobs and organizational units (see Figure E.6) are linked to functions and they indicate who carries out the functions in question or, in which organizational unit they are carried out.

Figure E.6 ARIS© Symbols: Job and Organizational Unit

Connectors

Connectors represent a logical link between functions containing decisions and the results of these decisions. The relationship between an event and functions resulting from it is also represented by connectors. The following connectors are used in the process examples shown:

▶ The *AND connector* (see Figure E.7) means that after an event or a function, several functions are executed in parallel. It is used if *all* functions that emerge after an event or function *must* be carried out.

Figure E.7 ARIS© Symbol: AND Connector

▶ If, on the other hand, not all functions that crop up after a function always need to be carried out, then the *AND/OR connector* (see Figure E.8) is used.

Figure E.8 ARIS© Symbol: AND/OR Connector

▶ The *XOR connector* (see Figure E.9) is used to show that decisions must be made in a function. Figure E.10 shows an example of how the XOR connector is used.

Figure E.9 ARIS© Symbol: XOR Connector

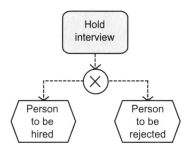

Figure E.10 Example XOR Connector

F   Recommended Reading

If you would like further information on any of the themes dealt with in this book, we can recommend the following publications.

Brochhausen, Ewald; Kielisch, Jürgen, Schnerring, Jürgen; Staeck, Jens: mySAP HR: Technical Principles and Programming. SAP PRESS 2003.

Buck-Emden, Rüdiger: mySAP CRM: Solution for Success. SAP PRESS 2002.

Buckingham, Coffman: First, Break All the Rules: What the World's Greatest Managers Do Differently. Simon & Schuster 1999.

Davis, Rob: Business Process Modelling with ARIS. Springer Verlag 2001.

Egger, Norbert: SAP BW 3.1 Professional. SAP PRESS 2004.

Fitz-Enz, Jac: The ROI of Human Capital: Measuring the Economic Value of Employee Performance. AMACOM 2000.

Huselid, Mark; Becker, Brian; Ulrich, Dave: The HR Scorecard: Linking People, Strategy, and Performance. Harvard Business School Press 2001.

IBM Business Consulting Services: SAP Authorization System. Design an Implementation of Authorization Concepts for SAP R/3 and SAP Enterprise Portal. SAP PRESS 2003.

Keller, Horst; Krüger, Sascha: ABAP Objects. SAP PRESS 2001.

Keller, Horst; Jacobitz, Joachim: ABAP Objects. The Official Reference. SAP PRESS 2003.

McFarland Metzger, Sue; Röhrs, Susanne: Change and Transport Management. The Official SAP Guide. SAP PRESS 2002.

Rickayzen, Alan; Dart, Jocelyn; Brennecke, Carsten; Schneider, Markus: Practical Workflow for SAP. Effective Business Processes using SAP's WebFlow Engine.

Scheer et al.: Business Process Change Management: ARIS in Practice. Springer Verlag 2003.

SAP Labs: System Administration Made Easy, 4.6C/D. 2002.

G   About the Authors

This book is the result of a team effort. The authors are grateful to many contributors, without whom this project would never have attained its current standard of quality. These include, in particular:

▶ Colleagues at *iProCon GmbH*—Anja Junold, Reinhold Luxenburger, and Jörg Edinger. They have made valuable contributions in the areas of role concept, reporting, workflow, and SEM. Over and above this, their assistance and suggestions were always helpful. Special thanks to Anja for producing approximately 200 screenshots for the U.S. edition!

▶ The many helpful members of staff at *SAP AG* and *SAP Deutschland GmbH,* who have contributed much detailed information, particularly in the area of new developments. They include Simone Buchwald, who was able to provide the information necessary, from an early stage, for Chapter 17, *E-Learning and Learning Management*.

▶ The technical support team at *PIKON International Consulting Group* (*www.pikon.com*), who ensured that we always had access to the IDES system, which was used as a source of numerous examples.

▶ Our Partners in the HR consulting network AdManus (www.admanus.com), who always are prepared to share their wisdom.

▶ Last but not least, we want to thank the team at *Galileo Press and UCG*, and in particular, Wiebke Hübner and Nancy Etscovitz. They not only put up a brave fight against the dreaded typo monster; they also supported the authors in the conception of the book and have shown great confidence since the launch of the project. By producing a book devoted specifically to the processes of personnel planning and development with mySAP HR, we are treading new ground, which other publishers have avoided to date. In so doing, Galileo Press further embraces its role as an innovative knowledge transmitter in—among other things—the world of SAP AG products.

We shall now briefly introduce the authors themselves (in the following order of appearance: "age before beauty"):

Christian Lübke

Christian Lübke is founder and director of *iProCon GmbH*. He has worked on various projects to optimize the implementation of mySAP HR, particularly in the areas of personnel controlling and personnel cost planning. His other areas of interest include payroll and the company pension scheme. Until early 2000, he was a senior manager at *IDS Scheer AG*, where he headed the area of Human Resource Consulting.

Sven Ringling

Sven Ringling is also a founder and director of *iProCon GmbH*. He has worked on many projects aimed at optimizing the implementation of mySAP HR, with a focus on personnel development, among others. He also has experience in managing personnel processes and in the selection of HR software and outsourcing service providers. He was a senior manager at *IDS Scheer AG* until early 2000, where he was second-in-command in the area of Human Resource Consulting.

Christian Krämer

Christian Krämer has been working as a senior consultant at *iProCon GmbH* since early 2001. He supports several customers in the area of mySAP HR. He has also developed extensive projects on process-oriented design for the implementation of mySAP HR and has experience in e-learning projects. Until early 2001, he was a senior consultant in the area of HR at *IDS Scheer AG*.

iProCon GmbH

Since early 2000, *iProCon GmbH (www.iprocon.com)* has set for itself the mission of optimizing personnel processes throughout their customer's enterprises and in so doing, has achieved a sustainable improvement in competitiveness for their customers. In addition to process-oriented consultation, the implementation of modern HR systems and in particular, mySAP HR, forms the core of their business. The idea of allowing requirements to flow directly from processes to the IT implementation is also the foundation of this book. In addition to their high-quality project work (conducted in German as well as in English), the consultants of iProCon have written several publications on mySAP HR and on HR process management. They are in great demand as speakers in various conventions and workshops. To strengthen its leading position in the HR area, iProCon—together with other small companies—established the HR consulting network AdManus (**www.admanus.com**).

Index

Numerics
360-degree appraisal 287
360-degree feedback 303

A
Account assignment 78, 447
Account assignment features 48
Accounting 21
Accounting for foreign services 21
Accounting for services 21
Activity fees 21
Activity group 109
Activity-based costs 21
Ad-hoc query → see Infoset query
Adjustment → see Compensation
  adjustment
Adjustment reason 425
Adjustment type 425
Age structure 238
ALE 517
ALE scenario 462
Analyst 518
Analytic functions 26
Anonymity 304, 313
Anonymous individual appraisal 289
Anonymous multisource appraisal 289
Appraisal 204, 287
Appraisal form 307, 379
Appraisal meeting 313
Appraisal model 288, 292, 298
Appraisal overview 307
Appraisal period 291
Appraisal process 290
Appraisal result 288, 422
Appraisal scale → see Scale
Appraisal template 380
Appraisal type 289
Appraisals catalog 288
Appraiser 292, 303
Approval process 438
Assessment center 246
Attendee appraisal 295
Audit 239
Author (BW) 518
Authority 407, 536
Authorization 48, 112, 313

Authorization administration 48
Authorization concept 116, 134, 162
Authorization level 118
Authorization main switches 117, 133
Authorization object 112, 116
Authorization profile 112
Award → see Long-term incentive

B
Balanced Scorecard → see BSC
Basic pay 444, 453
Basic system 21
Benchmark job 427
Benchmarking 26, 419, 427, 440
BI → see Business Intelligence
Blended learning 488
Bottom-up 181
Bottom-up appraisal 303
BSC 26, 176, 185, 522
Budget 395
Budget deduction 437
Budget structure 424
Budget type 424
Budget unit 424, 433
Budget value 433
Budgeting 417, 423
Business area strategy 519
Business Content 517
Business development 397
Business event appraisal 295
Business Explorer 516
Business Explorer Analyzer 516
Business Explorer Browsers 516
Business Information Warehouse 515
Business Intelligence 515
Business process 178, 207
Business process change 179
Business processes 198
Business Workflow 155
BW → see Business Information Ware-
  house

C
Cafeteria survey 310
Calculation base 425
Calculation method 289, 300, 422

Interested in reading more?

Please visit our Web site for all
new book releases from SAP PRESS.

www.sap-press.com